NEW BRITISH FASCISM

The British National Party (BNP) is the most successful far right party in British political history. Based on unprecedented access to the party and its members, this book examines the rise of the BNP and explains what drives some citizens to support far right politics. It is essential reading for all those with an interest in British politics, extremism, voting, race relations and community cohesion. The book helps us understand:

- how wider trends in society have created a favourable climate for the far right;
- how the far right has presented a 'modernised' ideology and image;
- how the movement is organised, and has evolved over time;
- who votes for the far right and why;
- why people join, become and remain actively involved in far right parties.

Matthew J. Goodwin is a Lecturer in the School of Politics and International Relations at the University of Nottingham.

Routledge Studies in Extremism and Democracy

Series Editors: Roger Eatwell, *University of Bath* and **Matthew Goodwin**, *University of Nottingham*.

Founding Series Editors: Roger Eatwell, *University of Bath* and **Cas Mudde**, *University of Antwerp-UFSIA*.

This new series encompasses academic studies within the broad fields of 'extremism' and 'democracy'. These topics have traditionally been considered largely in isolation by academics. A key focus of the series, therefore, is the (inter-)*relation* between extremism and democracy. Works will seek to answer questions such as to what extent 'extremist' groups pose a major threat to democratic parties, or how democracy can respond to extremism without undermining its own democratic credentials.

The books encompass two strands:
Routledge Studies in Extremism and Democracy include books with an introductory and broad focus, and which are aimed at students and teachers. These books will be available in hardback and paperback. Titles include:

Understanding Terrorism in America
From the Klan to al Qaeda
Christopher Hewitt

Fascism and the Extreme Right
Roger Eatwell

Racist Extremism in Central and Eastern Europe
Edited by Cas Mudde

Political Parties and Terrorist Groups
Second edition
Leonard Weinberg, Ami Pedahzur and Arie Perliger

The New Extremism in 21st Century Britain
Edited by Roger Eatwell and Matthew Goodwin

New British Fascism
Rise of the British National Party
Matthew Goodwin

Routledge Research in Extremism and Democracy offers a forum for innovative new research intended for a more specialist readership. These books will be in hardback only. Titles include:

NEW BRITISH FASCISM

Rise of the British National Party

Matthew J. Goodwin

Routledge
Taylor & Francis Group

LONDON AND NEW YORK

First published 2011 by Routledge
2 Park Square, Milton Park, Abingdon, Oxon OX14 4RN

Simultaneously published in the USA and Canada by Routledge
711 Third Avenue, New York, NY 10017

Routledge is an imprint of the Taylor & Francis Group, an informa business

British Library Cataloguing in Publication Data
A catalogue record for this book is available from the British Library

Library of Congress Cataloging in Publication Data
Goodwin, Matthew.
  New British Fascism: Rise of the British National Party/Matthew J.
  Goodwin.
    p. cm. — (Routledge Studies in Extremism and Democracy)
  Includes bibliographical references and index.
  1. British National Party (1982–)   2. Fascism—Great Britain.   I. Title.
  JN1129.B75G66 2011
  324.241′0938—dc22
  2011002708

ISBN: 978-0-415-46500-7 (hbk)
ISBN: 978-0-415-46501-4 (pbk)
ISBN: 978-0-203-80804-7 (ebk)

Typeset in Times New Roman
by RefineCatch Limited, Bungay, Suffolk

MIX
Paper from
responsible sources
FSC
www.fsc.org   FSC® C004839

Printed and bound in Great Britain by
CPI Antony Rowe, Chippenham, Wiltshire

**Dedicated to the memory of F.G. Holliday
1922–2010**

So despairing of the status quo are the majority of Britons, that time for a radical change in political thinking is being demanded and actively sought. The British National Party with its comprehensive, articulated and common sense approach seeks to be the vehicle for that change. Our time is approaching.

BNP General Election Manifesto (2005)

The major task of social science, whether motivated by fear or fascination with the right wing, is not argument and prescription – or even proscription – but understanding and prediction.

Robert A. Schoenberger (1969) *The American Right Wing: Readings in political behavior*, New York: Holt, Rinehart and Winston, p.2

CONTENTS

LIST OF FIGURES AND TABLES

Figures

Tables

PREFACE

The story of the British extreme right has long been one of failure. Unlike events in other European democracies, the inability of the extreme right to attract a large and sustained following has meant that politicians, civil servants, academics and observers have not been forced to think too seriously about this form of extremism, and the roots of its support. Instead, the extreme right was often dismissed as nothing more than a minor political irritant. This view was shaped by the performance of extreme right parties in elections: between the election of Margaret Thatcher in 1979 and the re-election of Tony Blair in 2001, Britons sent only one candidate from an extreme right party into local government.

That candidate represented the British National Party (BNP) in the Millwall ward of Tower Hamlets in 1993. Despite generating considerable alarm, the isolated breakthrough proved to be a false dawn. The BNP promptly lost the seat the next year, which led one journalist to summarize the traditional view of the movement: 'It won Millwall by only seven votes. It may pick up a few more council seats next May but its long-term destiny is the same as Mosley's Blackshirts and Martin Webster's National Front, which is as a short footnote in the slender history of the British far-right.'[1]

There is, however, a different view of the extreme right. Seen from an alternative perspective, there exists in British politics a sizeable amount of latent support for the extreme right which is far greater than is apparent at the polls. Put simply, extreme right parties in Britain have consistently failed to realize their potential.[2] Particularly since 2001, this latent support has been revealed by a resurgence of support for the BNP. Contrary to the prediction above, in only a short time it has gone from a party used to political obscurity to the fifth largest party in British politics, and at the time of the 2010 General Election had good reason to claim it was one of the fastest-growing parties. It has established a significant presence in elected office that includes representation in local government, the Greater London

Assembly (GLA) and the European Parliament. In short, it is the most successful party in the history of the extreme right in Britain.

The leader of the BNP is Cambridge-graduate Nick Griffin, who has been actively involved in extreme right politics for over 30 years. Griffin claims to have transformed the BNP from 'a bad political joke into a major factor in British politics', and has made clear his goal to turn the party 'from a potential footnote in history into a serious contender for power'.[3] Having entered public office and attracted an impressive number of voters, Griffin's BNP rejects the suggestion that it will emulate its ancestors as a 'flash-in-the-pan' that will soon fade from the horizon.

The rise of the BNP has met a hostile reaction. Politicians and leaders of faith communities share a consensus that the party is not a legitimate player in democratic politics: Prime Minister David Cameron brands it a 'completely unacceptable' organization that 'thrives on hatred'; former Prime Minister Tony Blair described it as a 'nasty, extreme organisation'; former Home Secretary David Blunkett urged voters not to support 'the vile, racist politics of the British National Party'; and Bishops of the Church of England warned voters that supporting a racist party is 'like spitting in the face of God'. The most strident condemnation of the party and its supporters came in 2004 when Michael Howard, then leader of the Conservatives, described them as a 'stain' on British democracy: 'This is not a political movement,' said Howard, 'this is a bunch of thugs dressed up as a political party.'[4]

The origins of this book lie in two observations about this topic. First, despite attracting considerable interest and debate, there is a striking absence of reliable research on the BNP and its supporters. Few would dispute the assertion that it is 'a phenomenon that needs to be taken seriously', and that 'it is essential that as many people as possible understand the party in order that racism can be countered effectively'.[5] Yet both the party and its support remain under-researched and are poorly understood. Writing about its main predecessor, the National Front (NF), the academic Christopher Husbands once observed that while there was much speculation about the NF, there was remarkably little evidence.[6] The same could be said of its successor. We know little about the BNP and even less about the citizens who are fuelling its rise, either by voting for the party or demonstrating a greater level of commitment by becoming members.

While the book examines BNP voters, it draws mainly on extensive interviews with grassroots members. A more detailed study of the BNP electorate can be found elsewhere.[7] In this book, the author had unparalleled access to key players inside the party, individuals who have been dismissed as a 'ragbag of ageing skinheads, slick wannabe politicians and ditzy women with chips on their shoulders'.[8] Their qualitative accounts provide rich and unique insights into the party and its appeal among ordinary Britons. How can we ever understand the attraction of extreme right parties like the BNP unless we talk to those involved?

A second observation is that right-wing extremism has recently acquired much greater policy relevance. Much of this interest has focused on the question of how to prevent *violent* extremism, or tackle processes of radicalization within *Muslim* communities.[9] As highlighted by the bombings in London in 2005, Glasgow in 2007 and Stockholm in 2007, given current challenges to national security this heavy focus on violent Islamism and its 'circle of tacit support' is understandable.[10] At the same time, however, this almost exclusive focus on one form of extremism has generated a sense of unease. This anxiety was expressed by one select committee on preventing violent extremism in 2010, which concluded that 'any programme which focuses solely on one section of a community is stigmatising, potentially alienating, and fails to address the fact that no section of a population exists in isolation from others. The need to address extremism of all kinds on a cross-community basis . . . is paramount.'[11]

The rise of the extreme right has not gone unnoticed, but it has received much less attention. Aside from its failure to mount a major electoral assault, this also owes much to the way in which national and local government are often unsure about how (or even whether) they should research what drives support for parties that, on the one hand, are democratically elected but, on the other, undermine 'community cohesion'. An additional aim behind the book is to make the research accessible to a wide audience. References to the academic literature have mostly been consigned to endnotes and a description of methodology can be found in Appendix 1.

The book is based on doctoral and postdoctoral research undertaken at the University of Bath (2004–2007) and the University of Manchester (2009–2010).[12] A special debt of gratitude is owed to the Department of European Studies and Modern Languages (ESML) at the University of Bath, the Economic and Social Research Council (ESRC; grant PTA–026–27–2117) and the British Academy for providing financial support required to undertake the interviews, archival research and writing. I am also particularly grateful to colleagues who have provided support and advice, namely: Bruce Morrison, Kevin Deegan Krause, Anna Cento Bull, Sue Milner, Jocelyn Evans, Jonathan Tonge, Tim Bale, Elisabeth Carter, Andrej Zaslove, Stefan Wolff, Jim Shields, Jonathan Boyd, Darius Byrne, Jack Veugelers, Chris Wlezien, Bobby Duffy, Joe Twyman, Robin Niblett, Alessandra Buonfino, Joelle Adams, Mike Waite, James Bethell, Tim Montgomerie, Steve Wilkinson, Marilyn Eccles, Graham Archer, Andrew Hobbs, Steven Fielding, Philip Cowley, Vivien Lowndes, Lauren McLaren and M. Brands. A debt of gratitude is also owed to colleagues at the University of Manchester, mainly David Cutts and Robert Ford, whose research on BNP voting contributes to Chapter 5 and will appear in a future book.[13] Alan Harding, Peter John, Shaun Bevan, Will Jennings, Andrew Russell, Paul Hepburn and Rod Ling offered comments on earlier drafts. Roger Eatwell, Nicola Parkin, Craig Fowlie and three anonymous reviewers offered invaluable suggestions for improving the manuscript; and Naweed Khan for his help in the book's promotion. Fiona offered her continued support, love and patience.

Last, I would like to thank the members who pushed initial suspicions to one side and participated in the research. In virtually every case, members gave up many hours to answer questions about their backgrounds, motivations, beliefs and involvement. In some cases, activists provided literature; in others they took a risk and put me in touch with fellow members. As promised throughout the fieldwork stage, their names and locations have been kept anonymous.

Matthew J. Goodwin
University of Nottingham
January 2011

Notes

1 'A case of muscle over mind', the *Daily Telegraph*, 22 September 1993.
2 On this perspective see, for example, R. Ford (2010) 'Who might vote for the BNP? Survey evidence on the electoral potential of the extreme right in Britain', in R. Eatwell and M.J. Goodwin (eds) *The New Extremism in Twenty-First Century Britain*, Abingdon and New York: Routledge, pp. 145–168; P. John and H. Margetts (2009) 'The latent support for the extreme right in British politics', *West European Politics*, 32(3): 496–513.
3 Nick Griffin leadership election statement 2010. Available online: www.bnp.org.uk (accessed 10 September 2010); N. Griffin (2006) 'The convergence of catastrophes', *Identity*, 68: 6.
4 M. Tempest, 'Howard attacks BNP "thugs" in Burnley', the *Guardian*, 19 February 2004.
5 'We cannot be complacent in the face of the BNP's minor electoral success', the *Independent*, 4 May 2002.
6 C.T. Husbands (1983) *Racial Exclusionism and the City: The Urban Support of the National Front*, Abingdon: Routledge.
7 R. Ford and M.J. Goodwin (2011) *Voting for Extremists* (forthcoming with Routledge).
8 B. O'Neil, 'What's driving the BNP?' *New Statesman*, 1 May 2008.
9 On this point and the wider gap between research and public policy, see Eatwell and Goodwin, Note 2 *supra*.
10 On tacit support, see S. Saggar (2006) 'The one per cent world: Managing the myth of Muslim religious extremism', *Political Quarterly*, 77(3): 314–327.
11 Communities and Local Government Committee (2010) *Preventing Violent Extremism: Sixth Report of Session 2009–2010*, London: House of Commons.
12 M.J. Goodwin (2007) 'Examining the role of party actors in extreme right party development: The British case', PhD thesis, University of Bath. Dr Matthew Goodwin (2009–2010) Economic and Social Research Council (ESRC) Postdoctoral Fellowship, 'Pathways toward participation in the contemporary extreme right' (Grant number PTA–026–27–2117).
13 Ford and Goodwin, Note 7 *supra*.

LIST OF ABBREVIATIONS

ABEX	Association of British Ex-Servicemen
AENM	Alliance of European National Movements
AFBNP	American Friends of the British National Party
ASF	Aryan Strike Force
BDP	British Democratic Party
BES	British Election Study
BF	British Fascisti
BFP	British First Party
B&H	Blood and Honour
BM	British Movement
BNP	British National Party
BPP	British People's Party
BSA	British Social Attitudes survey
BUF	British Union of Fascists
C18	Combat 18
CPGB	Communist Party of Great Britain
DN	Democratic Nationalists
EDL	English Defence League
EFP	England First Party
FAIR	Families Against Immigrant Racism
FN	National Front (Belgium)
FN	National Front (France)
FP	Freedom Party (UK)
FPÖ	Freedom Party of Austria
FT	Tricolour Flame (Italy)
GWR	Great White Records
ITP	International Third Position

LEL	League of Empire Loyalists
LN	Northern League
MSI	Italian Social Movement
MSR	Republican Social Movement (Spain)
NA	Nationalist Alliance (UK)
ND	National Democrats (England)
ND	National Democrats (Sweden)
NESB	National European Social Movement
NF	National Front
NFSG	National Front Support Group
NHS	National Health Service
NLP	National Labour Party
NNP	New Nationalist Party
NP	National Party
NP	Nationalist Party
NPD	National Democratic Party of Germany
NSDAP	National Socialist German Workers' Party (Nazi Party)
N9S	November 9th Society
PFNE	Nationalist Party of France and Europe
PNR	National Renewal Party (Portugal)
PPERA	Political Parties, Elections and Referendums Act
REP	Republikaner (Germany)
RVF	Racial Volunteer Force
RWB	Red, White and Blue festival
SD	Sweden Democrats
SPLC	Southern Poverty Law Centre
SRP	Socialist Reich Party
UKIP	UK Independence Party
UM	Union Movement
UN	United Nations
VB	Flemish Block
VM	Voting Membership scheme
WDL	White Defence League
WRP	Workers Revolutionary Party
YBNP	Young British National Party
YN	Young Nationalists
YNF	Young National Front

INTRODUCTION

Britons have been betrayed by the old parties and their politicians; they have been fleeced to pay for public services which do not deliver, and they have been gagged by political correctness. The British National Party has the policies, plans and people to put the great back into Britain.

BNP General Election Manifesto, 2010[1]

The message from Barking to the BNP is clear: get out and stay out. You're not wanted here, and your vile politics have no place in British democracy. Pack your bags and go.

Labour MP Margaret Hodge, Barking, May 2010

As Britons went to vote at the 2010 general election, they might have cast their minds back over the campaign. These memories would have included the first televised debates between the leaders of the three main parties, a subsequent surge of support in the polls for the Liberal Democrats, and footage of Labour Prime Minister Gordon Brown describing a supporter of his party who raised concern over immigration as a 'bigoted woman'. Some voters would also have focused on a different story which did not involve the main parties but still simmered throughout the campaign. The story concerned the British National Party (BNP) and the prospect of it achieving something which had eluded the extreme right: a national breakthrough.

Since 2001, the BNP has attracted rapidly growing and striking levels of support for a minor party in an electoral system which favours two main parties. With little money or manpower, the party established a significant presence in elected office, including more than 50 councillors, a seat on the Greater London Assembly (GLA) and two Members of the European Parliament. Seeking to build on these gains, in 2010 the party confidently set its sights on entering Parliament and achieving several second finishes.[2] It stood an impressive 338 candidates, the largest number of candidates fielded by an extreme right party in British history.

The breakthrough appeared especially likely in one seat in outer-east London where leader of the BNP, Nick Griffin, was challenging the incumbent Labour MP Margaret Hodge in what became known as the 'Battle for Barking'. Although residents of Barking had elected Labour candidates uninterrupted since 1945, there were good reasons to take the BNP seriously. Since the late 1990s, it had shifted its focus onto Labour's deprived heartlands where it sought to provide 'former traditional Labour voters with a new party to give them fresh hope'.[3] It was in these working-class districts where the BNP was pitching specifically to disaffected Labour supporters through slogans such as 'We are the Labour Party your grandfather voted for'.

In Barking, the effectiveness of this strategy was apparent at the 2005 general election when the BNP polled a record 16 per cent (while also polling a respectable 9 per cent in neighbouring Dagenham). It continued to cultivate support in local elections and, in 2006, was rewarded when 12 of its 13 candidates were elected onto Barking and Dagenham Council. One headline following the result reflected the way in which this particular borough was becoming synonymous with a toxic tradition in British politics: 'Welcome to Barking – new far right capital of Britain.'[4]

It was against this backdrop that observers of the 2010 election watched anxiously as the BNP set its sights on a breakthrough. The party also anticipated gains in local elections being held on the same day. Numerous commentators pondered whether it might take control of Barking and Dagenham Council. While some labelled the goal as a political fantasy, others acknowledged that the BNP had become a serious force, as one newspaper told its readers: 'It is far from unthinkable that the citizens of this London borough will wake on 7 May to find the British National Party running their council.'[5] Meanwhile, one poll suggested most Britons had grown worried about the BNP's advance.[6]

In its quest to rally support, the party launched the most detailed manifesto in its history. Voters were offered an end to immigration and the war in Afghanistan, opposition to 'Islamism' and withdrawal from the European Union (EU). Among others, these policies were delivered on more than 18 million leaflets and a television broadcast that presented Griffin against images of Winston Churchill and the Second World War. By the time its date with destiny arrived, the BNP claimed to have run its most professional campaign which, even before results were announced, generated some 10,000 enquiries from prospective new joiners.

The breakthrough, however, failed to arrive. As each result was declared, it seemed the extreme right was experiencing yet another false dawn. In Barking, which Griffin claimed was a two-horse race between himself and Hodge, the BNP leader finished third and some 18,000 votes behind Labour. Griffin never came close to realising his ambition. He was even forced to watch Hodge *increase* her majority in an election that saw almost 100 Labour MPs lose their seats. The BNP vote was swamped by increased turnout which was mainly the result of strong campaigns by Labour and anti-fascists, which even he conceded: 'Out of those who voted, we won the white working class vote in Barking, there's no question of it. But not enough of them voted, and the Labour Party's campaigning was brilliant.'[7]

Further disappointment followed in local elections: the BNP lost every one of its councillors in Barking and Dagenham. It had gone from being tipped to take control to being completely thrown out in one fell swoop. Across the country, the number of BNP councillors slumped from over 50 to 28 in a set of elections which Griffin admitted were 'disastrous'.[8] As the scale of these losses became clear, Hodge delivered an unequivocal message to the BNP: 'The message from Barking to the BNP is clear: get out and stay out. You're not wanted here, and your vile politics have no place in British democracy. Pack your bags and go.'

During the campaign, numerous commentators had predicted a breakthrough. But in its aftermath, many were quick to dismiss the BNP and its future prospects: some argued the party was 'wiped out', others that it had taken a 'mortal blow', and some pointed to 'indications of a national collapse in the BNP vote'.[9] The view that dominated post-election analysis was one that has long been applied to the British extreme right: while it may be an occasional cause for concern, the movement is foremost one of failure. Extreme right parties like the BNP will never attract and sustain mass support, and will never be more than a flash-in-the-pan.

This book argues against this view. It does so by examining the BNP and its most committed supporters. There are numerous competing arguments about the extreme right and the roots of its appeal: some see parties like the BNP as a temporary by-product of rapid and destabilizing economic change; others view them as a short-lived outlet for political protestors who are dissatisfied with the main parties; and still others argue they are driven by racist voters concerned only about immigration. These arguments, however, fail to provide a convincing explanation for why a rising number of Britons are shifting their support behind the extreme right. The picture of BNP support is far more complex. Drawing on new and unique data, this book shows how specific trends have enabled the BNP to rally a growing band of supporters who are socially distinct and deeply concerned about a specific set of issues. The BNP has not attracted the same level of support as similar parties elsewhere in Europe, and nor is it likely to become a major electoral force. However, the party is forging ties with members of particular social groups who are driven by clear political goals. For this reason, the extreme right looks set to become a permanent fixture on the political landscape.

Few topics in politics attract as much interest and debate as the extreme right. Across Europe, the rise of extreme right parties has reignited concern over the continuing appeal of racism and sparked debate over whether these parties and their often charismatic leaders herald the resurrection of interwar fascism. As these arguments continue, what remains unquestionable is that large numbers of citizens are supporting parties which fiercely oppose immigration, adopt ambiguous if not hostile positions toward liberal democracy and, in some cases, are associated with neo-Nazism. Nor have these parties been fleeting phenomena. On the contrary, their continuing ability to rally support led one academic to observe that 'the proliferation and political advance of organized anti-immigrant groups, movements and political parties are among the most disturbing and intractable challenges of post-1970 Western European politics'.[10]

The rise of these parties is important because of their impact on society and public policy, and the questions they raise for social scientists. In wider society, parties like the BNP often seek to enact exclusionary policies that entail negative consequences for minority groups, whether immigrants, Muslims, Jews or the Roma. The fact that a growing number of citizens are endorsing these campaigns has sparked a great deal of anxiety about the impact of the extreme right on inter-group relations, levels of racial or religiously motivated violence, and community cohesion. These parties have also impacted on public debate and policy. This is reflected in their role in the emergence of new debates, for example, the role of Islam in the Netherlands or Switzerland, and the continuation of older debates, for example, the impact of immigration across Western Europe. It is also reflected in the response of established mainstream parties. On the centre-right, some parties have openly flirted with the extreme right electorate by co-opting policies and rhetoric on the issues of immigration, law and order, or the integration of minority communities. On the centre-left, some parties have been forced to switch positions in response to parties which have increased the salience of right-wing issues while also appealing to working-class voters.[11]

For social scientists, the extreme right also raises important questions about the evolution of party systems, social norms and voting behaviour. In some countries, these parties forced some of the most profound changes in their party systems in the postwar era.[12] While further eroding traditional political loyalties, the rise of successful extreme right parties also challenged popular notions about the values and attitudes of citizens in modern Europe. As others observe, these parties surfaced in established democracies, affluent post-industrial societies and cradle-to-grave welfare states which have some of the most highly educated and secure populations in the world. Rather than provide a fertile breeding ground for racism and xenophobia, these conditions might be expected to reduce racial prejudice, encourage tolerance and promote liberal attitudes.[13]

An additional puzzle concerns the way in which these parties have not risen to comparable levels across the continent, despite the fact that West European democracies have experienced broadly similar socio-economic change. Instead, their fortunes have varied widely from one country to the next. In Austria, Italy and the Netherlands, they joined government coalitions. In France, the extreme right failed to achieve national power but has controlled large towns and co-governed regions. Even in countries long considered immune to the extreme right such as Sweden, similar parties polled strongly in elections in 2010 and entered the national parliament. Elsewhere, however, in countries like Germany, Ireland, Portugal and Spain, parties on the extreme right wing have so far failed to attract a sizeable and stable following.[14] Confronted with these divergent trends, what has become clear to social scientists is that explaining *why* extreme right parties arise is far more complex than conventional wisdom would have us believe.

Britain has traditionally been associated with the latter group of countries that remain without a successful extreme right. This was particularly apparent during the first two 'waves' of fascist and extreme right activity, the interwar British Union of Fascists (BUF) and postwar National Front (NF). Despite generating publicity, both movements failed to mount a sustained challenge through the ballot box. Neither sent a single candidate into Parliament or even gained a noticeable presence in local government. In fact, over the entire period stretching from the election of the first Labour government in 1923 until the re-election of 'New' Labour in 2001, Britons sent only five candidates from fascist or extreme right parties into local government.[15]

This record of failure meant that studies of British elections were often quick to dismiss the extreme right as the 'dog which didn't bark'.[16] Despite experiencing considerable levels of non-European immigration, Britons, it seemed, were uninterested in anti-immigrant parties that were attracting considerable support elsewhere in Europe. Since 2001, however, this situation has begun to change. While the extreme right has not mounted a major electoral assault, rapidly growing numbers of Britons have showed themselves willing to support a seemingly 'new' party in British politics; the third wave British National Party (BNP). Before charting the rise of the BNP, we should first pin down exactly what it is that we are talking about.

What is right-wing extremism?

There are four relatively distinct types of organization on the extreme right wing. A first type is represented by parties registered with the Electoral Commission, based on dues-paying memberships and which pursue power through the ballot box. Aside from the BNP, other examples in recent years include the England First Party (EFP), Democratic Nationalists (DN), Freedom Party (FP), British Freedom Party (BFP), National Democrats (ND), National Front (NF) and New Nationalist Party (NNP). These parties rely on minuscule memberships and few resources. Some are so weak they have been confined to specific areas, for example, the DN in Bradford or the NNP in the Midlands. Although they aim to operate within legal frameworks, individual members have been linked with violence.[17] In earlier years, for example, a BNP activist was jailed after setting off a bomb close to offices of the Workers Revolutionary Party (WRP) and more recently supporters have been imprisoned after throwing a Molotov cocktail into a mosque and harassing minority ethnic groups.[18]

A second type is the English Defence League (EDL), a grassroots social movement which also aims to mobilize mass support but avoids elections and the trappings of a formal political party. The EDL was formed in June 2009 and differs from 'traditional' extreme right parties in several respects. While parties regularly contest elections, campaign on a range of issues and favour an ethnically defined 'whites only' membership, the EDL prioritizes confrontational rallies, campaigns almost exclusively on the single issue of opposing Islam and (at least publicly) claims to operate an inclusive membership which is open to 'to all races and faiths'.[19]

A third type are extra-parliamentary and more openly neo-Nazi groups that are less interested in mobilizing mass support than recruiting elite activist cadres. Groups like Combat 18 (so-called because the numbers 1 and 8 represent A and H in tribute to Adolf Hitler), Aryan Strike Force (ASF), Racial Volunteer Force (RVF), British Freedom Fighters (BFF) and Blood and Honour (B&H) express little interest in conventional forms of political participation. Instead, they focus on educating activists in 'pure' ideology, engaging in the pan-European skinhead music scene or undertaking 'direct action' methods against opponents and minority communities. While these groups are often ridiculed by opponents for having more initials than members, the potential for violence should not be ignored. In 2005, for example, five RVF supporters were imprisoned after conspiring to incite racial hatred which included encouraging followers to resort to violent methods, such as one article titled 'Roast a Rabbi' which detailed a recipe for an incendiary device and offered 'one hundred team points' to the first person who torched a synagogue.[20]

A fourth type consists of individual 'lone wolf' activists who may have links to the groups above but tend to act in isolation or small cells. Lone wolves draw inspiration from 'Oklahoma Bomber' Timothy McVeigh, 'London Nail Bomber' David Copeland and *The Turner Diaries*, a novel depicting a forthcoming race war. Belief in race war, for example, was one motive linked to a former BNP candidate who was jailed in 2007 after stockpiling chemical explosives. Two years later, a white supremacist was convicted after planning acts of terrorism and in 2010 a BNP supporter was jailed after stockpiling weapons (including over 50 improvised explosive devices and firearms).[21] In this book, we shall encounter evidence which suggests that belief in a forthcoming race war is relatively widespread among grassroots BNP supporters.

Classifying organizations in this way is a useful exercise but does not clarify what is meant by the underlying concept of 'right-wing extremism'.[22] This book follows political scientist Elisabeth Carter in considering right-wing extremism as *a particular form of political ideology that is defined by two anti-constitutional and anti-democratic elements*: first, right-wing extremists are *extremist* because they reject or undermine the values, procedures and institutions of the democratic constitutional state; and second, they are *right wing* because they reject the principle of fundamental human equality.[23]

In terms of the first element not all extreme right parties call for the overthrow of liberal democracy but most advocate policies, a form of populism, strategy and culture that undermine its legitimacy and functioning (albeit more indirectly than interwar fascists).[24] The populism of the extreme right dichotomizes issues into good and evil, and aims to position the majority against minority groups on sensitive issues such as asylum or human rights. The tendency to repress difference and remove dissenting voices from society undermines notions of bargaining and compromise, which are integral to representative democracy and pluralist society, or put in other words: 'Extremists are intolerant of ambiguity. There are no shades of grey between black and white. Further, those who hold differing views are not merely in error but they are also evil because of their failure to recognize the truth.'[25]

In terms of the second element, its rejection of human equality is a feature that differentiates the extreme right from alternative forms of extremism, for example, radical violent Islamism or left-wing extremism. Whereas supporters of the latter tend to accept human equality (even though their actions may negatively impact on other freedoms), right-wing extremists emphasize the *inequality* of individuals which they typically trace to ancestry, race or nationality. This is because parties like the BNP are *ethnic* nationalist and stress the importance of birth and blood to citizenship and belonging. Unlike *civic* nationalists who stress the importance of shared residency, political practices, rights and values, *ethnic* nationalists aim to restrict nationality only to citizens who share a primordial belonging to an original (or 'indigenous') ethnic group.

For the BNP, this ethnic in-group is comprised of 'the English, Scots, Irish and Welsh along with the limited numbers of peoples of European descent, who have arrived centuries or decades ago and who have fully integrated into our society'. Only members of this ethnically defined in-group belong to the nation, as the party makes clear: 'Being British is more than merely possessing a modern document known as a passport. It runs far deeper than that: it is to belong to a special chain of unique people who have the natural law right to remain a majority in their ancestral homeland.'[26] It is this emphasis on the importance of race to national identity that differentiates the BNP from other parties in British politics, as its leader elaborates:

> Every few years some ambitious charlatan comes along and tries to turn the BNP into a civic nationalist sell-out party. Frankly, if that was what we wanted, and if that was what was needed, we could all have left it to UKIP [UK Independence Party] . . . But it is not. Just because a featherless biped can speak English and knows how to sign on for benefits, that does not make it one of us. Nationality and identity are based on ancient roots and belonging, not on possession of a passport. And every new wave of new recruits must be taught this, or our struggle would be pointless.[27]

Its ethnic nationalism leads the extreme right to demand that the nation be inhabited only by members of the in-group, and that 'threatening' out-groups are either reduced in size (by halting immigration) or removed altogether (by repatriation). To attract support for these ideas, parties like the BNP employ *xenophobic* campaigns which frame immigrants and minority groups as different, problematic or threatening to the in-group. One way of galvanizing support, for example, is by claiming that out-groups threaten the economic resources, interests or even survival of the in-group.

While most extreme right parties are xenophobic, some like the BNP also have their roots in a tradition of *biological racism*, arguing that immigrants and minority groups are not only threatening but also biologically inferior to the white race. This strident and crude form of racism traces differences between groups – for example, their levels of intelligence or propensity to commit crime – to their biological characteristics while ignoring other factors such as socio-economic context. It also argues that racial integration and multiculturalism should be avoided in order to protect the racial purity of the in-group. Parties that subscribe to this more blatant form of racism are also often anti-Semitic, claiming for example that secretive Jewish-led groups control international relations, that the Holocaust never happened, and that Jews encourage multiculturalism to undermine the racial purity of other groups.

For Carter, parties which are xenophobic, biologically racist and reject or undermine liberal democracy are 'neo-Nazi' on the basis that their ideology is reminiscent of, and heavily influenced by, interwar Nazism. As others point out, the influence of interwar Nazism is often revealed in 'references to myths, symbols, slogans of the interwar fascist experience, often veiled as nostalgia, or in terms of a more explicit reference to at least part of the ideological corpus of fascism'.[28] While the ideological core of fascism is heavily contested, it is often associated with a strong emphasis on national crisis or decline, a myth of national rebirth or renewal, and populist ultra-nationalism.[29]

Not all parties on the extreme right, however, hold their roots in this tradition. Rather, neo-fascist and neo-Nazi parties are more accurately seen as branches within a larger extreme right family tree, as Carter explains: 'While fascist or neo-fascist movements or parties should indeed be considered right-wing extremist, not all right-wing extremist movements or parties may be considered fascist or neo-fascist.'[30] This is because some parties on the extreme right deliberately steer clear of those biologically racist, anti-Semitic and anti-democratic ideas above, which have become increasingly unacceptable to postwar populations. While large numbers of citizens in Europe have become anxious over immigration and rising ethno-cultural diversity, support for more strident forms of racial prejudice has declined and norms of racial equality have become increasingly widespread. Meanwhile, though large numbers of citizens are dissatisfied with their democratic institutions (notably political parties), few oppose democracy as a form of government.

Amid these broader trends, the most successful extreme right parties have been those which have distanced themselves from the toxic fascist brand, a strategy not lost on the BNP.[31] Rather than stressing biology, these parties seek to mobilize public opposition to immigrants and minority groups by framing them as a more diffuse threat to culture, values and ways of life. One argument advocated by the extreme right, for example, is that minority groups such as Muslims are not biologically inferior but do hold values which are incompatible with Western liberal democracy, and hence they should be excluded on this basis. The most successful parties also avoid direct attacks on the democratic system, instead advocating an anti-establishment but not overtly anti-democratic populist strategy.[32] These shifts from race to culture, and from anti-democratic to anti-establishment appeals, are important as they have enabled extreme right parties to attract politically dissatisfied citizens who are anxious over immigration but who 'never would have considered voting for an "old" right-wing extremist party promoting biological racism and/or anti-democratic stances'.[33]

Rise of the BNP

The historic failure of the British extreme right to match the success of its continental cousins has been traced to various factors.[34] Some point toward history, suggesting Britain's defeat of fascist regimes is an important episode in the national story and poses a formidable barrier to parties stained by the stigma of fascism. The enduring legacy of this tradition was suggested by one poll in 2005 which asked Britons to rank the defining characteristics of 'Britishness'; the number who chose the country's defiance of Nazi Germany as being 'very important' to this identity was only second behind the number who selected freedom of speech.[35] Others focus on Britain's tradition as a 'civic culture', arguing its strong liberal democratic heritage and citizens who were noted for their pride in the political system and deference to authority stifled opportunities for extremists.[36] An alternative third approach focuses on public opinion, arguing there is insufficient public demand for ideas and policies advocated by the extreme right. Still others focus on the mechanics of the majoritarian system, noting how it favours two main parties and makes it difficult for minor parties to convince citizens that a vote for them is not 'wasted'.[37] A fifth perspective stresses party competition, contending that at various points in recent political history support for the extreme right has been co-opted by the Conservative Party, which has delivered a more competent response to public anxiety over immigration.

While several of these arguments contain valid points, some of their assumptions and more general tendency to view the extreme right as a movement of failure have been challenged by the rise of the BNP. The BNP was born in the spring of 1982 and over the next two decades remained in the wilderness. It expressed little interest in fighting elections. Rather than knocking on voters' doors, it was more likely to be seen marching through the streets demanding 'Rights for Whites!'. When elections were contested, the BNP's campaigns were characterized by farce and failure: in 1983 it stood in 54 seats but could only campaign in five; in 1987 it was so weak it officially abstained; in 1992 it stood only 13 candidates, not even half as many as the Monster Raving Loony Party; and in 1997 it contested more than 50 seats but averaged a derisory 1.4 per cent. Given this dismal record, it is not surprising that one academic who set the BNP alongside its more successful European neighbours described it as 'a minute, gawky, earthbound, ugly duckling destined to scratch around indefinitely without ever coming out as a swan'.[38]

As the twentieth century drew to a close, however, there emerged more favourable conditions for the extreme right. Rising public concern over immigration, anxiety about settled Muslim communities and dissatisfaction with the performance of the main parties presented new opportunities for a movement struggling to find space. Under the new leadership of Nick Griffin, the BNP suddenly attracted rapidly growing levels of support which soon reached unprecedented heights. Between 1992 and 2010, the number of BNP votes in general elections increased more than 70-fold, rising from 7,000 to more than half a million. In the same period, its number of candidates surged from 13 to over 300 (see Fig. 1). This support is particularly impressive given that the party has lacked money and members, and operates in a system which is unfavourable toward small parties.

This growth commenced at the 2001 general election, at which the BNP polled over 10 per cent of the vote in two seats and 16 per cent in one seat in North West England.[39] These results were striking given that the party did not invest heavily in the campaign, telling activists beforehand it was 'not going to waste huge sums of money and time, just to get half a percent across the country'.[40] The BNP then turned to local elections, which offer more favourable conditions for minor parties: they are less expensive, tend to have lower turnout, exhibit lacklustre campaigns by the main parties; and heightened protest voting against the government. In its quest for local success, the party also began developing its own brand of pavement politics which put strong emphasis on face-to-face contact with residents and building a solid grassroots presence. The aim was to overcome the supposedly ingrained British resistance to fascism by replacing confrontation with community politics, and swapping boots for suits.

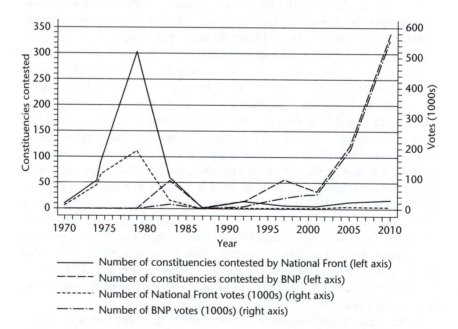

——— Number of constituencies contested by National Front (left axis)
– – – – Number of constituencies contested by BNP (left axis)
------- Number of National Front votes (1000s) (right axis)
—·—·· Number of BNP votes (1000s) (right axis)

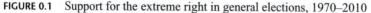

FIGURE 0.1 Support for the extreme right in general elections, 1970–2010

This led the party to expand its presence rapidly in local elections. In 2000, the BNP claimed only 17 local election candidates and 3,000 voters. Within a few years, the party was fielding over 700 candidates and attracting 366,000 voters (see Fig. 2). The local strategy gained momentum following the election of three councillors in Burnley in 2002, a deprived borough that was recovering from urban disturbances the previous year. One journalist described the election as the moment Britons elected three councillors from the far right and a monkey to be Mayor of Hartlepool.[41] While the BNP had actually stood fewer than 70 candidates across fewer than 30 local authorities, its first breakthrough in almost a decade sparked a wave of anxiety; one poll suggested four out of ten citizens thought the result would 'harm race relations', and six out of ten favoured banning the party.[42]

This anxiety was fuelled at local elections in 2003, which saw the BNP gain over 100,000 votes and 13 new councillors, including a further seven in Burnley. As debate over the drivers of BNP support ensued, the party offered its own analysis which traced these gains to 'local campaigns against the unfair allocations of funding, whereby councils run by various other parties overlook poor white areas while spending large sums on Politically Correct projects for various minorities'.[43]

The party underscored its growing ambition at the 2005 general election, rejecting the suggestion it was simply a 'flash-in-the-pan'.[44] Seeking to prove the point, it increased its number of candidates more than three-fold to 119 and launched a targeted campaign that focused on West Yorkshire, the Lancashire mill towns, the Midlands, East London and South Essex.[45] The party saw its average vote in seats contested increase to a respectable 4.3 per cent, although

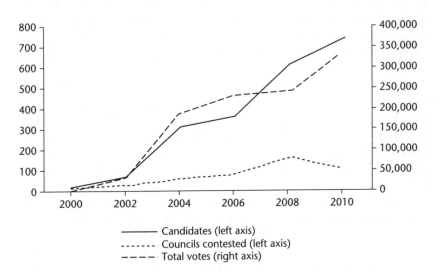

FIGURE 0.2   The BNP in local elections, 2000–2008

Source: BBC Election Archive

some candidates polled much stronger: almost 17 per cent in Barking; 13 per cent in Dewsbury; over 10 per cent in Burnley; and over 9 per cent in a further four seats.[46] One of these seats was Keighley in West Yorkshire which, according to a local Labour MP, needed the BNP 'like a hole in the head'.[47]

Overall, the number of BNP voters reached almost 200,000 which, as some of its activists were quick to point out, was more than the NF had attracted in 1979.[48] The targeted strategy also helped save more deposits, which is important for minor parties. At general elections, candidates or their parties are required to submit a deposit of £500 which is returned only if they poll at least 5 per cent of the vote. During its infancy, the BNP routinely lost every deposit it put down, saved only three in 1997 and seven in 2001. In 2005, however, it met or surpassed the threshold in a total of 34 seats.

The strategy had been to use the 2005 campaign as a springboard into local election success the following year, and it reaped dividends: the party received over 220,000 votes, averaged 18 per cent and gained 30 councillors in an election which it described as its 'biggest electoral and political breakthrough to date'.[49] There also emerged evidence of wider support; while BNP candidates finished first in 28 wards, they finished second in over 80.[50] The aim behind contesting these local elections was to build an image of credibility at community level, as Griffin explains: 'We fought local elections because they were the easiest to win. In fact, they were the only ones we could win.'[51] Yet the reach of the BNP was about to extend beyond local councils.

In May 2008, Londoners went to the polls to elect members of the Greater London Assembly (GLA) and over 130,000 of them voted BNP. After polling more than 5 per cent of the vote, the party gained one seat in City Hall and hailed the result as 'the single [most] significant political achievement attained by the British National Party since its inception' and 'easily the most significant electoral and political victory in the entire history of British nationalism'.[52] One journalist offered a more sombre assessment, remarking that 'as electoral advances go, this was hardly a blitzkrieg'.[53]

While the party might not have launched a lightning assault on the party system, its rise was proving stubbornly persistent. In each set of local elections since 2005, the BNP had rallied more than 200,000 Britons. Their support enabled the party to establish a foothold in councils in a diverse range of areas, including Amber Valley, Bradford, Broxbourne, Broxtowe, Calderdale, Charnwood, Dudley, Epping Forest, Havering, Hertfordshire, Kirklees, Leeds, Leicestershire, Lincolnshire, Nuneaton, Pendle, Redbridge, Redditch, Rotherham, Sandwell, Sevenoaks, Solihull, Stoke and Thurrock. In Burnley (in 2003) and Barking and Dagenham (in 2006), it recruited enough support to become the main opposition group on the council.[54]

In 2009, these advances were overshadowed by a breakthrough of much greater magnitude. Griffin had first predicted representation in the European Parliament while campaigning in 2004. Attempting to realize this prediction, the BNP invested more than £200,000 into its campaign and even brought Jean-Marie Le

Pen, leader of the National Front (FN) in France, across the Channel to help attract publicity.[55] Despite polling over 800,000 votes under a more proportional electoral system, the BNP failed to enter Europe. Some organizers turned their frustration on local branches which 'took things easy' and had not undertaken enough canvassing.[56] Nonetheless, the failure to progress onto the European level was only temporary.

The next set of European elections was held in June 2009 and amid continued public concern over immigration, outrage over a parliamentary expenses scandal and anxiety about a financial crisis. The BNP responded by anchoring its campaign in two themes; it urged voters to 'punish the pigs' in Westminster and promised 'British jobs for British workers'. Meanwhile, at the local level its literature sought to attract support by tapping into a sense of unfairness and a perception among some voters that immigrants were threatening resources: 'It's not a matter of race, it's wrong that people who've worked for this country and paid taxes for years are shoved to the back of the jobs, health and housing queues behind newcomers who've done nothing for Britain.'[57]

When all votes were counted it was revealed that almost one million citizens voted BNP. In two regions, BNP support was sufficient to send two candidates (Andrew Brons and Nick Griffin) into the European Parliament.[58] Nor were these candidates alone; across Europe voters in Austria, Belgium, Bulgaria, Denmark, Finland, France, Greece, Hungary, Italy, Romania and Slovakia had sent candidates from extreme right-wing parties to represent their interests in Europe.[59] For the BNP, the result was a major watershed which delivered significant resources, a platform in European politics, an opportunity to establish links with similar parties and unprecedented media coverage. The extent of the latter became clear four months later when Nick Griffin sat down alongside mainstream politicians on the popular BBC One programme *Question Time*.

Although the main parties had long refused to share a platform with the extreme right, newly elected Griffin was now given an opportunity to present himself and his party to over eight million viewers, and a hostile studio audience. Some compared the event to Le Pen's appearance on the French equivalent *L'Heure de Vérité* in 1984 which, after the French FN subsequently polled strongly in elections, was described by Le Pen as 'the hour that changed everything'.[60] In the end, *Question Time* did not change everything for the BNP (although in its aftermath one poll suggested 20 per cent of the population might at least consider supporting the party.)[61] Some observers traced this result to the way in which the BBC had seemingly altered the format of the show to enable the audience to focus almost exclusively on Griffin, or as he puts it: 'That [poll] was astounding. I was expecting a bounce but not a bounce on that scale. But there again they [the BBC] did spectacularly cock up on what they did.'[62]

At the 2010 general election, the BNP aimed to build on its growing profile and gains in 'second order' elections by entering Parliament. It was not the only extreme right party fighting the election, but it was easily the most prominent.[63] However, unlike its campaigns in 2001 and 2005, its attempt at a breakthrough was consistently undermined by internal problems. Proposed changes to its 'whites-only' membership policy and rumours of financial corruption among its leadership had sparked a wave of discontent among the grassroots. The party's attempt to appear to voters as a credible alternative was further undermined by allegations that its director of publicity had threatened to kill Nick Griffin, then footage of a BNP councillor brawling in the street with Asian youths, and then the temporary closure of its Internet site by a disgruntled activist.

Events in the wider campaign also appeared to be conspiring against the breakthrough. In Barking, Griffin met strong opposition from Labour and the anti-fascist network Hope Not Hate, which claimed to have recruited 140,000 supporters and 20,000 regular online campaigners.[64] These attempts to halt the rise of the BNP focused mainly on mobilizing women and minority ethnic groups who do not tend to vote for the extreme right (see Chapter 5). One 'day of action' saw more than 500 anti-fascist volunteers deliver 90,000 newspapers across Barking and Dagenham, while on election day teams of activists helped mobilize a targeted list of non-BNP voters in key wards. Opposition to the BNP was also evident in national media; the *Mirror*, the country's only left-leaning tabloid newspaper, ran a story titled 'five reasons not to vote BNP'.[65] While the party continued to muse over the possibility of entering Westminster, opinion polls told a different story according to which only 1 per cent of the electorate was about to vote BNP.[66]

While the party ultimately failed to realize its ambition, its support remained impressive. Despite internal problems and a lack of resources, the BNP's number of votes more than doubled to over half a million. It polled almost twice as many votes as the Greens who entered Parliament, and received more votes than the Scottish National Party (SNP) and Plaid Cymru who similarly won seats. It polled more than twice as many votes as the NF had received in 1979 and confirmed its status as the fifth largest party in British politics. It also attracted more votes than similar parties elsewhere in Europe that benefit from different electoral systems and have entered national parliaments, including Flemish Interest (VB) in Belgium and Sweden Democrats (SD).[67] Griffin's campaign in Barking was promptly branded a failure, but it had actually mobilized more votes than in 2005, and more than any extreme right party candidate in British history. BNP candidates also polled strongly outside the target seats of Barking and Stoke Central. They polled over 10 per cent in three seats; over 8 per cent in nine seats; and met the 5 per cent threshold in over 60 seats. It might not have achieved a visible breakthrough, but Griffin's BNP still rallied the largest number of Britons in the history of the extreme right.

What this book is about

How can we explain the rise and sustained appeal of the BNP? This book addresses that question by drawing on new and unique data which provides unprecedented insight into the party and its support (on methodology, see Appendix 1). This includes extensive interviews with BNP leaders and grassroots members, which allow us to explore their backgrounds, motivations and beliefs. These voices are surprisingly absent in studies which ostensibly seek to understand what 'pushes and pulls' some citizens to support the extreme right. Combined with analysis of party literature, the data provide unparalleled insight into the appeal of the extreme right among ordinary Britons. In addition, the book analyses BNP voters between the years 2002 and 2010, including their profile and attitudes toward various social and political issues.[68] When seen as a whole, this combination of qualitative and quantitative data sheds much light on a topic that arouses much interest but remains poorly understood.

The book shows how trends in the wider environment have enabled the BNP to rally a growing band of Britons who are socially distinct and concerned about a specific set of issues. It does so by adopting an integrated framework which simultaneously considers what political scientists label the *demand-side* and *supply-side*.[69] The demand-side focuses on the impact of large-scale social and economic change, such as globalization, immigration and rising ethno-cultural diversity, and how these processes shape the attitudes of citizens and create public *demand* for ideas and policies offered by political parties. While acknowledging that these trends are important, the supply-side is critical of a tendency to view parties as simply 'hapless victims' of their surrounding environment, as if they are boats amid stormy waves which are unable to influence their direction. Also important is how parties themselves respond to events around them, by modifying their message, strategy and organization.[70] A common starting point in these accounts is the argument that globalization and immigration have created a reservoir of potential support for extreme right parties in most established Western democracies, and so these movements become masters of their own fate. The extent to which this potential is translated into actual support will depend much on the actions of the main parties and the extreme right, such as whether the latter delivers a resonant and credible message, develops an effective organization, appeals to particular social groups and distances itself from the stigma of interwar fascism.

These approaches have produced numerous arguments, but three are particularly important. The first 'losers of modernization model' argues that the shift toward a globalized post-industrial economy has essentially left behind members of a marginalized and disaffected 'white working class'. Amid rapid and destabilizing socio-economic change, more deprived, less-educated and hence less flexible citizens have fallen susceptible to feelings of insecurity, economic pessimism, alienation and resentment toward the main parties. In response, some switch their loyalty to more extreme parties like the BNP, which campaign to halt these changes, protect the interests of native citizens and launch populist attacks against the mainstream parties.[71]

A second 'racial threat model' puts stronger emphasis on the impact of immigration and rising ethno-cultural diversity. Seen from this perspective, financially insecure citizens who occupy more precarious positions in society – such as skilled and semi-skilled workers – are more likely than their affluent employer and unemployed neighbour to feel they have 'something to lose' from immigration and rising diversity. They may feel their economic resources (e.g. jobs, social housing, regeneration funding, etc.) or culture, values and ways of life are under threat from immigrants and more culturally distinct minority groups, such as Muslims. In response to this sense of threat, citizens shift behind parties which seek to curb or halt immigration, and as a way of expressing their hostility toward these 'threatening' out-groups.[72]

A third 'political competence model' focuses more heavily on the actions of political parties, contending that parties like the BNP have profited from a sense of dissatisfaction among some citizens over the perceived failure of mainstream parties to deliver a competent response to key issues. This draws on the argument that what matters most to citizens when making decisions about whom to support are their evaluations of which party will deliver the most competent performance on issues which have become increasingly important in recent years, such as immigration and rising ethno-cultural diversity.[73] In response to their anxiety over these issues and dissatisfaction with the response of the mainstream parties, some citizens switch to more ideologically extreme parties as a way of 'sending a message' to their representatives about issues they care deeply about, but which they feel are not being competently addressed.

Rather than juxtapose the demand-side and supply-side, this book takes both into account.[74] It shows how each of the models above has something to say about the rise of the BNP. In terms of public demand, it shows how changes to the wider issue agenda and climate of British politics have created particularly favourable conditions for the extreme right. The BNP could not have chosen a more promising time to launch an electoral challenge and, in many respects, the extreme right has never had it so good. The increased importance of immigration in the public mindset, profound anxiety over this issue and concern over settled Muslim communities have shifted the agenda firmly in favour of parties which campaign against immigrants, Muslims and rising diversity. At the same time, there is significant dissatisfaction among Britons over the perceived failure of recent governments and the main parties to deliver a competent performance on these immigration-related issues. While there are other important factors, including longer-term trends in the party system which have loosened bonds between voters and the main parties, these two core opportunities are the most important to understanding the sudden emergence of the BNP.

On the supply-side, the BNP has met these opportunities by adopting an electoral strategy and launching a concerted attempt to widen its appeal. This has entailed modifying its message, targeting specific social groups in particular areas of the country and attempting to professionalize its internal organization. Despite favourable conditions, however, this strategy has met only limited success. The appeal of the BNP does not extend across society, and the party has struggled to realize its wider potential. Large numbers of Britons are deeply anxious over immigration and sceptical about its effects on society, but most remain unwilling to endorse the BNP. In ancient Greece, the mark of 'stigma' was a literal one, whereby citizens were burnt or scarred to brand them as beyond the pale. In modern politics, the mark of stigma is revealed in surveys and polls. Put simply, most Britons have never associated the extreme right with normal democratic politics, and nor do they consider the BNP an acceptable alternative.

Yet while the party is unlikely to build mass support, it *is* rallying supporters who are socially distinct, reside in particular social contexts and are motivated by their concerns over specific issues. Popular stereotypes tell us that extreme right parties are bastions of irrational fanatics, ignorant racists, isolated loners and the direct descendants of interwar fascists. BNP supporters have been dismissed as 'ignoramuses and bigots', 'troglodyte thickoes', 'fantasists and oddballs', 'toxic little Blackshirts' and 'knuckle-dragging skinheads'.[75] These citizens, however, are not motivated simply by crude racism, political protest or irrational impulses. Nor are they responding in knee-jerk fashion to economic deprivation. Rather, they are driven to support the BNP by clear and coherent preferences. First and foremost, they are motivated by a 'potent combination' of hostility toward immigration and dissatisfaction with the main parties. They are deeply hostile toward immigration, Muslim communities and rising ethno-cultural diversity, but they are also extremely dissatisfied with their current political options. The BNP does not have mass appeal, but the evidence in this book suggests it is forging ties with 'angry white men': middle-aged and elderly working-class men who have low levels of education, are deeply pessimistic about their economic prospects and live in more deprived urban areas close to large Muslim communities. Foremost, these citizens are sending a message about their profound concern over issues which they care deeply about, but which they feel are not being adequately addressed by the main parties.

Structure

The book is organized in two sections. The first four chapters examine the anatomy of the BNP, including its history, evolution and more recent attempts to modify its message, strategy and organization. The next four chapters explore the supporters: the voters, members, their initial motives for joining, and how the party attempts to sustain their loyalty over the longer term.

Chapter 1 sets the BNP in historical context by examining the evolution and support for fascist and extreme right movements. Chapter 2 examines the development of the BNP during its formative years, from its birth in 1982 until a change of leadership in 1999. The next chapter situates the rise of the BNP and its attempt at 'modernization' against the backdrop of wider trends in British politics. This has also entailed changes to its internal organization, which are examined in Chapter 4. The next chapter shows how these factors have enabled the BNP to recruit voters who share a distinct social and attitudinal profile, and also investigates perceptions of the party among the wider electorate. Chapter 6 examines the evolution of its membership, including who joins the party and how they first became involved. Chapter 7 explores the motivations which initially 'pushed' these citizens to enroll, while the final chapter shows how the party attempts to build on these initial motives and 'pull' supporters into active participation. In a concluding chapter, the book summarizes the main findings and discusses their implications for the BNP, the extreme right and British politics more broadly.

For reasons discussed throughout this book, the BNP is unlikely to achieve a wider breakthrough. But nor does the party or the extreme right more generally look set to vanish from the landscape. In Britain and other European democracies, the trends which are fuelling public demand for ideas and policies offered by right-wing extremists are unlikely to subside. It is important, therefore, that we examine these organizations, their appeal and supporters more closely and, above all, in an objective manner. This book is intended as a contribution to that process.

1

THE LEGACY OF HISTORY

If you say BNP to me, I think National Front.
Resident in Barking and Dagenham.[1]

The roots of political parties are important as they can profoundly shape their longer-term development. A new party which builds on a tradition that most citizens consider legitimate is unlikely to find it difficult to attract some initial support. A party which builds on a tradition that is considered illegitimate, however, may struggle to present itself as a credible alternative. The enduring influence of historical legacies on political parties is particularly apparent in the evolution of the postwar extreme right. As others have shown, the most successful of these parties have generally been those which have built on diverse ideological currents and distanced themselves from the stigma of crude racism and interwar fascism. Conversely, the parties which tend to poll less well are those which have built on overtly fascist or neo-Nazi foundations, and are stigmatized in wider society as a result.[2]

These varying fortunes owe much to the way in which postwar European populations have increasingly subscribed to social norms of racial equality and support for democracy as a form of government. While in recent decades there has emerged a sizeable reservoir of public anxiety over immigration and its effects, and public distrust of the main parties, most citizens are unwilling to endorse the most strident forms of crude racism, anti-Semitism and anti-democratic appeals. As a consequence, parties which have sought to build on these traditions have struggled to attract a large and sustained following, and instead have been forced to rely on small rumps of racist voters. For these reasons, it is impossible to understand the rise of the BNP without first setting it in historical context and exploring its roots. The importance of these roots has been underscored by its current leader,

Nick Griffin, who has talked of the constraints imposed on a party which 'already has its own traditions, expectations, and complexities'.[3]

British Union of Fascists (BUF)

Before the outbreak of the Second World War, the extremist fringe in British politics was littered with minuscule and electorally irrelevant groups. Among others, the Britons Society, Fascist League, Stamford Fascists, Yorkshire Fascists, National Fascisti, Nordic League and British Fascisti all tried unsuccessfully to rally Britons under the banner of fascism.[4] Rather than look toward German Nazism and its fanatical obsession with race, many of these groups took their inspiration from Italian fascism and accompanying ideas about how to reorganize authority and the state. Despite what their names implied, however, few grasped the core pillars of fascist ideology. Rather, the significance of groups like British Fascisti (BF) owed more to their role as a training ground for activists who, in later years, assumed leading positions on the extreme right.[5]

The only serious attempt at fascist mobilization was undertaken by the British Union of Fascists (BUF), which was founded by Oswald Mosley amid economic crisis in 1932. Unlike other figures on the extremist fringe, Mosley emerged out of the 'mainstream' establishment and had strong links to political and media elites. Even after switching allegiance to fascism, for a short period Mosley recruited support from the *Daily Mail* newspaper which, in 1934, ran with the headline 'Hurrah for the Blackshirts'.

Among academics, there is a general consensus that the most interesting feature of the BUF was its ideology. Mosley was anything but a novice ideologue. In the 1920s he had worked on Keynesian-type economics and thereafter developed one of the most comprehensive articulations of fascism in interwar Europe.[6] Through his tireless writing and speeches, the BUF leader made clear his desire to transform Britain into a single-party authoritarian regime based on corporatist economics and a strongly technocratic ethos.[7] As others note, while this interest in corporatist economics did not necessarily make Mosley a fascist, his belief that people were necessarily unequal, his desire to destroy class differences and his 'more general attempt to synthesize key aspects of the old with the new, especially in the quest to produce a new fascist man' did.[8]

The BUF saw little need to question the aggressive foreign policies of Hitler and Mussolini, so long as Britain's imperial interests were not threatened. Throughout the 1930s, it also came to embrace anti-Semitism, arguing for example that 'alien Yiddish finance' was undermining national prosperity.[9] The fascist credentials of the BUF were also reflected in its paramilitary-style approach to campaigning, which put strong emphasis on organized rallies for its Blackshirted activists and frequent detours into political violence against opponents (the tactic was effectively neutralized following the Public Order Act in 1936).[10] While the BUF and its followers dreamed of national power, their attempt to mobilize mass support through the ballot box was a total failure. Mosley had first sought to lure voters away from the main parties through the New Party (NP), which was founded in 1931 but met little success.[11] The performance of the BUF was similarly dismal and there appeared little public demand for Mosleyite fascism. Nor was this encouraged by its grassroots organization. As one historian notes, the BUF's emphasis on paramilitarism and populist demagoguery meant it struggled to recruit a 'better type' of activist, and found it 'extremely difficult to build efficient constituency and ward organisations in a locality'.[12] Its ambitions were also increasingly checked by anti-fascists, most notably at the notorious Olympia rally in 1934 which was marred by violence.

Internal weakness was one reason why the BUF abstained from the general election in 1935. Though Mosley sought to sustain morale through the slogan 'Fascism next time', the reality was that his movement was heading into electoral oblivion.[13] In fact, the electoral performance of British fascism more generally was disastrous. The sum of elected representation amounted to only three councillors: two from the BF in Lincolnshire in 1926; and one from the BUF in Suffolk in 1938. The BUF proved unable to build a large base of support. Instead, it was restricted to a small number of working-class enclaves in London, the South East and, to a lesser extent, northern England. Its limited appeal was especially apparent in the mid-to-late 1930s when it fell heavily dependent on one area of the country for support, which was quickly earning itself a name as the heartland of fascist and extreme right politics.

Even before the First World War, residents of the East End of London had lent their support to organizations such as the anti-Semitic British Brothers League (BBL), which was mainly active in Bethnal Green, Limehouse, Stepney and Shoreditch. Between 1902 and 1905, and amid 'prophecies of impending doom and racial conflict', the BBL sought to galvanize opposition to Jews by claiming that Britain was being invaded by 'alien swarms', and that minority groups were receiving preferential treatment from local authorities.[14] The movement did not endure, but as Britain passed through the 1930s, Eastenders continued to turn out in disproportionately large numbers for the BUF (although this support should not be exaggerated given that it did not elect even one councillor in the area).[15] Nonetheless, and despite receiving financial support from Mussolini, the BUF failed to transform these small enclaves of sympathy into a national movement. This failure owed much to 'supply-side' factors, though mainly its chosen strategy; Mosley never seriously committed the BUF to an electoral strategy. Rather than engage with electoral politics, he pinned his hopes on being invited into power amid a period of national crisis. The result was that few resources were invested in electioneering.

While the BUF rallied few voters it did attract a sizeable membership which, according to some estimates, peaked at 40,000–50,000 followers in 1934. With the exception of an inner cadre of diehard Mosleyites, however, few members appeared active on a regular basis. One historian estimates that only seven of 200 members in Cardiff and 10 of 66 members in Leeds were active. By the end of the 1930s, there were no more than 100 members in the North West and only one full-time worker in the entire north of England.[16] Where was the movement strongest?

Unfortunately, a lack of reliable data makes it extremely difficult to respond convincingly to this question. Academics suggest the largest and most active branches were in London, Manchester, Lancashire and Yorkshire and, to a lesser extent, some seaside towns along the South Coast.[17] Yet as the outbreak of the Second World War approached, it was London's East End which emerged as its 'stronghold'. According to one estimate, in 1936–1938 more than half of the entire membership was concentrated in this area.[18]

It is also extremely difficult to shed light on the questions of who joined the movement and why. Some suggest early recruits arrived from the New Party, British Fascisti or Imperial Fascist League (IFL), and were drawn mainly from the armed services, middle classes, self-employed and fringes of the Conservative Party. In contrast, members of the more active Blackshirts and branches in the East End appear to have come from the working classes.[19] A similar picture emerges from the most comprehensive study of BUF membership, which suggests there were two distinct factions; on one side were unemployed members of the working classes; on the other were more affluent members of the professional classes, such as ex-army officers. It seems likely that the former were recruited from the textile and shipping industries in Pennine Lancashire, Liverpool and the East End, while the latter were concentrated more heavily in southern England.[20]

While the BUF attracted a significant grassroots base, its associations with continental fascism and propensity for political violence almost certainly alienated large sections of the electorate and mainstream establishment. In elections and the streets, Mosley never came close to producing his much anticipated seizure of power and, following the outbreak of war, was interned alongside his loyal lieutenants.

National Front (NF)

The political realities of postwar Europe rendered any attempt to return to the fascist blueprint futile. Nazi-style claims of racial supremacy, anti-Semitic theories and calls to overthrow the democratic system sparked little interest among weary, war-torn populations.[21] Amid the rubble of war and knowledge of the atrocities which had been committed in the name of fascism and Nazism, political parties that were associated with this legacy found themselves stripped of legitimacy. In several cases, such as the openly neo-Nazi Socialist Reich Party (SRP) in Germany or National European Social Movement (NESB) in the Netherlands, parties were banned outright. Elsewhere, parties which advocated similar ideas but did not breach constitutional law were branded pariahs and put into political quarantine (a *cordon sanitaire*). Across the continent, parties which held their roots directly in the fascist tradition were sent back into the electoral desert along with their grandiose visions of racial supremacy and national rebirth.

British fascists who resurfaced after the war similarly encountered a hostile environment and few opportunities. Britons had emerged victorious from war, and anti-fascism was now a key ingredient of their national identity. Mosley, however, failed to grasp that he was damaged goods and gathered together 1,500 followers in the Union Movement (UM). After changing track by calling for European unity, in the 1950s he then targeted signs of anxiety among Londoners over the emerging issue of immigration. While the issue would later become the *raison d'être* of the postwar extreme right, the UM's demands for a 'white Brixton' failed to resonate and the veteran agitator finally withdrew from British politics.[22] The vacuum left by the departure of Mosley was soon filled by a new generation of activists, who advocated an alternative and less sophisticated strand of right-wing extremism. The new realities of postwar politics were seemingly lost on these 'racial nationalists' who clung to the core pillars of interwar Nazism. The doctrine of racial nationalism marked less a quest to forge a new ideological synthesis than a crude attempt to mobilize voters through anti-immigrant, anti-Semitic and anti-democratic appeals.

As their name implied, these activists thrust issues of race and nationalism to the forefront of campaigns, preaching crude racism and anti-democratic appeals to the few citizens who seemed willing to listen. Racial nationalism was emblematic of a particular type of extreme right ideology that combined three elements: biological racism; virulent anti-Semitism; and a revolutionary critique of the liberal democratic system.[23] The seeds of this tradition had been nurtured by figures such as Arnold Leese, an obscure yet highly influential figure, who was described by one historian as the 'most fanatical, uncompromising and idiosyncratic of fascists'.[24] Inspired by the rise of continental fascism, Leese underwent a bizarre transition from a veterinarian who specialized in camel diseases to joining the British Fascisti and becoming one of the first fascist councillors in England.

Leese subsequently became a leading advocate of racial nationalism, though in particular anti-Semitism. In his autobiography, for example, he recollects becoming aware of a 'Jewish plot for world domination' and issued vitriolic tirades against the 'Jew Menace'.[25] To some extent, Leese sought to cloak these ideas with a veneer of intellectual respectability by preaching pseudo-scientific theories about race and the alleged biological inequalities that differentiate groups. Like elsewhere in interwar Europe, Darwinian ideas about natural selection and the 'survival of the fittest' were manipulated and cited as evidence for the biological supremacy of the white race. Given these views, it is not surprising that some considered the former camel doctor to be the nearest equivalent to an 'English Hitler'.[26]

In the 1920s, these ideas found their expression in the Imperial Fascist League (IFL), an organization characterized by an 'uncompromising crude racial fascism, extremist policies, and a language and style of propaganda that often bordered on lunacy'.[27] Reflecting the influence of German Nazism, Leese's IFL ordered its few hundred followers (most of whom arrived via the Britons Society) to adorn themselves with Blackshirts and an armband that featured a swastika superimposed on the Union Jack. The influence of National Socialism was also evident in the IFL's emphasis on Nordic racial supremacism and claims that Jews were encouraging racial integration to undermine the British Empire.[28] The activists who emerged from under the shadow of Leese marked an important departure from the first wave. Leese had considered Mosley too moderate in his views toward the 'Jewish question', and encouraged his followers to subscribe more forcefully to eugenic ideas. One proposal was to use the instruments of the state to prevent the purity of the white race from being 'contaminated by inbreeding with inferior racial stocks'.[29] While the IFL made no impact in elections whatsoever, Leese would exert such an influence over racial nationalists that some suggest he supplanted Mosley as the Chief mentor of the extreme right.[30] It was the legacy of Leese and not Mosley which breathed new life into postwar currents.

Leese was not the only source of inspiration for racial nationalists. The ideas of A.K. Chesterton, who was previously a prominent member of the BUF, were also absorbed, including by some Conservatives who lamented the decline of Empire.[31] By the mid-1950s, Chesterton was playing a key role in the League of Empire Loyalists (LEL) which was more pressure group than political party and campaigned to preserve the British Empire and end non-white immigration. The contribution of the LEL to the evolution of the extreme right was two-fold: first, it dressed its murkier anti-Semitic ideas in a more respectable overcoat in an attempt to appeal to disillusioned members of the Conservative right-wing fringe; and second, despite attracting only 3,000 followers at its peak in 1957 it also served as an incubator for racial nationalists like John Tyndall, who would later establish the BNP.[32] In fact, Tyndall drew a straight line from his own knowledge of politics to Chesterton.[33]

After the LEL, Tyndall passed through numerous movements on the extremist fringe, including the openly neo-Nazi National Socialist Movement (NSM). Rather than seeking mass support, the NSM put strong emphasis on recruiting an elite cadre of activists, even attempting to establish a small paramilitary formation. In 1961, Tyndall and other NSM members were arrested after police uncovered stockpiles of pistols, uniforms, Nazi flags, swastika armbands and recordings of speeches by Hitler.[34] Tyndall saw the NSM as a direct continuation of the IFL, and the neo-Nazi tradition continued to cast a long shadow over his political career.[35] When Harold Wilson's Labour Government was elected in 1964, Tyndall had moved on to establish the Greater Britain Movement (GBM), the aim of which was 'to uphold, and preach, pure National Socialism'.[36] Tyndall reaffirmed his ideological heritage when establishing his own political journal the next decade, which was described from the outset as 'an organ of National Socialist opinion in Britain'.[37]

Also active in the LEL was John Bean, who first entered politics under the influence of Mosley. Bean also became a leading advocate of racial nationalism and took these ideas into various groups, the most significant of which was an earlier incarnation of the BNP that was launched in the 1960s. Like the BNP that would be established by Tyndall some two decades later, this earlier version called for the compulsory repatriation of immigrants, warned of the threat posed by international Jewish financiers and stressed the biological superiority of the white race. Bean's BNP relied on a minuscule membership and never posed a serious challenge, although its leader took some comfort from polling a respectable 9 per cent in Southall at the general election in 1964.

Ideology of the NF

Neither Leese nor Chesterton had a track record of electoral success, yet their ideas were still absorbed by activists like Tyndall and Bean and carried into the second-wave National Front, which was born in February 1967. The NF was the result of an uneasy merger between rival groups. While most of the early recruits arrived from the LEL and Bean's BNP, additional members also came from the Racial Preservation Society (RPS), Anglo-Rhodesian Society and, after some discussion, Tyndall's openly neo-Nazi GBM.[38] These roots ensured that most leading activists were socialized in racial nationalism, and had a long history of involvement with the extreme right. For example, aside from Bean and Tyndall, Martin Webster had been active in the LEL, NSM and GBM; Andrew Fountaine was involved with the National Labour Party (NLP), the BNP and had fought for Franco in the Spanish Civil War; and numerous other NF organizers had been involved with either the BUF or IFL.[39] Although electoral growth would later attract more experienced and respectable recruits from the Conservative fringe, for much of its short life the NF was dominated by racial nationalists. This was reflected in the fact that each of the five activists who controlled the party during its heyday in the 1970s had a long history of involvement with extreme right politics.[40]

From the outset, these networks ensured that the NF adhered to the core pillars of racial nationalism and quickly took the form of a neo-Nazi party. As discussed in the Introduction, neo-Nazi parties are a subset in the wider extreme right family that are characterized by three core features: radical xenophobia; biological racism and anti-Semitism; and overt hostility toward liberal democracy.[41] The radical xenophobia of the NF was revealed in its overwhelming preoccupation with issues of race and immigration; for example, more than 80 per cent of available space in its newspaper was devoted to race-related issues.[42] The party consistently sought to mobilize intolerance toward immigration by framing immigrants and minority groups as a 'threat' to the resources and even survival of white Britons. One example was a National Front march in the mid-1970s which followed a banner claiming that 80 per cent of muggers were black and 85 per cent of their victims were white.[43] In another campaign, the party claimed 'thousands of immigrants pouring into Britain ... have been given immediate priority over homeless British families'.[44] In response to these perceived threats, the NF demanded that immigrants be forcibly removed from the country through a policy of compulsory repatriation.

Given wider trends in public opinion (see below), the xenophobic appeals of the NF may have resonated with a large section of the electorate that was increasingly concerned about a new phase of immigration and its effects. However, its racial nationalist roots ensured that the NF offered citizens more than simple racial populism. Its second ideological feature was crude biological racism, which led the party to argue that different groups can be divided into superior or inferior categories based on their genetics. The argument was that 'the nature of man as a physical and social animal was predominantly, if not exclusively, determined by his genetic inheritance'.[45] The world of racial nationalism is principally one of race and nation, where groups are organized into hierarchies and their behaviour and social status are explained on the basis of their biological characteristics. Though white Britons are racially supreme, their racial purity is threatened by Jewish-led plots to encourage multiculturalism and racial integration. These ideas were communicated to supporters through historical examples, such as the fall of the Roman Empire, which the NF traced to a decision by weak leaders to grant non-Romans citizenship. In turn, the purity of the racial group was weakened and so was its resolve when under attack from foreign invaders.[46]

This crude racism spilled into election literature, such as the demand for an alliance between 'white' Commonwealth states and to focus the British state on improving the purity of white Britons. Intertwined with this biological racism was virulent and conspiratorial anti-Semitism. One claim, for example, was that Jews were promoting immigration and internationalism to encourage the mixing of racial groups and apocalyptic-style race war. These conspiratorial plans were orchestrated by secretive Jewish organizations, such as the Bilderburg group, the Rockefeller and Rothschild families, and institutions like the World Bank. Confronted with these threats, the NF urged members to become 'Jew wise' and familiarize themselves with revisionist arguments, such as that millions of Jews were not gassed in the Second World War and the Holocaust was the 'Hoax of the Century'.[47] Writing in his autobiography, John Tyndall (who led the NF on two separate occasions) described his own awareness of an alleged Jewish-led conspiracy as follows: 'it started to come home to me . . . that there was present in Britain and around the world a definite Jewish network wielding immense influence and power . . . The truth was inescapable.'[48]

The NF also expressed overt hostility to the values, procedures and institutions of the liberal democratic state, and often hinted at the need to overthrow the system. For the NF, liberal values and democratic governance undermined racial purity, the quality of political leadership and encouraged the degeneration of British society. Though more disguised than its racist attitudes, the NF offered voters a revolutionary critique of the democratic system and advocated that conventional party politics and special interests be subordinated to the primary interests of race and nation. Its literature often outlined the case for a strong leader and dictatorship, ridiculed liberal values for encouraging multiculturalism and advocated that the state be reorganized around the goal of upholding and improving the purity of white Britons.

Rise of the NF

While the NF held its roots in a longer tradition, it was born into a particularly turbulent period in British politics. In economics, the postwar boom had been replaced by slow growth, recession and growing industrial unrest. Meanwhile, in the political arena the two main parties were facing new challenges. The bonds between citizens and the main parties were loosening and the former were becoming increasingly volatile in elections. Whereas partisan loyalties had once guided their behaviour, issues were now playing a more important role. There had also emerged a new and potentially explosive issue on which both the Conservatives and Labour were unsure about how to respond.

Before the 1960s, the average voter had little or no direct experience of immigration. Though some immigrants had followed employment opportunities in areas like Cardiff, Liverpool and London, the numbers were low. In fact, most Britons in the 1950s were unable to detail a personal encounter with immigrants. According to one survey, for example, more than half of the population had never personally seen or interacted with a 'coloured colonial subject'.[49] This situation was about to change radically. The birth of the NF coincided with a new phase of immigration which partly stemmed from labour shortages created by the postwar boom and a lack of formal restrictions on entry. For immigrants, dismal socio-economic conditions and political unrest in their home countries also provided an incentive to move. The result was that New Commonwealth immigrants from the West Indies and then Bangladesh, India and Pakistan arrived and settled in growing numbers, rising from approximately 2,000 in 1953 to more than 136,000 in 1961. Many of these early immigrants were joined by family members and moved into urban areas which offered the most opportunities for skilled and semi-skilled workers, mainly Greater London, the Midlands and parts of Yorkshire.[50] Despite some legislative attempts to curb the number entering the country, such as the 1962 Commonwealth Immigrants Act which revoked the right of Commonwealth citizens to enter without restriction, there was not a dramatic decline. Even as economic growth slowed and unemployment rose, between 1969 and 1978 more than half a million immigrants arrived and settled.[51]

While attracting alarmist and frequently hostile media coverage, this change was followed by a striking increase in the importance of immigration in the minds of ordinary Britons. From the late 1960s, surveys revealed the extent to which the population had become profoundly anxious about immigration and its effects: large majorities thought there were too many immigrants in the country and made clear their preference for a more restrictive immigration policy. In fact, through much of the 1960s and 1970s, more than 80 per cent of voters thought too many immigrants had been let into Britain while 20 per cent went further by supporting the idea of sending immigrants back to their countries of origin (the core policy of the NF). In one survey, citizens felt so strongly about the issue that they elaborated beyond the closed question to express their view that immigrants were having a negative impact on housing, jobs and living standards. Some academics who were observing these trends were unable to escape the conclusion that not only was there considerable public support for reducing immigration, but that strong and overwhelmingly hostile attitudes toward immigrants were quite widespread among the population.[52] At the same time, there were also signs of uncertainty among Britons over which party would deliver the most competent performance on this issue. Between 1964 and 1966, voters were asked which of the two main parties was most likely to stop immigration and more than half said there was not much difference between them.[53]

It was amid this climate that the maverick Conservative MP Enoch Powell delivered his infamous 'rivers of blood' speech in 1968, which called for a halt to immigration and floated the idea of using financial incentives to encourage the repatriation of immigrants. Though Powell was promptly sacked from the Shadow Cabinet, three quarters of Britons expressed agreement with his ideas and two thirds thought the Conservative leader (Edward Heath) had been wrong to demote the rebel MP.[54] Yet beyond the immediate humdrum of party politics, Powellism had a more profound impact. The intervention generated considerable interest in the NF's core issues, and there is some evidence that it profited from the publicity. Interviews with NF organizers suggest Powell's speech sparked an influx of new recruits, most of whom arrived from the Conservatives.[55] Some also argue that Powell fuelled a more favourable climate for the extreme right by legitimizing the consideration of repatriation, a policy which until this point remained the exclusive property of right-wing extremists and ultra-Conservatives.[56] Though the NF advocated *compulsory* rather than *voluntary* repatriation, by the time voters received its literature they would at least have heard about the policy. An additional effect of Powellism, however, was less beneficial for the extreme right. While Powell emerged as a dissenting voice within his own party, there is evidence that his intervention actually strengthened a link in the minds of voters between the centre-right Conservatives and opposition to immigration. As one political sociologist points out, it is likely that Powell played a key role in the increased willingness of Britons to identify with the Conservatives on immigration. Between 1966 and 1979, the percentage considering the Conservatives as the preferred party on immigration more than doubled from 28 per cent to 61 per cent (meanwhile, the percentage favoring Labour plummeted by 18 points to just 2 per cent).[57] By the end of the 1970s, the Conservatives had assumed ownership over the issue which offered the most opportunities to the extreme right.

While the 1960s had seen the birth of the NF and Powellism, the 'explosive possibilities' of immigration had still been only partially recognized.[58] Over the next decade, political opportunities stemming from this issue came into much sharper focus. Britons remained firmly opposed to immigration and in favour of tougher restrictions. The percentage who felt strongly that 'coloured' immigration should be reduced peaked at 77 per cent in 1970 and remained at high levels thereafter.[59] In fact, between 1964 and 1979 this figure never dropped below 70 per cent, while 20 per cent continued to express support for repatriation. Nor was immigration a fleeting concern; more than 80 per cent of Britons polled said they felt strongly about the issue.[60]

Aside from the increased salience of immigration, there was also a more specific opportunity for the NF. Though Powell helped marry Britons who were hostile toward immigration with the Conservatives, in the mid-1970s there emerged signs of doubt among citizens about the sincerity of this partnership. Powell openly criticized the Conservative record on immigration and even broke ranks in 1974 by urging his supporters to vote Labour. For Britons who were anxious over immigration, dissatisfied with the performance of the Conservatives and unconvinced that Labour could do a better job, there appeared few obvious homes for their vote.

The failure of the NF to take full advantage of these conditions owed much to the way in which it arrived late on the scene. It was entirely absent at the 1964 general election which might otherwise have yielded promising returns. Similarly, though public concern over immigration reached its zenith in 1970, at the general election that year the NF stood only 10 candidates and failed to invest seriously in the campaign. Even when it began contesting elections on a more consistent basis, bitter infighting and a continual lack of resources stifled its attempts at election-eering. Some minor cause for optimism arrived two years later when the NF polled 8 per cent in a by-election in Uxbridge, but it remained unclear when or even whether a breakthrough would take place.

The demoralized racial nationalists were then unexpectedly reinvigorated following the arrival of 27,000 Ugandan Asians. The event further fuelled anxiety among Britons and encouraged the NF to throw all of its weight into a by-election in West Bromwich in 1973. Benefitting from the absence of a Liberal candidate which might otherwise have split the protest vote, the NF polled over 16 per cent of the vote. It was the first and only time the party saved a deposit. It was also in this period when membership peaked at 15,000, although some estimate that as many as 60,000–70,000 passed through the NF during the 1970s.[61] Few members, however, were regularly active and most watched the two general elections in 1974 from their armchairs. The NF commenced these campaigns in a bad state. Prior to the first contest in February, over half of its 30 branches were complaining about a lack of money to fund deposits and literature. The situation became so dire that some branches could not even afford envelopes required for the free delivery of election addresses.[62]

The NF sought to attract voters by stressing its total opposition to immigration, overseas aid and preferential housing for the Ugandan Asians who had fled Idi Amin.[63] It also adhered to a confrontational strategy of 'march and grow', organizing provocative rallies to attract publicity and, hopefully, some new recruits. In the end, however, the 54 NF candidates averaged just over 3 per cent in seats contested (see Table 1.1).[64] The NF continued to poll strongly in the West Midlands, where it attracted more than 7 per cent in West Bromwich West, but a lack of progress in the target areas of Leicester, Wolverhampton and London was a bitter disappointment.

Nor did the party perform much stronger in the second election in October. Confrontational marches over the summer helped establish the NF as a household name but a lack of money continued to hamper progress. Despite increasing its number of candidates to 90, it invested less money into the campaign than every other party, including the Communists.[65] Furthermore, while the party had expe-rienced membership growth it was failing to convince supporters to get active and knock on doors. The Birmingham branch, for example, complained how despite a three-fold increase in members the number of *activists* was exactly the same as at

TABLE 1.1 Support for the NF in general elections, 1970–2010

Election	Votes	Candidates	Average vote in seats contested (%)	Highest vote (%)
1970	10,902	10	3.6	5.6
1974 (Feb)	76,865	54	3.2	7.8
1974 (Oct)	113,843	90	3.1	9.4
1979	191,719	303	1.3	7.6
1983	27,065	60	1.1	3.7
1987	286	1[a]	0.6	0.6
1992	3,984	14	0.7	1.2
1997	2,716	6[b]	1.2	1.2
2001	2,484	5	1.5	2.2
2005	8,079	13	1.6	2.6
2010	10,784	17	1.4	4.9

Source: R. Eatwell (2000) 'The extreme right and British exceptionalism: The primacy of politics', in P. Hainsworth (ed.) *The politics of the extreme right: From the margins to the mainstream*, London: Pinter; J. Yonwin (2004) *Electoral performance of far right parties in the UK*, London: House of Commons Research Report SN/SG/1982; BBC Election Archive.

Note: (a) An unofficial candidate from the NF Flag Group contested the constituency of Bristol East. (b) A rival extreme right party – the National Democrats (ND) – fielded 21 candidates who, combined, received 10,829 votes and averaged 1.2 per cent (the highest vote was 11 per cent).

the previous election in February.[66] Compared with the election eight months prior, it attracted only an additional 37,000 votes while its average vote in seats contested dropped to 3.1 per cent and every deposit was lost.

With little progress being made nationally, the party switched its attention to local glimmers of hope. In 1976, the much-publicized arrival of Malawian Asians who had been expelled from their home country (and who were British passport holders) became a new target for the NF's opportunism. In local elections that year, the party polled strongly in Blackburn, Bradford, Sandwell, Leicester and Wolverhampton – areas where it had been active for some time.[67] These local enclaves of support, however, failed to produce elected representation. To make matters worse, it was a breakaway party – the National Party (NP) – which gained two councillors in Blackburn and the first elected representation for the extreme right in more than three decades.

Where was the NF strongest? Its support was not distributed evenly across the country but was concentrated heavily in urban working-class districts in regions that experienced a significant influx of immigration – mainly London, the Midlands and, to a lesser extent, Yorkshire. Within these regions, the NF recruited most of its support from more deprived districts in North East London, Bradford, Leicester, Sandwell and Wolverhampton. It struggled to build a presence outside of these areas and was virtually non-existent beyond the borders of England.[68] Like its predecessors, the NF was based mainly in London where it built on a legacy of anti-immigrant campaigns. In the immediate period preceding its birth, the League of Empire Loyalists, the National Labour Party and John Bean's BNP had all focused on London and so the NF simply picked up from where they left off. London hosted more than half of its electoral 'strongholds' and, between 1967 and 1974, almost two thirds of NF candidates in general elections.[69] This owed much to the way in which the NF's internal organization was skewed heavily toward the capital. During its heyday in the mid-1970s, the NF relied on approximately 30 branches and 54 smaller groups, although most were in London or surrounding areas in the South East.[70]

Drilling down further, it becomes clear that the NF's real heartland was London's East End, where it became heir to a particular tradition in British politics. While polling strongly in the East End and along the Lea Valley, 'the real NF heartland was confined to a relatively restricted area within the old East End – in fact, the western part covering Bethnal Green, Shoreditch, Hoxton and Haggerston, an area of two to three square miles'.[71] The party also had lingering appeal in the capital; in elections to the Greater London Council (GLC) in 1977 it attracted support from 120,000 Londoners. Despite the respectable result, however, a wider breakthrough seemed increasingly unlikely. In the same year, the NF averaged less than 1 per cent in county council elections, which was 'hardly the signal for those opposed to the NF to leave the country'.[72]

Who voted National Front?

Unfortunately, there is a lack of reliable data on who voted for the NF and why. Citizens who vote for extreme right parties are often reluctant to 'confess' their choice, and as a result they seldom appear in surveys in large numbers. Because of these difficulties, studies often relied on aggregate-level rather than individual-level data. These analyses concentrate on aggregations of individuals, for example, the relationship between levels of unemployment, education and immigration in a particular area and levels of support for the NF. While aggregate studies throw light on these relationships, they tell us little about the motivations driving *individual* National Front voters.

With these limitations in mind, aggregate-level studies traced NF support to urban working-class areas which had lower than average levels of education and large immigrant communities.[73] The party performed strongest in areas where there were sizeable immigrant populations, and which were located in more diverse regions of the country. For example, at the 1974 (February) general election, it polled on average 2 per cent higher in constituencies with large numbers of New Commonwealth immigrants. Similarly, at the 1979 general election, virtually all of the 49 seats where it polled over 2 per cent of the vote were located in three areas of the country that had large concentrations of immigrants: North East London, Leicester and the Black Country.[74] Building on these studies, one academic suggested that it is 'only one further step to the conclusion that primarily economically marginal, culturally threatened white workers in heavily working-class districts felt attracted to the National Front'.[75] Individual-level studies of NF voters supported this interpretation, revealing NF supporters to have a relatively distinct social profile: they tended to be young, employed men from the skilled working classes. According to one study, seven out of ten were male, the same portion was working class and five out of ten were 15–34 years old (see Table 1.2 below). They also tended to be based in areas which had experienced higher than average levels of immigration, mainly Greater London and the West Midlands.[76]

The fact that NF supporters shared a similar social profile and tended to congregate in particular social contexts provides some evidence that the party was not simply a by-product of political protest. If this were the case, then we would expect its support to be distributed more widely across different social groups. Instead, the NF received support mainly from citizens who occupied more precarious positions in society – young and employed skilled male workers in urban and more diverse areas of the country – and who felt threatened by immigration. Unlike more affluent citizens or the unemployed, it is the skilled working classes who are most likely to feel they have 'something to lose' from immigration and rising ethno-cultural diversity.[77] Because of their precarious position, skilled workers are more likely than other groups to encounter competition from immigrants and feel their resources or ways of life are under threat. This is exacerbated by the fact that immigrants also tend to be more deprived, often entering labour and housing markets on the same step of the social ladder as semi-skilled and skilled workers.

To probe whether this is the case, it is necessary to examine the attitudes of NF supporters. Elsewhere in Europe, it has been shown that while extreme right supporters share a distinct profile, the most powerful predictor of whether somebody will vote for a party like the NF are their attitudes toward particular issues, especially immigration. Rather than simply voting in knee-jerk reaction to socio-economic change or political protest, some citizens choose to endorse the policies offered by the extreme right.[78] Although there is a lack of data on the attitudes of NF supporters, the evidence which is available points in a similar direction. One study of NF sympathizers suggested there was a strong ideological basis to their support; in areas where the NF polled strongly, its supporters expressed disproportionately high levels of concern about the presence of blacks. They were also more likely than other survey respondents to perceive that the local neighbourhood had deteriorated, and to attribute this community decline to the presence of immigrants.[79]

NF support in the East End was similarly traced to economic insecurities among working-class residents which, it was suggested, were partly a by-product of the casual labour system of the old docklands. Subsequent waves of immigration had led some workers in traditionally ethnically homogenous areas to perceive that traditional close-knit communities were under threat from immigration. The argument put forward by Husbands was that these local conditions had fuelled the development of a laager mentality about the neighbourhood, and a propensity to support exclusionary anti-immigrant campaigns. While these traditions of racial

TABLE 1.2 Demographic characteristics of NF voters

	English adult population (%)	*NF support (%)*
Sex		
Male	48	71
Female	52	29
Age		
15–20 years	10	21
21–24 years	8	16
25–34 years	18	16
35–44 years	15	15
45–54 years	15	14
55 years or more	34	18
Social class		
Higher non-manual (AB)	16	6
Lower non-manual (C1)	22	22
Skilled manual (C2)	35	46
Semi-/unskilled manual and residual (DE)	27	26
Region		
Greater London	16	25
South East	20	17
South West	9	12
East Anglia	4	3
East Midlands	7	5
West Midlands	12	23
North	31	15
Working status		
Full time	47	68
Not full time	53	32
Property		
Owner/mortgage	55	53
Rented	34	41
Privately rented/other	11	6
Social class by age and sex		
Male, 15–34, ABC1	7	13
Male, 15–34, C2DE	11	25
Male, 35 or more, ABC1	11	9
Male, 35 or more, C2DE	19	24
Female, 15–34, ABC1	7	3
Female, 15–34, C2DE	11	11
Female, 35 or more, ABC1	13	3
Female, 35 or more, C2DE	21	11
N	*37,302*	*270*

Source: Adapted from M. Harrop, J. England and C.T. Husbands (1980) 'The bases of National Front support', *Political Studies*, 28(2): 271–283. Divergences from a total of 100 per cent are due to rounding error. The random omnibus surveys were conducted between October 1977 and April 1978. NF voters defined as anyone who mentioned the National Front (or its short-lived offshoot, the National Party) when asked 'How would you vote if there were a general election tomorrow?', and then 'Which party are you most inclined to support?' (if they refuse to answer the first).

exclusionism may have laid dormant for decades, they were reignited by an influx of immigrants or campaigns by the NF which sought to embellish a sense of racial threat.[80] The only other attempt to probe the attitudes of NF voters suggested they were characterized by disproportionately high levels of dissatisfaction with the performance of the government and leaders of the three main parties. Almost 75 per cent of NF supporters were dissatisfied with the government (compared to 46 per cent of the sample overall), and they were also more likely to express dissatisfaction with the Labour and Conservative leaderships. This suggests NF support was driven mainly by members of the 'white urban working class' who felt under threat from 'coloured' immigration and shared a 'sense that the existing political structure is incapable of responding to the perceived threat'.[81]

Demise of the NF

By the end of the 1970s, several factors had combined to stifle the NF's prospect of a wider breakthrough. The Conservatives had been assuming ownership over the immigration issue and, in the late 1970s, this lead was reinforced by the emergence of a new leader. In response to the increased salience of the issue as well as voices within her own party, Margaret Thatcher pitched specifically to NF supporters when she expressed sympathy for Britons who felt they 'might be rather swamped by people with a different culture' and raised the prospect of 'an end to immigration'.[82] The intervention almost certainly attracted significant numbers of volatile NF supporters back into the fold of mainstream politics.[83] For Britons anxious over immigration, the Thatcherite brand of right-wing populism offered a more credible response.

This image of competence contrasted sharply with the stained image of the NF. Its stigma was revealed in a range of surveys and polls, for example: almost 70 per cent held unfavourable views of the Front and thought it was deliberately stirring up racial problems to gain support; more than 60 per cent thought it would be bad for Britain if NF candidates entered the House of Commons; and more than 50 per cent rejected the suggestion that it expressed the views of ordinary working people. Most Britons were also unconvinced by the party's lacklustre attempts to downplay its roots and images of leaders dressed in Nazi regalia: more than 60 per cent thought the NF had a 'Nazi side' and more than half thought it wanted 'a dictatorship not a democracy'.[84]

Particularly from the mid-1970s onward, this extremist baggage was increasingly publicized by an organized anti-fascist movement. Labour banned the NF from using municipal buildings in more than 100 councils under its control and, in 1977, the Joint Committee against Racialism (JCAR) and the Anti-Nazi League (ANL) were formed with the goal of highlighting its Nazi sympathies.[85] The NF's negative image was further entrenched in the minds of voters by the ineptitude of its leaders. In 1974, for example, the NF Chairman John Tyndall was interviewed on prime-time television and watched by more than eight million viewers. As one commentator noted at the time, Tyndall made clear 'that the NF opposed mixed marriages, and that coloured people would go to the bottom of every queue for housing and social services before they were repatriated'.[86] Some of his fellow members were so dismayed with the performance that they subsequently voted Tyndall out of the leadership.

Most Britons reached the conclusion that the NF did not belong to normal democratic politics, and so it is difficult to see how it might have mobilized mass support. It fought the 1979 general election under the slogan 'It's Our Country, Let's Win It Back', but watched its support continue to slide. The campaign was marred by violence, notably at one riot in Southall which ended with more than 300 arrests and the death of anti-fascist campaigner Blair Peach. Despite fielding an impressive 303 candidates, the NF lacked the resources which might otherwise have minimized electoral losses.[87] Instead, it was forced to explain to supporters why it had polled a derisory 0.6 per cent of the total vote. The result was a disaster and confirmed the demise of the second-wave National Front.

2

IN THE GHETTO

1982–1999

Through the streets now we are marching
Like an army as to war
For the cause of race and nation,
With our banners to the fore.
Into battle, into battle, into battle BNP!
Into battle BNP!
                    BNP marching song (1982)[1]

The British National Party (BNP) was formed on 7th April 1982. As the party recalled some three decades later, it was the result of 'a merger of like-minded patriotic organisations'.[2] Those who were most active in setting up the party came from either the National Front (NF) or the New National Front (NNF), a break-away party established by Tyndall following his departure from the NF and which became a bridge between the second and third waves.[3] Strong continuity with the past was reflected in the fact that at least 40 per cent of the BNP's 54 candidates who contested its first general election in 1983 had previously represented the NF at the previous election in 1979. Continuity was also apparent in the lineage of activists awarded with leading positions. Most had previously been influential players in the NF and were socialized in the racial nationalist tradition. Before standing for the BNP in 1983, Charles Parker represented the NF in elections in 1974 and 1979, and organized its activities in Surrey and Sussex. David Bruce, who became BNP organizer in North London (a position he retained until his death in 1998), had previously served as NF treasurer. Before being made responsible for the BNP youth wing, the Young Nationalists (YN), Richard Edmonds stood for the NF in elections, sat on its national directorate and led recruits in London. Similarly, John Peacock, who became BNP organizer in the

East Midlands and its main point of contact with similar parties elsewhere in Europe, had also been active in the Front.

Like these early recruits, numerous other activists had cut their political teeth in the NF: Len Walker organized the NF in Plymouth; Robert Rhodes led recruits in Cheltenham and Gloucester; Roy Sinclair ran the NF in Thurrock; Tony Braithwaite was regional agent in Yorkshire; Michael Easter organized activities in Kent; Kenneth McKilliam contested elections; Ronald Rickord supervised campaigns in Buckinghamshire; Colin Bayliss ran the NF in the East Midlands; and Terry Fitzgerald stood in elections.[4] In fact, each of the five activists made responsible for the BNP's general election campaign in 1983 had played active roles in its parent party.[5] From its birth, therefore, the BNP was dominated by ex-members of the NF who profoundly shaped its ideological and strategic direction. There was little incentive to abandon racial nationalism and set out in a new direction.

Ideology of the early BNP

Like his followers, the founder of the BNP and its inaugural Chairman had assumed a leading position in the NF and saw no reason to cut off or conceal these roots. For Tyndall, the establishment of the BNP marked the third serious attempt to build a 'nationalist' movement in British politics. Both its 'style and spirit' were seen as a continuation of its predecessor.[6] Rather than pursue a new ideological model, the aim behind the establishment of the BNP was to provide racial nationalists with a more effective vehicle through which they could pursue their goals, as Tyndall explained: 'British nationalism inherited from the 1970s an ideology that was quite adequate to all demands. Instead, what was needed was a form of organization that would enable the movement to promote these ideas more effectively.'[7]

Under Tyndall, the BNP's commitment to racial nationalist principles was continually underscored. Even shortly before his removal as leader in 1999, the veteran wrote to the few diehard loyalists who remained in the moribund NF, in the hope of encouraging their defection. The latter were assured that there was 'scarcely any difference in ideology or policy save in the minutest detail' between the two parties. The BNP, Tyndall continued, remained firmly loyal to the tradition which had come to dominate the postwar extreme right: 'The BNP is a racial nationalist party which believes in Britain for the British, which is to say racial separation.'[8] Like its grassroots base, there was little in the ideology of the early BNP that marked a departure from the 1970s. It clung rigidly to the core pillars of biological racism, radical xenophobia and anti-democratic appeals. Yet with Tyndall at the helm, the party had also absorbed a more overt tradition of neo-Nazism. While this tradition was present in the NF, it had been forced into an uneasy coexistence with a more ultra-conservative populist wing. But with Tyndall now firmly in control and no populists to appease, the BNP was free to indulge in Nazi nostalgia and express allegiance to a political legacy which similar parties elsewhere in Europe were actively seeking to avoid. During its formative years, for example, it devoted scant effort to concealing the source of its ideological inspiration: it praised Nazi Germany's 'fine blend' of private enterprise and socialism, and encouraged followers to subscribe to *The League Review*, which was described as a 'pro-National Socialist' journal.[9]

The belief system of the BNP was anchored in ethnic nationalism, under which meant questions of national identity and belonging were defined along the lines of race, or as Tyndall explained: 'Race and not geographical location, is the cement that binds nations.'[10] As some of its more successful continental cousins began modifying their discourse on issues of immigration and race, the BNP continued to espouse crude racism and claims of racial supremacy, arguing for example that 'Whites, and Whites alone, must hold power . . . [and] appoint as their political leaders only those who will be ruthless in eliminating alien races from their society.'[11] Reflecting the enduring legacy of Chesterton and Leese, the party also sought to validate its claims by recruiting pseudo-scientific theories. Even at the time of the 1997 general election, its monthly newspaper was highlighting research in psychology when suggesting that differences in intelligence between whites and non-whites provide an understanding for 'inter-racial social problems', and was quoting a Professor of Law when claiming that 'black students cannot match the academic achievements of white students'.[12]

This biological form of racism was offered to Britons during sporadic campaigns. At one election, the party sought to entice voters by drawing their attention to quotes such as the following: 'The everlasting truth about race is that breed is everything . . . our race should fight . . . to keep its gene pool holy, unsullied and inviolable.' At another, it explained to potential supporters how its main goal was 'to hand down to future generations the genes and the blood' of figures like William Shakespeare.[13] The party also offered voters a government that would use the instruments of the state to improve the racial stock of indigenous white Britons and protect them from inferior racial groups. If Britons had received BNP literature in the early 1980s, they would have been asked to endorse plans to 'build a political and social order conducive to the breeding and development of a better population', take action against 'inferior strains within the indigenous races of the British Isles', and forcibly sterilize citizens with 'a family legacy of disease, imbecility or mental or character disorder'.[14] If they had returned to take a second look at the party the next decade, they would similarly have encountered articles titled 'Race Mixing Doesn't Work' (1997) and been told that their existence was threatened by racial integration. If there remained uncertainty about the party's position on intergroup relations, then it would have been removed by statements such as the following: 'As to the question of racially mixed couples, the party has made its position very clear. We neither want the racially alien parent, the mixed-race offspring nor the white renegade responsible for such offspring. They can all go.'[15]

Alongside biological racism, the party also inherited a tradition of anti-Semitism. Unlike other parties in Europe, which were steering clear of anti-Semitic conspiracy theories or restricting them to inner circles, the BNP saw little need to conceal this ideological element. From the outset, at the 1983 general election the party detailed its policies to voters while also complaining how the 'Government's grovelling attitude towards Jewry seems to be boundless'.[16] To a certain extent, it sought to follow its predecessor by attempting to package anti-Semitism as anti-Zionism, or opposition to the movement of Jewish nationalism. As others point out, the strategy marks an attempt to present anti-Zionism as an ordinary political viewpoint rather than an emotional hatred of Jews.[17] In one article, for example, it was argued that '*Zionist influence* in the United States, Britain and elsewhere must be eradicated [emphasis in original]', while at other times the party ominously calculated the number of Jews in Britain.[18]

More often than not, however, the BNP simply indulged in explicit anti-Semitism. This was reflected in the titles of articles which appeared in its newspaper throughout the 1980s and 1990s: 'Jews in the Ascendant', 'Where Do They Stand?', 'MORE "HOLOCAUST" HOGWASH' and 'Israel back-pedals on "Holohoax" toll'. It also advertised books which promised to expose 'fake Holocaust photos'.[19] These ideas were additionally communicated to rank and file members through recommended readings, which included *The Controversy of Zion*, *Did Six Million Really Die?*, *The Hoax of the Twentieth Century*, and *Is the Diary of Anne Frank Genuine?* Others focused on the alleged mysterious activities of a secretive Jewish-led 'Bilderberg Group' which, the party claimed, was controlling international relations.[20]

In an attempt to attract Britons hostile toward immigration, the party also retained the radical xenophobia of the NF, including its core policy of compulsory repatriation. In the early 1990s, the BNP sought to sell the policy to voters on stickers which read simply: 'Our Final Solution: Repatriation.'[21] While the policy would eventually be modified after a change of leadership, Tyndall remained firmly committed to the idea, as he explained in one interview shortly before his death in 2005: '. . . it's really no different to when a court has passed an injunction against a person, for example to vacate a property they're living in . . . at the end of the day if everything else hasn't succeeded, the police arrive one day and say "Mr Jones we've come to take you away from the property". Of course, if he gets violent some kind of forcible means have to be used . . . but in reality it very seldom comes to that.'[22]

In an attempt to cultivate public support for these policies, the party employed xenophobic campaigns which aimed to cultivate a perception among Britons that immigrants and minority groups were different, problematic and threatening. These persistent attempts to frame minority groups as a 'threat' took several forms. First, it was argued that immigration and disproportionately high birth rates among immigrants and minority ethnic groups had thrust ordinary white Britons into a battle for racial survival. This survivalist discourse was reflected in articles titled 'The last invasion?', 'WHITES FACING EXTINCTION', 'SUICIDE OF THE WEST' and 'The silent genocide'.[23] Typical of most was one article – 'Black Population Growth: The Horrifying Truth' – which informed supporters how 'the present birthrate among non-white immigrants in the UK is 112 per 1,000, as compared with 59 per 1,000 among Whites – in other words, *the coloured birthrate is almost double* the white birthrate [emphasis in original]!'[24] In other articles the party similarly claimed that 'by 2000 we will be outnumbered by non-whites, who will have a majority of 10 to 1'.[25] This emphasis on survivalism was often accompanied by apocalyptic themes and predictions that intergroup tensions would soon escalate into race war, for example: 'Race War on the Way', 'Media hushing up race war', 'Race war spreads', 'Is multi-racial Britain on the brink?', 'Tribal War on the Streets', 'London's East End Erupts After Vicious Attacks on Whites', 'Another Race Riot – When Will We Learn?'[26]

Second, it was also argued immigrants and minority ethnic groups threaten law and order and the physical security of white Britons. In virtually every edition of its newspaper, the BNP sought to cultivate a perception of minority groups as threatening social order and the main source of crime, for example; 'Vicious black crime in London', 'Blacks on looting rampage', 'Black criminals get green light', 'More horrific black crimes', 'Black terror stalks London borough', 'Black rape: The horrifying facts', 'White teacher raped in Black Ghetto hell school', 'Boy's face burned off by black maniac', and 'Black Gunmen Let Free'.[27] Meanwhile, local BNP branches were offered leaflets which drew attention to 'muggings, rape and other violent attacks on defenceless people'.[28]

Third, it was argued immigrants and minority groups threaten socio-economic resources, such as jobs, social housing and welfare. Reflective of this discourse was the claim that Britain is 'ruled by bleeding hearts anxious to give away the country's wealth built up by generations to undeserving foreigners'.[29] This welfare chauvinist discourse was often adapted to meet specific events. In the mid-1980s, for example, its youth wing distributed leaflets which asked voters to compare 'the way young Whites have been left on the scrapheap with the specially favoured treatment given to Britain's coloured racial minorities'. Over a decade later, leaflets called for an end to positive discrimination against whites and demanded local authorities prioritize white Britons when distributing resources. Similarly, at the time of the 1997 general election citizens in Dover were told that migrants from Central and Eastern Europe would soon be 'eligible for income support, child benefit and housing benefit totalling at least £260 per week', and so they should tell 'these latest scroungers to clear off'.[30] These attempts to amplify feelings of injustice often included emotive themes, such as one leaflet which contrasted refugees eating an English breakfast with pensioners who 'have to choose whether to eat or to put the fire on and keep warm'.[31]

While offering a toxic combination of biological racism, anti-Semitism and xenophobia, the BNP also absorbed the NF's hostility toward the liberal parliamentary system. During its early years, its renunciation of the democratic system was often unequivocal. Tyndall, for example, defined political power as 'the capability to bring about a revolutionary transformation of British society by dismantling the national institutions . . . and by substituting entirely new institutions in their place'. While the nature of these new institutions remained vague, it was clear the BNP leader was calling for the overthrow of the system: 'I am talking now about institutions of industry, commerce and finance, of education, of mass communication, of culture, of religious worship and, not least, of politics.'[32] Internal bulletins to members shed some light on how these arguments were communicated to the grassroots. At one meeting, the leader called on followers to 'repudiate this system root and branch'.[33] If there remained lingering doubts about the BNP's anti-democratic credentials, these were laid to rest by articles which asked readers the following: 'In which country has the popular will prevailed more in the actions of government – Spain under Franco or Britain under Parliament and the multi-party system? There is not the slightest evidence that the latter has been the case.'[34]

Strategy: the 'no-to-elections' party

The BNP's biologically racist, xenophobic and anti-democratic message situated it among a dwindling band of unsuccessful neo-Nazi parties in Europe. Amid increasingly affluent and better-educated populations, this toxic ideological brand was failing to attract significant support. While European populations had certainly become more distrustful of their established mainstream parties, they remained supportive of democracy as a form of government. While they had also become anxious over immigration and its effects, majorities were increasingly unlikely to endorse the most strident forms of racial prejudice. Political parties which remained blind to these trends struggled to carve out space and tended to remain on the fringes of their party systems.[35]

Nor was the BNP's attempt to rally support helped by its strategy. During the early stage of their life-cycle, political parties often devote much of their energy to 'identity-seeking' goals – they need to: communicate a message; build an image in the minds of citizens; and recruit a stable of committed followers.[36] Only after having met these goals will parties turn their attention toward the more complicated task of widening their appeal and attracting votes. Although the BNP was founded as a political party, for much of its first two decades it steered clear of electoral politics. There was little enthusiasm for chasing votes. If elections were fought, the aim was less to attract voters than to stand enough candidates to qualify for broadcasts which, it was hoped, might attract some new activists. Instead of the ballot box, a distinctly unfavourable environment forced the party to focus on the more pressing goal of political survival. To this end, it prioritized the goals of attracting publicity, recruiting new members, building a presence in different parts of the country and getting its hitherto unknown name into the minds of ordinary Britons. The view from inside the party was that elections could wait.

This strategy was also partly a response to a distinct lack of money and manpower. At the 1983 general election, for example, the party was so weak it was unable to deliver election addresses in 49 of the 54 seats it had chosen to contest. Most branches were left alone to undertake 'ghost campaigns' which involved little more than standing paper candidates, crossing fingers and hoping for the best.[37] Even before results were announced the leadership prepared the ground for disappointment, warning members to avoid the naïve expectations which had accompanied the NF's campaigns in the 1970s.[38] As expected, a series of dismal results reflected a lacklustre effort. Overall, the BNP attracted fewer than 15,000 voters and averaged a paltry 0.6 per cent in seats contested.[39] Nor could the party take comfort from an influx of new blood: while it claimed that its first foray into elections had generated some 3,000 enquiries, membership remained below 2,000.[40]

The result and a subsequent increase in the cost of contesting elections led the cash-strapped party to put its electoral ambitions on hold. While the Representation of the People Act in 1985 reduced the threshold which parties had to meet to save their deposits (from 12.5 to 5 per cent), it also increased the cost of deposits to £500, thereby placing an additional hurdle in front of minor parties. From here on, the BNP announced its strategy would consist of 'very limited involvement' in elections.[41] Although candidates occasionally emerged to contest the odd election, some inside the organization noted how it was becoming known as the 'no-to-elections' party.[42] If the decision to avoid elections attracted dissenters, they would have been silenced in 1987 when a candidate who popped his head above the parapet polled a derisory 0.3 per cent to contest a parliamentary by-election. Later that year, and after looking across the landscape of British politics, the BNP considered its prospects for growth to be so bleak that it officially abstained from the general election.[43]

Aside from internal weakness, the decision to formally withdraw from the electoral arena was also shaped by events in the party system. In particular, the emergence of Thatcherism combined with public interest in the newly formed Liberal–SDP Alliance (established only one year before the BNP) convinced the leadership that any serious investment in electoral campaigning would be futile. The view from inside the party was that Thatcher's tough stance on immigration had, at least in the eyes of ordinary Britons, removed the *raison d'être* of the BNP.[44] The Conservatives had already emerged as the preferred party on immigration (see Chapter 1). While Thatcher had talked tough on the issue in opposition, once in power her Conservative Government implemented new restrictions, including the British Nationality Act in 1981 which tightened citizenship rights and imposed new limits. As its activists were aware, the BNP was operating amid a quite different environment to that which had given rise to the NF. The issue of immigration subsequently slid down the list of salient public concerns, and provided the BNP with few obvious opportunities. Over the long period of Conservative rule which commenced in 1979 and ended 18 years later, the number of citizens considering immigration one of the most important issues facing the country remained low. When Thatcher was elected in 1979, around 16 per cent of citizens considered the issue important; when she was re-elected in 1983, the figure had slumped to 3 per cent; when John Major was elected in 1992, it was only 5 per cent; and when Tony Blair came to power in 1997, it had fallen back down to 3 per cent.[45] Even if the BNP might still have been able to mobilize support among the extreme right's core constituency of white working-class men in deprived urban districts, the changing dynamics of party competition had led it to abandon electoral politics. Pointing toward the failure of the NF to sustain a challenge when confronted with Thatcherism, the BNP branded elections 'an almost total waste of time' and turned its attention elsewhere.[46]

Tactics: 'march and grow'

With elections sidelined, the BNP faced the difficult question of how to sustain the loyalty of followers who had little prospect of achieving a tangible outcome. In the first instance, it announced a strategy of long-term organizational growth while also warning supporters that any progress would be 'slow and laboured'.[47] At least for the time being, the grassroots would have to suffice with mundane activities like leafleting, which in areas such as Essex sought to mobilize opposition to the 'upkeep of Vietnamese "boat people" ' at the taxpayers' expense.[48] Pushing leaflets through doors, however, was unlikely to sustain the commitment of foot soldiers in a supposedly revolutionary party. In the search for a tactic which might prove more effective at strengthening a sense of collective identity, the party looked back into history and recycled an approach which had long served this purpose.

The BNP's first organized march took place on 24th April 1982 and attracted around 400–500 activists who marched through the streets of London in celebration of St George's Day.[49] The march set a precedent for much that was to follow. While the BNP had talked of starting 'an entirely new approach to politics', the tactic of 'march and grow' was far from original.[50] On the contrary, it heralded a return to the NF's confrontational style of campaigning which, following several riots and the death of an anti-fascist campaigner, had become firmly associated in the minds of citizens with political violence. As the name implied, the tactic involved staging provocative marches and rallies to attract publicity, boost morale and recruit new followers. Implicit in the tactic was a particular view of how political power would be achieved, namely that 'a party like the BNP must first win power on the streets if it is to achieve power at the ballot box'.[51]

It is difficult to assess the extent to which the tactic strengthened bonds between the party and its activists, although the recollections of long-term followers suggest it assumed an important role, as one recalled: 'I think it would be untruthful to say that sort of thing didn't actually excite me, to be standing up with what at the time you perceive as your fellow man in a fight for the survival of this country. It's all a bit cranky. I do find that sort of thing actually exciting. I suppose it's the warrior in me.' BNP marches focused on a disparate array of issues and varied in size. In 1983, for example, a march in Leeds attracted over 200 activists who sought to draw attention to the decline of the textile industry. In London, however, a similar event attracted a 'frankly disappointing' number of followers.[52] Over the ensuing years, these events targeted a diverse range of issues, such as opposing the Irish Republican Army (IRA) and a conference on international war crimes, or what the party described as 'Zionist persecution of ageing Eastern Europeans on trumped-up "war crimes" charges'.[53] It even introduced a selection of marching songs to help boost morale.

While organizers came to favour indoor rallies over the more violence-prone outdoor events, throughout the mid-to-late 1980s small columns of BNP activists would have been seen marching through towns and cities such as Birmingham, Bradford, Darlington, Glasgow, Ipswich, Liverpool, Manchester and York.[54] As in the 1970s, these events frequently descended into violence, for example in Bradford in 1985 where one demonstration ended with 13 arrests.[55] In the same year, an internal membership bulletin explained how a march in Liverpool had been invaded by a 'mob of Blacks' who had to be 'fought off'.[56] Four years later, a clash between activists and anti-fascists in Dewsbury ended in 80 arrests.[57] One activist who attended this event described the basic premise of the tactic as follows: '[I] still consider it one of the best propaganda stunts we ever pulled . . . For less than a couple of hundred pounds we received WORLD WIDE news coverage!'[58] While the marchers did generate publicity, this was almost always negative and rein-forced an association in the minds of citizens between the BNP, political violence and the legacy of history. This was perhaps best reflected in one headline which followed a clash in the early 1990s and read simply: 'Blackshirts on Rampage.'[59]

Overtaking the NF

Aside from the need to attract publicity, the BNP's early strategy was also guided by the need to emerge as the dominant extreme right party. The BNP had consist-ently struggled to attract members and money, and these problems were reinforced by competition from the remaining rump of the National Front, though especially in London where the two parties were most active. This internecine rivalry ensured competition for new recruits, financial donations and, to a lesser extent, votes. Even though the NF had entered its demise, it was still able to outperform the BNP in elections. In 1983, it mobilized more candidates, received a higher average vote share in the seats it contested, and polled the strongest constituency result (3.7 per cent in Newham South compared to the BNP's 1.3 per cent in Walsall South; see Table 2.1). The BNP acknowledged that its parent party was more than a capable competitor. As its leader reluctantly conceded, not only did the NF have an appre-ciable electoral record but it had also become a 'brand name' in British politics.[60] The rivalry which ensued hampered the growth of the BNP, and was also about more than resources. BNP newsletters talked of meetings being disrupted and hostile confrontations in pubs between rival groups of activists.[61] When a suggested merger tabled at a meeting in Leeds in 1987 failed to materialize, it appeared that both parties might have to coexist in an already restricted political space.

Fortunately for the BNP, however, the NF had never truly recovered from infighting which precipitated its fall. Eventually, this enabled the party to begin pulling away from its old rival. In the mid-1980s, the NF's implosion into separate warring factions led some of its activists to switch allegiance to the BNP, subse-quently helping it reach a position of dominance.[62] The BNP also sought to do

TABLE 2.1 Performance of the NF and BNP in general elections, 1979–2010

Year	Total seats	BNP candidates	NF candidates	BNP votes	NF votes	BNP average vote (%)	NF average vote (%)	BNP lost deposits (cost)	NF lost deposits (cost)
1979	635	–	303	–	191,719	–	1.3	–	303 (£45,450)
1983	650	54	60	14,611	27,065	0.6	1.1	54 (£8,100)	60 (£9,000)
1987	650	2	1	553	286	0.5	–	2 (£1,000)	1 (£500)
1992	651	13	14	7,005	3,984	1.1	0.7	13 (£6,500)	14 (£7,000)
1997	659	56	6	35,832	2,716	1.4	1.2	53 (£26,500)	6 (£3,000)
2001	659	33	5	47,129	2,484	3.9	1.5	28 (£14,000)	5 (£2,500)
2005	646	118	13	192,746	8,079	4.2	1.6	85 (£42,500)	13 (£6,500)
2010	650	338	17	564,331	10,784	3.8	1.4	265 (£132,500)	17 (£8,500)

Sources: J. Yonwin (2004) *Electoral performance of far right parties in the UK*, London: House of Commons Research Report SN/SG/1982; Electoral Commission.

business with what was left; in 1987, for example, it announced a working alliance with the National Front Support Group (NFSG), one faction that had emerged from the debris of the NF split. In areas like Doncaster, NFSG branches simply rebranded themselves BNP and continued their activity.[63]

The BNP was quick to gloat over its new status as 'the No.1 Racial Nationalist Party in the UK'.[64] In reality, however, it was more of a street gang than a political party. It had only recruited a paltry membership and had few resources to its name. Nonetheless, in the early 1990s its growing confidence led to an announcement that much greater effort would be devoted to fighting elections.[65] The decision to dip its toes into electoral waters did not signal a complete change of direction; marches continued to be organized and it reaffirmed the need to establish an identity in the minds of voters, without which it would remain 'practically invisible'.[66] Yet it was in this period when the party commenced its slow drift toward elections, and began sowing the seeds of a future electoral strategy.

The shift was a response to several factors. Revisions to the Public Order Act meant it was more difficult to organize confrontational rallies. The legislative revisions required parties to provide police with advance notice of these events and enabled authorities to ban them if serious disorder appeared likely. BNP organizers thus found their ability to mobilize a streets-based presence was seriously curtailed, as one recalled: 'Marches were out of the question as every one we planned for . . . was immediately banned by the authorities.'[67] The shift was also prompted by changes in the wider arena. In particular, activists pointed toward the Salman Rushdie Affair in 1988–89, the first Gulf War in 1990–91, the creation of the European Union (EU) in 1993 and the opening of the Channel Tunnel in 1994 as evidence of more favourable conditions for ethnic nationalist parties. For a small number of 'modernizers' inside the party, these events underscored the need for an electoral strategy. While modernizers remained firmly committed to racial nationalism, they also shared a consensus that the BNP would need to modify its approach if it was to escape from the electoral ghetto. For activists like Eddy Butler, Tony Lecomber and Mike Newland, the party needed to shift its attention to local politics and begin building an image of credibility at grassroots level. It would tailor campaigns around the concerns of white working-class communities and, rather than waste resources by contesting costly general elections, would focus on being *respected* as being *credible*.[68]

This emphasis on local credibility led modernizers to advocate that the party embrace community-based campaigns, as one explained: 'We must stop talking just about what we like to talk about and start talking about the things that local people are crying out to hear.'[69] Community-based campaigning was seen as the vehicle through which the BNP might begin forging ties with members of particular social groups and countering its negative image. In turn, local success would provide a springboard into a wider breakthrough and enable the party to circumvent the barrier of the majoritarian system. Between 1990 and 1993, activists began experimenting by targeting local issues and sinking roots in communities, though mainly in the inner East End where most were based.[70] Much of this activity was geared toward cultivating a perception of threat among working-class communities. Organized around the slogan 'Rights for Whites', these campaigns claimed the economic resources and physical safety of white working-class residents were threatened by immigrants and minority ethnic groups. One activist described the community-based model as follows:

> It was never a case of going on the street and bellowing 'Rights for Whites' while striking a nationalist posture; it was one of actively going into the community and talking to people, listening to what *they* had to say and then articulating *their* problems, identifying solutions and presenting those solutions in an easily understood form that appealed to the people. Put simply, it was community politics [emphasis in original].[71]

This more intensive style of campaigning was applied to a string of local by-elections and soon met improving results. In 1993, these efforts culminated in the election of the first BNP councillor in the party's history. While the breakthrough triggered a wave of optimism, it was short lived. The next year, and in the face of increased turnout and vigorous opposition from local faith groups, the seat was lost and the party would not enter local government again for almost a decade.

Nonetheless, while it was not sustained the isolated breakthrough marked an important watershed in the evolution of the BNP for two reasons. First, the result encouraged the party to keep strong emphasis on the theme of 'anti-white racism' which had proven effective at cultivating a sense of injustice and racial threat among working-class communities. Throughout the remainder of the 1990s, this theme was placed at the core of campaigns and reflected in articles such as 'Racial Attacks against Whites Continue', 'Will Labour End the Race Attacks?', 'Stop the Race Attacks', 'Whites – Victims of Race Hate Attacks', 'White Boy Loses Finger in Racist Machete Attack', 'Race Attacks in Oldham', 'Race Hate Attack Puts Boy in Hospital', 'No Let Up in Race Hate Attacks Upon Whites', and 'Race Tribunals Value Blacks 50 Times that of Whites'.[72] These 'rights for Whites' campaigns would also gather pace as the party shifted its focus toward Labour's deprived heartlands in northern England (see below).

Second, modernizers saw the breakthrough as vindicating their decision to experiment with a community-based strategy. The result, they argued, provided clear evidence that the BNP had been wrong to focus on 'street politics alone'.[73] These activists subsequently began exerting growing influence over the party's direction. This was evident at one rally in 1994 which adopted canvassing as the main theme and stressed to activists 'the importance of door-to-door paper sales in areas where elections were to be fought'.[74] The architects of the East End campaigns continued urging the party to develop closer ties with residents and explore ways of establishing a more positive image, 'particularly in relation to standards of dress and appearance'.[75] Some went further by advocating that the party revise its core policy of compulsory repatriation. While large numbers of

Britons were once again becoming anxious over immigration, few seemed enthusiastic about the idea of forcibly removing immigrants and settled minority ethnic
groups out of the country. Rather, it was argued the BNP might appeal to these
citizens by adopting a Powellite policy of *voluntary* repatriation, whereby financial incentives would be used to encourage immigrants to return to their countries
of origin. Writing in 1995, one activist proposed giving each repatriated adult
£10,000 and each minor £2000–£3000.[76]

The demonstration effect

The BNP's growing interest in community-based politics was partly inspired by
the tactics of the Liberal Democrats, who were also faced with the difficult question of how to appear credible in an electoral system which favoured two main
parties. The latter's attempt to overcome this hurdle by concentrating resources in
key target areas was not lost on the BNP, as one of its activists noted: 'Analyses
were made, lessons were learnt and the Liberals adopted community politics and
presented a fresh face to the public.'[77] Yet while the Liberal Democrats sparked
interest in community politics, they offered few insights into how the BNP might
overcome a more fundamental barrier.

While all minor parties in majoritarian systems face the challenge of appearing
to voters as a credible alternative, extremist parties must also convince them that
they are legitimate players in the democratic process. As discussed in the last
chapter, one important factor in the demise of the NF was its failure to fulfil this
task. Most Britons simply did not associate the NF with liberal democratic politics. The result was that while large numbers of voters were concerned about the
NF's core issue of immigration, few were willing to endorse its stigmatized
message. Instead, the party found its appeal limited to small working-class
enclaves in specific parts of the country. Its failure to provide a more resonant
message arguably owed much to the timing of its rise and fall. As others point out,
the NF arose before the emergence of similar but far more successful parties
across Western Europe throughout the 1980s and 1990s. By the time these more
successful parties arrived, the NF had begun its descent into the extreme right's
favourite pastime, infighting. It was therefore unable to learn and benefit from a
more resonant message which steered clear of ideas which most voters considered
beyond the pale.[78]

By the mid-1990s, however, the landscape of European politics had altered
radically. The BNP saw an altogether different environment from that which met
its parent party. Since the 1980s, charismatic figures such as Jörg Haider in
Austria, Gianfranco Fini in Italy and Jean-Marie Le Pen in France had been
downplaying toxic legacies and widening their parties' appeal. The rise of parties
like the Austrian Freedom Party (FPÖ), National Front (FN) in France, Flemish
Bloc (VB) in Belgium and Progress Parties in Scandinavia demonstrated how
parties which opposed immigration and established mainstream parties could
mobilize impressive and durable levels of support.[79] While building effective

organizations, the most successful of these parties also sought to avoid the biologically racist and anti-democratic appeals of the 'old' extreme right. Instead, and as the NF clung rigidly to these more socially unacceptable ideas, they developed a more potent formula.

First, at least in their public appeals, parties such as those above distanced themselves from crude biological racism which most citizens refused to endorse and saw as a relic of the interwar years. Rather than emphasize racial supremacism, they sought to mobilize hostility to immigration by stressing the alleged cultural threats posed by immigrants and minority ethnic groups. In contrast to older arguments based on biology, the new discourse claimed minority groups are culturally incompatible with Western liberal democratic values, and hence should be excluded on this basis. While biological racism contends that inferior outgroups threaten the racial purity of the in-group, the new discourse claims rising ethno-cultural diversity generates value conflicts and threatens group identities.[80] Second, they also distanced themselves from overtly anti-democratic appeals and instead invested more effort in presenting themselves as 'a populist response to current anxieties'.[81] While significant numbers of citizens had grown dissatisfied with their main parties, few were willing to overthrow the entire system. The rise of parties like the Austrian Freedom Party (FPÖ), however, had shown that citizens were receptive to populist campaigns which attacked the main parties and avoided direct assaults on democracy. While this populism took different forms in different party systems, most parties at least stressed their tolerance of democracy even if their campaigning and rhetoric shook its foundations more indirectly.

These changes may appear slight, yet they are important to understanding the rise of parties which are similar to the BNP but have been far more successful. As one academic points out, the shift from race to culture enabled them to mobilize anti-immigrant hostility while avoiding the stigma associated with crude racism. Meanwhile, the embrace of populism enabled these parties to ferment political dissatisfaction and mobilize protest votes while not appearing as revolutionary anti-democrats.[82] As several studies would later reveal, parties which adopted these elements performed much stronger at the polls than those which remained committed to the toxic anti-democratic and biologically racist message.[83]

Partly for these reasons, from the mid-1990s the BNP sought to respond to its dilemma by looking beyond the borders of British politics. The party had long attempted to forge cross-national ties with similar movements: in 1992, for example, one of its rallies was addressed by the leader of the Nationalist Party of France and Europe (PFNE); the next year, the BNP crossed the Channel to return the favour; in 1994, it was the turn of the neo-Nazi National Democratic Party of Germany (NPD) to visit the BNP; and two years later, the latter organized a camping trip in the Peak District with members of the Antwerp-based *Vlaams Duits Kultur Verbond*, 'with everyone around the flames taking turns to propose a toast to a white future'.[84] These links, however, seldom involved more than the exchange of pleasantries.

The rise of parties like the Austrian FPÖ and French FN offered a more detailed blueprint for how the BNP might escape from the electoral wilderness. The view from inside the party was that these 'Euro-nationalist' parties had developed a 'distinctly modern nationalist flavour' and were 'presenting thoughtful nationalist policies that are all the more persuasive because of their common sense approach and moderate language'.[85] Modernizers were especially impressed, and argued that parties similar to the BNP were enjoying elected office because they had replaced the 'old, stale and unsaleable fascism' with a more moderate message and appealing image.[86] In particular, it was the rise of Le Pen's FN which became the main source of inspiration, as one modernizer explained:

> Le Pen understood back in the early 1980s that any association with past nationalist regimes is the kiss of death. Le Pen devised a whole new suite of nationalist policies that were practicable and had voter appeal . . . Nationalists in all these countries, particularly Austria, France, Belgium and Italy, are on the electoral motorway. *It is no coincidence that* all *these nationalists are* modern *nationalists* [emphasis in original].[87]

Eager to learn from its French cousin, in 1997 the BNP sent a delegation to the FN's annual *Bleu-Blanc-Rouge* (Blue, White and Red) festival.[88] In the same year, modernizers coalesced around their own publication, *Patriot*, which was described as a journal 'packed with colour, history, analysis and racial nationalist views'.[89] In the first issue they sought to familiarize readers with parties like the FN and how their electoral rise had demonstrated the effectiveness of 'suits, smiles and good presentation'.[90]

Modernizers used *Patriot* to set out their vision of how the BNP should change: it would need to: moderate its official discourse on issues of race, immigration and asylum; develop a wider ideological agenda that appealed to different groups in society; and explore more innovative ways of building a 'viable and attractive' BNP.[91] As part of this process, the party would need to downplay its roots, including the 'mega-phone and placard demo-culture' and attempt to emulate the NF's strategy of 'kicking its way into the headlines' (which modernizers dismissed as a 'stupid statement').[92] More generally, the party would need to jettison its 'unhealthy obsession' with the interwar years and stop 'harking back to the 1930s with outdated street tactics'.[93] In short, if it was to move from the margins to the mainstream then the 'old' politics of fascism would need to make way for the 'new' politics of 'Euronationalism'.[94]

Aside from demanding suits and smiles, modernizers also sought to widen the BNP's appeal in specific ways. First, rather than remain an urban single-issue party which focused exclusively on immigration, they argued the BNP should extend its reach by targeting rural issues and communities. This meant that, toward the end of the 1990s, more coverage was devoted to a crisis in the farming industry, the 'New Labour attack' on rural sports and opposing plans to build on greenbelt land.[95] This attempt to sink roots into rural communities also led activists to attend the Countryside Rally in 1997, a fish festival in Cornwall, a country show in Cumbria and demonstrations by farmers.[96] These initiatives were small scale but they reflected the underlying aim of transforming the BNP from an anti-immigrant party into a movement with broader appeal, or as one activist explained: 'The key to the party's current growth and publicity is its new focus on issues other than race.'[97]

Second, the attempt to attract new supporters led the party to begin shifting its focus toward Labour's more deprived heartlands in northern England. In earlier years, the NF and BNP sought to recruit dissatisfied members of the Conservative and Eurosceptic right-wing fringe by targeting more divisive issues such as immigration and European integration. Over the mid-to-late 1990s, however, the BNP shifted its emphasis and began pitching more seriously to disaffected white working-class voters in Labour areas. This change of strategy was reflected in a new range of leaflets designed for areas where Labour dominated local politics and there were large numbers of residents dependent on welfare. These areas included Glasgow, Liverpool, parts of the North East and Yorkshire, where the BNP sought to tell residents that Labour had 'abandoned ordinary working people' because it was 'more interested in "gays", ethnics and their rich money-bags backers'.[98] This search for a more receptive audience led the party to focus increasingly on areas in northern England which were characterized by high levels of deprivation, low education levels and large Muslim communities of Bangladeshi and Pakistani heritage.

It was in these types of areas where the party aimed to mobilize supporters through its 'Rights for Whites' campaign. The strategy was particularly evident in areas like Oldham in 1997–98, where the party seized on remarks by a local police chief to claim that 'race-hate attackers' and 'anti-white racial extremists' were operating 'almost with impunity'.[99] It then quickly distributed tailored leaflets which aimed to cultivate anxiety over 'Asian racist violence' and demanded 'Rights for Whites'.[100] These campaigns were also evident in more traditional areas of strength, such as the Midlands where in Stoke-on-Trent the party focused on the murder of a white youth, or 'another victim of the multiracial "experiment" '.[101] Further south in Tipton, a rising star in the party named Nick Griffin organized a demonstration against a 'race-hate attack' by an Asian gang on a white youth.[102] Improving electoral results fuelled the growing interest in northern areas. A promising result in Dewsbury in 1997 prompted one organizer to deliver the following message to activists: 'Don't let anyone tell you that you can only get good results in London.'[103] When a new branch in Halifax polled over 7 per cent in local elections the next year, activists began discussing the idea of relocating the party to the more industrial north.[104] Shortly afterward, an important branch emerged in the town of Burnley and announced its arrival to residents by organizing a barbecue.[105]

Third, to recruit support in these areas it was also argued the BNP should develop more professional campaigning methods. By this time, the party had already begun experimenting with ways to present a more moderate image. For example, it had replaced the NF-inspired slogan on its newspaper 'For Race and Nation' with the more voter-friendly 'Voice of the British People' (it was suggested the former wouldn't connect with first-time readers).[106] More innovative campaigning techniques were also being employed in local elections. Branches had begun distributing *Patriot* leaflets which targeted local issues, and one campaign in London distributed videos to households which contained large numbers of white voters.[107] It is important not to exaggerate this activity. The BNP remained poorly organized and lacked a sizeable membership. Moreover, most branches were not regularly active and were slow to adopt community-based campaigns. However, in some areas of the country branches had begun tailoring their campaigns around issues of local interest. In the Midlands, for example, activists targeted schooling, speed limits and the quality of the local environment, even liaising with residents' associations.[108] Meanwhile, activists in Burnley were being encouraged to write letters to the local newspaper to give the impression of a strong grassroots movement.[109]

Modernization stalled

While modernizers were advocating a change of strategy, they were not demanding a break from racial nationalism. They remained firmly committed to the ideological tradition and were quick to criticize rival parties for seemingly compromising their core principles. For example, one small rival party – the National Democrats (ND) – was criticized on the grounds that 'in the race for respectability [the ND] lost the very meaning and defining principle of racial nationalism, that of re-creating a mono-racial nation, which in the final analysis can only be achieved by compulsory repatriation'.[110] Also, despite calls to downplay extremist baggage, there remained clear links between the BNP and more violence-prone extra-parliamentary groups. In 1998, for example, the party continued to advertise videos of 'White Pride' concerts featuring supremacist skinhead bands such as Skrewdriver. It also encouraged members with an interest in 'White Resistance' music to write to Blood and Honour (B&H), a neo-Nazi group with links to the European skinhead scene. Meanwhile, Coventry and Warwick branches of the BNP raised funds for the 1999 European elections by holding an event featuring skinhead bands.[111]

The aim behind the strategy of 'modernization' was not to abandon racial nationalism, but rather to distance the BNP from the legacy of history in the hope of attracting Britons who had not previously supported the extreme right. By downplaying its roots and offering a more resonant message, the party hoped to appeal beyond the extreme right's core electorate and mobilize a larger pool of potential supporters who had become anxious over immigration and dissatisfied with the performance of their main parties (see Chapter 3). As one activist explained, the impetus behind the demand for a change of strategy was political expediency rather than ideological conviction: 'We need to realise that we are a race teetering upon an abyss of extinction, and that the time for feuding amongst ourselves over obscure political points and semantic ambiguities is way past. The racial principle will always be the engine that drives the party forwards, but the ideological baggage that surrounds it has to succumb to the dictates of reason and utility.'[112]

Yet even though modernizers were not proposing ideological change, they still encountered fierce opposition from the BNP leadership. Tyndall saw little need to abandon confrontational tactics and was unlikely to endorse calls for change which undermined his own authority.[113] He sought to stem the growing influence of modernizers by warning members that 'Modernization becomes the course of prudence which in turn is the rationale for cowardice'.[114] The reality, however, was that leading activists had become exasperated with their ageing leader and his inability to grasp the need for a new direction, as one organizer explained:

> He [Tyndall] lost the crowd completely. He didn't have a common touch, he couldn't really identify with the average person. He couldn't grasp what the rights for whites campaign was about, partly 'cause that is saying that we're like the civil rights movement and we're more like the partition of black people say in the Southern states . . . like Martin Luther King. He wouldn't be able to go that way 'cause he'd want to be the boss, the colonial master type . . . He couldn't make that adjustment from being the empire loyal type of thing to being the community politician.

Tyndall proved unable to quieten a wave of discontent that was rumbling through the grassroots. His attempt to fend off the challenge was further weakened by results at the 1997 general election. When over 50 BNP candidates polled fewer than 36,000 votes, Tyndall may have realized his position had become untenable. Despite all the talk, few candidates had been supported by grassroots campaigns while the party also failed to mobilize a significant presence in local elections that were held at the same time. There were only four BNP candidates and three stood in Newham. More disappointment followed a parliamentary by-election in Uxbridge at which the BNP polled 0.6 per cent. As one activist explained, while they could just about stomach finishing behind the Socialist Party, 'finishing behind the Official Monster Raving Loony Party is quite a different matter'.[115] These dismal results meant that calls for change soon escalated into calls for a new leader, as one organizer recalled: 'People who wanted to go somewhere knew his time as leader was over and a new leader had to come forward. Tyndall's days were finished.' The question which remained unanswered was who would step up. In March 1999, the BNP newspaper announced that the director of publicity had been nominated to contest the leadership. The candidate's name was Nick Griffin.

As we have seen in this chapter, the BNP was born into a quite different environment from that which gave birth to the NF. As the party would later recall, the 1980s was 'an entirely different decade from the one preceding it'.[116] Britons were less concerned about the extreme right's core issues and the rise of Thatcherism left it with little space. In response, and with few resources, the BNP abandoned electoral politics, returned to confrontational tactics and focused on the goal of survival. As similar parties elsewhere in Europe explored ways of detoxifying their message, the BNP continued to offer Britons a toxic formula of biological racism, anti-Semitism and anti-democratic appeals. Like other parties on the continent which clung to these ideas, the party remained firmly in the electoral ghetto. However, it was also in this period when the BNP commenced its slow drift toward an electoral strategy. While the seeds of this new approach had been planted in the East End, they would not blossom until the arrival of a new leader and more favourable conditions for the extreme right.

3

FROM STREET GANG TO POLITICAL PARTY

1999–2009

I said at the [founding of the BNP] meeting that the British National Party, if it were to succeed, must be a party of revolution, dedicated to the service of Race and Nation, and that we must never again be hampered by the trappings of any pseudo-democratic policies . . . We must never offer watered down propaganda in order to attract mass membership. We must never shirk from our duty to cause and creed. We must never moderate, for moderation is liberalism and liberalism is stagnation and defeat.

BNP founding member (1982)[1]

The BNP has genuinely changed enormously over the last few years, and our victories . . . are partly the reward for those changes.

Nick Griffin (2002)[2]

In October 1999, the BNP held the first leadership election in its history. The two candidates fighting for control of the party were its founder and leader of 17 years, John Tyndall, and its director of publicity, Nick Griffin. Under Tyndall, the BNP had stood brazenly in the shadow of racial nationalism and steered clear of making a serious commitment to electoral politics. This reluctance to invest in elections was reflected in the sum of its elected representation; since its birth, the party had seen the election of only one councillor. Though Griffin was considered a supporter of Tyndall, he now sought to usurp his mentor by reaching out to the disillusioned grassroots and promising improved administration, financial transparency and greater support for local branches.[3] The outcome of the contest would determine whether the party would continue on its course, or set out in a new direction. Eighty per cent of members cast a vote and almost two thirds backed Griffin. With a new leader who was determined to embrace an electoral strategy and learn from the experience of the failed NF, the BNP set out on a period of change. This chapter examines these internal changes but first sets them against the backdrop of wider trends in British society which combined to produce a favourable climate for Griffin's BNP. The party could not have chosen a more promising time to launch an electoral challenge. In many respects, the extreme right had never had it so good.

A more favourable issue agenda

The 1980s and 1990s had been unprofitable years for the BNP. In the public imagination, issues of race, immigration and asylum were much less important than they had been during the heyday of the NF. Even if these issues continued to spark anxiety among some quarters, the party which most voters favoured to manage them – the Conservative Party – was in government. Starved of opportunities and resources, the BNP abandoned elections and returned to marching in the streets. As it approached the end of the 1990s, however, its core issues once again began climbing the ladder of salient public concerns. In fact, among ordinary Britons the perceived importance of immigration would soon reach historic levels.

Unlike the 1970s, several factors had combined to ensure that Britons were now living in a country of net immigration rather than net emigration. The most important were the more liberal immigration policies of 'New' Labour, rising numbers of applications for asylum due to foreign conflicts, and the accession of Central and East European states to the European Union (EU) in 2004 and 2007.[4] The result was a large and unprecedented phase of immigration into the country. Between 2000 and 2008, the number of people arriving and settling in Britain each year increased more than four-fold, rising from approximately 125,000 to almost 600,000.[5] Applications for asylum also increased, from 30,000 in 1997 to over 100,000 in 2002.[6] Then, over the three years following the accession of countries like Estonia, Lithuania and Poland to the EU in 2004, an estimated 683,000 people applied to work in the country.[7] As a consequence, some later estimated that around 2.5 million foreign-born people were added to the population following the election of New Labour in 1997.[8]

As the level of immigration increased, its sources diversified. Earlier immigrants who came mainly from Commonwealth countries were joined by new arrivals from parts of Africa, the Middle East, Latin America and Central and Eastern Europe. The rising ethno-cultural diversity of the population was reflected in one report in 2008, which estimated that for every ten migrants entering the country only one was born in Britain, three were born in one of the remainder 27 EU member states and six were born elsewhere in the world.[9] It was also apparent at the local level, where in some areas of the country councils began grappling with the onset of 'super diversity', which refers to the complexity arising from a striking increase in the number of migrants, languages, faiths, identities, cultural values and practices.[10] Not every citizen could detail a direct experience with immigration, but most were aware that the country was experiencing historic rates of demographic change. Immigrants and asylum-seekers were often the subject of alarmist and hostile coverage in tabloid newspapers such as the *Daily Mail,* the *Sun*, and *Daily Express*, and also found themselves the focus of inflammatory statements by mainstream politicians who were seeking to accrue political capital or satisfy anxiety among their own camps. As one academic observed, the relative tranquillity on the immigration front which had emerged in the 1980s and 1990s appeared to be ending.[11]

In 2000, the Conservatives were criticized for using words such as 'swamped', for claiming the number of asylum-seekers was 'out of control' and that criminals are 'flooding our country with bogus asylum-seekers'.[12] The party similarly thrust these issues to the forefront of its 2005 general election campaign by demanding an annual limit on immigration, greater investment in border security and withdrawal from the Geneva Convention to allow more restrictive asylum policies. If citizens came across Conservative Party billboards or speeches by its then-leader Michael Howard, they would have been told: 'It's not racist to talk about immigration. It's not racist to criticize the system. It's not racist to want to limit the numbers. It's just plain common sense.'[13] Nor was the centre-right alone in adopting strident rhetoric on these issues: in 2002, Labour Home Secretary David Blunkett refused to apologise after suggesting asylum-seekers were 'swamping' British schools; in 2006, Labour MP Jack Straw sparked debate after suggesting Muslim women who cover their faces with veils were having a negative impact on community relations; the next year, Labour MP Margaret Hodge was criticized for 'using the language of the BNP' after suggesting British families have a sense of entitlement over immigrants; and shortly afterward, Prime Minister Gordon Brown created a furore after pledging to create 'British jobs for British workers'.[14] As some commentators pointed out, the slogan had previously been used by both the NF and BNP.

While partly an attempt to appease a hostile media and core supporters, these statements also marked a response to changing tides in public opinion. Though immigration was not politicized in Britain to the same extent as in other European states, it still moved onto the core agenda of British politics. As Britons entered the twenty-first century, the issue was quickly moving to the forefront of their minds. The growing salience of immigration was reflected in the finding that, between 1990 and 2000, the proportion of letters sent to Members of Parliament about the issue increased more than three-fold.[15] It was also revealed in numerous surveys and polls. For example, when Britons were asked between 1990 and 2007 to rate the most important issues facing the country, the percentage choosing immigration rocketed from under 2 per cent to a record peak of 46 per cent.[16] In fact, at various points in 2006 and 2007, immigration was considered more important than education, crime, the National Health Service (NHS) and foreign affairs. There was also a striking increase in the percentage considering immigration the *most* important issue. While in 2001 the figure was 2 per cent, by 2005 it had jumped to 20 per cent (see Fig. 3.1).[17]

Most Britons considered immigration one of the most important issues and reached the same conclusion about what should be done: the number of immigrants should be reduced.[18] Immigration, in other words, became a 'valence issue'

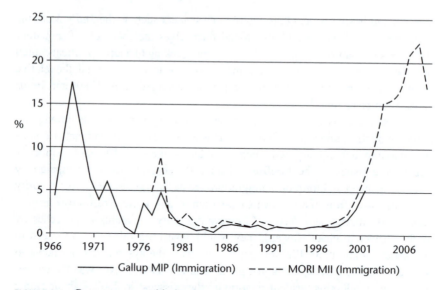

FIGURE 3.1   Percentage considering immigration as the most important issue

Source: W. Jennings and C. Wlezien, 'Distinguishing important issues and problems', presented at the Annual Meeting of the Elections, Public Opinion and Parties (EPOP) Specialist Group of the U.K. Political Studies Association, September 2009.

on which there was strong agreement. The textbook example of a valence issue is the economy, as most people want a healthy economy and agree this is what politicians should deliver.[19] By the time Griffin's BNP began investing more seriously in elections, a large portion of the electorate not only considered its core issue to be one of the most important but also expressed their desire for a reduction in the number of immigrants entering the country. Between 1995 and 2003, the proportion of Britons favouring a reduction increased from two thirds to three quarters.[20]

Importantly, while Britons became profoundly anxious over the issue, they also distanced themselves from more open forms of racism and discrimination. In 2003, for example, citizens were asked their views about the most important attributes to being 'truly British'. While over 70 per cent considered birth and long-term residence important criteria, only 15 per cent thought 'being white' was a key requirement. In other words, while there emerged significant levels of xenophobic hostility toward immigration (among citizens who might be termed 'immigration sceptics'), levels of support for harder forms of racism and prejudice which stressed the importance of race (among citizens who might be termed 'hostile racists') were much lower.[21] Behind this scepticism was deep anxiety about the impact of immigration on wider society. When Britons were asked their views about the effect of immigration on public services, culture and society, most took the opportunity to register negative feelings (see Table 3.1). One example is a poll in 2006 which indicated that two thirds of Britons thought the country was 'losing its culture' because of immigration.[22] Two years later, another poll carried

TABLE 3.1 Public opinion on immigration, 2000–2010

Question/Source	Positive (%)	Negative (%)	Neither/Don't know (%)
Too much done to help immigrants?	63	22	16
Ipsos-MORI/*Reader's Digest* 2000			
Large numbers of asylum-seekers are cheats?	59	28	13
Ipsos-MORI/*Mail on Sunday 2001*			
Immigrants integrate and make a positive contribution to Britain or not?	26	54	20
ICM/Race poll 2002			
Immigration benefitted or damaged British society over the past 50 years?	30	44	26
ICM/Race poll 2002			
Concerned Britain is losing its own culture?	57	29	14
Ipsos-MORI/Migration Watch 2003			
Immigration improves cultural life of Britain?	28	62	10
YouGov/*Mail on Sunday* 2004			
Asylum/illegal immigration reason why public services are overburdened?	54	42	4
Populus/*News of the World* Aug 2004			
Number of immigrants has overstretched National Health Service?	54	36	11
Populus/*News of the World* 2005			
Immigrants make a positive contribution to the economy of Britain?	59	34	7
Populus/*Daily Politics* 2006			
Immigrants having a good or bad influence on Britain?	34	52	15
Ipsos-MORI/The *Sun* 2007			
Pleased or worried about the impact of immigration on Britain?	7	71	21
YouGov/Migration Watch 2009			
Impact of immigration on British culture?	25	58	17
YouGov/Juniper TV 2008			
Parts of this county don't feel like Britain anymore because of immigration?	58	38	3
Ipsos-MORI/BBC *Rivers of Blood* 2008			
Worried immigration will cause problems for you and your family over the next few years?	53	43	4
YouGov/The *Sun* 2010			

out on the fortieth anniversary of Enoch Powell's 'Rivers of Blood' speech suggested six out of ten thought some parts of the country 'don't look like Britain anymore because of immigration'. It also suggested that five out of ten Britons supported the idea put forward by Powell some four decades earlier, namely that the government should encourage immigrants to leave the country.[23]

Despite the onset of economic recession, immigration remained a top priority for Britons at the 2010 general election. As issues like education, pensions and the NHS slid down the agenda, immigration emerged as the second most important issue and eight out of ten voters remained in favour of reducing the number of immigrants.[24] It featured in all three televised leadership debates and attracted renewed attention following 'Duffygate' (when Prime Minster Gordon Brown dismissed a labour voter who raised concerns over immigration as 'bigoted'). Even after the campaign, and as the impact of recession continued to dominate headlines, immigration was considered more important than unemployment.[25] Against this backdrop, it is perhaps not surprising that one Labour MP who surveyed how the issue had evolved reflected as follows: 'Immigration, the elephant in the room? Not any more. Now it's parading down the high street, garlanded in ribbons, leading a three-ring circus.'[26]

Unlike previous decades, the increased salience of immigration was only one of several security-related issues which, following terrorist attacks in New York City on 11th September 2001, also climbed the issue agenda. Alongside immigration and asylum, crime, terrorism and the war in Iraq were issues that formed a 'new security agenda' which became a top concern for the electorate. In fact, by the time of the 2005 general election, this new security agenda was just as important to voters as more traditional issues like the economy and public services.[27]

One additional development often glossed over in discussion about the growing importance of security-related issues has been the emergence of a more specific form of hostility toward settled Muslim communities. Unfortunately, there is a striking absence of research on the drivers of anti-Muslim sentiment in modern Britain, but its growing importance can be seen in various surveys and polls. One poll in 2002, for example, suggested that 56 per cent of respondents thought their values had little or nothing in common with those of British Muslims, 32 per cent did not think Muslims play a valuable role in society, 26 per cent thought it was not possible for Islam and Western values to coexist peacefully and 17 per cent would be disappointed if Muslims moved in next door.[28] More recent research similarly points toward a significant reservoir of anti-Muslim sentiment among the population. One poll conducted in the aftermath of terrorist attacks in London on 7th July 2005 suggested that one quarter of Britons consider the beliefs of Islam and Western liberal democracy to be fundamentally contradictory.[29] Three years later, another poll indicated that more than half of Britons thought Muslims should do more to integrate into society while almost the same portion thought Britain was in danger of losing its identity if more Muslims settled.[30] In 2009, and at the same time that Nick Griffin and Andrew Brons were elected into the European Parliament, 44 per cent of respondents to another survey agreed that 'even in its milder forms Islam poses a danger to Western civilization'.[31]

Opinion polls provide a useful snapshot of public opinion but their questions can sometimes be misleading, particularly on sensitive issues.[32] That said, more systematic research similarly reveals significant levels of anxiety over Muslim communities, and suggests this stems from a perception that Muslims threaten British culture, values and ways of life. One example was the response to the British Social Attitudes (BSA) survey in 2003: more than 60 per cent of Britons held the view that Muslims are more loyal to other Muslims around the world than to their fellow Britons; more than half thought Britain will begin to lose its identity if more Muslims arrived and settled; almost the same number thought Muslims could never truly be committed to Britain; and one quarter would feel unhappy if a close relative married a Muslim. Further analysis of these data concluded that there has emerged 'a considerable degree of hostility to Muslims in Britain and concern that this group poses a threat to the values and identity of non-Muslim citizens'.[33] Nor is there much evidence that anti-Muslim sentiment has since subsided; in a more recent edition of the survey, only one in four Britons expressed positive views of Islam and more than half said they would feel 'bothered' if a mosque was built in their community.[34]

Dissatisfied democrats

When seen as a whole, the trends above have created opportunities for the extreme right to rally Britons anxious over immigration, rising diversity and more culturally distinct Muslim communities. These more immediate opportunities have also been reinforced by deeper and longer-term trends within the political system. While the rise of extreme right parties across Europe has taken place amid increased public concern over immigration, it has also coincided with intensified dissatisfaction with, and distrust of, established political institutions.[35] As elsewhere in Europe, though few citizens in Britain oppose democracy as a form of government there is ample evidence of 'dissatisfied democrats': citizens who are supportive of democratic governance and norms but are also dissatisfied with the performance of their political institutions, mainly political parties.[36]

Falling turnout in elections, dwindling party memberships, declining levels of trust in parties, the dominance of issues over partisan loyalties and the unwillingness of large sections of the electorate to identify with the two main parties are commonly cited as evidence of this political dissatisfaction. While similar trends are evident across Europe, in the aftermath of the parliamentary expenses scandal which broke in 2009, some political scientists pointed to a broader malaise among the electorate, arguing that 'Britain might, sadly, be a world leader in terms of the extent of the current crisis of confidence in the political class and political practice'. Drawing on a wealth of empirical data, Gerry Stoker contends that while Britons are neither less informed nor less interested in politics than in previous years, they 'have less confidence in their ability to influence decisions, less pride in the political system, and less belief in the fairness and responsiveness of government'.[37]

Of course, bonds between Britons and the established main parties were weakening long before the expenses scandal. This is reflected in the fact that contemporary Britons are much less likely than their parents and grandparents to identify with the main parties. For instance, when Harold Wilson came to power in 1964, 44 per cent of voters identified strongly with one of the main parties and only 18 per cent did not. When Tony Blair came to power in 1997, these figures had almost reversed; only 16 per cent identified with the main parties and 42 per cent did not. From here on, the percentage of strong identifiers continued to slide to 13 per cent in 2001 and 9 per cent in 2005.[38] One process that has been integral to this trend has been the way in which the main parties have gravitated toward the centre ground, in search of the median voter. This process of convergence has arguably fuelled a sense among voters that there is little difference between the main parties, or as Stoker puts it: 'The feeling that someone in the system was on your side has given way to a sense that they are all the same.'[39] This is supported by evidence that as Labour and the Conservatives have embraced more 'catch-all' ideological appeals, voters increasingly perceive there to be little difference between them. When the NF contested the second general election in 1974, for example, 40 per cent of Britons thought there was a 'great deal' of difference between the two main parties. But by the time Griffin's BNP appeared at the 2001 general election, the figure had plummeted to a record low of 17 per cent (increasing by only 4 points in 2005).[40] One consequence of this trend is that citizens who are dissatisfied with a tendency among the main parties to avoid divisive issues may shift behind more ideologically extreme parties which *do* campaign on these issues and attack the main parties for being 'all the same'.

There is, however, a more specific opportunity for the extreme right. According to recent research on voting behaviour, what matters most to citizens when deciding who to support in elections is their judgement about which party will deliver the most competent performance on important issues.[41] While most Britons may agree that a particular issue is important, they may disagree about which party is the 'best' performer on that issue. They will seek to reward parties which are competent on the major issues of concern, while punishing those which are not. In 2001, for example, most voters concluded that Labour was most competent on the important issues at that time, which were the economy and public services (although Tony Blair was also a major asset).[42] As detailed above, however, since 2001 traditional issues like the economy have been joined by a new set of security-related concerns, including immigration and asylum.

As these issues became more important to voters, there also emerged considerable dissatisfaction over the way in which recent governments and the main parties have performed on these issues. Numerous surveys and polls provide the window through which the extent of this dissatisfaction can be seen. Despite extensive legislative action in these areas, they reveal considerable public discontent with the performance of the 1997–2010 Labour governments: large majorities consistently rejected the suggestion that the government was controlling immigration and asylum; was making progress in these areas; or was simply being open and honest about the scale of immigration into Britain (see Table 3.2). Even at the

TABLE 3.2 Views towards government performance on immigration

	Positive (%)	Negative (%)	Neither/Don't know (%)
Gvt has immigration under control?	6	85	9
Ipsos-MORI/Migration Watch 2003			
Gvt has asylum under control?	6	85	9
Ipsos-MORI/Migration Watch 2003			
Gvt is open and honest about scale of immigration?	12	76	12
Ipsos-MORI/Migration Watch 2003			
Gvt policy to control immigration is working?	7	84	10
YouGov/The *Sun*			
Gvt is open and honest about scale of immigration?	11	78	11
YouGov/The *Sun*			
Immigration improved or got worse since Labour elected in 1997?	8	66	26
ICM/*Guardian* 2003			
Gvt has illegal immigration under control?	13	82	6
Populus/*News of the World* 2004			
Do you believe Gvt statistics showing fall in asylum applications?	19	77	4
Populus/*News of the World* 2004			
Labour Gvt been successful in tackling illegal immigration?	12	80	7
Populus/*News of the World* 2004			
Gvt is open and honest about the scale of immigration?	11	80	9
YouGov/*Mail on Sunday* 2004			
Asylum system is getting better or worse?	11	49	40
ICM/Cabinet Office 2004			
Immigration system getting better or worse?	10	50	28
ICM/Cabinet Office 2004			
How do you rate Gvt policy on immigration and asylum?	12	78	11
YouGov/*Mail on Sunday* 2005			
Gvt immigration policy is about right?	28	64	8
Populus/*News of the World* 2005			

(*Continued overleaf*)

TABLE 3.2 Continued

	Positive (%)	Negative (%)	Neither/Don't know (%)
Progress on implementing sensible policies on immigration/asylum?	19	76	5
YouGov May 2005			
Labour Gvt policies on immigration success or failure?	18	72	10
Populus/*Daily Mirror* 2005			
The British Gvt has immigration under control?	4	84	12
YouGov/*Tonight with Trevor McDonald* 2006			
Satisfied or dissatisfied with Gvt performance on immigration/asylum?	15	72	12
Ipsos-MORI/The *Sun* 2007			
Gvt is open and honest about the scale of immigration?	14	80	5
Ipsos-MORI/The *Sun* 2007			
Mainstream parties have no credible policies on immigration?	62	32	5
ICM/*News of the World* 2009			
Progress on implementing sensible policies on immigration/asylum?	15	79	6
YouGov March 2010			
Labour Gvt handling of immigration good or bad?	21	69	10
YouGov/The *Sun* 2010			

time of the 2010 general election, and after 13 years of Labour rule, eight out of ten voters rejected the suggestion that progress had been made on implementing sensible immigration and asylum policies, and seven out of ten thought Labour managed these issues badly. When Britons were asked in another survey to rate the performance of Labour on immigration, most did so negatively: among Labour supporters, negative ratings of its performance outnumbered positive ones by 30 percentage points; and among *all* voters, irrespective of who they voted for, negative ratings outnumbered positive ones by almost 60 points. While concern over how immigration is managed appears widespread, it is concentrated most heavily among white working-class voters who traditionally identified with Labour.[43] There also emerged evidence that Britons were less confident in the ability of their government to integrate immigrants than their American, French, German, Italian and Spanish counterparts.[44]

Given that the electorate has long preferred the Conservatives on immigration, negative ratings of Labour are perhaps not surprising. In more recent years, Britons have continued to express their clear preference for the centre-right to manage this issue (see Table 3.3). Importantly, however, this support is slightly lower than in previous decades. For instance, when voters were asked shortly after Thatcher's 'swamping' remark in 1978 which party had the 'best' policies on immigration, 50 per cent rallied behind the Conservatives. When voters were

TABLE 3.3 Which party has the best policies on immigration/asylum?

	Con (%)	Lab (%)	Lib Dem (%)	BNP (%)	Other (%)	None of them/Don't know (%)
Ipsos-MORI Oct 1977**	34	20	4	–	–	38
Ipsos-MORI Apr 1978	51	22	3	–	–	19
Ipsos-MORI Aug 1978**	50	21	3	–	–	21
Ipsos-MORI Jan 2001*	19	18	5	–	2	56
ICM May 2001***	42	29	5	–	–	23
ICM May 2001	23	23	6	–	–	48
Populus Feb 2003*	23	22	21	–	1	23
Populus Aug 2004***	24	15	7	3	3	48
Ipsos-MORI Apr 2005	36	18	10	–	–	33
ICM Apr 2005	34	22	9	–	2	31
YouGov May 2005	42	19	13	–	5	21
ICM May 2006	36	18	11	–	6	29
Ipsos-MORI Sep 2006	28	11	9	–	–	49
ICM Jun 2007	25	21	7	–	4	42
Ipsos-MORI Sep 2007	21	17	7	–	–	50
YouGov Aug 2007	34	17	7	–	7	35
Ipsos-MORI Aug 2008**	35	14	10	–	–	34
YouGov Sep 2008	37	11	8	–	7	36
Ipsos-MORI Sep 2009	29	15	10	–	–	36
ICM Oct 2009	27	18	16	11	–	27
YouGov Mar 2009	38	14	10	–	9	29
YouGov Feb 2010	41	14	9	–	8	28
Ipsos-MORI Mar 2010	28	17	9	–	–	35
ICM Apr 2010	26	17	9	–	14	36

* Asks about the specific issue of asylum-seekers
** 'None' was not recorded as a separate response category in this survey
*** Asking about most effective on *illegal* immigration

asked the same question in more recent years, the figure was significantly lower (19 per cent in 2001, 36 per cent in 2005 and 28 per cent in 2010). Over the same period, the number of citizens who do not associate *any* of the main parties with the best policies on immigration has increased. Even in 2005, when the Conservatives adopted a particularly tough position on immigration and asylum, between 20 and 33 per cent of the electorate remained unwilling to endorse any of the main parties on these issues.[45] In fact, since 2001 several polls suggest the number of citizens unable to credit any of the main parties with the best policies on immigration has been higher than the number choosing one of the main parties. Also, while the Conservatives remained the favoured party on these issues, they were not expected to win either the 2001 or 2005 general elections. For voters anxious over immigration and dissatisfied with the performance of the Labour government on this issue, there appeared few homes for their vote.

These wider trends suggest some Britons may have turned toward the BNP to 'send a message' about their profound concern over issues which they care deeply about, but they feel have not been competently addressed. They also suggest that hostility toward immigration and political dissatisfaction will be the most important drivers of BNP support (the motivations of BNP voters are examined in Chapter 5). Seemingly 'new' parties like the BNP, however, do not emerge 'simply because the circumstances may be ripe'.[46] Rather, their ability to take advantage of these more favourable conditions and translate potential into actual support will depend much on their own actions: the message they offer voters; their attempts to appeal to a wider audience; and how they attempt to mobilize support. The next section turns to examine these 'supply-side' factors.

A 'modernized' BNP

While his election as party Chairman sparked a period of change, for Griffin it marked the latest stage in a longer commitment to 'nationalist' politics. Griffin holds his roots in the NF, after which he became involved with the obscure factions Political Soldiers and International Third Position (ITP).[47] As a result of his lineage, before taking control of the BNP Griffin was considered a 'hardliner' who devoted considerable effort to questioning the events of the Holocaust and claiming that Jews wield disproportionate influence over British media. In the late 1990s, however, opportunism led Griffin to downplay these hardline positions. He had been particularly impressed by the modernizers' isolated breakthrough in the East End, as he recalls: 'Winning the seat made a number of people within the party realize that it was possible for the party to actually make advances and move out of its little ghetto. But there were no resources put in whatsoever and of course it was lost so I would say it was a missed opportunity which made people realize what could be done if they got it right.'[48] He was also influenced by the rise of similar but far more successful parties on the continent. Like others inside the party, Griffin took particular inspiration from Le Pen's FN which, he argued, underscored the need to invest in developing an electoral strategy.[49] Seeking to learn from the French example, in 1998 Griffin and his wife visited the FN head-quarters in Paris to discuss strategy with its then-deputy leader, Bruno Mégret. After buying a book which detailed the rise of the FN, he returned to Britain deter-mined to follow the blueprint and draw on his experiences in the failed NF.[50] He subsequently withdrew support for Tyndall, shifted behind modernizers and was elected BNP chairman with their support.

Ethno-nationalist xenophobia: From race to culture

Since 1999, Griffin's BNP sought to widen its appeal in mainly three ways: it appealed to Britons anxious over immigration but who might not have previously supported the extreme right; devoted more effort to shedding its status as a single-issue party; and attempted to reach these voters by developing community-based campaigns. In terms of the first, the party launched a concerted effort to rally citi-zens hostile toward immigration but who also distance themselves from more socially unacceptable forms of racism. As part of this attempt to reach beyond its core base and rally immigration sceptics, the BNP sought to follow the example of more successful parties on the continent by downplaying crude biological racism and emphasizing the alleged cultural threats posed by immigrants and minority ethnic groups. Rather than divide groups into superior and inferior categories according to their biology, the party began stressing the 'threats' which immigrants and minority ethnic groups pose to British culture, values and ways of life.[51]

At least in its outward-facing campaigns, Griffin's BNP devoted more effort to advancing the argument that there are irreconcilable cultural differences between groups, and multiculturalism should be opposed to protect ethno-cultural diversity. Though some activists had first become interested in these ideas in the 1970s, it was not until the late 1990s when the party began to embrace this discourse, as its news-paper explained in 1998: 'The BNP is not a "race supremacist" party. The BNP does not claim that any one race is superior to any other, simply that they are different. The party merely wishes to preserve those differences which make up the rich tapestry of human kind . . . To protect and preserve the racial and cultural integrity of the British people – and of others too – the party believes in separa-tion.'[52] The shift gathered pace and, by 2005, the party was claiming it had devel-oped an 'entirely new critique of multiculturalism' which was anchored in its desire to preserve diversity.[53] Underlying the change of discourse was an attempt to rally Britons who have long considered the BNP beyond the pale, as Griffin explains:

> The formula we've developed now there's at present six thousand unique cultural and ethnic groups in the world, by the end of the century ecologists say there are going to be eight hundred . . . that's a huge die-off of human diversity which is the thing which gives people their sense of identity and belonging . . . Now I can defend that on *Newsnight* or *Question Time* in a way that everyone of vaguely goodwill or independent thought out there will think 'yeah, that's reasonable enough, that's not racist bigotry'.[54]

The party's new discourse marked a departure from the crude racial nationalist rhetoric of its early years. At various points, Griffin's BNP has: talked about ensuring 'peaceful co-existence with the maintenance of cultural and biological separation'; argued that 'the only thing that can prevent human diversity vanishing into an antheap of rootless coffee-coloured consumerism is the celebration of difference'; told Britons it wants to protect biological diversity and guard against the loss of languages; and outlined its goal to defend 'the rights of indigenous cultures and peoples to preserve their territorial and cultural integrity'.[55] Attempting to downplay the legacy of history, the party also announced to voters that it was no longer interested in 'Nazi-style claims for racial supremacy'.[56] This led it to soften its core policy of compulsory repatriation. While the party retained its demand for an immediate halt on further non-white immigration and the deportation of illegal immigrants, it moved to advocate a system of 'voluntary resettlement', whereby 'non-white immigrants who are legally here will be encouraged, but not compelled, to return to their lands of ethnic origin'.[57] In more recent elections, it has advocated using the foreign aid budget to finance this voluntary resettlement scheme.

At the same time, however, the party moved to reassure its core base that the switch owed more to pragmatism than principle. Shortly after Griffin's election, the grassroots were informed the underlying rationale for shifting that from race to culture was that the latter raises 'no alarming or debatable questions of superiority or inferiority'.[58] As one organizer elaborated at the time of the 2001 general election: 'Take the race and immigration issue, our principle is, bottom line, the restoration of an overwhelmingly white Britain. Whether it is the old policy of compulsory repatriation of everyone descended from the non-whites who arrived here after 1948, or the new more voter-friendly voluntary proposals, they both seek the same end – that of a white Britain – and thus both are in accordance with our principles.'[59]

The shift from racial to cultural threats also led the party to devote more energy to mobilizing anti-Muslim sentiment. While the BNP sought to mobilize Islamophobia in earlier years, these efforts pale in comparison with more recent attempts to own the issue.[60] As part of this quest to exploit anxiety over settled Muslim communities, the party turned its attention toward areas with large Muslim populations of Pakistani or Bangladeshi heritage, mainly in the North West and Yorkshire (see Chapter 4).[61] Within hours of the terrorist attacks on 11th September 2001, the party launched a 'Campaign against Islam' and quickly developed leaflets which featured quotations from the Koran and warned voters that Britain was being turned into an Islamic republic.[62] In the same year, the party formed an Ethnic Liaison Committee, with the aim of highlighting links with Sikhs who supported its anti-Islam stance. This attempt to attract Britons anxious over the perceived threat posed by Muslims has since been pushed to the forefront of BNP campaigns, as Griffin explains:

> It's [Islam] the public's raw nerve at present. The media have made people think about this because it's exciting, it sells stories. So they've set the button up and there's no one to press it except us, so we'd be very foolish

not to press it. But there's a longer term strategy. There's no doubt that over the next 25 years that is going to be the core issue at the heart of European politics, so we've worked very hard over the last couple of years to make this *our* issue. This is a piece of ground that they [mainstream parties] can't follow us onto, not least because if you criticize Muslims you lose enormous block votes, you get very heavy lobbying against you and you risk having your throat cut, so it's ground which is tactfully good for us. It's like Churchill in 1937; warning about Nazi Germany didn't do him any good at all in 1937. It's further down the line when people say 'yeah, these people said this was the case, they were right, presumably by extension they're the ones that can now sort out the problem'. So it's a long-term gambit. (Interview with Nick Griffin, October 2006.)

The strategy was evident during the 2004 European elections, when the BNP broadcast was introduced by a Sikh who told viewers he was voting BNP because it was the only party 'with the courage to speak out about the biggest danger facing this country today, Islamic extremism'.[63] The following year the party reiterated that its primary issue of concern was 'the growth of fundamentalist-militant Islam in the UK and its ever-increasing threat to Western civilization and our implicit values'.[64] The shift was also evident in local communities such as Keighley in West Yorkshire, where attempts to galvanize support centred on amplifying local concerns that Muslim men were 'grooming' young white girls. At the 2005 general election, the party similarly sought to mobilize anti-Muslim sentiment by warning Britons about the 'danger posed to our democracy, traditions and freedoms by the creeping Islamification and dhimmitude of Britain'.[65] Four years later, while campaigning in elections to the European Parliament, its election broadcast warned that the rise of militant Islam fosters 'contempt for women, vandalism against Christian churches, attacks against Jews, a heroin epidemic and terrorism'.[66]

By the time of the 2010 general election, the BNP was not the only movement in British politics attempting to exploit public anxiety over Muslims and Islam. The emergence of the English Defence League (EDL) and similar demands by the UK Independence Party (UKIP) to ban the burka and niqab highlighted how the party was not the only organization seeking to mobilize anti-Muslim sentiment. The BNP once again attempted to assert its ownership over this specific issue by devoting an entire section of its manifesto to detailing policies for 'confronting the Islamic colonisation of Britain', which included banning the burka, ritual slaughter, the building of further mosques and immigration from Muslim countries. It also called for the immediate deportation of radical Islamist preachers, and 'any other members of their community who object to these reasonable security measures'.[67]

Anti-establishment populism

Under Griffin, the BNP also sought to widen its appeal by devoting greater effort to attracting politically dissatisfied voters. While distancing itself from its anti-democratic roots, it has attempted to incorporate the populist strategy of its more successful continental cousins, claiming to speak for the 'silent majority' against the corrupt 'old gang' parties. This populism has included three main elements. First, the party has downplayed its anti-democratic heritage by anchoring campaigns in more voter-friendly themes, such as Democracy, freedom, culture and identity.[68] It has also downplayed its earlier calls for a large state and strong leader and support for 'the Big Government mania of the 1930s'.[69] Instead, it began advocating the devolution of power to local communities, revival of county councils and citizens' initiative referenda based on the Swiss model. At the 2010 election, it similarly sought to attract voters who favoured a stronger defence of civil liberties, the creation of a Bill of Rights and an English Parliament.

Second, it has devoted more effort to embedding campaigns in nativist themes and stressing the 'British' credentials of the British National Party. While criticizing its ancestors for advocating a 'foreign way of doing things' that was 'against our own traditions', the party has sought to wrap campaigns with references to domestic traditions.[70] In 2002, for example, Griffin encouraged followers to adopt Churchill's 'V for Victory' salute which would promote 'impeccably British credentials' while resolving the 'right-arm problem'.[71] The party has since continued to appropriate images and figures from British political history; in its European election broadcast in 2009, for instance, it compared itself with Second World War heroes 'fighting like lions to stop Britain being swamped by foreign invaders'.[72]

Third, as part of its attempt to shed its single-issue image and extend its reach into new social groups, the party has targeted a diverse array of issues. Since 2001, its newspaper, *Voice of Freedom*, which is tailored for an external audience, has targeted a plethora of different issues: rising tuition fees and fuel costs; the 'foot and mouth' crisis; calls to reintroduce capital punishment for paedophiles; the need to protect greenbelt land; the decline of British pubs; and opposition to the Euro, civil partnerships, wars in Iraq and Afghanistan, and fox hunting. In 2005, for example, its core policies of ending immigration, deporting illegal immigrants and voluntary repatriation were offered to voters alongside detailed policies on crime, environment, transport, education, food production and foreign policy. While seeking to attract Britons hostile toward immigration, the party has attempted to rally a broader coalition of supporters: those who favour withdrawal from the EU; protectionist economic policies; capital punishment; a return to traditional teaching methods; the creation of an English parliament and Bill of Rights; and the abolition of CCTV and plans to introduce identity cards.[73] This strategy has also been evident at the local level, where BNP campaigns target a range of community-based issues (see below). In 2008, for example, its local election campaign offered voters lower council tax, free weekly bin collections, more police, priority for white Britons when allocating social housing, a sensible immigration policy, a secure future for their children and the promotion of traditional Christian values. While contesting county council elections the following year, it similarly pledged improvements to the 'Meals on Wheels' service for pensioners, free housing for police, the removal of speed cameras and opposition to the creation of 'super-schools' which, the party claimed, were 'riddled with tension between pupils from an Islamic background and everyone else'.[74]

Community-based activism

While modifying the message, the shift toward elections also necessitated a change of tactics. A successful electoral strategy is one that mobilizes a broad and stable coalition of supporters. It requires parties to explore new ways of attracting followers, invest more seriously in fighting elections and develop more effective campaigning techniques. The extreme right had never committed fully to a ballot box strategy. Instead, it had long sought to project an image of strength in the hope of coming to public office amid a period of crisis. For reasons discussed in the last chapter, the BNP reached a different conclusion. If it was ever to escape from the lunatic fringe then it would need to embrace a vote-seeking electoral strategy, as Griffin explained: 'We deliberately haven't built our theoretical model anymore on the certain reliance that at some stage in the future there will be an economic catastrophe and then as long as we're there they'll all turn towards us.'[75] Shortly after taking control, Griffin criticized the tactics of his predecessors for fuelling a public image of the BNP as comprised of 'thugs, losers and troublemakers', and entrenching an association in the minds of voters between the party, the NF and the BUF.[76] Though Griffin had at one time defended these tactics, he was also aware from his days in the NF of their potential to have a profoundly negative impact:

> One of our strongest [NF] units of all was Bury St Edmunds, that was the place where we finally realised that marches were a counter-productive waste of space because we had this tremendous march and ruck with the reds and so on. We had great fun. But the people that we sold papers to in the market place the next week were saying 'well don't do that again because we couldn't trade, we couldn't come into town, my granny got knocked over by those scum, you know, it's crazy the support here but don't spoil our town again'.[77]

While modernizers experimented with community-based campaigns, Griffin now sought to place the tactic at the heart of party strategy. The underlying rationale was three-fold. First, community-based activism was considered essential to what the party termed its 'ladder strategy', which prioritized local campaigning and success as a crucial prerequisite to achieving a wider break-through. By concentrating efforts on local and European elections, the BNP hoped to build an image of credibility from the grassroots upward. Second, in some areas of the country the adoption of pavement politics would enable the BNP to take advantage of 'rotten boroughs' which were characterized by a long history of Labour dominance, moribund mainstream party branches and stagnant campaigning. While the BNP was unable to build a nationwide organization (see Chapter 4), in some areas of the country it sought to forge ties with voters through intensive and targeted campaigns. For Griffin, the tactic is also one way in which the party can outmanoeuvre rivals like the UK Independence Party (UKIP), which tend to be less active at the grassroots.[78] Third, by sinking roots in local communities and building relationships with residents, the party might also begin countering its stigma in wider society, as Griffin explained: 'We don't have to be in an area very long just doing grassroots work for us to overcome that [negative image] completely in that area and we're doing it on a borough by borough basis.'[79]

In its quest to achieve these goals, the party began developing more professional and localized methods. These methods were developed through an iterative process of trial and error, although specific campaigns played an important role (Fig. 3.2). In 2000, for example, branches were instructed to 'double-drop' leaflets that simultaneously pushed an anti-asylum message and targeted local issues.[80] Strong results in Burnley and Oldham at the 2001 general election and, the following year, the election of three BNP councillors in the former were also important; these campaigns saw the party distribute CDs to young people, tailor leaflets around local issues, target local workers through the Yellow Pages and launch a local website. The grassroots philosophy of the BNP organizer in Burnley reflected the broader mood within the party: 'It wasn't just a matter of actually contesting elections; it was a question of actually campaigning vigorously and wanting to produce a result, whereas historically in nationalism people have just stood in elections and thought that, maybe to solve their conscience, they've done their duty, they've stood and got a bad result.'

First Stage

- Select suitable candidate
- Target local ward
    - preferably Labour dominated
    - avoid strong Con/Lib Dem wards
    - avoid ward with high immigrant population/strongly middle class

Second Stage

- Identify local issues via leaflet
- Establish localized newsletter
- Establish candidate via community work

Third Stage

- Organize election team/appoint campaign manager
- Delegate responsibilities

FIGURE 3.2   BNP community politics model

Source: BNP literature.

Thereafter, campaigns increasingly targeted local issues and sought to establish a presence at community level, as another strategist explained: 'You've got to start right at the grassroots. The way that we cocked up in the eighties, where [the BNP] tried to go straight in and run before it could walk, well we have to walk before we can run. To do that, we've got to be seen within the community and to be seen that we aren't the people we are perceived to be in the media. We actually go out there, meet people, and let people talk to us.' Between 2002 and 2003, a string of local election gains led the party to reassess its target wards. Much like its ancestors, the BNP had never invested much effort in targeting particular social groups. Instead, it tended to focus simply on deprived districts where it had a local branch. Yet, when several of its candidates polled unexpectedly strongly in slightly more affluent areas, the party began revising its approach. Rather than target the working classes *per se*, its attention began turning toward the *skilled* working classes and disaffected Labour voters, as Griffin explains:

> So after that we've always told people 'don't go for the sink estates. If you've got a ward with a sink estate in it you've got to work it, but don't give it much attention because it's places where people have bought their own homes, where they've got something to lose. If you're canvassing and you're pushed for time and the house has got uncut grass and half-burnt mattresses in the front garden, don't do it because they won't vote for us even if they say they are going to', which is, I suppose, effectively Labour-vote territory . . . those are the areas.[81]

In an attempt to reach these voters the BNP began developing increasingly sophisticated campaigns. During one local by-election in Blackburn in 2002, it focused on rumours that a nursing home was being turned into a hostel for asylum-seekers and that Muslims were receiving disproportionate amounts of funding from the local council. It also drafted in members from nearby branches to help deliver a coordinated and intensive campaign, as one recalled: 'When the whole ward had been canvassed and second and third re-knocks done to make sure we had spoken to as many people as possible, we then drew up lists of all those households where at least one person had said they would be voting BNP. On the day before polling day each of these houses received a personally delivered thank you leaflet reminding them to vote.'[82] Another important campaign took place in the town of Halifax in 2003, when videos were sent to households with large numbers of white voters or influential local opinion-makers. The party also kept a local focus: it targeted the closure of a large employer, a pay rise for local councillors, and delivered seven different leaflets designed for middle-class areas and apathetic white voters. The party claimed it was active in the ward for six weeks prior to polling day and that almost 100 activists descended on the town. This strong presence led one Labour activist to observe: 'The BNP were the new kids on the block here, and boy were they on the block.'[83] Griffin hailed the Halifax campaign, which culminated in the election of a fifth BNP councillor, as the most sophisticated in its history, as he explains: 'What we'd learned by Halifax was that we could actually go head-to-head with the other parties' election machines and beat them on their own turf.'[84]

From then on, an increasingly confident BNP sought to apply the community-based model to other areas: in Burnley it campaigned for lower speed limits on housing estates and against the closure of local swimming baths; in Suffolk it sought to mobilize opposition to asylum while calling for the protection of rural bus services and local shops; in south Birmingham it targeted concerns among pensioners over youth gangs by distributing a local newsletter and presenting itself as a 'go-between' between residents and police; and in Halifax it returned to campaign to keep a primary school open.[85] By 2006, organizers were instructing activists to purchase 'high visibility' jackets to draw attention to their local work. They were also urged to embed local election candidates into community issues 'well before elections are called'.[86] This approach was evident in areas across the country: in Loughborough activists cleaned up a children's play area and claimed 'the BNP are the community party willing to help the local people'; in Havering they improved a boxing gym that was popular among young people; in Nuneaton they attended a protest in support of a popular local greengrocer who was 'being forced out of business by corporate bullies'; and in Leicestershire they became involved in a campaign against a proposed camp for travellers.[87] Griffin claims it was around this time that community-based activism became more firmly entrenched in the party's collective mindset and branches began employing the tactic on their own initiative: 'We identified canvassing very early on as being crucial to breakthrough the image of the BNP, you know outside, thuggish and not interested in local issues. We spent probably three years writing articles and running seminars and going places to canvass, and still virtually no-one outside of Tony Hardcore canvassed. Then about two-and-a-half years ago something switched in the party's collective brain and it's now very usual for people to canvass.'[88]

Local organizers were then issued with more detailed instructions: they should target areas with a history of Independents on the basis that this might have weakened the loyalty of voters to the main parties; and they should focus on seats which alternated regularly between parties as this reduced the likelihood of there being a popular local incumbent and improved the prospect of the BNP winning the seat on a lower percentage.[89] These tactics were evident during the party's 'one hundred seat campaign' at the 2005 general election. Rather than contest constituencies in sporadic fashion, the strongest regions were ordered to heavily canvass only one target seat. They were also provided with more specific selection criteria: the seats should be in areas where: the party had polled at least 8 per cent at elections to the European Parliament in 2004; it had elected councillors; or there was evidence of habitual BNP voting within local communities. By targeting seats in this way, the party aimed to consolidate its presence in emerging strongholds and used the campaign as a springboard into local election success the next year. Though some activists criticized the strategy and made clear their desire to contest more seats, Griffin reminded them how the record of 'nationalist' parties since the mid-1970s had been 'a cross between the Charge of the Light Brigade and a very expensive Chinese meal – one fart and it's all gone'.[90]

Some branches were more willing than others to embrace the new tactics. In Barking, the BNP polled over 16 per cent following a particularly intensive campaign; activists canvassed the borough daily and were joined at weekends by activists from nearby branches who carried out additional leafleting and canvassing.[91] Although the branch was only formed in 1999, it had quickly built a presence by contesting a string of local elections. In 2004, for example, it distributed nine different leaflets, canvassed voters on three separate occasions and used the electoral register to avoid inadvertently mobilizing Labour voters and minority ethnic groups.

Following the 2005 election, Griffin further encouraged local campaigns by urging activists to spend their time selling the BNP newspaper door-to-door, and 'while doing this you will quickly become aware of something in the ward which is crying out for a few hours' work by a BNP Community Clean Up Team. Perhaps a stream that's used as a rubbish dump, a playground littered with the dangerous litter left by junkies, or graffiti that needs painting out'.[92] While it might be tempting to dismiss this activity as overstated, there is evidence that it played an important role in attracting support. One study in London found that the party performed strongest in areas where it had previously been active. Another study of voting behaviour in three northern towns suggested that, in some wards, residents experienced more face-to-face contact with the BNP than the main parties.[93]

Conclusions

By the time the BNP turned its attention toward elections, there had emerged particularly favourable conditions for the extreme right. While Britons have long favoured a more restrictive immigration policy, in the early years of the twenty-first century this issue moved to the forefront of their minds and became a major concern. While large numbers of citizens considered the issue important and expressed anxiety about its effects, significant numbers were also dissatisfied with the perceived failure of the main parties to deliver an adequate response. The BNP sought to meet these opportunities by launching a concerted attempt to rally citizens hostile to immigration and resentful toward their mainstream representatives. The change of strategy meant modifying the racial nationalist message and confrontational tactics which had failed to convince ordinary Britons that the party was an acceptable alternative. Instead, and in an attempt to realize its potential, the party offered a message that put stronger emphasis on cultural rather than racial conflicts, populist rather than anti-democratic appeals and community politics rather than violence-prone marches. Similar to strategies employed by more successful extreme right parties elsewhere in Europe, the aim has been to attract citizens who 'never would have considered voting for an "old" right-wing extremist party promoting biological racism and/or anti-democratic stances'.[94]

4

ORGANIZING FOR ELECTIONS

We can win in all sorts of areas; middle class, working class, we know we can win. So that's not stopping us winning. What's stopping us winning is local credibility, lack of money, lack of campaign teams and so on, not the ideology.

Nick Griffin

As detailed in the last chapter, the search for wider appeal has led the BNP to pursue three main goals: attract the large number of Britons anxious over immigration and rising ethno-cultural diversity by putting stronger emphasis on cultural rather than racial conflicts between groups; mobilize politically dissatisfied citizens by launching populist attacks against the main parties; and replace confrontational tactics with community-based activism. While modifying the message, however, the shift toward elections also entailed consequences for how the party is organized.

A successful electoral strategy requires parties to undertake some basic organizational tasks: they must ideally establish strong leadership; build an infrastructure in different parts of the country; and provide their members with opportunities and incentives for getting actively involved. To translate initial gains into durable success, parties will need to overcome additional challenges: they will need to extend their reach into new areas; absorb new recruits; transform novice ideologues into skilled activists; establish a steady stream of income; and minimize factionalism and dissent.[1]

While there is some evidence that the most successful extreme right parties are those with strong leaders, effective organizations and unified memberships, their internal life largely remains an enigma.[2] Some describe the functioning of political parties more generally as 'an endless frustration' to academics, and this is especially true on the extreme right wing where parties are notorious for their intense secrecy, paranoia over infiltration and reluctance to grant outsiders access.[3] Nonetheless, a combination of interviews with activists and analysis of party documentation makes it possible to obtain insight into the internal workings of the BNP.

Structure and evolution

Fascist parties were once described as tightly centralized organizations based on a system of vertical links which protect against infighting and ensure strict discipline from their followers.[4] Extreme right parties in contemporary Europe are often portrayed in similar terms: highly authoritarian; lacking internal democracy; and operating according to the whim of a strong and charismatic leader. While leaders of the BNP have lacked popular charismatic appeal, their party has long been organized along these lines. From the outset, decisions about how to organize the BNP were influenced strongly by the NF and its committee-rule system of collective leadership.[5] Following repeated outbreaks of infighting, it became clear that the NF's structure had failed to fulfil an especially important task for a small and heavily ideological party: to discourage factionalism and minimize dissent.

Seeking to avoid the problems that befell its predecessor, the BNP adopted the 'leadership principle', a hierarchical structure that maximized the powers of the Chairman while minimizing the role of members. While the grassroots were expected to distribute literature, organize campaigns and contribute money, they were given no formal power in return. Instead, complete power was awarded to the leader. While the structure reflected the party's ideological emphasis on the need for strong leadership, discipline and service, it also marked a response to its early stage of development. During their infancy, political parties are often dominated by a strong leader who draws on his personal authority to compensate for a lack of established rules and procedures. This tendency for leaders of new parties to adopt an authoritarian style and rely only on an inner circle of loyalists is further encouraged by a lack of resources and experienced personnel.[6]

For the BNP, the total absence of internal democracy was justified on the grounds that if it was to survive then its leader would require the freedom to 'cut to a minimum the possibilities of faction, schism and subversion', and 'purge the ranks of disrupters the moment they showed their faces above the ground'.[7] The result was that, during the Tyndall era, there was no annual conference which might otherwise have enabled members to influence party affairs. Instead, followers were summoned to an annual rally where they heard a speech by the Chairman and were permitted no substantive involvement. As the party later recalled, during the early days it was little more than a 'one-man band', or as one activist remarked: 'The BNP is John Tyndall and there is no contesting his leadership or the constitution.'[8]

While keenly aware of the NF's flawed model, like its parent party the BNP failed to grasp the basics of party management. For much of its first two decades, a continual lack of members and money left a skeleton organization which attracted no more than 2,000 members, most of who were not regularly active. Internal fragility meant that opportunities for growth were frequently stifled, and a culture of amateurism pervaded the party. For example, though one of its main goals was to recruit new members, through much of the 1980s it remained without a telephone line through which it could take enquiries. The party was also ill-equipped to stem factionalism and exploit opportunities which followed the election of its first councillor in 1993. Instead of taking advantage of the publicity and enquiries which ensued, it became embroiled in a dispute with its rival, Combat 18.[9] Through much of this period it also lacked a regular newspaper, and when publications appeared they seldom had more than 500 subscribers.[10]

An inability to employ full-time staff meant that members were often told they would have to be patient and wait for a response to their orders and enquiries. These problems owed much to the fact that, at least until the late 1990s, the party's entire administrative structure rested almost exclusively on the shoulders of one activist, which severely constrained its ability to make progress:

> And throughout all this time the administration was Richard Edmonds, who was a nice, honest, very, very sincere fanatical man. But his organization was literally a big table. The party's administration was literally a pile of paper, letters and forms and so on just on the table. It was a most awful shambles. Basically, Richard's organization of this in terms of the membership cards and everything else could cope with about 600 people. The moment it got beyond that, everything collapsed. You're out leafleting and the follow-ups, responses, don't come back for six months because they're buried somewhere in this heap of paper. Once it gets beyond a certain size, that's it, it couldn't cope.[11]

Some significant attempts at internal reform followed the election of Nick Griffin in 1999, who sought to downplay the party's 'near dictatorial arrangement' and extremist image.[12] Like his predecessor, Griffin came of political age in the NF and viewed its committee-style structure as a 'guaranteed recipe for factionalism'.[13] The result was that, during his tenure as Chairman of the BNP, he expressed little desire to remove or modify the leadership principle. While responsibility may be delegated, the party made clear that 'the underlying Leadership Principle is unaffected', and '[r]esponsibility and liability for all decisions save those made by local officials acting on their own initiative rests with the Chairman and the Chairman alone'.[14] This was reaffirmed when the party revised its constitution in 2009, stating that 'the elected National Chairman shall have ultimate and final authority upon any decision made'.[15]

The arrangement awarded Griffin with full executive power, including the power to: appoint and create party officers; determine internal structures; shape rules and procedures; and make all executive, administrative, policy and tactical decisions. The dominance of the leader was further enforced through a constitutional provision which ensured he could only be removed following a postal ballot of the membership, and provided the challenger met certain criteria – they must: have been a member for at least five years; have status as a 'voting member' (see below); and have received support from at least 20 per cent of members with two years continuous service.

As Griffin took control, however, the shift toward an electoral strategy also required the party to strengthen and expand its apparatus. From 1999, several internal bodies were established to facilitate this process, including: a Department for Group Development to support the growth of branches; Administration and Enquiries Departments to manage membership and literature subscriptions; a Communications Department to handle media relations; a Legal Affairs Department to provide advice; a Security Department to manage events and ensure the safety of personnel; and Departments to help manage publicity and information technology. More significant was the formation of an Advisory Council (AC), which was tasked with providing the Chairman with guidance. The AC is comprised of leading activists who meet several times each year, and typically includes the deputy Chairman, regional organizers, full time staff and other members appointed by the Chairman. While AC members appoint an auditor and are able to call an extraordinary general members meeting (providing they assemble a two-thirds majority), their powers are limited. It is the Chairman who sets the agenda for meetings and retains the power to determine who sits on the Council. Shortly after its creation, the party was also careful to underscore that its tasks are to be undertaken 'without hindering the Chairman's ability to make the final decision on all matters'.[16]

Expansion

During its early years the BNP prioritized survival over electoral success (see Chapter 2). This meant there were few incentives or resources to invest in organizational development. Its growing involvement in elections, however, called for more effort to be devoted to nurturing the growth of branches, groups and contacts, or what the party terms 'units'. For the BNP, units have three core functions: to recruit followers; to raise funds; and to work toward elections. Since its birth, units have been divided on a regional basis and then subdivided into branches, groups and contacts. Typically, they are organized around constituencies, cities or villages. Branches are managed by a local organizer and a fundholder who coordinate activity and are supervised by regional organizers. Below branches are smaller and less active groups, which are formed when two people agree to act as organizer and fundholder. Groups are promoted to branch status only when they have recruited sufficient memberships, achieved stability and are deemed sufficiently active (i.e. regularly contesting elections). Below groups are individual contacts, described as 'one-person units [who are] given permission to be the party's contact in that area with the intention of taking details of local members and applicants and so building a group thereafter'.[17]

Under Griffin, the party retained this core structure while also setting out more specific assessment criteria. National and regional organizers are encouraged to hold regular meetings with local organizers to monitor their performance, including: the amount of literature being distributed; whether campaigns are targeting local issues; and the rate of enquiries being converted into actual members. Branches are also expected to fulfil certain criteria – they should: have at least 50 members; hold six meetings each year; sell 150 copies of the party newspaper and magazine each month; stand at least four candidates in local elections; and have at least £300 in their bank account. Within six months of being formed, groups should be selling 50 copies of party publications each month and holding two meetings each year. Contacts, meanwhile, are expected to be promoted to group status within one year by pursuing local enquiries and leafleting. While some anecdotal evidence suggests this assessment is more regular than in the past, it is impossible to assess the extent to which it actually takes place.[18]

Internal literature provides some useful insight into the evolution of units. One example is the Southend unit which was formed by four activists in 1989–90, but soon disintegrated when leafleting drives failed to attract new recruits. The unit was relaunched in 2001 by an ex-Conservative member. After recruiting a small band of activists, the group contested local elections in 2003 and attracted the attention of local media. Its recruitment strategy put strong emphasis on leafleting and face-to-face meetings with residents who had enrolled or enquired about membership. These local sympathizers were given a newsletter that included information about meetings, and were encouraged to purchase the newspaper (*Voice of Freedom*) and magazine (*Identity*). This produced a paper round of over 100 newspapers which were delivered by six activists on weekly leafleting drives. In an attempt to sustain the loyalty of its activists, the group initiated a voting system which enabled them to determine what activities they would undertake. The unit was awarded branch status in 2004.[19]

Other examples, however, highlight the fragility of BNP units. While the Bradford branch performed strongly in local elections between 2002 and 2004, it was weakened when it was revealed that an organizer had been working undercover for anti-fascists. Its growth was further hampered by the resignation of a key activist in 2006. Soon afterward, the branch lost one of its council seats in a by-election, three of its councillors in local elections and gained only one new seat. At local elections in 2007, support continued to decline and, the following year, infighting culminated in the departure of several activists who established a rival party, the Democratic Nationalists (DN).

While they are useful, these anecdotal examples tell us little about the broader evolution of the party to which we now turn. From its birth, a distinct lack of resources prevented the BNP from building a national network of branches. Instead, it focused on areas where its predecessor had been most active and received higher than average levels of support. Across Europe, extreme right parties often anchor their campaigns and organizations in local or regional strongholds, such as Flemish Interest (VB) in Antwerp or the Austrian Freedom Party (FPÖ) in the southern province of Carinthia.[20] While less successful, the BNP similarly sought to anchor its organization in areas where there was a legacy of campaigning and support.

This meant that although five activists were initially entrusted with the task of building a national infrastructure, little activity took place outside of the East End of London, where they hoped to build on a longer tradition of anti-immigrant campaigns (see Chapter 1). Some of the earliest and most active BNP units emerged in places like Hackney and Tower Hamlets, where ex-members of the NF and British Movement (BM) shifted support behind the new party. These early recruits were most active in North and South East London, in areas such as Enfield, Hackney, Redbridge and Waltham Forest. To a lesser extent, the party also sought to build on an existing presence outside of London as in Bristol or Carmarthen where, in the latter, an entire NF branch switched allegiance to the BNP.[21]

While the level of activity was almost certainly low, by the time of the 1983 general election the party claimed to have established branches in several areas across the country, including: Liverpool and Manchester in the North West; Hull and Leeds in Yorkshire, as well as smaller groups in Bradford, Wakefield and York; Gateshead in the North East; and Plymouth and Bournemouth along the South Coast. In contrast to these more promising prospects, the party considered itself weak in West London and complained that factionalism or stagnation had set into units in Essex, East Anglia, Kent and Glasgow.[22]

If there was a 'stronghold' of the early BNP then it was London. The party's heavy concentration in the capital becomes clear by examining seats it contested at the 1983 election, which were selected on the basis of where there were active BNP units (see Table 4.1).[23] Almost one third of BNP candidates stood in London, while there was also a noticeable cluster in surrounding areas which would provide higher than average support to the party some two decades later, for example, Broxbourne, Epping Forest and Thurrock. One possible explanation for this presence in outer London is that members of the more established branches in London spilled over into neighbouring areas to help campaigns. It was

TABLE 4.1 Location of BNP parliamentary candidates, 1983–2010

	1983	1987*	1992	1997	2001	2005	2010
Region							
Greater London	19	1	4	22	14	12	34
Eastern	–	–	1	3	1	5	41
South East	12	1	–	5	0	5	27
South West	4	–	–	4	0	3	19
East Midlands	5	–	2	5	3	7	33
West Midlands	2	–	–	6	5	22	38
Yorkshire and Humber	5	–	1	5	2	33	48
North West	5	–	1	3	5	17	38
North East	–	–	1	–	2	11	28
Scotland	1	–	2	3	0	2	13
Wales	1	–	1	–	1	2	19
Total	**54**	**2**	**13**	**56**	**33**	**119**	**338**

* The party officially abstained from the general election of 1987.

London-based branches which tended to benefit from more experienced and active organizers, many of whom earned their political stripes in the NF. For example, it was the Islington branch which raised the largest donation during the 1983 campaign (£1000) and, two years later, the Lewisham branch which was hailed as the top door-to-door seller of the party newspaper.[24]

At least until 2001, the BNP remained essentially a phenomenon of London and, to a lesser extent, surrounding areas in the South East. While activists were encouraged to devote their weekends to building a presence in 'virgin' territory, the reality was that few ventured beyond the borders of London.[25] Toward the end of the 1980s the party declared London its stronghold, with this 'strength' drawn mainly from enclaves of support in Enfield, Hackney, Lewisham, Southwark and Tower Hamlets, and then smaller units in Bexley, Camden, Greenwich, Hillingdon, Lambeth and Redbridge.[26]

It was in Tower Hamlets where the election of the first BNP councillor in 1993 kept its focus fixed firmly on the capital. This was apparent the next year when activists in Newham actively contested local elections at a time when few branches seemed interested in elections. In 1996, it was again two London-based branches that were applauded for distributing the most literature and becoming the strongest areas; they covered the inner East End, North London and East Hertfordshire.[27]

Toward the end of the 1990s, however, this geographical focus began to shift. The new topic of conversation inside the party was votes, and how to get them. The growing interest in electoral politics meant more energy would have to be devoted to extending its reach into new areas. This would be achieved by relaunching older units in decline and building new units in previously uncharted territory. As the BNP entered the twenty-first century, the result was steady albeit not spectacular growth.

According to a combination of party literature and data submitted by the party to the Electoral Commission, between 1985 and 2008 the number of BNP units increased more than six-fold, rising from 30 to over 200 (see Fig. 4.1).[28] Much of this growth, however, has taken place since 2001 and amid rising support in elections. Between 2001 and 2003, for example, relaunched or new units emerged in a diverse array of areas across the country, including Basildon, Brighton, Bristol, Dorset, Eastbourne, Gateshead, Hastings, Hull, the Isle of Man, North Wales, Portsmouth, Sedgefield, Southampton, Southend, Sussex, Swansea, Swindon, Teesside, Thurrock, Watford, Weymouth and Woking.[29] Though not all units would have been active, stable or supported by large memberships, the fact that they were listed alongside contact information suggests at least some basic level of organization in these areas.

Rather than expanding across the country, the BNP was moving in specific directions. While building on a legacy of extreme right party campaigning in the Midlands and London, it also began moving into the North West and Yorkshire. The Midlands had been the birthplace of Powellism and also provided disproportionately high levels of support to the NF. Some two decades later, the BNP sought to build on this tradition by relaunching groups in areas like Coventry and Birmingham, while also poaching influential activists from the West Midlands

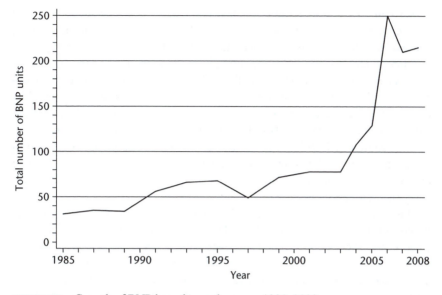

FIGURE 4.1 Growth of BNP branches and groups, 1985–2008

Source: BNP literature/interviews.

branch of a rival party, the National Democrats (ND).[30] At one meeting of a relaunched group in 2006, for example, residents donated £500 while listening to a speaker give 'a blistering account of the many failures of the main parties with particular reference to the massive wave of immigrants that are now coming to Britain'. One local shopkeeper offered members a 10 per cent discount, provided they show their BNP card.[31]

While the party also remained active in the East End, its interest in its historic bastion of support was waning. Its continued presence was apparent at local elections in 1998, which saw almost 80 per cent of the 34 BNP candidates contest either Newham or Tower Hamlets.[32] The reality, however, was that local organizers were finding it increasingly difficult to mobilize and sustain support in an area that was rapidly diversifying. As activists struggled to mobilize support among white working-class communities which voted Labour, were apathetic, or were at ease with their increasingly diverse surroundings, they began withdrawing from the inner East End, as Griffin explains:

> There are no whites left, or at least there are no whites left with any fight or capabilities. All the younger, brighter ones got their families out. Lots of them [residents] are elderly; they feel that it's too late and all of the rest of it. You couldn't leaflet, you couldn't possibly leaflet in Tower Hamlets without sooner or later having people killed. It's simply too dangerous, the area's gone, that's it. The FN [*French* Front National] has the same trouble in parts of Paris.[33]

Searching for a more receptive audience, the party turned its attention toward outer London, in particular to areas such as Barking, Bexley, Dagenham, Havering and Greenwich. This shift gained momentum following the 2001 general election which saw the BNP poll strongly in Barking, Dagenham and Poplar and Canning Town. Respectable results in these areas led one activist to summarize the party's changing direction: 'While the party is witnessing the death of the old East End, on election night we saw the birth of the new East End in Barking and Dagenham.'[34] In fact, the BNP had first arrived in the area in 1999 and quickly built a community-based presence. The next year, the importance of grassroots campaigning was underscored at the first meeting of the newly formed Lewisham and Bromley branch:'posturing and posing are out', one organizer told the audience, and 'hard graft is in'.[35]

While shifting eastward along the Thames, the party had also begun moving northwards toward more deprived heartlands of the Labour Party (see Chapter 2). Historically, the extreme right had never built a strong presence in northern England. In the 1980s, for example, the BNP dismissed its units in the North West and Yorkshire as 'bottom of the league'.[36] Though some areas of Yorkshire such as Dewsbury and Halifax bucked the trend, for much of its history the party avoided making a serious commitment to the north.[37] In the late 1990s, however, this reluctance loosened as there emerged signs of opportunities in Pennine Lancashire and West Yorkshire. These favourable conditions followed the decline of traditional industries and the onset of post-industrialism, which had left several councils grappling with stagnant economies, deprivation and anxiety among some residents over how regeneration grants were being distributed. There was also direct evidence of intergroup tension, which had surfaced in Bradford in 1995 and then amid urban disturbances in Bradford, Burnley and Oldham over the summer of 2001.

Particularly from 1999, the BNP's determination to exploit these opportunities was reflected in the birth or relaunch of units in towns like Bradford, Burnley, Preston, Rochdale and Rossendale.[38] In Burnley, the party found its path into local politics cleared by the failure of mainstream parties to stand full slates of candidates in elections, and also populist Independents who claimed Muslim communities had received the bulk of regeneration funds. In Burnley and other nearby towns, the historical dominance of Labour combined with a lack of vibrant party competition, grassroots campaigning and responsive local governance had led some observers to point toward signs of 'rotten boroughs'. As one study pointed out, even when the mainstream parties sought to address the decay of grassroots democracy by fielding full slates of candidates, the presence of names on ballot papers was 'of limited relevance if the local party is not running anything like a recognisable campaign in most of the local authority district'.[39]

Seeking to take advantage of these conditions, the BNP began investing more energy in building a presence in northern England. In 2001, for example, it held its first meeting in Liverpool for almost a decade and, the following year, around 200 residents attended the first meeting of a group in Blackburn. Meanwhile, the party also began strengthening its presence in parts of West Yorkshire, such as

Bradford, Halifax and Keighley. In 2001, its relaunched Dewsbury branch claimed that around 50 residents attended its first meeting and promptly organized a petition against 'anti-white racist attacks' in the town.[40]

By the time the party celebrated its twentieth birthday on 7th April 2002, its northward shift was gathering pace and it appeared increasingly disinterested in its birthplace of London. This was evident at the 2002 local elections, which saw the election of three BNP councillors in Burnley and strong results in Oldham contrast with a disappointing night in London. The party attributed its poor performance in the latter to the disintegration of branches in the East End, which it traced to the departure of key organizers and 'white flight'.[41] In fact, the party had become so preoccupied with northern England that it felt the need to reach out to supporters in London and assure them they were 'not forgotten'.[42] Further north, however, between 2002 and 2003 it continued expanding its presence by launching new units in areas such as Barnsley, Clitheroe, Halifax, Hyndburn, Keighley, Pendle, Sheffield and Wakefield. For Griffin, unlike large cities, these 'close knit' towns and communities were considered 'easier to work' for a small and relatively active party.[43]

This picture of organizational expansion is supported by analysis of BNP literature, which suggests that during its early years the party was strongest in London, the Eastern region and Yorkshire, but weaker in the North East and South West (see Table 4.2). From the late 1990s, however, its presence in the North West and Yorkshire strengthened considerably. While in 1985 these two regions hosted only 10 BNP units, two decades later the number had risen to 35 and they had become its two strongest regions. As shown in the next chapter, this northward shift is also evident in the party's social bases of support.

Extending its reach

Like social movements, extreme right parties in Europe often attempt to extend their reach in society and rally large coalitions of supporters by establishing affiliated networks and organizations. In the 1970s, for example, the NF attempted to rally young Britons and supporters overseas through a youth wing and affiliated groups in Commonwealth countries. To widen its appeal and achieve power, Griffin similarly advocates that the BNP should develop a social movement model of campaigning, and invest more effort in extending its reach, as he explains: 'We have no cultural base; we have no extra-parliamentary base. I'm not talking about illegality or insanity. I'm just talking about straightforward practical things such as the Countryside Alliance. We're *behind* in terms of developing those.'[44]

By developing a network of affiliated organizations, the aim has been to transform the BNP from a conventional political party into a broader movement, and to mount a more durable challenge which is not restricted to elections, as supporters were told: 'Vital though contesting and winning elections remain, this Islamist juggernaut cannot be opposed by electioneering alone. Sinking roots in community work, youth clubs, popular culture and pressure groups must all become as

TABLE 4.2 BNP branches and groups in England's regions, 1985–2006

Region	Year											
	1985	*1987*	*1989*	*1991*	*1993*	*1995*	*1997*	*1999*	*2001*	*2003*	*2005*	*2006*
Eastern	6	7	4	6	5	5	3	6	9	10	7	14
East Midlands	1	3	3	7	8	8	3	5	8	7	9	16
Greater London	3	4	3	9	9	12	9	15	10	7	10	12
North East	1	2	3	4	4	3	1	2	4	4	4	6
North West	4	5	5	8	13	9	10	14	14	19	19	21
South East	2	3	3	5	8	11	7	8	9	7	8	15
South West	3	1	1	3	3	5	2	5	4	5	5	8
West Midlands	5	4	2	5	7	7	8	9	8	6	11	14
Yorkshire and Humberside	6	6	10	9	9	8	6	8	12	13	16	19
Total	**31**	**35**	**34**	**56**	**66**	**68**	**49**	**72**	**78**	**78**	**89**	**125**

Note: The total number of BNP units combines branches and groups but does not include local 'contacts', which are typically one-person units. The data has been compiled from December issues of *Spearhead*, *British Nationalist* and *Voice of Freedom*.

much a part of the BNP's normal activity as leafleting and canvassing.'[45] Griffin describes the strategy as cultivating 'the water in which the fish swim'.[46]

While one element of the strategy has been community-based activism, another has been the establishment of affiliated networks. Shortly after taking power, for example, Griffin attempted to recruit a network of overseas supporters through the American Friends of the BNP (AFBNP).[47] Since then, the party has launched an annual festival – the Red, White and Blue (RWB) – which has become an important event in the BNP social diary. In 2003, for example, more than 1,000 members attended the festival where branches were awarded for recruiting the largest number of members in one year (Bradford), and raising the largest donation (Leicester).[48] Among activists, the RWB is considered important in helping to normalize the BNP in the eyes of the wider public, as one explained: 'We're probably more of a family I think than some of the other parties, and I think that's important for us because part of the thing that obviously we're trying to promote is that we do represent the white population of this country. That isn't a racist thing. It might be a *race* thing in that, you know, we're looking after our own but, as far as we're concerned, if we don't look after our own then who the hell is going to do?' While an additional aim is to present a more family-friendly image, the event has hosted bands connected to the white power skinhead scene, such as Stigger, Nemesis and Warlord, which have attended party events and contributed merchandise.[49]

Other initiatives are similarly designed to appeal to members of social groups who might not previously have supported the party, and to strengthen bonds of loyalty among existing members. These have included an attempt to recruit support among rural constituencies (through the group Land and People), families and women (through a Family Circle), members of minority ethnic groups (through an Ethnic Liaison Committee), ex-members of the armed services (through an Association of British ex-Servicemen), Britons concerned over 'anti-white' racism (through the group Families Against Immigrant Racism), military veterans (through the Veterans Group) and young people and students (through the Young BNP). Reflecting its shifting discourse, in 2010 the youth wing was renamed BNP Crusaders 'to pay homage to our ancestors from the Middle Ages who saved Christian Europe from the onslaught of Islam'.[50] The party has also established an associated record label (Great White Records), trade union (Solidarity) and radio station.[51]

For Griffin, while extending the party's reach these initiatives are also geared toward reducing the rate of membership dropout, as he explains: '[We] constantly have to give them [members] the idea that we're going forward; that in some way they can be empowered to make a contribution to that. So it's their success and not our success, and evolving some way on a social level so if they leave politics they also leave friends.'[52] It is important, however, not to overstate the strength of these affiliated groups. Most have few members and resources. In 2001, for example, and following claims the BNP had received substantial donations from supporters in the United States, it was revealed there were only 100 members of the AFBNP.

Seven years later, the party claimed to have recruited only 108 overseas members.[53] Between 2004 and 2007, its Land and People group had an annual budget of less than £2,000, and, in 2005, Families Against Immigrant Racism had less than £300 in its bank account.[54]

While lacking resources, these initiatives reflect a broader attempt to emulate models of organization developed by similar parties elsewhere in Europe. The RWB, for example, was directly inspired by the festival of the French Front National (FN) – the *Bleu Blanc Rouge* (Blue, White and Red). The BNP has since strengthened ties with the FN, as well as other extreme right parties such as Jobbik in Hungary, the National Democratic Party of Germany (NPD) and National Democrats (ND) in Sweden. These links have been evident at numerous events, for example: the former leader of the NPD, Günter Deckert, was invited to speak to BNP's Croydon branch in 2001; the leader of Young BNP attended an NPD event in Hamburg; in 2004 Griffin attended a rally of the Swedish ND to help publicize its European election campaign; in the same year, Jean-Marie Le Pen attended a BNP fund-raising dinner; in 2005, Griffin returned the favour by speaking at the FN's annual Joan of Arc parade; three years later, he was the guest speaker at a rally by Jobbik and joined the Swedish ND at another rally in Prague by the Czech National Party (NS); the NS leader was then invited to speak at the RWB; and in 2009, the BNP Deputy Chairman attended an international conference alongside members of the French FN and Italian Forza Nuova.[55]

These cross-national links have been strengthened further following the election of Griffin and Andrew Brons to the European Parliament in 2009. The next year saw the BNP join several other parties in the Alliance of European National Movements (AENM), with Griffin appointed Vice President of the group. Other members include the French FN, Hungarian Jobbik, Swedish ND, Tricolour Flame (FT) in Italy, National Front (FN) in Belgium, National Renewal Party (PNR) in Portugal, Freedom (Svoboda) in the Ukraine and Republican Social Movement (MSR) in Spain. In 2010, a high-ranking member of the BNP joined representatives from these parties at an international conference in Japan, scheduled as the first of regular meetings between the parties.

Attempts at professionalization

While attempting to learn from its European neighbours, the BNP has also sought to invest more seriously in its infrastructure and grassroots base. Influenced strongly by his experience in the NF and its history of infighting, Griffin has attempted to build a more professional party machine capable of sustaining a long-term challenge. Since 2005, this has included four main elements: devoting more energy to educating and training members; providing these members with incentives for getting actively involved; establishing a steady stream of income; and overcoming the extreme right's traditional weakness of factionalism and dissent. Not all of these goals, however, have been achieved.

In terms of the grassroots, during its infancy and in the quest to survive, the BNP prioritized the recruitment of loyal foot soldiers over skilled administrators. Lacking the resources and inclination to build a respectable and well-trained activist cadre, the party instead recruited the bulk of early members from within the extreme right. As the party would later discover, most of these novice ideologues lacked the experience and skills required for successful electoral campaigns. When, in the late 1990s, it became more involved in elections, its heavy reliance on the extremist fringe for volunteers undermined its attempt to appear to Britons as a credible alternative, as Griffin explained: 'Once you reach that level on the downward spiral, they [activists] can't recruit, because even if they are going out campaigning and someone sends in for an information pack, they go and see them, the ordinary Jo Public, and they think "oh my god, this bloke is barking mad".'[56] As Griffin elaborated, the negative impact of inexperienced racial nationalists on electoral campaigns has remained clearly evident, such as during the general election in 1997:

> We don't regard general elections as a place where we're going to win. The party wanted to fight enough seats to get a broadcast which is over 50. It does involve a certain degree of organisational capability and still in those days, it was 'oh god how many of them [activists] are going to fowl up their nomination papers?' It's a very simple thing to do, but if you'd never done a nomination before . . . Next to 'description', you get people putting in 'five foot nine inches, brown hair' instead of 'British National Party'. You're thinking, 'how many of these fools are going to cock things up?'[57]

Because of its minuscule membership, however, the party remained heavily dependent on these longer-term activists, as Griffin continues 'But at the same time we can't afford to just alienate everyone from the past, or who regard themselves as a principled nationalist. We simply can't afford to do that. The organizational costs would be too catastrophic.'[58] These internal problems were further exacerbated when, after rising support in elections, an influx of previously unaffiliated new recruits presented an additional challenge. While new recruits brought much-needed money and labour, they lacked understanding of the party and the racial nationalist tradition. As Griffin warned the BNP faithful, in the quest for electoral success the potential danger was that they might suddenly become 'swamped by an ideologically incoherent wave of naïve new recruits'.[59]

In response to this uneasy coalition of inexperienced racial nationalists and ideologically unaware new recruits, the party began devoting more effort to activist training and education. As the wife of Nick Griffin (who is also active in the party) explained during one interview, by investing more seriously in these tasks, the party has attempted to overcome the problem of an ideologically committed but inexperienced grassroots base: 'To get anywhere, you have to have your civil service. The biggest problem that's gone on is we've been putting square pegs in round holes: we've been using political people to push paper.'[60]

In response, the party held its first 'annual college' for activists in 2001, providing them with training in community-based activism, postal ballots, using the electoral register and databasing results. By the time of the 2005 general election, it had launched a regular strategy conference for activists in the North West, and an annual conference for members. This growing emphasis on membership development was formalized in 2007, when the newly formed Education and Training Department was tasked with 'turning enthusiastic amateurs into professional volunteers equipped with the ideological and practical skills needed to take the BNP to the next level of political success'.[61] Annual 'summer schools' for high-ranking officials followed in 2008 and 2010, providing training in recruitment, legal issues, ideology and treasury skills. The party also increased efforts to improve ideological and strategic awareness among members through a magazine, website, internet television service and regular DVDs.

Trained and educated members, however, are useless unless they are active. At the core of the second goal – to provide members with incentives for becoming active – is the Voting Membership (VM) scheme. The VM scheme holds its roots in Griffin's research on the evolution of other radical movements, such as the early labour movement, Sinn Fein and Hizb-ut-Tahrir. The dilemma which the scheme aims to resolve is how to transform passive members into committed activists, while also restricting influence inside the party only to those loyalists who have 'an effective understanding of our core aims'.[62] This attempt to create 'a self-selecting elite' commenced at the 2005 annual conference, at which organizers, fund-holders, major donors and members with at least ten years' service were allowed to debate and influence policy and constitutional reform. Shortly thereafter, leading activists visited the Swedish ND to explore how its organization had been modified to encourage an active membership.[63] The mechanics of the scheme were further developed at the 2007 annual conference, and then formally adopted.

The scheme entitles members who have been enrolled for two years to register to become a voting member, at which point they enter a one-year probationary period. Members commit themselves to attend education and training seminars, undertake a set amount of activism and provide regular donations (although some 'recognised' activists are exempt from these requirements). In return, the most active members are permitted to vote on certain matters at general members' meetings and annual conferences. They are also able to participate in policy debates, become eligible for appointment to intermediate or senior positions and, after five years' continuous service, be nominated as a candidate in a leadership election. In this way, by the time active members achieve senior positions and influence, they have been fully trained in BNP ideology and electoral strategy.[64]

Finance and factionalism

Internal reform and election campaigns require money. Unlike mainstream parties, the BNP attracts few donations from businesses, trade unions or wealthy donors.

Instead, it has long relied almost exclusively on members for money. In the early days, it attempted to supplement this income by selling literature and recordings of speeches by prominent activists. A total lack of transparency, however, it impossible to obtain insight into its financial health, as one activist recalled: 'John Tyndall used to run the party's finances effectively out of his own back pocket. No-one knew what the party's finances were, whether they were good or bad. People would die and leave their money to him personally in their will and not to the party.'

What appears certain is that, during its formative years, the BNP operated on a financial shoestring. Its sporadic general election campaigns were typically supported by paltry war chests: in 1992 for example, it collected only £5,000, and in 1997 only £10,000.[65] Its attempts to overcome this persistent weakness tended to end in failure: a bookshop that opened in 1989 was closed in 1996 after attracting opponents and proving too costly; then, while the party launched a dining club for more affluent members in 1992, six years later it continued to complain how it was yet to receive a donation of more than £5,000 (the club was renamed the Trafalgar Club in 2000). By the time of the 1997 general election, the party admitted expenses were 'far out-stripping' income.[66] The response from members failed to silence concerns. Later that year, the party issued an urgent appeal for donations to help pay back £8,000 of loans which remained from the 1990s.[67]

The party remained in a weak financial state, managing to survive by drawing on what it called its 'strategic reserve', a fund of around £100,000 left by a supporter in the North East. In 1999, however, Griffin and his supporters encouraged the Chairman to invest as much of the fund as possible into the European election campaign, in the hope of recruiting some new members and easing his rise to power.[68]

As leader, Griffin has sought to remedy the problem by devoting more energy to generating income. According to data submitted to the Electoral Commission, these attempts have met some success. Since 2001, the party's annual turnover has increased more than six-fold, with much of this income coming from members (see Table 4.3). Between 2001 and 2008, income from membership subscriptions increased almost five-fold, rising from £35,000 to £166,000. Meanwhile, over the same period the party claimed its income from donations surged from £38,000 to

TABLE 4.3 Financing the BNP, 2001–2008 (£,000s)

	2001	2002	2003	2004	2005	2006	2007	2008
Members' subscriptions	35.6	59.6	92.0	129.0	114.6	145.4	201.4	166.0
Donations	38.0	77.0	100.0	270.0	217.0	289.0	198.0	662.3
Total income from all sources	145.0	228.0	370.0	718.0	672.0	726.0	611.0	985.7
Profit/loss		+14.8	+24.8	+27.6	–20.2	–94.7	+18.9	–50.6	–82.6

Source: Electoral Commission (figures rounded).

over £660,000.[69] One recruit described her willingness to respond to the party's persistent appeals for donations as follows: 'But you just accept that you have to do these things, you have to raise the money. I myself gave, I think, £700 toward the European election, £500 toward the General Election. You know, you send your £50 or £100 quid for Nick's legal fees. You have to do it, what good is money to me if I'm not free?'

While the financial base of the BNP is easily dwarfed by those of the three main parties, since 2003 it has generated more income from its membership than the Greens and Plaid Cymru and, in 2007, the UK Independence Party (see Table 4.4). Despite this rising income, however, its financial base remains weak and is a constant source of tension inside the party. While revenue has increased, the party has recorded significant deficits following costly election campaigns and numerous court cases. In fact, deficits in 2004 and 2005 prompted auditors to express doubt over the longer-term financial viability of the BNP. Even Griffin conceded the fledgling party had 'seriously overstretched itself'.[70]

One major contributory factor to these problems was the party's costly but ultimately unsuccessful attempt to enter the European Parliament in 2004 which, according to Griffin, left it 'crippled' for the next 18 months.[71] In response, subscriptions were increased in 2006 and members were given a grim assessment: 'Unless we increase our regular, reliable income, the British National Party faces a simple and disastrous choice: Either cut back on the things we do . . . or continue to do what we need to do and go bankrupt next summer.'[72]

The dismal financial position was clearly impacting on the party's ability to sustain its electoral and organizational growth, as Griffin explained during this period: 'The crucial bottleneck is key organizational stuff. There was a time when that was because the people weren't there. We've now got people coming over ears. It's purely a matter of money. We don't have the resources to employ the

TABLE 4.4 Party membership and subscription fee revenues compared, 2001–2008 (£,000s)

	BNP	Con	Lab	Lib Dem	Green	Plaid Cymru	SNP	UKIP
2001	35.6	–	3,399	589.7	–	15.0	–	–
2002	59.6	665	3,093	680.0	78.1	41.6	136.4	119.4*
2003	92.0	814	3,452	680.2	87.4	53.3	126.1	209.6
2004	129.0	814	3,492	709.5	99.5	86.1	169.1	198.8
2005	114.6	843	3,685	768.5	113.7	93.9	195.4	181.4
2006	145.4	1,191	4,376	832.1	118.0	81.8	244.0	148.1
2007	201.4	1,121	4,447	803.7	142.2	98.2	310.8	167.1
2008	166.0	1,229	3,930	807.8	141.1	88.5	367.1	193.7

Source: J. Marshall (2009) *Membership of UK political parties*, House of Commons Library Research Standard Note SN/SG/5125; Electoral Commission.

Notes: *16-month period starting from 09/2001; revenues for the year to 31 December; Conservative and Labour figures only available to the nearest thousand.

people that we should be employing to achieve what we easily could achieve, some of which would bring in extra resources. So it's purely a lack of money.'[73] These views were echoed by a national organizer who drew attention to the difficulty of building an effective party machine with little financial support: 'If we had the money, we should have much better regional structures of organization, you know, people who are paid in every region and who are accountable to members in that region. But we don't have that because we don't have that kind of money. It's the one thing that holds us back – the inability to pay local officials and the reliance upon volunteers. It's very difficult to tell volunteers to change their ways, to improve their efficiency or make sure they inform more people about what they're doing when they're giving up their own time.'

The BNP had been forced to grow while managing without full-time staff. At least until the late 1990s, it relied on only a handful of unpaid regional organizers who were scattered across the country.[74] It also lacked a permanent base, and was instead forced to operate a 'virtual headquarters' whereby party affairs were managed through meetings, telephone calls and e-mail. Even at the time of the 2001 general election, the party was supported by only three full-time members of staff. Six years later, and despite a rising profile in elections and media, this number had risen to only 13.[75]

While the party managed to stabilize its position, in 2007 it was forced to borrow funds from a regional accounting unit, which prompted auditors to raise further concerns. Then, at the end of the year, several high-ranking activists and members of the Advisory Council were expelled after criticizing Griffin and the lack of financial transparency. Several of these 'December rebels' subsequently launched an unsuccessful leadership challenge, which included demands for transparency and internal democracy.[76] The activists coalesced under the banner 'voice of change', and called for a 'fresh and democratic structure' that would ensure the BNP 'is financially solvent, politically astute, credible and electable, truly represents family values in everything that it does and maintains democratic management . . . in a fair and transparent manner'.[77]

While the challenge failed, Griffin moved to appease dissenters and stabilize the party's financial base by employing an external business consultant to coordinate a series of donation appeals and help strengthen administrative structures (an earlier attempt stalled when the organizer made responsible died suddenly). Within one year, the consultant was hailed for increasing annual turnover to almost £1 million and achieving more than a three-fold increase in donation income, which jumped from £200,000 to £660,000. Some of this income was redirected into the party's successful campaign in 2008 to achieve representation in the Greater London Assembly (GLA).

While the consultant became the target of considerable criticism among some activists who alleged financial corruption, the next year he was applauded for helping increase turnover to over £2 million and donation revenue to over £1.6 million.[78] It is almost impossible to assess the validity of these claims, as the BNP has (at the time of writing) failed to submit its 2009 accounts to the Electoral

Commission. Its rising income, however, was evident during elections to the European Parliament in 2009. At the launch of its campaign, the party detailed to members how increased revenue had financed the establishment of several administrative sites around the country. These included an administrative centre, data-inputting centre and call centre for enrolling and renewing membership subscriptions.[79] The subsequent election of two BNP candidates to the European Parliament secured additional resources; both Brons and Griffin were able to employ eight members of staff (most of whom had a history of involvement with the BNP or NF).

Since the election, however, financial problems and discontent among the grassroots have continued to surface. Internal tensions were fuelled further by the party's failure to achieve a breakthrough at the 2010 general election, as well as a series of costly legal disputes with organizations such as the Equalities and Human Rights Commission (EHRC; see Chapter 6). In its aftermath, influential activists attempted to mobilize another leadership challenge to Griffin. One of the leading rebels was Eddy Butler, the party's chief election strategist and who, in the early 1990s, had orchestrated the isolated breakthrough in Tower Hamlets.

Alongside a growing number of supporters, who included new recruits and founding members of the BNP, Butler anchored his campaign in a series of demands for reform, including: greater financial transparency; competent leadership; internal democracy and a separation of powers between the Chairman and administration; more resources for branches; and a relaunched BNP with a modern public image. The campaign to oust Griffin also included further allegations of financial corruption, that the consultant had made inappropriate advances toward a young female member, that Griffin was leading the BNP into costly and unnecessary legal cases, and had approved the distribution of over 20 million leaflets which featured an obsolete phone number. Griffin responded by arguing the rebels would lead the BNP 'back to amateurism' and toward 'organisational and financial suicide'.[80]

When Butler failed to secure the required number of nominations to contest the leadership (20 per cent of the membership), the rebels divided into two camps: some abandoned the BNP to establish a rival party named the British Freedom Party (BFP); while others attempted to exert influence through the Reform Group, an internal pressure group.[81] Their concerns over party finances were then partly validated by the response of the Electoral Commission to the party's accounts for the year 2008. The conclusion was that BNP treasurers had breached the Political Parties, Elections and Referendums Act (PPERA) by failing to keep records which adequately demonstrate the party's financial position.

Griffin moved to quell the growing rebellion by announcing he would stand down as Chairman by 2014 and, in the meantime, implement new controls on party finance. While rebels branded the announcement disingenuous, Griffin considered their challenge serious enough to offer concessions. Over the summer of 2010, the party established a national scrutiny committee to examine the treasury department and improve transparency.[82] Following accusations of foul play during the nomination process and criticism of the lack of internal democracy, the AC was also instructed to undertake a review of the party constitution, in particular rules governing leadership elections, and to explore whether decision-making bodies (mainly the AC) should be supplemented by an executive. Andrew Brons, a respected figure within the party and BNP Member of the European Parliament, was made responsible for the consultation process.

The attempt to quieten dissenters continued at the annual conference in December 2010, which was organized under the slogan 'moving forward together'. While claiming that the party was back on the road to financial recovery, the leadership conceded it had been 'surviving from appeal letter to appeal letter'. These persistent appeals for donations had been a necessary response to the fact that, between 2007 and 2009, the cost of BNP operations increased by almost £900,000. In the process, the party had accumulated debts of approximately £500,000. Activists who attended the conference were told the debt had fallen to less than £250,000, and that the party was moving toward a system of sustained income. The attempt to achieve internal stability, however, entailed negative consequences for party development: the monthly cost of running the BNP was reduced from £100,000 to £28,000; monthly staff costs were slashed from £40,000 to £8,000; new initiatives such as the call centre, which had played an important role during the 2009 European elections, were downscaled; the number of employed party staff fell from over 20 to only seven; and the number of offices was cut from five to two.[83]

While the outcome is yet to be decided, the conference also voted on four proposals for constitutional reform, which were put forward by leading activists and marked a response to the rebels' dissatisfaction over the lack of grassroots influence. The proposal which received most support, and was advocated by a Griffin loyalist, was for the AC to be replaced by an indirectly elected national executive. While the Chairman will still be elected directly by members and for a fixed four-year term, the aim behind the executive is to 'ensure that the party hierarchy becomes representative of the activist base'.[84] The governing executive committee will be comprised of the Chairman, two representatives from each region, and three additional members who are appointed by the Chairman. Concluding the outcome of the consultation, and reaching out to the disgruntled rebels, Brons expressed his hope that the proposal 'will please sufficient alienated members to reinvigorate the Movement', and 'is something that we can all accept'.[85] The proposed revisions will be put before the membership for ratification in June 2011.

Conclusions

The BNP's shift toward elections has entailed important consequences for how it is organized. As noted at the outset, a successful electoral strategy requires a strong and stable organization, a well-trained activist cadre and incentives for members to get actively involved. Since 2001, the BNP has experienced significant internal growth and has devoted more energy than its predecessors to fulfilling these tasks. Its organization has expanded, building on a tradition of extreme right campaigning in the Midlands and London, while also establishing a stronger presence in the North West and Yorkshire. The party has also sought to extend its reach among a wider range of social groups, by developing an affiliated network of organizations and, in the hope of learning lessons, cultivating cross-national links with similar parties elsewhere in Europe. Unlike its early years, it has also invested more seriously in strengthening its administrative and grassroots base. This includes a Voting Membership scheme which is designed to reward the most active members, restrict influence to loyalists and transform the BNP into an activist party.

Strategies, however, are useless without resources. Despite internal growth and the arrival of particularly favourable conditions, internally the BNP remains a weak and divided party. Its electoral strategy and attempt to convince voters it is an acceptable and credible alternative have been consistently undermined by internal problems: a lack of strong and stable finances; structures which have proven unable to resolve factionalism; and a leader who has become a highly divisive figure within the movement. Yet despite these problems, the party has still attracted striking levels of support in elections. Indeed, the internal fragility of the BNP is one reason why its rise in elections has been so remarkable. But who actually votes for the BNP and why? It is to this question that our attention now turns.

5

VOTING FOR THE BNP

If this City of ours is so great in its multiculturalism and its diversity, why is it that a small minority gets a large percentage of the finance paid by every taxpayer in this capital city? Why is it broken down that the majority that fund this City get the lowest return for the work they put in day in day out? This is Britain. It is for the British people . . . It is not for people to enter into this land dictating what will or will not happen to the people that created it and built it over generations.

Richard Barnbrook's acceptance speech, London Assembly, May 2008

In May 2008, the BNP contested elections to the Greater London Assembly (GLA). The party polled over 5 per cent of the vote and gained one seat in city hall. While the result was described by one journalist as 'the biggest prize the extreme right has ever won in British politics', it was soon overshadowed by a breakthrough of greater magnitude.[1] The next year saw Britons head to the polls to elect Members of the European Parliament (MEPs). Supported by an expanding organization and rising income, an increasingly confident BNP invested £500,000 into its campaign which focused mainly on the North West, West Midlands and Eastern regions. It was in these areas where it hoped to benefit from particularly favourable conditions. Continued public concern over immigration, anxiety about a financial crisis and outrage over a parliamentary expenses scandal had created a perfect storm for the extreme right. When all votes were counted, it was revealed that almost one million citizens had voted BNP. In the North West and Yorkshire, its level of support was sufficient to send two candidates, Nick Griffin and Andrew Brons, into the European Parliament.

Griffin promptly declared his party had 'breached a dam of lies' erected by the main parties, and that 'waters of truth and justice and freedom are once again flowing over this country'.[2] On reflection, however, he would have realized the result did not signal a breakthrough into the mainstream of British politics, and that the party should have polled stronger. It failed to match the performance of its main rival, the UK Independence Party (UKIP), which was the main beneficiary of the favourable conditions. UKIP attracted 2.5 million votes and finished in second place, above the Labour government and with 13 Members of the European Parliament (MEPs). The result, however, still marked an important watershed in the evolution of the BNP. Representation entailed lucrative funds and unprecedented access to media. The latter became evident four months later when over eight million citizens watched Griffin make his debut performance on the flagship television programme *Question Time*.

Who votes for the BNP and why? As noted in the Introduction, numerous competing arguments have been put forward in response to this question: some argue that citizens who vote for extreme right parties are responding in knee-jerk fashion to socio-economic deprivation; others contend they are political protestors driven by dissatisfaction with the main parties; and still others argue they are simply racists who are concerned only about immigration. As we shall see, the picture of BNP support is far more complex.

1. The losers of modernization model

Various theories have been developed to explain why some citizens vote for extreme right parties, but three are particularly important. A first approach which draws on older arguments suggests that voters are influenced strongly by their position in society, for example, their age, gender, level of education and social class. As a result of these long-term social influences and group loyalties, members of particular social groups are predisposed to support particular parties but not others. One example is social class, and the way in which particular classes (e.g. the working class) have traditionally leaned toward particular parties (e.g. Labour) as a means of protecting their interests and expressing loyalty to their group.

This sociological model has since been adapted to explain why some citizens support extreme right parties. The starting point in these accounts is the impact of disruptive socio-economic change, mainly the decline of traditional industry and the arrival of globalized post-industrial economies. This rapid and destabilizing change has produced two distinct groups: on one side are better-educated, highly skilled and economically secure 'winners' who have adapted and prospered; but on the other are less well-educated, less skilled and more insecure 'losers of modernization' who have struggled amid the new climate. Financially insecure working-class men, the unemployed and less well-educated are particularly susceptible to feelings of alienation, pessimism about their future economic prospects and resentment toward the main parties. In response, some of these 'angry white men' shift behind parties that promise to halt this disruptive change, return to a bygone era, protect their position in society and punish the mainstream politicians.[3]

In British politics, this argument focuses on members of a disaffected 'white working class' who have been most exposed to socio-structural change but at the same time have felt abandoned by the policy priorities of 'New' Labour which focused more on the middle classes. It suggests that, in some areas, the BNP has profited from Labour's inability to satisfy an uneasy coalition of supporters: on one side are younger and better educated members of a 'new left' who work in middle-class public sector jobs and subscribe to progressive post-material values; on the other are older, more deprived and insecure members of an 'old left' who hold their roots in the union and labour movement and are more concerned about right-wing issues like immigration.[4] It is these latter 'Labour losers' who have been the focus of BNP campaigns, as reflected in its slogan 'we are the Labour Party your grandfather voted for'. This leads us to expect that its support will be concentrated most heavily among these angry white men: middle-aged and elderly working class men, who have low education, are pessimistic about future prospects and previously identified with Labour.

2. The racial threat model

Rather than responding in knee-jerk fashion to socio-economic change, it might be that extreme right party voters are similar to voters more generally in being driven by specific ideological or policy preferences. Because parties like the BNP focus mainly on opposing immigration, their supporters may be motivated by a desire to endorse calls for a more restrictive immigration policy, or to express their opposition and hostility toward rising ethno-cultural diversity. In other European states, for example, it has been shown that anti-immigrant hostility is a particularly strong predictor of whether somebody will vote for the extreme right, even after controlling for their social characteristics.[5]

The racial threat model suggests that what is most important is not opposition to immigration *per se*, but rather a perception that immigrants and minority ethnic groups threaten resources or interests. This sense of threat may stem from anxiety about intergroup competition over scarce economic resources, such as jobs or social housing. Alternatively, it may stem from more diffuse concerns over perceived cultural threats to values, identities and ways of life. For instance, one recent trend discussed in Chapter 3 is public anxiety over settled Muslim communities, and a perception this group threatens 'British' values and culture. There is evidence elsewhere in Europe which suggests that anti-Muslim sentiment has become an important driver of support for the contemporary extreme right.[6] Seen from this perspective, parties like the BNP are rallying citizens who foremost feel threatened by immigration and more culturally distinct minority groups.

This model leads us to expect that BNP voters will be driven primarily by their hostile attitudes toward immigration and minority groups, even after we allow for their background characteristics. It also leads us to expect that they reside in more ethnically diverse areas, though especially areas where there are large Muslim communities. Importantly, this theoretical model is not entirely inconsistent with arguments that stress the role of economic deprivation, as it is the less skilled, less well educated and financially insecure who are most likely to feel their precarious position is under threat from immigrants and members of minority groups. This is exacerbated by the fact that minority ethnic groups also tend to be located on the same step of the social ladder as the typical extreme right party voter. In Britain, Pakistani and Bangladeshi Muslims experience disproportionately high rates of deprivation and hence have similar economic interests as BNP voters (see below).[7] Encounters between these groups need not be direct, but their proximity in more deprived and diverse areas may fuel perceptions that resources or ways of life are under threat.

3. The political competence model

An alternative argument is that parties like the BNP are simply a by-product of protest politics. The protest model traces support to citizens who are dissatisfied with the existing political options and devotes little attention to their attitudes toward other issues. Because political protest tends to be distributed quite widely across society, it suggests BNP support will not be socially distinct. This model, however, does not appear very convincing. In earlier decades, supporters of the NF *did* share a distinct profile and also expressed concern over the presence of blacks and their impact on local communities. Research elsewhere in Europe has also demonstrated that, while it is important, political dissatisfaction is only one ingredient of the extreme right vote.[8]

A more convincing argument is offered by the 'political competence model', which argues that voters are strongly influenced by their evaluations of which party is the most competent on the important issues.[9] When citizens share a consensus that a particular issue is important, their decision about whom to support is influenced by their calculation of which party will deliver the 'best' performance on the issue. It suggests that the rise of a seemingly 'new' party might owe much to a perception among voters that the main parties have failed to deliver an adequate response to concerns about a particular issue. Clearly, it is unlikely that voters will associate an extremist party like the BNP with credible policy solutions. But it may still be the case that citizens who are hostile toward immigration *and* dissatisfied with the performance of the main parties are willing to shift their support to the extreme right as a way of 'sending a message' to their representatives about an issue which they care deeply about, but which they feel is not being competently addressed. This leads us to expect that BNP voters are not driven solely by anti-immigrant hostility or political dissatisfaction, but are motivated by a potent combination of the two.

A note on data and methods

Traditionally, a lack of reliable data on extreme right voters in Britain has meant that examining their characteristics and concerns has never been straightforward. One post-election survey, for example, produced a sample of only six BNP voters and one exit poll was based on 22 voters, samples which are too small for meaningful analysis.[10] These problems can be overcome by drawing on two sets of individual-level data: the first are data on 965 BNP voters gathered over the period 2002–2006, a period when the BNP was enjoying its first local level gains; the second are data on 985 BNP voters collected in June 2009, at the time of its breakthrough into the European Parliament.[11] Further confidence in our findings can be drawn by setting them alongside several other academic studies of the BNP vote.[12]

Social profile: who votes BNP?

The evidence reveals that the BNP recruits the bulk of its support in elections from 'angry white men': middle-aged and elderly working-class men who typically have few educational qualifications and are deeply pessimistic about their economic prospects. Compared with other political parties, the BNP is most likely to draw support from skilled or unskilled workers, the unemployed, citizens over 34 years old, those with no formal qualifications and who are based in the north of England (see Table 5.1).

The fact that BNP support has a distinct social profile provides some evidence that the party is not simply a by-product of protest politics. Further insight into who these supporters are can be gained by examining their core characteristics. The popular portrayal of extreme right parties as being male-driven is an accurate one. BNP support is driven mainly by men and its strong male bias is one of its most striking aspects. Between 2002 and 2006, seven out of every ten BNP voters were male. Given broader trends in Western democracies, this gender gap is not surprising. In recent decades women have drifted to the left wing of the spectrum, becoming more concerned than men about issues like public services.[13] At the same time, there has emerged evidence of a steep generational decline in racial prejudice among Britons, which is particularly pronounced among young women. Unlike their male counterparts, women are significantly less likely to endorse prejudiced views.[14]

The age profile of a party's electorate can tell us much about its future prospects. A stable of young recruits suggests a promising future, whereas a greying base of supporters casts doubt over its longer-term survival. In the 1970s, the NF recruited most of its support from young working-class men. Support for the BNP has similarly been traced to young Britons, with some suggesting that 'the trouble with the BNP is that it reveals among us a younger generation that is willing to embrace hatred out of choice rather than from inherited prejudice'.[15] The reality, however, is quite different. Rather than a bastion of young radicals, the BNP is a party of the middle-aged and elderly. Between 2002 and 2006, three quarters of its voters were over 34 years old and only one quarter were aged 18–34 years. This suggests that supporters of the extreme right in Britain are ageing, a trend which is especially apparent when we consider 18–24-year-olds. In the 1970s, this group provided the NF with almost 40 per cent of its support. It now provides only 11 per cent of support to the BNP (see Table 5.2). Nor did young people turn out in large numbers to vote BNP at the 2009 European elections: more than 40 per cent of its voters were aged 34–55 years old and over 30 per cent were aged over 54.[16]

TABLE 5.1 Social characteristics of BNP voters and other voters (%)

	BNP	Lab	Con	Lib Dem	UKIP	Non-voters
Sex						
Male	**69**	48	50	45	60	44
Female	**31**	52	50	55	40	56
Age						
18–34	**25**	26	17	24	14	40
35–54	**39**	37	30	37	35	36
55+	**36**	37	54	39	51	24
Social class						
(AB) Professional/managerial	**11**	18	31	31	18	12
(C1) Routine non-manual	**19**	26	33	32	31	23
(C2) Skilled manual	**32**	23	19	18	24	24
(DE) Semi-/unskilled manual/ residual	**38**	34	18	19	26	41
Education						
No qualifications	**34**	32	24	18	26	32
GCSE/O-level	**34**	27	27	22	32	35
A-level	**11**	12	14	14	12	11
Degree/postgraduate	**6**	17	19	31	15	11
Property						
Owner/mortgage	**68**	68	86	78	79	57
Local authority rented	**24**	24	8	12	15	30
Privately rented/other	**8**	8	6	9	6	13
Region						
Greater London	**6**	11	9	11	8	11
South (exc. London)	**29**	31	47	47	53	34
Midlands	**23**	19	19	15	22	21
North	**41**	39	25	27	18	34
N=149,655						

Source: MORI 2002–06, adapted from R. Ford and M.J. Goodwin (2010) 'Angry white men: Individual and contextual predictors of support for the British National Party', *Political Studies*, 58(1): 1–25; white English respondents over 18 only.

This suggests that the appeal of extreme right parties among a more recent generation of Britons is dwindling, and that the BNP's attempt to widen its appeal among young people has met little success. There are two possible explanations which might explain this trend. The first is a 'life cycle effect', which suggests that as people grow older they assume more responsibility, become more socially conservative and are more likely to feel threatened by social change like immigration. Older citizens, who now provide the bulk of support to the BNP, are more susceptible to the appeals of parties which express right-wing values, demand a return to a bygone era and oppose social change like rising ethno-cultural diversity. A second and not inconsistent explanation is a 'generational effect', which suggests that what matters most is not the age of voters today but their age when they first became interested in politics.[17] In 2009, the average BNP voter was in his mid-50s

TABLE 5.2 NF and BNP voters compared

	NF voter 1977–78 (%)	BNP voter 2002–06 (%)	Difference BNP-NF (%)
Sex			
Male	71	69	–2
Female	29	31	+2
Age			
15–24	37	11	–26
25–34	16	13	–3
35–54	29	39	+10
55+	18	36	+18
Social class			
Higher non-manual (AB)	6	11	+5
Lower non-manual (C1)	22	19	–3
Skilled manual (C2)	46	32	–14
Semi-/unskilled manual and residual (DE)	26	38	+12
Region			
Greater London	25	6	–19
South East	17	11	–6
South West	12	7	–5
East Anglia	3	11	+8
East Midlands	5	9	+4
West Midlands	23	14	–9
North	15	41	+26
Working status			
Full time	68	45	–23
Not full time	32	55	+23
Property			
Owner/mortgage	53	68	+15
Local authority rented	41	24	–17
Privately rented/other	6	8	+3
Social class by age and sex			
Male, 15–34, ABC1	13	4	–9
Male, 15–34, C2DE	25	17	–8
Male, 35 or older, ABC1	9	13	+4
Male, 35 or older, C2DE	24	36	+12
Female, 15–34, ABC1	3	2	–1
Female, 15–34, C2DE	11	7	–4
Female, 35 or older, ABC1	3	6	+3
Female, 35 or older, C2DE	11	16	+5

Source: Adapted from M. Harrop, J. England and C.T. Husbands (1980) 'The bases of National Front support', *Political Studies*, 28(2): 271–283. R. Ford and M.J. Goodwin (2010) 'Angry white men: Individual and contextual predictors of support for the British National Party', *Political Studies*, 58(1): 1–25.

and so would have been eligible to vote in the early 1970s, a period characterized by intense debate over immigration and its effects (see Chapter 1). Socialized under the shadow of Powellism, the rise of the NF and Thatcher's tough stance on immigration, it seems plausible that members of this particular generation have retained higher concern over immigration, and sympathy toward the extreme right.

An alternative view is that young Britons are simply more detached from politics and that surveys are underestimating their support for extremist parties. The continued willingness of young people to endorse extremist movements is apparent at rallies of the English Defence League (EDL), which are attended by large numbers of young working-class men, some of whom are linked to football hooligan firms and extra-parliamentary right-wing extremist groups. It might also be the case that the BNP recruits support from young people in areas where there is a longer tradition of support for the extreme right, and where 'family socialization effects' transfer this sympathy from one generation to the next.[18] These arguments, however, tend to gloss over wider evidence of generational change in modern Britain. Unlike their parents and grandparents, young Britons have grown up since the onset of mass immigration, are better educated and experience more social contact with members of other ethnic, religious and cultural groups. As decades of research in social psychology has demonstrated, this social contact can have important and positive effects, such as reducing perceptions of racial threat and promoting tolerance.[19] Pointing toward these trends, one academic convincingly argues that more recent generations of Britons 'seem to have been completely socialized into a tolerant set of "multicultural" norms, and rarely express any discomfort about social contact with ethnic minorities'.[20] While some young Britons will continue to endorse the extreme right, particularly those who are more deprived and less well educated, when seen from a broad perspective more recent generations are increasingly unlikely to support parties which are associated with open racism and prejudice.

The importance of education is revealed in the profile of BNP voters. Most have no formal educational qualifications, while the party polls strongest in areas where the average level of education is low.[21] During its initial local gains between 2002 and 2006, two thirds of BNP voters had no formal qualification or had left school after sitting their GCSEs/O-levels. Only one out of ten had an A-level while the portion with a degree or postgraduate qualification was even smaller.[22] Individuals who remain in the education system for longer tend to adopt more liberal values, are less likely to endorse ethnic nationalist and authoritarian policies, and are more likely to build ties with members of different groups. In contrast, citizens who are less well educated are less flexible and less competitive in the labour market, and more likely to feel threatened by immigration and rising diversity.

Like its European cousins, the BNP draws most of its support from members of the more insecure lower social classes. Between 2002 and 2006, seven out of ten BNP voters were skilled or unskilled workers or unemployed. In 2009, six out of ten similarly came from the lower social classes.[23] While the party is more likely than other parties to recruit semi- and unskilled manual workers, it is especially more likely to attract the *skilled* working classes (see Table 5.1). Unlike their unemployed neighbour and more affluent employer, skilled workers occupy an especially precarious position in society. While they have some assets they are not particularly secure, and hence are more likely than most to feel they have 'something to lose' from immigration and rising diversity, and to feel threatened by these processes. The BNP is recruiting significant levels of support from the unskilled and the unemployed, but it has been most successful in areas where there are large concentrations of employed skilled workers.[24]

The financial insecurity of these voters is reflected in their pessimistic outlook. BNP voters are far more negative than other voters about future economic prospects. The financial crisis has generated considerable uncertainty among Britons about whether their future financial position will be an improvement on the past. BNP voters appear absolutely convinced that their financial position will worsen. For instance, almost seven out of ten expected their economic prospects to deteriorate compared to four out of ten voters overall.[25] In 2009, almost three quarters of BNP voters were similarly dissatisfied with their family's financial situation, and almost half were fearful that either they or a close relative would lose their job. Nor was their pessimism restricted to economics: almost half were dissatisfied with the safety of their community and over two fifths were dissatisfied about access to local services, such as schools and hospitals. In all of these areas BNP voters were more pessimistic than supporters of other parties.[26] These findings suggest the BNP is recruiting support from similar social contexts as Labour. As we have seen, in recent years it has shifted its focus to Labour heartlands in the North, Yorkshire and, to a lesser extent, outer-east London. This change of strategy is reflected in its social bases of support which reveals a clear northward shift. In the 1970s, 15 per cent of NF voters came from northern England but in 2002–06 more than 40 per cent of BNP voters did so. In fact, while the extreme right has long considered London its stronghold, in recent years it has become the weakest region for the BNP (see Table 5.2). This pattern remained evident in 2009 when BNP voters were more likely than voters of other parties to come from the North West, Yorkshire and West Midlands. On the contrary, they were less likely to come from more ethnically diverse London.

The BNP's attempt to invade Labour's heartlands is reflected in the political context of its rise. As detailed in Table 5.3, its strongest performances have all been in seats controlled by Labour. At the 2005 general election, for example, 33 of the 34 seats where the BNP saved deposits had Labour incumbents and, over the period 2005–09, 52 of the 58 council seats won by the BNP came at the expense of Labour. Further evidence that the BNP is recruiting support heavily among Labour's losers is presented in Table 5.4, which reveals that in 2009 the percentage of BNP voters who came from Labour backgrounds was only second behind *actual* Labour voters. Closer examination, however, reveals that only 47 per cent of BNP voters came from Labour-voting families, meaning more than half came from other backgrounds (in fact, one quarter came from Conservative backgrounds and 20 per cent said their parents were apolitical or did not know whom they supported). Moreover, the percentage of BNP voters coming from Labour families is only 5 per cent higher

TABLE 5.3 Top ten BNP constituencies, 2001–2010

Constituency	Region	BNP vote (%)	Incumbent
2010 general election			
Barking	London	14.6	Labour
Dagenham and Rainham	London	11.2	Labour
Rotherham	Yorkshire	10.4	Labour
Stoke-on-Trent South	West Midlands	9.4	Labour
West Bromwich West	West Midlands	9.4	Labour
Burnley	North West	9.0	Labour
Barnsley Central	Yorkshire	8.9	Labour
Barnsley East	Yorkshire	8.6	Labour
Normanton, Pontefract & Castleford	Yorkshire	8.4	Labour
Leeds Central	Yorkshire	8.2	Labour
2005 general election			
Barking	London	16.9	Labour
Dewsbury	Yorkshire	13.1	Labour
Burnley	North West	10.3	Labour
West Bromwich West	West Midlands	9.9	Labour
Dudley North	West Midlands	9.7	Labour
Dagenham	London	9.3	Labour
Keighley	Yorkshire	9.2	Labour
Stoke-on-Trent South	West Midlands	8.7	Labour
Bradford South	Yorkshire	7.8	Labour
Stoke-on-Trent Central	West Midlands	7.8	Labour
2001 general election			
Oldham West and Royton	North West	16.4	Labour
Burnley	North West	11.3	Labour
Oldham East and Saddleworth	North West	11.2	Labour
Barking	London	6.4	Labour
Poplar and Canning Town	London	5.1	Labour
Dagenham	London	5.0	Labour
Pendle	North West	5.0	Labour
Dudley North	West Midlands	4.7	Labour
Bradford North	Yorkshire	4.6	Labour
West Bromwich West	West Midlands	4.5	Labour

Source: BBC Election Archive.

TABLE 5.4 Voting habits of BNP voters' parents

	Total	BNP	Con	Lab	Lib Dem	Green	UKIP
Parents voted Conservative	27	25	47	11	23	24	32
Parents voted Labour	42	47	25	66	38	43	42
Parents voted Liberal	5	3	4	3	12	7	5
Parents voted for other party	1	1	1	1	1	2	1
Parents didn't support one party	12	12	11	9	14	13	11
Don't know	13	11	12	9	11	12	10

Source: YouGov/Channel 4.

than the percentage of respondents who did overall. In other words, while its voters are more likely to come from Labour backgrounds, the BNP is not overwhelmingly more likely than other parties to recruit ex-Labour voters.

In this respect, it is also interesting to note that BNP voters are most likely to identify themselves with right-wing politics. When asked to position themselves on the left–right spectrum, four out of ten positioned themselves on the right wing, two out of ten considered themselves centrist and only one out of ten saw themselves as left wing.[27] However, while most BNP voters identified with right-wing politics, they were also profoundly hostile toward Labour. When asked their views toward the main parties, more than half thought 'Labour used to care about the concerns of people like me but doesn't nowadays', and they were more likely than other voters to think so.[28] This dissatisfaction with Labour appears to stem from a perception that it has prioritized immigrants and minority ethnic groups over white Britons. BNP voters were more likely than other voters to endorse the view that Labour is mainly interested in helping immigrants and minority groups (a striking 78 per cent of BNP voters endorsed this view, compared to 44 per cent of the sample overall). In fact, BNP voters more generally were most likely to agree that: immigrants and minority groups have been prioritized at the expense of white Britons; white Britons suffer from unfair discrimination; and Muslims, non-white groups and homosexuals benefit from unfair advantages.[29]

Before examining the attitudes of BNP voters in more depth, we can also explore some of their other characteristics. One popular claim is that extreme right voters are more isolated in their communities than other citizens, and turn to parties like the BNP in the search for a sense of belonging. There is some tentative evidence to support this claim. BNP voters are less likely than other voters to be involved in civic and religious organizations, including trade unions, sports clubs and churches. Yet the evidence is also mixed: while BNP voters appear less integrated into civil society, they are *more* likely to participate in political activities, such as boycotting products, writing to newspapers or phoning talkback radio stations.[30] One qualitative study of BNP voters in a northern town also challenges the suggestion they are especially isolated; at least one quarter of those interviewed personally knew the BNP councillor they were supporting in elections, or as one councillor explained: 'I think in the area, everybody knew me . . . they practically knew everything about me . . . so they knew I weren't Nazified, so they thought [name] is not bad so they [the BNP] can't be so bad.'[31]

Another claim is that the BNP has profited from tabloid media, which often feature negative coverage of immigrants, Muslims and asylum-seekers. BNP voters are no different from voters more generally in gathering the bulk of their news and information from television, newspapers, websites and radio.[32] Yet there is evidence to support the claim: citizens who vote for the BNP tend to read tabloid newspapers which are hostile toward immigration, namely the *Daily Mail*, *Daily Express* and the *Sun*. In 2009, more than half of BNP voters read one of these newspapers (or the *Daily Star*), suggesting that xenophobic coverage is an important factor in understanding what drives support for the extreme right.[33] What remains unclear is whether supporters are selecting newspapers which reflect their views, or whether these newspapers are shaping their views.

Which of these characteristics are most important in explaining the BNP vote? One technique that enables social scientists to identify the factors which are most important in predicting voting behaviour is logistic regression analysis.[34] Results from a logistic regression analysis of BNP voting confirm it is a male, working class phenomenon that is most likely among those aged 35–54 years, and is significantly higher in the northern and Midlands regions. The significance of this particular age group provides further evidence that those who came of political age in the 1960s and 1970s have retained sympathies toward extreme right parties. The results also reveal that BNP support (see Table 5.5) is extremely rare among those who have a university education, while the finding that working class and unemployed citizens are more likely to vote for the party suggests that perceptions of racial threat and competition are particularly important. Citizens who read 'anti-immigrant' tabloid newspapers are also more likely to vote BNP, even after allowing for their social characteristics.

Attitudes: what do they think?

The findings above reveal that the BNP is forging ties with a socially distinct group of Britons. What remains unknown are their attitudes toward various issues, and whether these are strong predictors of their support after we control for their social characteristics. The prominence of insecure working-class men from more deprived areas, who read anti-immigrant newspapers and who are hostile toward Labour suggest that hostility toward immigration and dissatisfaction with the main parties may be important motivations. We shall now examine the extent to which this is true.

Mobilizing intolerance: anti-immigrant hostility

Perhaps unsurprisingly, BNP voters are overwhelmingly concerned about immigration. Yet what is surprising is the extent of this concern. When supporters of all parties were asked to rate the most important problems facing Britain, a large number selected immigration. BNP voters, however, expressed striking levels of concern about this issue; 60 per cent considered immigration the most important problem facing the country. While other voters divided their attention between several issues, supporters of the BNP focused almost exclusively on immigration (see Table 5.6).

Nor was their concern about this issue temporary. In 2009, they remained profoundly concerned about immigration and were more likely than other voters to rate it as one of the most important issues facing the country. In fact, almost nine out of every ten BNP voters rated immigration or asylum as the most important issues, and almost six out of ten rated them the most important issues facing their families. It would be mistaken, however, to view BNP supporters as single-issue voters. In fact, they are motivationally diverse, although they are mainly concerned about right-wing issues: they are more likely than average to rate law and order,

TABLE 5.5 Demographic predictors of BNP support 2002–06*: logistic regression model

	Model 1: Demographics
Intercept	–6.94***
Survey year (ref: 2002)	
Linear trend (2002=0)	0.24***
2005 (Election year)	–0.75***
Sex	
Male	0.94***
Age (ref: 18–24)**	
25–34 years	0.17
35–54 years	0.32**
55 years +	0.03
Class (ref: AB)	
Lower non-manual (C1)	0.11
Working class (C2DE)	0.76***
Housing tenure (ref: owner-occupier)	
Rent privately	0.11
Rent from council	0.08
Deprivation	
Unemployed	0.31*
No car in household	–0.33***
Media	
Reads anti-immigrant tabloid	0.30***
Education (ref: No qualifications)	
GCSE/NVQ	0.03
A-level	–0.21
Degree	–0.88***
Postgrad	–1.24***
Region (ref: London/S. East/S. West)	
East Anglia	0.41***
East Midlands	0.42**
West Midlands	0.69***
North West	0.33**
North East	0.49**
Yorkshire/Humber	1.01***
Model fit (pseudo- R square)	*0.065*
N	*149,655*

Source: R. Ford and M.J. Goodwin (2010) 'Angry white men: Individual and contextual predictors of support for the British National Party', *Political Studies*, 58(1): 1–25.

* White English respondents over 18 only.
** This variable is coded using deviance coding, so the coefficients show deviations from the overall mean.

TABLE 5.6 Issue priorities of BNP voters compared (by voting intention, %)

	BNP	Lab	Con	Lib Dem	UKIP	Full sample
Issues in 2002–06*						
Immigration	59	13	21	11	28	16
Defence/foreign affairs/terrorism	10	24	17	24	15	21
Crime/law and order	5	10	12	9	9	11
Health/NHS	5	12	11	12	8	11
Education	1	6	5	8	2	6
Economy	2	4	5	4	2	4
European Union	1	3	6	4	15	4
Others/don't know	17	28	23	28	20	27
Issues in 2009**						
Immigration and asylum	87	34	57	33	76	49
Economy	60	72	73	74	67	70
Crime/law and order	50	39	46	35	46	42
Prices and cost of living	33	35	35	35	28	34
Europe	27	6	15	10	39	15
Pensions/social security/poverty	26	37	29	38	30	33
Afghanistan/Islamic extremism	25	17	17	16	18	16
Health/NHS/hospitals	22	45	34	40	28	36
Taxes	19	14	23	16	20	18
Housing market and interest rates	13	24	20	21	12	20

* Ipsos-MORI/adapted from R. Ford and M.J. Goodwin (2010) 'Angry white men: Individual and contextual predictors of support for the British National Party', *Political Studies*, 58(1): 1–25; white English respondents only.
** YouGov/Channel 4; Respondents asked, 'Which three or four of these issues do you think are the most important facing the country? [Allowed to pick up to four issues.] I include only the top ten issues for BNP voters.

Europe, and Afghanistan/Islamic extremism the most important issues facing the country. Meanwhile, they are less likely than other voters to rank the economy, pensions, National Health Service (NHS) and housing market as important.

The survey in 2009 also asked a series of questions about their attitudes toward a range of other social and political issues. Consistent with the public opinion trends discussed in Chapter 3, most voters – irrespective of whom they voted for – expressed considerable anxiety over immigration and its effects. In fact, almost half of all voters rated immigration the most important issue facing Britain (see Table 5.6). Large numbers of voters also made clear their preference for a more restrictive immigration policy, and scepticism about the effects of immigration: more than six out of ten thought all further immigration should be halted; more than five out of ten said councils let immigrants 'jump the queue' when allocating social housing; the same portion rejected the idea that immigration has helped the British economy grow faster; and almost four out of ten rejected the suggestion that the country has benefitted from the arrival of people from different countries and cultures. In short, large numbers of respondents overall expressed anxiety about immigration, favoured reducing the number of immigrants and thought immigration is having a negative impact on the country (see Table 5.7).

TABLE 5.7 Attitudes of BNP voters

Statement	BNP voters	Full sample
All further immigration to the UK should be halted		
Agree	94	61
Neither agree nor disagree	2	13
Disagree	3	23
Local councils allow immigrant families to jump the queue in allocating council homes		
Agree	87	56
Neither agree nor disagree	4	12
Disagree	6	18
Britain has benefitted from the arrival of people from different countries and cultures		
Agree	8	38
Neither agree nor disagree	10	20
Disagree	81	38
Immigration has helped Britain's economy grow faster than it would have done		
Agree	4	24
Neither agree nor disagree	11	21
Disagree	82	48
Most crimes are committed by immigrants		
Agree	58	22
Neither agree nor disagree	28	27
Disagree	11	44
Employers should favour whites over non-whites		
Agree	49	15
Neither agree nor disagree	26	24
Disagree	22	58
Gvt should encourage immigrants and their families to leave Britain (inc. members born in UK)		
Agree	72	27
Neither agree nor disagree	14	24
Disagree	12	45
Non-white British citizens born in this country are just as 'British' as white citizens born in this country		
Agree	35	71
Neither agree nor disagree	20	14
Disagree	44	12
There is no difference in intelligence between black Britons and white Britons		
Agree	42	64
Neither agree nor disagree	24	18
Disagree	31	14
Even in its mildest form, Islam poses a serious danger to Western civilization		
Agree	79	44
Neither agree nor disagree	11	18
Disagree	7	32

Source: YouGov/Channel 4 'Megapoll' June 2009.

At the same time, however, while large numbers of voters were anxious about immigration, majorities also distanced themselves from the more socially unacceptable forms of racism; more than seven out of ten agreed that non-white citizens born in Britain are just as British as white citizens born in the country; more than six out of ten said there is no difference in levels of intelligence between black and white Britons; six out of ten rejected the idea that employers should favour white applicants over non-white applicants; less than three out of ten said the government should encourage immigrants and their families to leave Britain; and only two out of ten thought most crimes are committed by immigrants. Though large numbers expressed concern about immigration, most remained unwilling to endorse more openly racist and discriminatory views toward immigrants and minority ethnic groups.

BNP supporters were asked the same battery of questions and expressed much higher levels of hostility toward immigration: they were overwhelmingly more likely than other voters to: advocate halting all further immigration; endorse the view that immigrants receive preferential treatment from local authorities; reject the suggestion that immigration has helped the economy; and disagree that Britain has benefitted from the arrival of people from different countries and cultures. Importantly, however, BNP voters were also more likely than other citizens to endorse the more openly racist and discriminatory ideas; almost 75 per cent agreed the government should encourage immigrants and their families to leave Britain, including those born in the country; almost 60 per cent thought most crimes are committed by immigrants; almost 50 per cent thought employers should favour whites over non-whites; more than 40 per cent rejected the suggestion that non-white citizens born in Britain are just as British as white Britons born in the country; and over 30 per cent rejected the suggestion that there is no difference in levels of intelligence between black and white Britons. Not all BNP voters endorsed these harder forms of intolerance, but they were more likely than supporters of other political parties to do so.[35]

BNP supporters were also more likely to express anti-Muslim sentiment. In recent years the BNP has sought to mobilize this specific form of intolerance by claiming the cultural distinctiveness and incompatibility of Muslims and Islam with wider society. The evidence suggests this change of strategy has met some success; BNP voters are overwhelmingly more likely than other voters to subscribe to the view that Muslims benefit from unfair advantages (70 per cent agreed compared with 39 per cent of the full sample) and that 'even in its milder forms Islam poses a serious danger to Western civilization' (79 per cent compared with 44 per cent). The importance of anti-Muslim sentiment to BNP support is further underscored by studies which find a strong and positive relationship between higher levels of BNP support and the presence of Muslim communities. At the 2002–03 local elections, the BNP polled strongest in ethnically diverse local authorities where there were large Muslim communities. Within these more diverse areas, support for the party stemmed from more ethnically homogeneous 'threatened white enclaves', with the suggestion being that BNP voters have less social contact with members of other ethnic groups.[36] In 2004, the party was similarly most successful in more ethnically diverse authorities in northern England, many of which have large Muslim communities.[37] These findings suggest that perceived threats posed not only by immigrants but also by settled Muslim communities are an important driver of BNP support. This is confirmed by a more comprehensive multi-level analysis of BNP support, which finds that it is higher in constituencies where education levels are low and employment rates are high, even after allowing for individual education and employment status. It is also most successful in areas where there are large Muslim communities, although the presence of non-Muslim Asians (e.g. Buddhist, Hindu, Sikh communities) has no significant effect on BNP support while it is *lower* in areas with large black populations.[38] The implications of these findings are discussed below, but they provide strong evidence that the BNP is becoming a vehicle of anti-Muslim sentiment.

Mobilizing protest: political dissatisfaction

While BNP voters are profoundly hostile toward immigration and Muslim communities, they are also extremely dissatisfied with the government and main parties. As noted at the outset, the political competence model puts strong emphasis on voters' evaluations of which party will deliver the most competent performance on key issues. When making these evaluations, voters often take cues from party leaders, rating them 'in terms of characteristics such as competence, responsiveness and trustworthiness' that enable voters to choose a party whose leader will be a 'safe pair of hands'.[39] BNP supporters are a profoundly dissatisfied group of citizens: they are extremely negative about the performance of the government and the three main parties. Even before the parliamentary expenses scandal, which saw public opinion of the main parties sink to an all-time low, large majorities of BNP voters were dissatisfied with mainstream political elites; more than nine out of ten said they were unhappy with the government and they were also more likely than other voters to hold negative views of the main parties (see Table 5.8).

The later survey in 2009 asked a wider range of questions and provides insight into the nature of this political dissatisfaction. It is important to note that the

TABLE 5.8 Dissatisfaction and pessimism among party supporters (by voting intention)

	BNP (%)	Lab (%)	Con (%)	Lib Dem (%)	UKIP (%)	Full sample (%)
Dissatisfied with . . .						
Government	92	31	87	72	88	62
Labour leader performance	85	27	83	71	86	59
Conservative leader performance	64	42	31	51	55	40
Lib Dem leader performance	52	22	31	14	48	24
Economy (will get worse)	69	27	52	42	56	41
N	*263*	*9,997*	*8,257*	*5,961*	*432*	*38,358*

Source: IPSOS-MORI political polls, 2002–06; white English respondents aged over 18 only.

Bold: More dissatisfied than average.

survey was carried out in the context of a second-order European election and, unlike above, following the outbreak of the expenses scandal, which is likely to encourage protest voting. As detailed in Table 5.9, supporters of all parties expressed high levels of distrust toward their political representatives, including Members of Parliament, council officials and senior civil servants. BNP voters were more distrustful of their mainstream elites; more than 80 per cent distrusted their MP, council officials and civil servants.[40] They also expressed a more general sense of disaffection with a host of institutions in society, including judges, senior police officers, trade unions and BBC journalists. While less trustful, they are also more likely than other voters to think most politicians are personally corrupt.[41] They are also more likely than other voters to perceive there to be no

TABLE 5.9 Trust in institutions: BNP voters compared

	Total	BNP	Con	Lab	Lib Dem	Green	UKIP
Your local MP							
Trust	30	14	34	46	35	30	23
Distrust	63	81	60	48	60	64	73
Senior officials in the local council							
Trust	21	11	22	34	27	21	13
Distrust	73	85	72	60	68	74	85
Senior civil servants in Whitehall							
Trust	15	8	16	26	19	17	9
Distrust	77	86	78	67	75	78	88
Family doctor							
Trust	88	82	89	91	90	89	88
Distrust	10	15	9	7	8	10	11
Judges							
Trust	60	39	66	66	69	66	49
Distrust	36	58	31	29	28	31	49
BBC journalists							
Trust	59	44	58	63	70	72	53
Distrust	37	52	39	34	27	27	45
Senior police officers							
Trust	53	36	59	62	57	52	45
Distrust	43	61	38	35	40	45	52
Trade union leaders							
Trust	31	26	20	54	34	41	24
Distrust	61	67	73	39	58	54	72
Directors of big companies							
Trust	14	11	20	14	13	9	14
Distrust	81	84	75	80	83	88	83

Source: YouGov/Channel 4 'Megapoll' June 2009.

real difference between the two main parties, which suggests that the BNP is rallying citizens dissatisfied with the centrist mainstream options. For example, almost 70 per cent agreed 'there is no real difference these days between Britain's three main parties' (compared to 46 per cent of respondents overall).[42]

A potent combination

The findings above suggest that hostility toward immigration *and* political dissatisfaction are particularly important drivers of BNP support. The importance of this potent combination of motives is confirmed by more sophisticated analyses of the survey data. Table 5.9 presents results from a logistic regression analysis which tests for the impact of attitudes on the BNP vote between 2002 and 2006. Model 2 examines the impact of political attitudes alone, revealing that anxiety over immigration, dissatisfaction with the main parties and economic pessimism are strongly correlated with BNP support, and have a highly significant independent impact. Model 3 then tests for whether these effects are robust, while controlling for the social characteristics. The combined model confirms that anxiety over immigration, political dissatisfaction and economic pessimism continue to have a strong impact on BNP support.

In other words, during the period of its local electoral advance the BNP recruited support from socially distinct citizens who hold a distinct set of attitudes: they are overwhelmingly concerned about immigration, profoundly dissatisfied with the government and main parties, and extremely pessimistic about future economic prospects. To what extent have these motives remained important for BNP supporters? In 2009, at the time of its breakthrough into the European Parliament, the party's voters were similarly driven by this potent combination of motives. Results from a logistic regression analysis of the BNP vote in 2009 are presented in Table 5.10. Because the survey contains a larger number of

TABLE 5.10 Logistic regression model: political attitudes and BNP support, 2002–06

	Model 2 Political attitudes	Model 3 Political attitudes with demographic controls
Political attitudes		
Disapprove of the government	**1.54***	**1.70***
Disapprove of Conservative leadership	**0.49***	**0.58***
Disapprove of Lib Dem leadership	**1.04***	**0.90***
Don't know on Lib Dem leadership	**0.68***	**0.49***
Negative opinion of economic prospects	**0.57***	**0.53***
Immigration rated most important problem	**1.60***	**1.52***
Model fit (pseudo- R square)	*0.125*	*0.182*
N	*38,358*	*37,629*

Note: White English respondents only.

Bold figures: Denote significant effects: *p <0.05; **p <0.01; ***p <0.001.

questions, we first undertook exploratory factor analysis, a technique that enables researchers to create 'factors' comprised of items that are correlated and loaded onto a particular item. Put simply, each factor – for example, 'anti-immigration' – contains a set of attitudes that are connected with each other (see Appendix 2).

Model 1 examines the impact of these attitudes alone, and reveals that anti-immigrant hostility and political dissatisfaction continue to have the strongest impact on BNP support, although Islamophobia, Euroscepticism and homophobia also have significant effects.[43] In other words, while BNP supporters displayed a set of similar attitudes, the most important of these were hostility toward immigration and dissatisfaction with the government and main parties. For example, the second column in Model 1 tells us that citizens who subscribe to anti-immigration were more than three times as likely to vote BNP. Similarly, Britons who are dissatisfied with the mainstream parties were more than twice as likely to vote BNP (see Table 5.11). Model 2 then tests for whether these attitudes have an effect after including social controls.[44] Consistent with the findings above, it confirms that hostility toward immigration and political dissatisfaction are the most important predictors of whether somebody will vote BNP.

TABLE 5.11 Attitudinal influences on the BNP vote in 2009

Variables	Model 1 Attitudinal factors		Model 2 Attitudinal factors and demographic controls	
	β	$exp(\beta)$	β	$exp(\beta)$
Constant	–4.77*-		–4.17*	
Attitudes				
Factor 1: Anti-Immigration	1.30*	3.67	1.29*	3.65
Factor 2: Euroscepticism	0.30*	1.35	0.33*	1.38
Factor 3: Political dissatisfaction	0.72*	2.06	0.67*	1.94
Factor 4: Homophobia	0.28*	1.32	0.30*	1.36
Islamic Threat	0.48*	01.62	0.51*	1.67
−2 Log Likelihood	6,678.18		6,492.34	
Nagelkerke R2	0.25		0.27	

Note: Unstandardised Coefficients, * $p < 0.05$; $N = 29{,}169$. Examination of multicollinearity statistics (VIF and tolerance statistics) shows no evidence of collinearity present in either model.

Demographic controls used: Gender; Age (Young/Old – middle base); Social class (Prof/Man – base); Anti-immigrant papers; Political socialisation (Labour and Conservative separately); Associational membership; Political activism; Region (Yorkshire and Humberside and North West); Public sector employment; Financial expectations over the next 12 months.

The BNP and the 'credibility gap'

At the 2010 general election, the BNP continued to recruit most support among urban working-class areas where there were large numbers of manual workers, large Muslim communities and low education levels, though mainly in Pennine Lancashire, the Midlands and outer-east London. There is also evidence that the party has benefitted from the recent financial crisis as it performed strongly in areas which experienced large increases in unemployment since 2005.[45]

However, while it is continuing to forge ties with socially distinct citizens who hold a specific set of attitudes, the BNP has proved unable to engineer a wider breakthrough. One explanation for this limited success is the majoritarian electoral system which leans toward two main parties while penalizing minor parties.[46] This is because the system makes it difficult for minor parties to appear in the minds of voters as credible alternatives, and convince them that they have a realistic prospect of entering Westminster. Yet while all minor parties struggle to appear credible, we have also seen how extreme right parties like the NF have also failed to fulfil the more fundamental task of appearing simply as a legitimate democratic alternative. Though large numbers of Britons in the 1970s were anxious over its core issues, most were unwilling to endorse the stigmatized NF (see Chapter 1).

The legacy of history has left an indelible print on the BNP. Like its parent party, and despite persistent attempts to widen its appeal, the party is also failing to appear to voters as a legitimate and credible alternative. While it is forging ties with angry white men who are deeply hostile toward immigration and profoundly dissatisfied with the main parties, it has proven unable to convince the majority of voters that it is a legitimate player in the political process. Surveys and polls reveal the extent to which most voters hold negative feelings toward the party. At the time of the 2004 European elections, for example, seven out of ten voters said they would not ever consider voting BNP. Even when presented against the backdrop of immigration, the party remained 'off limits' to most voters. When asked whether 'the recent row over immigration' had made them more or less likely to vote BNP, almost 75 per cent said it made no difference; they would never have voted BNP anyway.[47]

The party's inability to detoxify its racial nationalist brand was similarly revealed in 2006 when the polling organization YouGov undertook an innovative quasi-experimental study. Two groups of voters were asked their views toward a range of policies but only one group was informed they were the policies of the BNP. Consistent with the findings in this chapter, most participants thought Britain should accept fewer asylum-seekers, halt all further immigration, deny immigrants the right to bring family members into the country and prioritize British families over immigrants when allocating social housing. When these policies were identified with the BNP, however, their level of support declined while opposition to them increased. For example, when a halt on immigration was presented as a BNP policy, its support dropped by 11 points. Similarly, when the idea of preventing immigrants from reuniting with their families was affiliated with the BNP its support dropped by nine points. In other words, while large numbers of voters expressed support for policies that regularly appear in BNP literature, the number who are willing to support these policies when they are associated with the BNP is much smaller.[48]

Despite its electoral advances, the BNP continues to generate negative feelings among the electorate. During elections to the European Parliament in 2009, only one out of ten citizens held a positive view toward the BNP.[49] Following Griffin's appearance on *Question Time* a few months later, there similarly emerged evidence of considerable hostility toward the party; according to one poll, 'under no circumstances' would two thirds of the population consider voting BNP. In fact, only 4 per cent said they would 'definitely consider' supporting the party. To underscore the point, this latter figure was lower than the percentage of voters in the 1970s who said they would seriously consider voting for the National Front.[50]

Concluding remarks

At the outset of this chapter, we considered three models that have been recruited to explain who votes for the extreme right and why: the losers of modernization model traces support to more deprived, less well educated and insecure citizens who feel left behind amid rapid and destabilizing socio-economic change; the racial threat model traces support to members of similar social groups who feel threatened by immigration and rising ethno-cultural diversity; and the political competence model traces support to citizens who are deeply concerned about key issues but feel that the main parties have failed to deliver a competent performance.

The findings reveal all three models have something to say about BNP support. First, rather than recruiting support from across society the party is appealing primarily to 'angry white men' who are socially distinct; they are older and economically insecure working-class men who have low levels of education and are located in particular regions of the country. The fact that these voters share a distinct social profile tells us that the BNP is not simply a product of protest politics. Rather, it is forging ties with members of specific social groups who congregate in particular social contexts. Like its predecessors, the BNP relies on a few regions for support: the North of England, the Midlands, parts of Yorkshire and, to a lesser extent, outer-east London. Within these regions, its supporters tend to congregate in more economically deprived urban districts where education levels are low and there are large Muslim communities. BNP voters, however, are not a mirror image of their NF-voting predecessors in the 1970s: they are older, less skilled, more northern and more dissatisfied with mainstream elites. This suggests it will be much more difficult for the main parties to lure these voters back into the fold of mainstream politics.

Second, we have also encountered evidence supportive of the racial threat model. While the BNP is most successful in areas where there are large Muslim communities, its voters are economically insecure and they are overwhelmingly hostile toward immigration and Muslims. This suggests the party is rallying citizens who feel their social positions or identities are under threat from immigration and rising ethno-cultural diversity. The prominence of anti-Muslim sentiment among BNP voters also suggests its appeal is more complex and subtle than the NF's crude 'anti-black' racism. In some areas of the country, the BNP is mobilizing anxiety over perceived conflicts between Muslim communities and white Britons. While this hostility may be fuelled by anti-Muslim campaigns in sections of the British tabloid media, the fact that BNP voters are often based in close proximity to large Muslim communities suggests that more direct experiences may be at work.

Third, while BNP voters are profoundly hostile toward immigration, they are also profoundly dissatisfied with the performance of the government and main parties. BNP voters are exceptionally distrustful of political institutions, hostile toward politicians and tend not to see a difference between the main parties. Though most voters do not consider the BNP a credible alternative, some citizens have been motivated to support the party by a potent combination of hostility toward immigration and dissatisfaction over the perceived failure of their mainstream representatives to deliver a competent performance on this issue.

The surveys analysed in this chapter have shed light on the characteristics and concerns of BNP supporters in elections. To probe the views of the party's supporters more closely, and the motivations which drive their support, the next three chapters draw on extensive qualitative interviews with its more committed supporters – the grassroots members.

6

MEMBERSHIP

The British National Party is an activist Party and activists are our most valuable members because we cannot rely on the media to promote our policies to the public. And, unlike the mainstream parties, we don't have millions of pounds to spend on advertising campaigns. We have to rely on our members to promote, recruit, campaign and win elections. This is why we prize our activists so highly.[1]

While most voters do not consider the BNP a legitimate alternative, it has attracted a growing band of voters who share a similar social profile, are overwhelmingly concerned about immigration and extremely dissatisfied with the mainstream parties. It would be very difficult, however, to mobilize this support in elections without a stable of committed grassroots supporters. Activists and members represent the heart of a political party: they spread the message, contest elections, recruit new followers, fulfil roles on a voluntary basis, provide access to networks of potential supporters, and are a source of finance and labour.[2] At the same time, however, party memberships have been declining across most European democracies. Britain has experienced one of the largest declines in the proportion of the electorate enrolled in parties, and has one of the lowest rates of party membership in Europe. Between 1964 and 2009, the combined memberships of the three main parties slumped from over 3 million to under half a million.[3] Attempts to account for this downward trend often point toward the changing nature of mainstream parties: their drift toward 'catch-all' ideological appeals; growing emphasis on political marketing techniques; and the embrace of web-based campaigns. These developments mean there are simply fewer incentives for parties to build and sustain a large grassroots base.

In the world of minor party politics, however, where resources are few and far between, grassroots members remain indispensable. This is especially true for extremist parties which not only lack resources but are often shunned by politicians and media. The result is they fall heavily dependent on their rank and file supporters to get out the message, the vote and money from their pockets. The BNP is no exception and describes its membership as its 'life blood'.[4] It relies almost exclusively on members for money and has placed its active followers at the core of its community-based strategy. But how has membership of the party evolved, who joins the BNP and how?

BNP membership, 1982–2010

As is the case with most parties, you have to pay to join the BNP. Standard members pay £30 each year or £60 if they enrol as 'gold' members and demonstrate greater commitment. There are also concessionary schemes for families (£40), pensioners, students and the unemployed (£15). Mainly in response to financial pressure, the party also introduced a life membership scheme which offers supporters a chance to become 'part of that elite that signs-up to the cause of British survival and national rebirth for life' (which is £495).[5] In return, life members receive literature, an engraved watch, certificate and signed portrait of Nick Griffin. In 2009, most members were enrolled under the standard scheme and were employed, although the party also claims to have recruited significant numbers of pensioners, families and, to a lesser extent, unemployed persons (see Fig. 6.1).

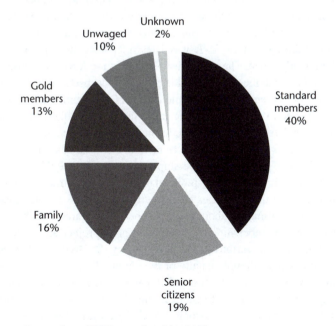

FIGURE 6.1 Categories of BNP membership, 2009

Source: Minutes of the Advisory Council (AC) Meeting, January 2009. Available online: www.bnp.org.uk (accessed April 2009).

On joining, members can attend meetings, assume formal positions and stand in elections. Following a two-year probationary period, they also become eligible to be a voting member and have some minor influence over internal affairs. Not every citizen, however, has been allowed to join. For much of its history, the BNP operated a restrictive and ethnically-defined membership that was specified within the terms of 'the legal ambit of a defined "racial group", this being "Indigenous Caucasian" and defined "ethnic groups" emanating from that Race . . .'.[6] The policy, which reflected the party's ethnic nationalist beliefs, essentially restricted membership to 'indigenous' white Britons. In 2009, however, the Equalities and Human Rights Commission (EHRC) claimed this membership criteria failed to comply with the Race Relations Act of 1976, and requested that the constitution be amended to ensure that potential or actual members were not discriminated against on racial grounds.

The BNP had actually begun discussing the possibility of allowing 'non-white' members in 2004, when Griffin hinted at the possible benefits that might accompany a more inclusive membership.[7] The intervention by the EHRC, however, forced the party to consider a change more seriously and, in early 2010, led members to vote to permit non-white members. Subsequent revisions proposed by the party included interviewing prospective members and requiring them to pledge 'to the continued creation, fostering, maintenance and existence of a unity and of the integrity of the Indigenous British'. Prospective members would also be required to support 'stemming and reversing the immigration and migration of peoples into our British Homeland that has, without the express consent of the Indigenous British, taken place since 1948, and to restoring and maintaining . . . the indigenous British as the overwhelming majority'.[8] It was later ruled that these proposed clauses remained indirectly racist. The party was instructed to remove the clauses from its constitution and also to meet substantial legal costs.[9] It subsequently complied with the ruling toward the end of 2010. While members of minority ethnic groups are technically allowed to join the party, the actual numbers are likely to be extremely small. During the 2010 general election, for instance, Griffin claimed the party had received only a 'trickle' of enquiries from members of Sikh communities.[10]

What is the size of BNP membership and how has it evolved over time? Gathering membership data on any political organization is difficult, but it is especially challenging in the case of extremist parties which have more reasons than most to conceal information about their members. They are also likely to artificially inflate their membership size in an attempt to project an image of legitimacy.[11] For instance, at various points in its history the BNP has claimed record rates of recruitment while not actually providing any figures. The task is further complicated by a tendency for extremist parties to experience high rates of membership turnover. A lack of resources, infighting and stigma are not conducive to building a cohesive grassroots base.[12] The difficulty of sustaining the loyalty of followers was particularly familiar to the National Front which, as one journalist observed, attracted a membership that was 'rather like a bath with both taps running and the plughole empty. Members pour in and pour out'.[13]

At its birth, the BNP gathered approximately 1,200 members from the NF or New National Front (NNF), and a handful of recruits from the League of St George and Leicester-based British Democratic Party (BDP).[14] By the time of the 1983 general election it had recruited approximately 2,500 members, although few were active. With elections sidelined, little energy was invested in building a large membership. Instead, efforts focused on recruiting a small and highly committed cadre of young working-class 'toughs' who could meet physical opposition from anti-fascists and deliver the confrontational tactic of 'march and grow'. This early recruitment strategy was geared toward poaching members from rival groups on the extremist fringe. At one of its first rallies, the leadership stressed the importance of 'reactivating' former NF members who had abandoned politics after the disappointment of the 1979 general election.[15] Ex-members of the NF and also members of the openly neo-Nazi British Movement (BM) found their way into some of the earliest BNP branches in Hackney and Tower Hamlets.[16]

Over the next two decades, the BNP continued to rely heavily on the extremist fringe for recruits: it poached NF organizers in the mid-1980s, members of the Nottingham-based Nationalist Party (NP) in 1991, activists from the National Democrats (ND) in the West Midlands, and in the late 1990s members of the NF who helped establish groups in areas like Norwich.[17] While the strategy ensured continuity with the past, it also had a profound impact on party development. Because of the weak and fragmented nature of the extreme right, the party struggled to attract a significant following. By the time Margaret Thatcher was re-elected in 1987, membership had slumped to under 1,000 and would not grow significantly until the early years of the twenty-first century. A distinct lack of resources and reluctance to invest in elections also meant the party was ill-equipped to convince its recruits to remain committed for the long walk through the wilderness. As one organizer would later recall, throughout the 1980s the party lost as many if not more members as a result of dissatisfaction and burnout as the number enrolled through its lacklustre recruitment campaigns.

The strategy also ensured that, in later years, when the party began moving toward elections, it would struggle to attract more 'respectable' recruits with the experience and skills required for a successful electoral strategy. Rather than draw support from the fringes of the Conservatives, the BNP was dominated by inexperienced novice ideologues who held their roots in racial nationalism and had little experience of electioneering. As it stumbled through the 1990s, it experienced no significant membership growth. Even in the inner East End, it failed to translate a local breakthrough in 1993 into new blood; while the party claimed an influx of 900 new recruits, subsequent infighting with Combat 18 stifled growth. The fallout was so severe that the leadership was forced to acknowledge a 'rumbling of discontent in party ranks', and that members were abandoning the party (membership of Combat 18 was eventually proscribed in 1994).[18]

The fact that only 100 foot soldiers attended a major event in 1994 suggested few were active.[19] Even when more favourable conditions emerged, the party saw little need to revise its strategy. At the 1997 general election, it continued to direct appeals toward the extremist fringe. It even held talks about a possible merger with the NF, assuring members of the latter they would 'find the warmest of welcomes in the BNP', while soon-to-be leader Nick Griffin reiterated they would be 'warmly welcomed . . . recognised and rewarded'.[20] The merger never materialized and after the election the party's dismal internal state meant it was unable to translate 3,000 enquiries into actual members.[21] It would not be until a change of leadership and growing support in elections that the situation began to change.

Some strong results at the 2001 general election and the gaining of three councillors in 2002 prompted Griffin to break with tradition and detail membership figures. In 2001, the BNP was supported by 2,173 members, a figure which would steadily rise alongside growing support in elections: 3,487 in 2002; then 5,737 in 2003; and then 7,916 in 2004. The growth temporarily stalled when the party failed to enter the European Parliament in 2004, meaning that at the general election the next year membership hovered at 6,281.[22] Publicized advances at the 2006 local elections in areas such as Barking and Dagenham triggered another influx. Media coverage of the party was also fuelled by the trial of Nick Griffin for incitement to racial hatred, who alongside another activist was acquitted. The next year saw the total number of BNP members reach a record 9,000 (an internal report put the exact figure at 9,297).[23]

Further insight came in 2008, when the BNP membership list was leaked onto the Internet by disgruntled activists who, it was claimed, 'didn't like the direction the party was going'.[24] The list detailed membership toward the end of 2007 and was described by Griffin as mostly genuine. Nonetheless, some leading activists could not conceal their anger about its release, such as the deputy party Chairman: 'If we find out the name of the person who published this list it will turn out to be one of the most foolish things they have done in their life.'[25] The list included the names and addresses of more than 12,000 members, though in the spring of 2009 the party claimed a total membership of 10,276 members (Fig. 6.2).[26]

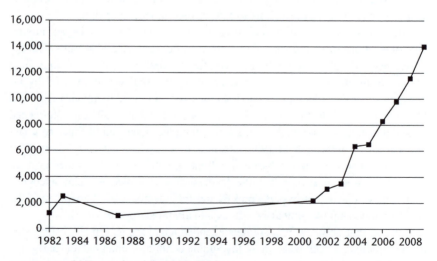

FIGURE 6.2   BNP membership, 1982–2009

Thereafter, the party has detailed additional growth, including approximately 5,000 membership enquiries following Griffin's appearance on *Question Time*, and 10,000 enquiries during the general election campaign in 2010.[27] Shortly after the election, the party announced it had surpassed the 14,000 mark, and had recruited a larger membership than the UK Independence Party (UKIP).[28] While there are good reasons to question these claims, since 2001 the party has experienced significant membership growth.

How does BNP membership compare to that of other parties? Since 2001, it has recruited a membership similar in size to that of other minor parties in British politics (see Fig. 6.3). As with parties such as the Greens and UKIP, the BNP has seen its number of members rise in a period when the main parties have seen memberships fall. In fact, since 2001 the BNP has experienced the most rapid membership growth of all minor parties.[29] Within the more immediate world of the extreme right, the BNP is easily the dominant force. Since 2001, the extreme right has expanded and diversified. Among others, organizations have included the British People's Party (BPP), Bradford-based Democratic Nationalists (DN), England First Party (EFP), Freedom Party (FP), National Front (NF), Nationalist Alliance (NA), New Nationalist Party (NNP), November 9th Society – British First Party (BFP), National Liberal Party – Third Way and the British Freedom Party (BFP). Most, however, have been based on only paltry memberships and few resources, for example: in 2009 the DN claimed only 22 members and an operating budget of £250; in 2008 the NF claimed only two operating branches, the EFP claimed less than 100 members and the FP had no paid-up

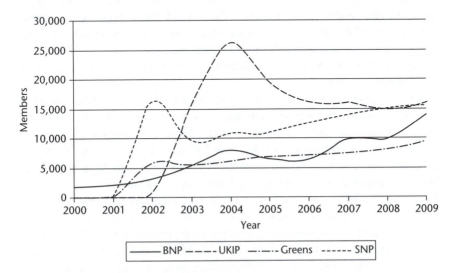

FIGURE 6.3   BNP membership compared

Source: Electoral Commission; J. Marshall (2009) *Membership of UK Political Parties*, House of Commons Library Research Note SN/SG/5125; Electoral Commission.

members after failing to collect subscriptions (it subsequently renewed its existing 42 memberships without charge); in 2007, the openly neo-Nazi BFP raised only £300 from membership subscriptions; and in 2006 the NNP claimed only 38 members and was eventually deregistered by the Electoral Commission due to statutory non-compliance.[30]

BNP members: who are they?

In the last chapter, it was shown that the BNP receives the bulk of its support in elections from 'angry white men': middle-aged or elderly working-class men who have low levels of education, are profoundly pessimistic about future economic prospects and are located in deprived urban areas where there are large Muslim communities.[31] Its more committed members have been traced to similar social contexts. Following the release of its membership list, some journalists claimed that 80 per cent of members were men who were typically employed as skilled workers or were ex-members of the armed services. Rather than spread across the country, it was claimed that members were concentrated heavily in specific areas: while the largest clusters were in Charnwood in Leicestershire, Pendle in Lancashire, Amber Valley in Derbyshire and Ashfield in Nottinghamshire, members were generally more prominent in the East Midlands, Essex and Pennine Lancashire.[32] More technical analysis of the party membership list confirms that BNP members congregate in particular types of areas and social contexts.[33] The constituencies and local authorities with the strongest concentrations of BNP members are revealed in Table 6.1. This suggests that membership is strongest in areas of Lancashire such as Burnley and Pendle, areas of Leicestershire such as Melton, Charnwood, North West Leicestershire, Hinckley and Blaby, and areas of Nottinghamshire such as Ashfield and Broxtowe. Epping Forest, an area where the extreme right has long been active, is the only local authority in southern England to feature in the list of areas with the highest BNP membership rates.

One possible explanation for the geographical distribution of members is that regions where membership is strongest have also long been targeted by the extreme right, and have tended to provide disproportionately high levels of support to these parties. Parties like the NF were particularly active in the Midlands, while in more recent years the BNP has shifted its focus toward the North West and Yorkshire, all of which have large concentrations of members. By contrast, regions with the lowest number of members (in descending rank order) are the North East, South West, Scotland and Northern Ireland, all of which have traditionally been weak regions for the extreme right. Further evidence for this 'legacy effect' is evident in Table 6.1. Most of the constituencies which now contain large numbers of BNP members were targeted by extreme right parties in earlier years – for example, the NF campaigned in: Ashfield at the 1979 general election; Blaby in 1979–83; Huddersfield in 1970–74; Luton in 1979; Oxford in (October) 1974; and Wanstead and Woodford in 1979–83 (which was

TABLE 6.1 BNP membership at the level of constituencies and local authorities

Constituency	Region	Members per 100,000
Luton South	Eastern	127
Broxbourne	Eastern	106
Oxford West and Abingdon	South East	97
Ashfield	East Midlands	97
Cambridgeshire SE	Eastern	95
Forest of Dean	South West	95
Barnsley East and Mexborough	Yorkshire	91
Batley & Spen	Yorkshire	89
Huddersfield	Yorkshire	86
Barnsley West and Penistone	Yorkshire	84
Leyton & Wanstead	London	83
Bolton West	North West	81
Tonbridge and Malling	South East	80
Amber Valley	East Midlands	80
Blaby	East Midlands	80
Local authority		
Pendle	North West	87
Burnley	North West	80
Melton	East Midlands	79
Charnwood	East Midlands	79
Barnsley	Yorkshire	67
North West Leicestershire	East Midlands	63
Blackpool	North West	59
Ashfield	East Midlands	58
Lincoln	East Midlands	57
Hinckley and Bosworth	East Midlands	57
Amber Valley	East Midlands	57
Blaby	East Midlands	57
Broxtowe	East Midlands	55
Calderdale	Yorkshire	55
Epping Forest	Eastern	53

Source: M.J. Goodwin, D. Cutts and R. Ford, 'Extreme right foot soldiers: Examining the factors that determine extreme right party membership', Paper presented to the Elections, Public Opinion and Parties (EPOP) Conference, University of Strathclyde, Scotland, 28–30 August 2009.

later amalgamated into Leyton and Wanstead). Some of the constituencies are located in areas previously targeted by *both* the NF and BNP, for example: Forest of Dean is located in Gloucestershire which previously hosted a Powellite candidate in 1974, the NF in 1979, and BNP in 1983; both parties have been active in Broxbourne and Epping Forest; and residents of Bolton were targeted by the NF in 1974 and 1979, and the BNP in 1983. Though further research is needed, it suggests that the contemporary BNP is continuing to benefit from earlier campaigns by the extreme right.

More technical analysis of the list also reveals that membership is most likely in particular types of areas: they tend to be urban, have low education levels and large numbers of economically insecure residents who are employed in the manufacturing sector.[34] This provides further evidence that the BNP is drawing much of its support from citizens who occupy a more precarious position in society. Consistent with findings presented in the last chapter, membership is also correlated with the presence of large Muslim communities, which further suggests that the party is attracting citizens who feel particularly threatened by Muslims and Islam. By contrast, the presence of non-Muslim Asians (e.g. Sikh, Hindu, Buddhist communities) has no significant effect while membership is lower in wards where there are large black populations, even after including prior social controls. Consistent with the last chapter, these findings suggest that the appeal of the BNP is more subtle than that of its parent party.

Findings from the interviews

> Some would say put a red rose on a pig and they would vote for it.

Qualitative life-history interviews with a sample of members provide further and richer insight into who joins the party, their backgrounds and routes into membership. Consistent with the evidence gathered so far, the findings suggest the party is appealing to a socially distinct group of citizens: older and working class men who affiliate themselves and their families with Labour. Men dominate every level of the BNP. In 2009, for example, more than 80 per cent of its Advisory Council members were male and, between 2002 and 2009, more than three quarters of its councillors were men. On the contrary, the percentage of female BNP candidates in elections was only 6 per cent in 2001, 13 percent in 2005, 14 percent in 2009 and 16 percent in 2010.[35] As in elections, the interviews suggest the BNP is recruiting older citizens and is struggling to entice young Britons: the average member was 47 years old, and stood in stark contrast to the stereotypical image of the NF member as a young working-class skinhead who wore Doc Martens boots.[36]

Although we do not have detailed information about their social class, the qualitative accounts provided by members tell us much about their backgrounds.[37] Most identified themselves strongly with the working classes and Labour. Members typically described their upbringing as 'working class Labour', 'staunch Labour', or supportive of '*old* Labour':

> When I were at school I was a Labour voter. All my family were working class Labour, you can't call it a Labour Party anymore. I don't know what it is to tell you the truth, it's a disgrace. We were all Labour. Everyone on the estate were Labour. You got the odd family who were Conservative which we thought there must be something madly wrong with them.

I didn't think that in this town in particular people were getting a fair deal. Labour had been in power in this town for as long as anybody can remember and the place has been an absolute dump and an eyesore. So they've [Labour] got to take some responsibility for that.

While elaborating on their dissatisfaction with Labour, several members drew a distinction between *old* and *New* Labour, such as a BNP councillor: 'When I was younger my mum always voted Labour. At that time it wasn't too bad, it was doing what it was supposed to do, looking out for the poorer people, not industry or rich people.' Others similarly described the election of 'New' Labour in 1997 as 'the moment when working hard for the working classes [went] out of the window'. Reflective of most, two organizers recalled:

As I say, my family particularly, and myself, voted predominantly Labour, the *old* Labour I might add. One of the things that I feel people have missed out on is that when the Tories lost the seat of power to this *New* Labour they didn't see this word 'new' in front of the title and they didn't question 'new'. I think most people thought it was the same party, but brighter and shinier, as though it had undergone some sort of hair-do or facelift or something. In fact, what it was, was a new party in its entirety.

I was born in . . . a big steel town and in that area there were also lots of coal mines. So it's your typically, what used to be, heavy industry area. Margaret Thatcher closed basically most of those steel plants, closed most of the mines as well. Not just my family but most of my friends' families suffered. My dad worked 30 years and was thrown on the scrap-heap, never had a job again. Basically it destroyed my dad, destroyed a few of my uncles. And when you open the *Evening Telegraph* you'd see how many people had hung themselves.

These accounts reveal how most members were raised in communities where politics was dominated by Labour. As one member explained, his town 'has always been a Labour town, you know jokingly some would say put a red rose on a pig and they would vote for it'. Typical of these supporters was Maggie, a 67-year-old pensioner who was born and raised in a mill town in Pennine Lancashire. Having retired, Maggie now volunteers in a charity shop and is well known in her community. As with most BNP supporters, she left school with no formal educational qualifications and like her neighbours went to work in the textile industry: 'I went straight into the factory, 'cause that's all there were, 'cause it were a cotton town.' Maggie explained how neither her family nor friends had ever been involved in politics. In fact, prior to becoming involved with the BNP she had little interest in politics generally: 'No I was never interested in it [politics] 'cause [Town X has] always been a Labour town because it's been a working class town . . . so everybody voted Labour.'

Three 'types': the old guard, wanderers and new recruits

The interviews also allow us to explore *how* some citizens first became involved with the BNP. Research elsewhere in Europe suggests there is not one uniform route into the extreme right but that individuals tend to follow one of three different paths.[38] Through a first route, longer-term influences within their family or social context predispose individuals to support the extreme right from a young age. These 'socialization effects' lead some people to absorb right-wing values and attitudes from family members, become susceptible to the extreme right and follow a route of *continuity* into the movement. Through a second route, individuals switch loyalty from other types of political parties to the extreme right following a critical event or experience which leads them to reassess their ideological outlook and search for a new political home. While they may still be predisposed to support the extreme right, in this case they are *converted* following a specific 'trigger'. Through a third route, individuals enrol not because of socialization or ideological affinity, but in response to pressure from significant others to join. Rather than being pulled into membership, individuals are effectively pushed in by partners, friends, neighbours and colleagues, and are *compliant* in following others into the movement.

Evidence elsewhere in Europe stresses the importance of family, suggesting continuity is the most important route. Given that countries such as France, Germany and Italy have stronger traditions of fascist and extreme right politics, this finding is not particularly surprising. Interviewees in these countries could often detail pre-existing links to the extreme right through their family members, and were already exposed to ethnic nationalist, authoritarian and conservative ideas 'long before they actually joined'.[39] In Italy, for example, some saw their involvement as 'a heritage' received from their families.[40] Given the historic weakness of the British extreme right, however, we might expect family to play a less important role. Indeed, not one member of the BNP claimed their family had ever been involved with 'nationalist' politics. Typical of most was one organizer:

> No there's been no real political involvement . . . we were never a political family in any way. I've got four brothers and two sisters, none of whom are involved in politics. As I said before, I've been away for a long time, fifteen years in the army. The army and politics don't really go together because you're not allowed to take part in political activity anyway so I mean I was never involved.

While activists were united in claiming their families had no prior involvement with the extreme right, they often differed in terms of their route into the BNP: the activist *old guard* arrived at the party after a much longer history of involvement with the extreme right; the *political wanderers* only converted to the party following a dissatisfying experience in another political party; and the *new recruits* joined suddenly and typically had no prior experience of political activity.

Combined, it is the wanderers and new recruits who have fuelled the party's recent membership growth.[41]

The activist old guard

While seeking to downplay its roots, the BNP continues to rely heavily on members who have a long history of involvement with racial nationalist politics. Most members of the old guard trace their lineage to the 1970s NF, and view their membership as the latest chapter in a longer commitment to 'nationalism' and 'the cause'. Two examples shed light on the old guard. Following Griffin's election in 1999, John Bean was appointed editor of the BNP magazine. Bean is a veteran of fascist and extreme right politics in Britain (see Chapter 1). In his early years, he served in the Royal Navy and recalls in his autobiography how the experience of visiting countries like India shaped his political outlook: 'I had become aware of the racial differences that had created the varied cultures of mankind. This made me a racialist, but certainly not a "race hater".'[42] After reading a pamphlet distributed by Oswald Mosley in the 1940s and witnessing the arrival of immigrants from the West Indies, Bean enrolled in the Union Movement (UM) and came to consider 'the race question to be the most important factor in post-war world politics'. After campaigning for the UM in Brixton and Putney, he left in 1953.[43] Thereafter, Bean passed through an 'alphabet soup' of movements, including the League of Empire Loyalists (LEL) which he joined in 1955 and then the National Labour Party (NLP) which aimed to appeal to voters 'concerned over the effects of immigration, who had traditionally voted Labour'.[44] In 1960, the NLP merged with the neo-Nazi White Defence League (WDL) to create an earlier version of the BNP, which advocated racial nationalist positions while also calling for the release of Rudolph Hess.[45] Seven years later, Bean amalgamated the BNP into the National Front and remained involved in the latter until the mid-1970s. Following a period away from politics, he then enrolled in the BNP after the election of Nick Griffin in 1999, and was rewarded for his loyalty by being appointed editor of *Identity*, its monthly magazine.

Another member of the old guard is Bill, who first became involved with the extreme right by joining the NF, and in response to immigration. Bill enrolled after returning from living abroad in Germany where he worked for the civil service:

> I was brought up not in a strict family but one where morals and responsibilities and respect for others, all that sort of thing, were quite well up in family life. But I think that I felt that the way society was going, those values that I had were being undermined through various routes and I just felt that unless somebody stood up and did something about it, things would just go from bad to worse. I actually lived in Germany for four years and I came back, I worked in London for a short time . . . it was only at that time that I felt that I wanted to actually *actively* get involved [emphasis in

original] . . . seeing the way that I perceived society was falling apart, that spurred me into doing that.

Bill began selling NF literature outside football stadiums and attending marches. While these activities attracted attention, he began advocating that the NF change its name in the hope of overcoming its 'boot-boy' image. Disillusioned with the lack of progress, Bill joined the rival National Democrats (ND), a break-away party that favoured a more moderate approach. Yet when ND literature became less frequent, Bill began subscribing to the BNP newspaper and soon followed other ND members into the party. He has since assumed various roles inside the BNP, including local organizer, regional secretary, election candidate and member of the Advisory Council. Typical of the old guard, Bill recalled how his decision to get involved was predetermined: 'I knew what I was about . . . I think I did it by a process of elimination in as much as I knew which ones [polit-ical parties] I didn't want to be with and that left me with the one or two that I needed to choose from and I just picked. I mean, it wasn't a process where one Saturday night with pen and paper, it was just a natural thing I think really.'

Like these activists, other members of the old guard have been rewarded for their loyalty with positions of influence, for example: Martin Wingfield first enrolled in the NF in 1976 and sat on its national directorate before joining the BNP in 2001 and being appointed editor of its newspaper; Simon Darby was a prominent member of the ND before joining the BNP and becoming its Deputy Chairman; Eddy Butler first became involved with the NF in 1979 in Manchester and Tower Hamlets before joining the BNP in 1986 and becoming its election strategist; Andrew Brons had previously been a member of the National Socialist Movement (NSM), Bean's BNP and briefly led the NF before joining the BNP in 2005 and being elected to the European Parliament in 2009; Lance Stewart had similarly been active in Bean's BNP in the late 1950s before joining the BNP in 2007 and being made responsible for its Intelligence Department.[46] While rewarding the old guard with senior positions, shortly following his election Griffin also purged members who were loyal to his predecessor, John Tyndall. 'Tyndallites' were encouraged to leave the BNP and join rival groups, and by 2003 it was estimated they comprised only 7 per cent of the membership.[47] The aim has been to replace the Tyndall faction with activists loyal to Griffin, as he explained in one interview in 2006: 'Right up to the top level there are more people now in the upper echelons of the party . . . there's more old NF cadres seri-ously involved than there are Tyndall BNP people.'[48] As he elaborates, an addi-tional goal has been to learn the lessons of the failed NF:

There was a shocking case, I think it was in Martin Walker's book *The National Front*, when Martin Webster went to a meeting of the newly formed Wolverhampton branch and a fellow on the top table proudly spoke about how they'd been doing all this local community work and one of the things they'd just done, they'd taken a party of old age pensioners to the seaside to which Webster exploded from the top table next to him, 'this is a political party not a fucking burial society' and basically ended the Wolverhampton branch. That kind of attitude to sinking local roots . . . they felt they were going to be in power in 10 years' time, this incredible naivety. When the NF was at its height, the average length of service in the nationalist movement of the people on its governing body was probably about three or four years, whereas the average length of service of the hardcore in the BNP now is more like 25 years. We've seen a lot more cock-ups.[49]

There have been some notable exceptions, however. In 2008, Richard Edmonds was temporarily invited to attend meetings of the Advisory Council and offer guidance to Griffin.[50] Edmonds first became involved with the extreme right by joining the NF, then the New National Front (NNF) and then briefly leading the BNP while Tyndall served a prison sentence for inciting racial hatred.

The political wanderers

Political wanderers bring a different kind of experience to the party. They typically joined the BNP after being involved with other parties, and following a dissatisfying experience which sparked a search for a new home. Typical of the wanderers is Pam, a 60-year-old retiree who lives in a 'white flight' area in outer London. Pam left school when she was 15 years old, after which she attended Trade College and then began work as a secretary. Over the years, she became heavily involved in her community by volunteering in a residents' association for almost two decades. Though her mother was a staunch supporter of Labour, her husband was a loyal Conservative and for a short time worked as an organizer for a Conservative Member of Parliament (MP). Influenced by her husband, Pam also had a 'little stint' with the Conservatives but soon left to join the Referendum Party, a Eurosceptic party that disintegrated shortly afterward. In 2002, her husband began attending meetings of a local BNP branch, and she found herself following him into the extreme right:

> My husband attended meetings and came back and said to me he'd heard nothing that was controversial as far as, you know, what had been reported that the party was about . . . there was a friend of ours who we'd known for years who was a member. He was pleased that we started going and we joined. He's [her husband] the catalyst. He didn't drag me along at all. The chaps who came to sign us up were again not stereotypes. One was quite old but very gentle, well spoken and the others were in suits, well presented, well spoken.

Another example of the wanderers is Val, who was born and raised in Norfolk. Val is 64 years old, and has lived in her village in the South West of England for almost 30 years. Her father served in the army and, unlike her fellow members, her parents voted Conservative. Like Pam, Val became involved in politics by joining the Referendum Party, and then the UK Independence Party (UKIP). However, she soon became disillusioned with UKIP, though mainly because its publications were becoming less frequent and it 'didn't seem to be dealing with the problem of all this immigration'. Like most wanderers, Val only converted to the BNP after being introduced to the party by a significant other: 'So in the end Len said to me, "Val what you should do, you should join the BNP." I said, "the BNP? The BNP? Why would I want to join them?" He said, "I'll give you a phone number to ring up and you can get some information about it and see what you think", and that's what I did. They sent me out a newspaper for three months.' Like virtually all of the members who were interviewed, and irrespective of their route into the party, Val claimed the BNP leader played no significant role in her recruitment. While the appeal of extreme right parties is often linked to charismatic leaders this was not the case, or as Val explains: 'I didn't know Nick [Griffin]. I think it was more or less going to that local meeting, at that particular one there was application forms, you could *do it*.' After enrolling, Val was appointed local organizer and now regularly stands on the party's behalf in elections: 'I spend nearly 24 hours a day at it,' she explains.

The new recruits

Over half of the interviewees were new recruits who share several features. New recruits typically joined the BNP from 2001 onward, and mainly in response to its growing electoral support. Before joining, most lacked political experience and had little interest in politics: George explained how politics 'garnered no interest'; Sue claimed politics 'wasn't something I was interested in'; Michael 'was never interested in politics'; and Dean 'never talked politics until I got involved with the BNP'. Most of these new recruits were also self-starters; they approached the party themselves, and often following a specific event:

> I went to Australia in '99 to live and work for a year . . . I was on public transport in Melbourne and I experienced racial abuse. It wasn't physical, it was verbal but it was from groups of Lebanese young men. Another time it was from young Asian men. I was called various names and things and I thought 'hang on a minute, this isn't really on. I wouldn't dream of saying something like that to anybody else because of the colour of their skin' . . . I came back to England and in the year I'd been away I found that my views had changed quite a bit. I went through the paper, I saw changes taking place in Brighton and I just thought I really don't like what England's becoming and how things are changing so much. I went onto the [BNP] party website and I read the policies and I agreed with [the] majority of them and I thought 'well, that's it. I'm going to join up and see what happens'.

Rather than being influenced by family or friends, new recruits often joined through the party website, a particularly important tool for minor parties. For many, the website assumed a central role in the recruitment process. One member, for example, recalled his decision to join as follows: 'So I decided I'd contact the British National Party 'cause I'd heard a bit about them, people talkin' at work. So I went to the website and had a look and I sent off for an information pack. Basically, it spiralled from there really.' The involvement stories of other members similarly focused on the critical importance of the party website:

> . . . then I came across the website. I was reading through the website and it seemed very different to what the media were saying . . . the next month or two I was doing a lot of research into the party, it was a very much sort of testing time for me because I didn't want to jump into it if it might be extreme and difficult to get out of.

> The Internet's been a bit of guide really. So I looked at Conservative, Labour, Lib Dem and all of that. I mean, the main three parties, you can't understand what they're saying anyway. The smaller parties interested me more. I think I read the UKIP website, I looked at the Green Party website as I said, and I looked at the BNP website eventually. I was absolutely amazed. I read all the news articles on there, I just kept on reading them for hours I think, just reading these articles trying to find something I disagreed with and I couldn't find anything. I read their manifesto and I actually agreed with everything that they said and I thought: 'Oh blimey, there's been this organisation there this whole time while I've been going absolutely crazy and they stand for exactly the same things that I stand for and they're open for me to become a part of that if I wanted to.' So I was a bit nervous because of course they have a bad reputation and all this but I joined anyway, sort of half-heartedly joined.

For new recruits, the website was often seen as an important tool through which they could explore the BNP, its policies and goals. More often than not, this stage of exploration was then followed by the crucial experience of the first party meeting. Because of its stigma in wider society, many members recalled their profound anxiety about contacting the BNP, for example: 'Basically I felt the same way as most people felt about the party when they hear the BNP, they think Nazis and thugs, criminal elements, nasty people really. So I didn't have a good view of the Party before I joined.' Others similarly described feeling shocked at the suggestion from friends that they should consider approaching the party.

This initial anxiety, however, soon evaporated following the first meeting. As one political scientist points out, for potential members collective events like party meetings can become nothing short of a 'vision-altering gestalt'; meetings can appear like a 'moral discovery' that offer 'some new insight into the nature of the world, with a new paradigm for understanding how one ought to act and live one's life'.[51] Numerous members highlighted the critical importance of this event:

I never really got anywhere at first. So after keeping on trying, and trying and saying I wanna help out, I wanna come to meetings, they invited me to a meeting in Bedfordshire which is a bit of a way really . . . But it was worthwhile. I went along and I was very nervous. I was worried that I'd turn up and there'd be a big gathering of skinheads or something. But it was just normal people in a little village hall and there was sort of magazines and papers on display for sale, and there was a guest speaker who was over from the East of England. And he gave a very good speech which I agreed with a lot. And after the speech in fact I went up to him and said 'any qualms that I had about joining the party you put them aside and I feel happy now about being a part of it'. So I had a good chat to him after the meeting over a couple of drinks and I really felt as though I'd found a party that stood for what I stood for.

When discussing his shift toward the party, members such as Michael similarly focus on the first meeting: 'I was made to feel very welcome. I wasn't asked to speak or anything. Lots of people made a point of coming up to me and introducing themselves and I think it was *that* which probably pulled me in, that feeling of, "yeah I've met some really good people here".'

After taking the decision to join, new recruits also tend to become heavily active inside the party. Because of its weak internal state, many members rose quickly through the ranks; several explained how they almost immediately became organizers because there was no BNP unit in their area. Typical of most, one activist recalled: 'When I decided to join the British National Party I wanted to play an active role in it. I knew straight away that I wanted to get involved and be a part of activism, of leafleting and actually going out and promoting the party, you know, physically.' While becoming active in the party, most new recruits also distanced themselves from its main predecessors. In fact, most saw the post-1999 BNP as a seemingly 'new' party in British politics that had little in common with either the NF or BNP of the Tyndall era:

> The BNP was formed in '82 officially but in my eyes the modern day BNP started with Nick Griffin's election. It's developed more in the last six years than it has in the last 26 years. John Tyndall held us back. I would never ever have joined the party with John Tyndall at the helm.

> It [the Tyndall era] has left a legacy that is quite difficult, or has been quite difficult to move on from. Particularly images of John Tyndall dressed in ridiculous uniforms and things like that. They have tarnished the party in some way and make it now difficult to get away from things we were once labelled as.

One example of the new recruits is Dean, a student who joined in 2003. Dean's parents were never involved in politics, and he describes his background as 'very much working class'. He traces his involvement to reading BNP literature and articles in the *Daily Mail*, particularly columns by Peter Hitchens. Like most new recruits, Dean approached the party via its website, which he used to order an information pack and obtain details about a local meeting: 'I went along thinking to myself one of two things are going to happen: either they are extreme or I'll see something different. I saw something different, you know they weren't sinister. I explored it a bit further and decided that the party was for me.'

Dean recalled feeling that he wanted to be 'very active' from the outset; he wanted to stand in elections 'right from the beginning'. Over the next four years, he assumed prominent roles inside the party and its youth wing, campaigning in general and European elections, and organizing activities in his community. Dean, however, firmly rejects the suggestion of any links between the BNP and organizations like the NF: 'Their [NF's] idea of political activism was going down the pub, getting drunk and then kicking a few people in. That's not something I wish to carry on. Nick Griffin has also softened up the BNP's views quite a bit' cause whereas before with John Tyndall you got the anti-Semitism, huge hardcore racism, Nick Griffin has completely got rid of all of that … It's good really because in effect it's got rid of the extremism and has made us more electable.'

Conclusions

While the BNP's shift toward elections has attracted a growing band of voters, it has also triggered an influx of new members. Like other minor parties in British politics, since 2001 it has experienced significant membership growth and there is some evidence that this growth has been most pronounced in areas where the extreme right has long been active. Consistent with findings in the last chapter, the evidence suggests BNP grassroots supporters share a similar social profile: they tend to be older working-class men who identify strongly with 'old' Labour. Not every member identified with Labour, but the fact that most did suggests that dissatisfaction over its perceived failure to respond to their concerns over particular issues is an important 'push' factor in the recruitment process. Despite its attempts to mobilize new groups of supporters, there is little evidence that the party is successfully recruiting large numbers of young people and women.

These activists have a relatively distinct social profile, but quite different political backgrounds. During its formative years, the party recruited heavily from within the extreme right but now appears to be drawing support more widely from across the political spectrum: some members spilled into the BNP from the second-wave NF; others switched loyalty from other parties; and still others enrolled after years of disinterest in all things political. While their accounts provide insight into *how* they first became involved with the party, the question of *why* they decided to join remains unanswered. It is to this question that our attention now turns.

7

INITIAL MOTIVATIONS
Why join?

> To be an activist in the BNP involves making a certain *commitment*. It has its pressures and it makes its *demands*. Such an activist puts himself in the *front line*, where there can on occasions be some troublesome repercussions.'[1]

The decision to become involved in a political party invites few obvious benefits and can entail many costs. The loss of evenings, weekends and money are familiar sacrifices for committed party supporters. For this reason, party members and activists are often considered rather peculiar creatures. Yet if the decision to become involved in a political party seems odd, then the decision to enrol in an extremist party appears especially puzzling. Because of their links to fascism and racism, parties on the extreme right wing are often condemned as political pariahs that do not belong to democratic politics. In several countries, this has resulted in a strategy of exclusion whereby mainstream parties seek to prevent right-wing extremists from entering office and influencing debate.[2] It also entails consequences for their supporters. As others point out, aside from the costs of time, energy and money, the disadvantages of joining an extremist party might include official punishments, threats from rival movements and group reprisals for participating.[3] In fact, those who join have been shown to experience abuse, jeopardize employment prospects and damage relationships with friends and family.[4]

In Britain, these costs became apparent following the release of the BNP membership list. Trade unions promptly called on public bodies to ban BNP members, while their ostracism was reflected in the dismissal of a police officer, a petition to sack a university lecturer, and withdrawal of work for a radio broadcaster. The police had already banned staff from joining the party, while the Fire Brigades Union and Church of England would follow suit. Even before the leaked list, affiliation with the BNP invited negative consequences: one school headmaster resigned when his membership was revealed; a caretaker was sacked after attending a party rally; and the father of Nick Griffin was ousted from the Conservatives after answering an enquiry for the BNP. Individuals who have represented the party in elections have been sacked, expelled from unions or urged to resign.[5] These examples reflect the way in which there appear to be more reasons to steer clear of the extreme right than to sign up.

Despite these costs, however, recent years have seen a significant rise in the number of Britons joining the BNP. The puzzle of who has joined the party was aptly summarized by one politician as follows: 'It says it all about the BNP that so many of those on their database seem to be worried about being revealed as members. Who would join a party where membership is a social and professional embarrassment?'[6] The findings in the last chapter suggest these members tend to be older, working-class men who previously affiliated with 'old' Labour. Rather than being distributed across society, they also tend to come from particular types of areas: deprived urban districts where education levels are low and there are large Muslim communities. Until this point, however, the question of *why* they first joined remains unanswered. Drawing on their own accounts, this chapter explores the motives which initially 'pushed' some citizens to join the BNP. The next chapter then turns to examine how the party attempts to 'pull' them into active participation.

Becoming a right-wing extremist

While academics have developed various theories to explain why some citizens vote for the extreme right (see Chapter 5), they have also sought to account for why others demonstrate greater commitment by joining as members. In the aftermath of the Second World War, some of the earliest approaches emphasized the importance of disruptive psychological states. One argument was that individuals enrolled in fascist and extremist movements to ameliorate psychological problems.[7] The decision to enroll involved 'the projection of interests and concerns, not only largely private but essentially pathological, into the public scene'.[8] Others similarly argued it was an attempt to remedy a 'sense of powerlessness and confusion, and to achieve a heightened sense of personal worthiness'.[9] While different arguments were made, many viewed support as a by-product of psychological problems.

An alternative approach focused on the effects of isolation and alienation. Seen from this perspective, isolated citizens flock to right-wing extremist parties because they offer a sense of belonging which is anchored in an ethnic in-group and defined against various 'others'. It holds its roots in the Tocquevillean (and later Robert Putnam's) view that citizens who are integrated into a robust civil society are more trusting of others, and less likely 'to be swayed by their worst impulses'.[10] On the contrary, citizens who lack these social ties fall susceptible to feelings of alienation and may 'engage in extreme behaviour to escape from these tensions'.[11] Academics such as Hannah Arendt talked of 'the completely isolated human being who, without any other social ties . . . derives his sense of having a place in the world only from his belonging to a movement'.[12] Others similarly contended that if the 'need to belong' goes unfulfilled, then 'urgent psychological pressures' produce a pathological response in which 'unsatisfactory types of integration – most explicitly revealed in fascism – are leaned upon for sustenance'.[13]

These early theories, however, soon fell out of favour. The argument that involvement was a knee-jerk reaction to 'unconscious urges and unmet psychological needs' appeared far from convincing, as did the suggestion that the millions of citizens who have joined fascist and extremist parties over the years have all suffered from psychological abnormality.[14] Nor were these arguments supported by later research. One study of extreme right party activists across Western Europe concluded that, on the whole, they appeared 'as perfectly normal people, socially integrated, connected in one way or another to mainstream groups and ideas'.[15] Research on other types of extremist movements such as the Ku Klux Klan (KKK) and German Nazi Party similarly challenged the assumption that supporters were irrational, isolated loners. On the contrary, most appeared well integrated into their communities.[16] BNP supporters who were interviewed for this book similarly appeared well connected to social networks; while some volunteered in charity shops, others were active members of local residents' associations.

Attention subsequently turned to alternative theories, including those outlined in Chapter 5. Seen from one approach, the extreme right mainly recruits support from among the 'losers of modernization': deprived, less well-educated and pessimistic male workers and the unemployed who are struggling to adapt to rapid and destabilizing socio-economic change. As we have seen, while the BNP draws support from members of these social groups and angry white men, its followers are also profoundly hostile toward immigration, feel threatened by settled Muslim communities and are extremely dissatisfied with the mainstream parties. In elections, these attitudes are also the most important predictors of whether somebody will support the BNP, even after we allow for their social characteristics.

The importance of these immigration-related concerns leads us to the racial threat model. According to this approach, it is actual or perceived competition between groups over resources which triggers negative attitudes among members of the in-group toward 'threatening' out-groups.[17] It is these negative attitudes toward immigrants, asylum-seekers or Muslims which drive citizens to endorse exclusionary campaigns, such as by supporting an extreme right party in elections or becoming a dues-paying member and involved in politics on its behalf. In this way, citizens who feel threatened by rising ethno-cultural diversity embark on an instrumental strategy to protect their resources or wider ethnic group from these threats.[18]

While the findings thus far suggest this feeling of threat is an important driver of BNP support, it has not been possible to explore the views of BNP supporters in-depth. The qualitative accounts provided by members enable us to explore their reasons for joining the party, and in their own words. They also allow us to explore the validity of three distinct perspectives within the racial threat model. Seen from a first perspective, the BNP is recruiting citizens who feel their individual resources are threatened by immigration, for example, their job or social housing.

When citizens feel their resources are under threat, they mobilize along ethnic lines in an attempt to protect them and prevent other groups from gaining access to them. Support for the BNP in Barking, for example, has been traced to a perception among residents that immigrants were threatening their access to social housing. If this is the case, then we might expect the motives for joining to focus on more objective concerns over individual economic resources.

Seen from a second perspective, the party is similarly recruiting citizens who feel resources are under threat but are concerned mainly about the resources of their wider ethnic *group*. It builds on evidence that individuals who favour a restrictive immigration policy are driven less by anxiety over personal well-being than concern that immigrants and rising ethnic diversity threaten the resources of their collective group, such as the national economy or regeneration grants for the community. Put in other words, even if individuals are not personally threatened by competition over jobs and social housing, 'they may worry that others within their key in-group are actually in such competition'.[19] Support for the BNP in Burnley, for example, has been traced to a perception among residents that their group's access to regeneration funding was threatened by competing demands from Muslim communities.[20] In this case, the motives for joining would stem more from concern over threats to the collective group, for instance, white Britons.

Seen from a third and slightly different perspective, the party is recruiting citizens who perceive that immigrants and minority ethnic groups are threatening British culture, values and ways of life. Rather than focusing on material resources, it suggests the extreme right is recruiting individuals who are primarily concerned about wider threats posed by culturally distinct minority groups, for example, Muslims, and a 'clash of cultural identities'.[21] It draws on evidence that individuals hostile to immigration are concerned mainly about value conflicts presented by more culturally distinct groups, or as a study of anti-immigrant attitudes in Britain suggests: 'Britons are clearly worried about the symbolic threats of immigrants – the threat of religions that are perceived to emphasise non-British values and a terminal community other than that of Britain, and the threat to shared customs and way of life.'[22] In this case, we would expect the initial motive to stem from more diffuse concerns over perceived threats to British culture, values and ways of life.

'I want to make sure my people are put first': initial motives

The task of understanding what drives citizens to join parties is complicated by the possibility that they may reconstruct their initial reasons for joining. By interacting with the party and other members, they may adopt a rationale for support that differs from the motives which initially prompted their membership.[23] The importance of this distinction between initial and longer-term motives will become especially apparent in the next chapter, which shows how the BNP attempts to sustain the loyalty of followers by cultivating a set of specific 'motivational vocabularies'. In response to this challenge, one way of separating out these motives and investigating what first pushed some citizens toward the party was to begin each interview with the question: 'Could you tell me what first brought you toward political activity?' The open-ended question was designed to focus the minds of supporters on their initial reason for approaching the BNP.

In common with BNP voters, most members traced their decision to join to a profound sense of anxiety over immigration and rising ethno-cultural diversity. In virtually every interview, activists expressed concern about the presence of immigrants and their impact on British society and culture. In most cases, these concerns were presented in more subtle terms than the crude biological racism associated with the extreme right. Rather than expressing racist hostility *per se*, most members emphasized the perceived threats posed by immigrants and minority ethnic groups. For some, these threats stemmed from concern over intergroup competition for material resources, such as jobs and social housing. Bill, for example, grew up in a heartland of the Labour Party and, in later years, enrolled in the Marines. After retiring from the armed services, Bill joined the BNP in the late 1990s and soon became a local organizer and councillor. Like several other members, he recalled how his initial motive for approaching the party owed much to his concern over intergroup competition in the local labour market: 'The people that run this country are Oxbridge educated. They've got nothing in common with people like myself. They don't know what people suffer. They go on about this, they go on about that, they chuck some money at this and chuck some money at that, but they don't know what it's like to live cheek by jowl with a Polish person, a Lithuanian person, an African person and then fight for a job.'

Like Bill, several other members traced their initial motive to a feeling that immigrants are threatening resources which should be reserved for white Britons, as one explained: 'On immigration, any people who come to this country because they are really running away from oppression then no problem. But I see that a lot of the people that come to this country are doing it for economic reasons and, consequently, the impact on our workforce, and our own social services, our health service, they're suffering because of that.' While most members expressed this welfare chauvinist outlook, however, it did not emerge as the dominant theme in the interviews. Rather, they put much stronger emphasis on the *cultural* threat posed by immigrants and settled Muslim communities. Seen through the eyes of the typical member, these 'threatening' out-groups are having a profoundly negative impact on British society and ways of life, and are the main source of value conflicts. While they are a strain on public services, immigrants, Muslims and, to a lesser extent, asylum-seekers pose a more serious threat to the values and national identity of white Britons. Integral to understanding these motives are more symbolic concerns over a threatened white British community, and threats to their values and ways of life.

In most cases, this sense of cultural threat was presented alongside ethnic nationalist beliefs, with most members defining national identity along the lines of birth and ancestry. One example was the response of Bob, when he was asked what initially brought him toward political activity: 'I don't want to live in a place where my culture is second place to immigrants' culture. I want to make sure my people are put first. That drives me forward because immigration is still continuing and these demographic trends are still continuing and I think it's wrong for white British people to be second place in Britain and to face becoming a minority in their own ancestral and sort of ethnic and racial homeland.' Another supporter who is typical of most is Martin, who traced his decision to join the BNP in 1999 to a view that immigration is threatening the demographic dominance of white Britons: 'The thing that drives me is the fact that when I first got involved there was a series of articles in the mainstream press, I think in *The Guardian* and *The Times* saying that basically white people would be an ethnic minority in Britain by 2050 or 2060.' For Martin, joining the BNP offered an opportunity to 'do something' in response to this threat.

Nor were the concerns of members divorced from direct experiences of immigration, as is often suggested. On the contrary, in most cases it was only after a specific event or experience that supporters took the decision to join. Typical of most was Clive, who recalled his initial motive as follows: 'I can remember the actual day when I first contacted what you might call a nationalist party. It was pretty close to St George's Day. I was living in Ealing, West London, and I saw a sticker on a lamp post. I was looking for a pub to celebrate St George's Day and I thought, you've got everything else going on, you know you get all your Diwalis and your this and your that, and St Patrick's Day with all the posters up and cheap beer and all the rest of that. I thought "no-one's doing anything for *us*", and that's what started me off.' A young new recruit similarly traced his decision to approach the BNP to a specific event:

> I've always felt that everyone had a certain responsibility for more than just themselves. I was at university and confronted with a situation that I wasn't really used to. I was living in an urban environment. I was living in a very cosmopolitan environment with people from all over the world, all in a small space . . . A lot of them were from other countries who'd come here to learn. One from Poland, two were from Nigeria, others were from other countries: Finland, France, and all this. I'd always felt proud to be British and I felt a part of something. A lot of people I lived with didn't seem to share those values and, in fact, some of them would sit in the kitchen and they would just sit about and just complain about British people and how awful we are and how stupid we are and how everything we do is useless and how everything we've achieved is pointless.

These concerns were not restricted to immigration. As discussed in Chapter 5, anti-Muslim sentiment has become an important driver of support for the BNP in elections, and the party polls strongest in areas where there are large Pakistani or Bangladeshi communities. The interviews provide rich insight into the nature of this anxiety over settled Muslim communities. Often without prompting, activists framed Muslims and Islam as a specific threat to British values and society. Many expressed the view that Muslims are unwilling or unable to integrate into British society, such as Pam:

> If you think in accordance with the country you're living in you contribute, you inter-relate, you are a part of that culture. You genuinely earn the right to be called a citizen. But if you go to a country, you take your old values with you, you reject any accepted values of that new country . . . Like I say, you couldn't go to Saudi and start opening up a chain of pubs could you? You'd have a load of headless waiters.

Alan, an ex-member of the armed services, similarly traced his involvement with the BNP to his concern over the growing presence of Muslims in Britain:

> When I left university I went to live in Algeria, a devout Muslim country which had been at war. I also travelled around the Middle East. It brings it home to you; the totalitarianism of a particular type of religion. I've seen how it effects people. It also impinged on me, my freedom of movement, what I was allowed to say, what I was not allowed to say.

As reflected in these accounts, most members expressed their belief that there are irreconcilable value conflicts between white Britons and settled Muslim communities. Some framed Muslims as threatening political institutions, claiming they seek to 'Islamify' Britain, or 'fly the flag of Islam over Westminster'. Others contended Muslims were the main source of drugs and criminality in their areas, or are intending to impose Sharia Law on white Britons: 'So this so-called moderate majority, I don't buy it because when they get their Islamic state in this country, which they will unless we [the BNP] have anything to do with it, they're already practising Sharia Law, that's a fact, it's not a secret, they've already said they want their own parliament.' While the sample is small, the findings are supported by evidence in other European states which reveals how extreme right members often perceive Muslims and Islam as being incompatible with Western liberal democratic values.[24]

The interviews provide further evidence that the BNP is rallying Britons who feel threatened by immigration and culturally distinct Muslim communities, and are dissatisfied with the current response offered by the main parties. Supporters consistently expressed the view that the government and main parties are unable or unwilling to deliver an adequate response to their anxiety over these issues. One example is Simon, who previously represented the Conservatives but explained how they were not 'hard hitting' enough on his main issue of concern: 'They were very liberal in their sort of approach to immigration which was not something I was interested in, the liberal approach I mean. At that time, the only other political party around that was even remotely interested in the subject was the British National Party and that's why I got involved with them.' Another interviewee recalled his decision to join as follows: 'On immigration, any people who come to this country because they are really running away from oppression then no problem. But I see that a lot of the people that come to this country are doing it for economic reasons, and that's another area that I don't think the Conservatives are addressing.'

For several members, their political dissatisfaction stemmed from the perform-ance of Labour, particularly in areas where it has historically dominated local politics. Maggie, who lives in a traditional Labour heartland, traced her involve-ment with the BNP to the performance of Labour on the local council: 'I think they [Labour] were going along lacksidaisically, just swimming along with the tide, *not* consulting the people and you can't do that. People have got to have a say in their town, they've got to do!' Rather than voicing their dissatisfaction about national politics, several other interviewees similarly focused on the performance of Labour in their community:

> The frustration is that local people, even though they vote Labour, are not getting the things that they want. There were issues like the asylum-seeker issue and that kind of stuff as well about which I felt kinda strongly. So having read output from quite a number of the parties I decided that I wanted to get involved and that I was going to get involved with the British National Party.

'So I decided to join the BNP': three motivational stories

The accounts of three members shed light on the initial motives for joining and reflect common themes that emerged in the interviews: perceptions of cultural threat; a desire to enact change in their local community; and the importance of specific events and experiences which 'triggered' the decision to join.

Threats: 'We're not in a country that is British anymore'

Peter began his membership by approaching a BNP branch in his town of Pendlebury, in West Yorkshire.[25] Like many other former mill towns in the area, in earlier decades labour shortages in Pendlebury attracted a small Pakistani community. By the mid-1960s, around 2,000 immigrants had settled and, over the years, their communities steadily expanded. Peter was born and raised in the town and, like most new recruits to the BNP, describes his family background as being mostly 'apolitical'. Though he was briefly a passive supporter of the Conservative Party, toward the end of the 1990s he became disillusioned: 'They just didn't seem to be reflecting my political views, and they didn't seem to be moving with the times and addressing issues which really affected myself.' When asked to elaborate, Peter explained how the Conservatives were failing to deliver an adequate response to his growing anxiety over immigration: 'Look at what happened before the [2005] general election. Six weeks before the general elec-tion they started talking really tough on immigration. Are you thinking what we're thinking? They're thinking alright, people can see that. Unless they actually pass a policy or be seen to be doing something then they ain't going anywhere.'

Following his dissatisfaction with the performance of the Conservatives on this issue, Peter explains how his decision to approach the BNP stemmed more from his anxiety over the cultural threat posed by immigrants and rising diversity: 'I've no objections to anybody coming into this country to be a part of it, but what we've got at the moment is people coming into this country and they want *their* country to be in *this* country.' While continually hinting at threatened material resources, his hostility to immigrants and culturally distinct minority groups is driven more by his concern over threats to culture and values: 'I haven't got an objection to anybody because of the colour of their skin; I've got an objection to people coming over and trying to force their culture on me.' These anxieties over threatened values and ways of life are integral to Peter's motive for joining the BNP, as he continues: 'We're not in a country that is British anymore, things are changing. When I say that, I don't mean that when I go out there I want to see white faces everywhere. I've got no problem with anybody else with a different colour skin. What I want to see out there is my country; you know the way I knew it as a Christian country.'

While retracing his steps into the BNP, however, Peter turns his attention to changes in the local community: 'I'd seen changes locally that I didn't like, and I didn't think that there was any party that was actually addressing my particular fears and also the fears of the people around me.' In particular, and against the backdrop of wider threats, the decision to join followed his growing concern over a 'threatening' Muslim community in the local area: 'They hide behind the Islam thing but all the drugs locally come in, we know where they come in from, I could take you to addresses now. The drugs around here is not *predominantly* coming, it's *coming* from the Muslim community.' While confronted with this threat, Peter was also profoundly dissatisfied with the failure of local political parties or the police to deliver an adequate response:

> But honestly, you can go to areas where you're just not safe, and that's the honest truth. That's probably why nobody was surprised when the London bomber came from Pendlebury. Since our last interview, there have been two arrests made. What's really not making the headlines is that the lad who's been arrested and is in custody, well his grandfather is the main community leader. He's the man who was on TV saying that he would root out extremists and make sure that Islam is seen as a peaceful religion. And yet his own grandson is doing this! The police are softly footing all the time because they're frightened of upsetting this particular part of our community.

Peter associates the threatening Muslim community with the broader deterioration of his community: 'We've got a town, Pendlebury, it's virtually gone. You couldn't go shopping down there by yourself as a white person. There's areas, if you stray out of the town centre in Pendlebury, be it day-time or night-time, you would not be safe just because of the colour of your skin. You would be beat up, and I mean beat up badly.' Asked when he first noticed these local changes, Peter recalls: 'Prior to me actually becoming involved with the party to be honest with you, because it was little things like that which were making me look in the first place for an alternative, a party that would actually stand up and address the issues.'

Peter's account reveals how perceptions of wider threats to British society were often linked with specific threats to the local community. Like most of the supporters interviewed, it was a specific local trigger which prompted Peter to approach the BNP: 'I can remember [a BNP candidate] being elected over in Halifax. It was following his election, really, that I actually looked up BNP on the website.' The strong performance led him to reassess his views of the party: 'That's what actually made me think, oh, there's some credibility there if they've got a councillor elected. That's what made me make some enquiries and that's what really got the ball rolling.' For Peter, joining the BNP offered an opportunity to take action against the perceived threats posed by immigration and rising diversity, though in particular the Muslim community in his local area. This motivation became particularly evident toward the end of the interview, when he was asked what being involved in politics means to him personally: 'I feel that I'm doing my bit to try and hold on to our culture, our religions within this country. I also believe that without any change, in 20 years' time we'll be looking at another Islamic state. It scares me that, it scares me.'

Enacting change: 'If this is what we've got to do to affect things, then so be it'

Simon was born and raised in Brunswick, a former stronghold of the manufacturing industry in Pennine Lancashire. Like most BNP supporters, he left school immediately after sitting his O-levels: 'Though I wanted to stay on and do A-levels the pressure was really on to go out and get a job and help with the family finances.' His town is a traditional heartland of the Labour Party, which in more recent years has struggled with the collapse of traditional industries and the onset of deprivation. Amid this decline, toward the end of the 1990s the council came under criticism from local Independent politicians who claimed it was awarding the bulk of regeneration grants from the government to Muslim communities. While the challenge would not last, the BNP soon filled the vacuum and began polling strongly in elections.

It was also in the late-1990s when Simon, who was employed as an accountant, first approached the party after reading one of its leaflets. Simon describes his shift toward the party as being 'just a question of really responding in the only way we could to the detrimental impact of left-wing policies upon British society and the country in general'. While expressing concern over immigration, Simon also reveals his ethnic nationalist beliefs:

For me it's nature based, and I believe that, personally, I believe that we're actually hard-wired from sort of, from birth. I think we are predisposed to think and feel and behave in certain ways basically from the time that you're born. I love the countryside, I love nature, so basically that's the bedrock, the starting point from which I became interested in politics. It's a reaction to [how to] protect not just the environment but also our racial and cultural environment as well. So for me it's just a natural progression. A love of one thing leads you to want to become active in defending that, that which you love. It was just a natural progression and actual evolution of me personally getting involved in politics from a basis of really loving nature and wanting to protect what I regard as our birthright.

For Simon, involvement with the BNP offered an opportunity to protect his collective ethnic group from threatening immigrants and minority ethnic communities: 'With the transformation of society, the mainstream politicians have travelled leftwards whereas the BNP really have stood firm and said "we aren't shifting, we still believe that it's Britain for the British and there's too many coloured people coming into the country".' Simon elaborates further on his concern that immigration poses a serious threat to the position of white Britons: 'Statistics have just been broadcast that say that whites are on course to become a minority by 2050, not 2060 as was previously thought because of the rate of immigration and differences in birth-rate between the coloured races and the white race. Some people might say "so what, it doesn't matter". We happen to think it does matter.'

While Simon is concerned about wider threats to British society, he is particularly anxious over changes in his local community, and it was these which first prompted him to contact the party: 'There's an old saying, "not in my back yard" [nimby], and I don't think there's anything wrong with that. I suppose I am a nimby on a bigger scale, you know not in my back yard, not in my town.' While deeply anxious about the impact of immigration on the country, Simon was extremely dissatisfied with the response of the local Labour-dominated council to perceived threats in the local community. Describing his move toward the party, he talks about the council's decision to open a drug rehabilitation centre in the town, claims non-white employees are receiving preferential treatment and that minority ethnic communities are receiving the bulk of regeneration funding: 'I don't really want to look beyond this town when there's enough going on in this town for me to get my teeth into.'

Several other interviewees were also based in Brunswick and framed their motives in similar terms. John was also raised in the town, and in a family that had little interest in politics. Though John later grew interested in politics, his employment in the armed services prevented him from getting actively involved. When asked what later prompted him to get more involved in politics, he recalls his profound concern over the impact of immigration and asylum on British society, and desire 'to retain whatever we can of the culture that we've got in this country'.

While deeply anxious over the effects of immigration, John was also extremely dissatisfied with the existing political options: 'I didn't go through any religious conversion or anything like that. I think over a period of years, like a lot of people I'd become disenchanted with the current political parties. There's a compression of political thought into the centre. It's very difficult to see what the difference is now between the Conservative Party, the Labour Party and the Lib Dems.'

When describing why he joined the BNP in 2001, however, John shifts his attention onto the decline of the local community:

> I think the biggest problem Brunswick faced, like lots of towns in this area where you see a decline in the cotton industry, is that other industries didn't move in. This is a very, very low-pay area, and it seems that every time another manufacturing unit closes, OK you get some jobs come in but they always seem to be low-pay type jobs, you know call centres. People cannot get a foothold on the housing ladder because they just don't earn enough money.

For John, while joining the BNP marked a response to wider threats, it also offered an opportunity to enact change in his local community, as he recalled: 'I don't think any of us would be described as brilliant politicians. But, you know, we're kind of ordinary people with ordinary jobs with a belief that things need to change. If this is what we've got to do to affect things then so be it.' In similar fashion, research on supporters of alternative types of right-wing movements, such as the John Birch Society in the United States, suggests citizens often joined not in response to an overarching ideological commitment, but because participation offered an opportunity to engage in collective action and enact change.[26] The findings are also supported by research on extreme right party activists in other European states: for many, the decision to enrol was seen foremost as an opportunity to take action against perceived threats to their wider group.[27]

Local triggers: 'Maybe this party has got a future'

Clive is a former Labour voter who joined the BNP in 2000. Since joining, Clive has been appointed branch organizer and elected as a BNP councillor in his community. When asked what initially attracted him to the party, Clive pauses and then responds: 'I mean you've got a lot of, I'd not say *outsiders*, but a lot of immigration coming in and people are worried about their own culture being destroyed.' Seen from his perspective, British culture and values are being 'eroded' as a result of immigration and rising ethnic diversity:

> I am not against total immigration fully. A small amount of multiculturalism isn't bad, it's never been bad in my eyes, a small amount. But I think we've just been dwarfed with it in certain areas, and people, they don't like it. They

don't like the culture, the taking away of traditions. But again, I blame the Government for allowing it in the first place.

Over the course of several interviews, Clive elaborates on his belief that immigration is threatening British culture and ways of life: 'People say, "well why not? Why does it matter?" Well it matters a lot because people enjoy their own culture. We built up a great nation because this is what we want, we want to celebrate our own Christian festivities and be around our own Christian type of people.' While Clive is firmly opposed to immigration, he is particularly anxious about the specific threat posed by settled Muslim communities:

> You have to admire this fella from down South, some Professor. He were actually saying that they [Muslims] have two languages. In front of the camera they'll tell you this language, but behind the scenes they speak a different language. I mean you've got this thing where they say they won't be happy until they fly the flag of Islam over Westminster, and I actually believe that they want to do that, really want to Islamify Britain.

Like most BNP members and also voters, Clive is profoundly concerned about the presence of Muslims in British society. When recalling his initial motive for joining, however, his attention shifts on to the deterioration of the community: 'I mean ten or fifteen years ago you'd never have gun crime in this town, you'd never have had the drugs to the extent that have been dealt in. I lived on the Estate. We never had much on that estate; you know quite a poor estate. But everybody watched out for everybody, you had community spirit.' Set against the backdrop of community decline, Clive explains how Muslims have received preferential treatment from the local council: 'They're getting post-offices, shops, take-aways, everything. So they don't need us. The Government's way of dealing with deprived areas is by giving the biggest regeneration grants to the poorest areas. Well they're getting it every time. They're winning hands down every time. We haven't got a chance. So they're getting their houses done up, new windows, new doors, new kitchens. They're making people angry.'

Like other interviewees, Clive traces a growing drug problem in the community to Muslims: 'It is mostly Asian males that are actually . . . Muslim males that are actually dealing the drugs but we do have [our] own as well.' When retracing his steps toward the BNP, he recalls how nobody in the community appeared to be 'standing up' and confronting this particular issue: 'It's easy pickings for them [Muslims] at the moment, they don't seem to be challenged. It were saying in the paper not so many months ago, a million pounds of drugs is being transported through Leeds-Bradford airport every day. If they know that, why aren't they stopping it? Why aren't they finding the root of the problem?' It was not until a specific trigger when Clive took the decision to contact the BNP:

I obviously saw the country, how it had changed, my town, a lot of things were happening, a lot of things I didn't agree with, a lot of unfair things. So it came to a point one day when I was coming home from work, my car actually got attacked. When I contacted the police they actually turned round to me and they said 'what ethnicity was the person?' You know, we are having these problems and they're not being dealt with all because of the colour of somebody's skin. So I decided I'd contact the British National Party.

Though he first contacted the party during the John Tyndall era, Clive recalls how it appeared too extreme: 'Although I enjoyed his speech, I thought it was a very good speech, I thought to myself well I can't really see me joining this party because although, like I say, he had a good speech his views were a little bit too strong.' A few months later, and after the election of Nick Griffin, Clive attended another meeting and recalled how his view changed: 'Now within a few months of that speech, Nick Griffin stood and it was a breath of fresh air, professional, it's like he just blew people's minds away.' Like other new recruits, Clive strongly disassociates the BNP from the National Front and interwar traditions: 'How can you call me a Nazi? My grandparents were in the War. My uncle were in the War. You know, they fought for this country. For them to say something like that, I find it quite insulting. Let them have their say because I'm sure I'll have the last laugh somewhere down the road.'

Like those members above, most interviewees described approaching the BNP in response to their views that immigration and culturally distinct minority groups are threatening British society, but also dissatisfaction with the failure of the main parties to deliver an adequate response to these threats. These perceptions of threat were often 'triggered' by specific events or experiences at the local level, such as Clive's experience with crime and the police.

Similar findings appear in research on the drivers of racially motivated hostility in other Western democracies, which highlight the importance of changes in the local neighbourhood. Whether stemming from immigration or growing minority ethnic communities, these changes often acted as a 'catalyst for action' that pushed white residents into an exclusionary attempt to defend resources and territory which they associated with their collective group.[28] For BNP members, these triggers took various forms: coverage of immigration in local media; experiencing crime; hearing about initiatives launched by the council; or a strong performance by the BNP in local elections.[29] Another example is Jim, who traced his decision to join the BNP to a trigger in local elections: 'What shook me out of my slumbers as it were was the May 2003 local council elections when the BNP did rather well. They came within 100 votes of success in a number of wards including the one that I happened to be in. When I saw they'd actually come that close, I thought "well maybe this party has got a future and it's not just a wasted vote".'

Sally similarly recalled how her decision followed a specific event, in this case hearing news that Muslim businessmen planned to open a shop opposite her own business. While attempting to protect her own interests, she explained how joining the BNP offered an opportunity to work for the interests of the local white community: 'The BNP seemed to care for the people in Brunswick,' she explained. For Sally, the party was a useful vehicle through which she could 'do something' for herself and also the local community. George similarly described his membership of the party as enabling him 'to make progress and do something for the town, something for the ordinary white people who were being put down'. As above, this perceived opportunity to take action against potential threats did not become clear until a strong performance by the BNP in elections: 'Now I'd had nothing to do with them up until then [the election of a BNP councillor]. Then I thought: "Well if these people, the British National Party, instead of being agitators on the outside were now looking like as though they actually wanted to *do* something, something important for the town . . ." So I offered my services to them.'

These interviews provide rich insight into the factors which initially 'pushed' some citizens to approach and join the BNP. At the outset, and building on findings in previous chapters, it was suggested that the racial threat model provides a particularly useful framework for understanding these motivations. This sense of threat has variously been traced to perceptions of competition between individuals or groups over material resources, or more symbolic concerns over threats to culture, values and ways of life. While competition over resources was clearly important, the findings suggest most members approached the BNP in response to the perceived cultural threat posed by immigration and Muslim communities. For several joiners, the decision followed a sense that immigrants and minority ethnic groups were posing a realistic threat to economic resources. For most, however, the decision followed a profound sense of anxiety over the way in which immigrants and Muslims are threatening British values, culture, and ways of life. As others note, when citizens perceive 'that their national community is somehow threatened, many feel a strong desire – or can be led to feel a strong desire – to defend what they believe to be their way of life'.[30] For these members, rather than joining to express their hostility to immigration, most framed their involvement with the BNP as an opportunity to 'take action' against these threats, and 'do something' for white Britons, both in wider society and in their local community. More often than not, the actual decision to join was triggered by a specific event or experience which drew attention to the 'threat'.

While we have explored the initial motives driving some citizens toward the extreme right, these push factors only take us so far. In particular, they tell us little about how the party attempts to 'pull' members into active participation and sustain their loyalty over the longer terms. One way in which political parties and social movements fulfil this task is by supplying followers with a convincing and compelling rationale for getting active. The next chapter turns to the supply-side of this recruitment process.

8

SUSTAINING COMMITMENT
Why stay?

> We are not a political party like the establishment parties whose success or failure merely adds to the CV of the career politicians that compose them. Success or failure for us will mean more than the difference between whether or not we have cheaper butter or slightly higher old age pensions. Success or failure for us means the difference between the survival or destruction of our people and culture.[1]

One puzzle familiar to most political parties is how to convince their passive members to become committed activists. Individuals rarely join a party outright. Instead, they first tend to offer a small level of commitment, such as signing a petition, donating some money or helping with a particular campaign. As discussed in the last chapter, most BNP members who were interviewed traced their initial motive to a sense of threat, and saw involvement with the party as an opportunity to take action against these threats in the local community. The challenge which faces parties is how to convince these initial supporters to become and remain loyal activists.

Framing and 'vocabularies of motive'

Parties pursue various strategies in an attempt to cultivate bonds of loyalty among their followers. Perhaps the most important is providing members with incentives for getting actively involved, as one political scientist points out: 'Research shows that members need incentives if they are to participate, and cheer-leading is not an adequate incentive to promote their involvement.'[2] Without incentives, supporters might as well stay in their armchairs and 'free ride' on the efforts of others who *are* prepared to get out and slog the streets.[3] In the world of party politics, these incentives are often referred to as 'selective incentives', as they are benefits which are only available to those who actually get involved. Selective incentives, such as a salary or realistic prospect of being elected to Parliament, encourage members to overlook the costs of involvement, such as time, energy and money.

Aside from these 'hard' incentives, however, it has also been shown that citizens respond to other types of incentives, such as feelings of individual and group efficacy (i.e. a feeling that they or the party can make a difference), a sense of moral obligation and a desire to work not only for themselves but also the interests of a wider group. As others point out, the basic idea behind these 'collective incentives' is that 'individuals can put themselves in the place of the group, and think about the group welfare rather than just their own individual welfare'.[4] For example, a party might encourage members to get active by encouraging them to look beyond their own well-being and consider how, collectively, they might achieve benefits for a wider group, whether a social class, region or race.[5]

Unlike established mainstream parties, however, the persuasive powers of minor parties appear more limited. Fringe parties often lack the money and machinery required to offer those hard incentives above. They might also struggle to convince supporters that their cause is serious enough to warrant their active participation, and that they can really 'make a difference'. Aside from these challenges, extremist parties also face the additional hurdle of having to persuade supporters to overlook the often serious costs which accompany active involvement. As noted in the last chapter, there appear to be more good reasons to steer clear of extreme right parties like the BNP than there are to sign up.

One way in which parties, and also social movements, attempt to overcome these problems is by developing 'collection action frames'. These socially constructed frames organize the experiences and perceptions of supporters, shaping how they define particular situations and conditions.[6] By developing frames, parties attempt to interpret and give meaning to events and happenings in the wider world in a way that is designed to motivate their supporters to get actively involved. Frames render events or experiences meaningful; they simplify and condense often complex trends in society; and they cultivate beliefs and meanings among supporters which legitimize their cause and inspire them to become active.[7]

This framing activity typically involves three main elements. First, much like a medical doctor, parties develop frames which provide supporters with a *diagnosis* of perceived problems in society, and attribute blame for these problems to other actors in society. Second, also like a doctor, these frames offer a *prognosis* in terms of what should be done to ameliorate the problems in society. As we have seen, in the world of the extreme right the perceived problems include immigration, Muslim communities and the economic and cultural threats they pose to white Britons. In response to this diagnosis, the extreme right advocates that the source of the threat is either reduced in size, by halting immigration, or removed from society altogether, by enacting a policy of repatriation.

If they are to convince their supporters to get active, however, parties will need to offer more than a diagnosis and prognosis. To return to the analogy above, while you might agree with your doctor that smoking cigarettes or drinking alcohol is having a negative impact on your health, this consensus may be insufficient to galvanize you into changing your lifestyle. It is similarly the case in politics, as one academic points out: 'Just because people agree with a movement's contention that a problem exists, does not guarantee that they will drop everything else in their lives and work on alleviating the problem.'[8] What is also required is a third element, namely a convincing and compelling rationale for becoming politically active to deal with 'the problem'.

One way in which parties fulfil this third task is by cultivating 'vocabularies of motive', which give supporters a specific call to arms for taking action. These vocabularies provide them with compelling reasons for becoming an activist, and convincing answers to questions such as 'why become active?' and 'will my actions actually make a difference?'[9] For these reasons, they are crucial to understanding how movements pull their supporters into active involvement.

While they are often delivered by leaders, these vocabularies are continually nurtured and disseminated through interaction between the grassroots and the party. Whether at events, campaigns or through literature, members continually discuss and share ideas about problems in society, how they should be resolved and why they decided to become involved to address them. The importance of this process was underscored by one recruit when asked why he has stayed involved with the BNP: 'There are lots of people who join the party for different reasons, but I suppose I came into the party for the reason I already described. But when I came in, I learned about other problems, and heard other opinions. I found that I agreed with most of them and that I adopted some of them as my concerns. We learn from each other.'

In order for these motivational vocabularies to be effective, they must resonate with the initial concerns of supporters and be sufficiently compelling to inspire their active loyalty. In particular, it has been argued that the extent to which vocabularies resonate among supporters will depend on three conditions: whether they draw on beliefs, traditions, myths and values that are culturally relevant; whether they resonate with the everyday experiences and concerns of supporters; and whether they are delivered alongside evidence which convinces supporters they are not fighting a 'lost cause'.[10] If a movement proves able to construct a set of vocabularies which are compelling and convincing, then they are likely to become an integral part of its internal culture.

The BNP: sustaining commitment to the cause

The BNP is keenly aware of the need to provide its members with incentives for becoming active. In an attempt to strengthen a sense of collective identity and loyalty among the grassroots, in recent years it has established an annual festival, conference, record label, trade union and Voting Membership scheme which rewards the most active supporters with some influence over party affairs. At the same time, however, it also lacks the resources required to invest heavily in these initiatives (see Chapter 4).

As part of its attempt to sustain the loyalty of followers, the party also devotes considerable effort to cultivating a specific set of motivational vocabularies. The party has emphasized the importance of providing supporters with a specific rationale for joining and remaining involved at various points in its history. During the early years, for example, the leadership identified one of its main tasks as cultivating belief among members in 'ideas of mighty force', which were capable of inspiring the 'strongest commitment of the strongest spirits'.[11] As its founder made clear, these interpretive techniques were considered of equal if not more importance than material resources:

> In the development of a political movement, psychological factors play a very powerful part. It is not as if we are constructing a building where purely material ingredients are called for. Foundation-stones, frames, bricks and mortar – these are mere inanimate objects with no thoughts or emotions of their own . . . With human beings, the structure has to be kept together by an appeal to forces of the mind and spirit. Here, as with the mustering and the whole enterprise: an objective, a target, a goal upon which minds and hopes are concentrated. If such a thing is lacking, there is boredom, demoralisation, and drift – with the compounding danger that . . . the whole enterprise will end in large-scale desertion.[12]

The party has since continued to stress the importance of this task. Before his election as leader, Nick Griffin called for greater attention to be devoted to providing members with 'a sense of purpose, a sense of belonging and a sense of destiny', and argued the party should 'hone these techniques to near perfection' to prevent followers from joining rival groups, such as religious cults.[13] As he continued, the party should 'satisfy the subconscious needs which could otherwise lead our people up religious dead ends'.[14] Since becoming leader, Griffin has elaborated on these ideas. During the 2005 general election, he identified the 'secret X-factor' to building a successful party as being the development of 'a set of compelling ideas and images that inspire a devoted membership'.[15] These ideas, he explained, would need to build on the initial motivations which first pushed some citizens to approach and join the party:

> Lack of ideological understanding among some local officials and key activists would . . . leave them vulnerable to a breakdown in their commitment . . . Quite simply, if someone is motivated to be involved in the BNP primarily by the fact that the presence of asylum seekers of Islamic gangs in their area has caused problems for their family or devalued their house, they are hardly well-placed to maintain their loyalty to the Cause if by doing so they find themselves jailed as prisoners of conscience, unable to see their children or pay the mortgage . . . Ideology is the X-factor which allows them to spend years locked in cells and come out even more committed to the Cause than when they went in.[16]

Griffin emphasized the importance of constructing a compelling rationale for taking action by comparing loyalist and republican groups in Northern Ireland. He criticized the former for having recruited supporters along reactionary lines, failing to inculcate them with a powerful enough motive, and leaving them susceptible to breakdown, collaboration, criminality and religious conversion. On the contrary, republicanism was praised as an exemplar of how to cultivate among followers strong bonds of loyalty, strict discipline, revolutionary fervour and a capacity for self-sacrifice.[17]

These ideas were set out in internal BNP literature, which is the main vehicle through which the party attempts to cultivate vocabularies of motive. The magazine, *Identity*, is designed primarily for an internal audience of members and activists, and is considered by Griffin the key resource for communicating messages to the grassroots, as he explains: 'It's a constant cycle. You can't just put it into print once and forget about it. You have to reiterate it a few months down the line. Not so much for trying to win over the old hands; you've either won them over, or they've accepted something they don't like, or they don't give a toss or they're away with the fairies. It's the new people, and there's a constant influx, you have to be constantly explaining to them hence the repetition.'[18] Analyses of the magazine and interviews with supporters suggest that four vocabularies are particularly important – a vocabulary of: survivalism; urgency; collective efficacy; and moral obligation.[19]

The severity of the problem: survivalism

During the 2010 general election, the BNP delivered the following message to supporters: 'At current immigration and birth rates, indigenous British people are set to become a minority well within 50 years. This will result in the extinction of the British people, culture, heritage and identity.'[20] The vocabulary of survivalism was similarly evident at the previous general election in 2005, when the party warned Britons that their country's 'very existence is threatened by immigration'.[21]

Political movements often attempt to persuade their supporters to get active by emphasizing the severity of perceived problems in society. Aside from ideological reasons, this is also because members are unlikely to throw themselves into action unless they consider the issue critically important. Therefore, movements will often attempt to emphasize the severity of the problem and amplify the initial concerns of their supporters 'in such a way that their audiences are persuaded that any response other than collective action is unreasonable'.[22] As detailed in the last chapter, most interviewees traced their initial motive for joining the BNP to threatening out-groups. More often than not, these feelings of threat were triggered by a specific event or experience in the local community, which heightened anxiety over the presence of 'threatening' out-groups. One way in which the BNP attempts to amplify these initial concerns and galvanize supporters into action is by framing immigrants and culturally distinct groups as threatening not only resources and values, but the very survival of white Britons.

Through this vocabulary, initial anxieties over immigrants and Muslims are conflated into a grander 'clash of civilizations' and struggle for racial survival. To underscore the severity of the threat, the vocabulary is frequently compelling and draws on apocalyptic themes, or what one academic terms 'doomsday framings'.[23] It is reflected in the persistent claim that immigrants, multiculturalism and variations in birth rates across different groups have thrust white Britons into a battle against racial extinction. One example is an article which predicts a 'convergence of catastrophes'. Supporters are warned that declining stocks of oil 'raises the spectre of a civilisational collapse at the worst, or of major economic and social dislocation at the best'. They are then informed that rising oil costs and other societal trends will soon produce 'political instability, Islamic radicalisation, and pressure for mass immigration to the world's lifeboat – our relatively rich West'. In conclusion, supporters are warned that the 'convergence of catastrophes' will have a greater impact on Western democracies than the First World War, deadly flu pandemic, Bolshevik revolution and 1930s depression combined.[24]

At other times, the party predicts the collapse of the United States between 2012 and 2018, water shortages and environmental catastrophes which will produce 'resource wars' in developing states. These resource conflicts will create 'waves of mass immigration that threaten to swamp the West like the fifth-century Roman Empire facing the Goths and the Vandals'. Meanwhile, the European continent will implode as a result of expanding Muslim communities and 'its insane Eurabia project'.[25] In Britain, rapidly expanding immigrant ghettos will fuel the proliferation of lawless areas and white Britons will find themselves dispossessed, deculturalized and forcibly transformed into a mongrel society.[26] In the aftermath of the terrorist attacks in London in 2005, supporters were similarly warned that, as Enoch Powell had predicted some four decades earlier, British rivers will soon 'foam with blood'.[27]

This survivalist discourse is similarly apparent in claims that immigration and multiculturalism will soon produce 'dangerous internal ethnic divisions' and 'brutal and bloody wars of ethnic cleansing', similar to conflicts seen in Yugoslavia and Rwanda.[28] Anxieties in local communities over the distribution of resources will soon lead to a conflict not 'between mismatched armies and militias in distant deserts, but between angry neighbours on familiar streets'.[29] In this way, various concerns which initially pushed some citizens toward the party are linked to the survivalist struggle. On joining the party, supporters concerned about asylum are informed that the policy is 'not about providing a safe haven from persecution' but is 'one more stratagem for destroying white Anglo-Saxon-Celtic Britain'.[30] Asylum-seekers are framed as the greatest threat to Britain since the possible German invasion in 1940, only 'the invaders did not come wearing steel helmets and jackboots but waving bits of paper saying "British subjects" and later chanting the mantra of "Asylum, Asylum" '.[31]

These examples reflect the way in which survivalism permeates the internal world of the BNP: grassroots members are warned that unless they become active they will 'surely die'; the party attributes its rising support in elections to Britons who have grasped the seriousness of the threat of extinction; party literature is presented as a tool in the resistance against 'genocidal pressures'; and suggested reading includes texts such as *March of the Titans*, which links the 'destruction' of white civilization to immigration.[32] These survivalist themes were similarly stressed by the National Front, which encouraged supporters to watch films like *Survival Ethics*, which outlined the requirements for 'racial survival'.[33] Some two decades later, the continuation of this tradition was evident in predictions of 'a timebomb of ethnic and religious mayhem', 'open racial gang warfare' and 'a struggle for control of the streets'.[34] Like the old NF, the BNP frames its supporters as the only 'resistance' to the threat of extinction, and itself as the only party in British politics which is capable of saving white Britons.[35]

When asked what sustains their commitment to the BNP, most of the activists who were interviewed referenced the vocabulary of survivalism. In several interviews, the theme was prominent throughout. One example is Chris, a 52-year-old organizer who was previously active in the NF. Typical of most, Chris framed his participation in the BNP not simply as a quest to oppose immigrants, but as part of an instrumental attempt to ensure the survival of white Britons: 'It's come to me down to a very simple, fundamental basic principal which is survival ... I realised over a period of time that ultimately, what we're fighting for is our very existence and survival as a race, as a nation, as a culture which I would defend for everybody.'

Like most interviewees, when explaining what sustains his political activism, Chris draws attention to the importance of his ethnic nationalist beliefs: 'You may not be able to develop arguments, but the fact is this is your ancestral homeland. We are a distinct race and culture; we've been here for a very long time. How anyone can argue with that I don't know.' At various points during several interviews, Chris returned unprompted to the theme of survivalism: 'Although some people might see it as a clash of civilizations, I don't. It's just pure survival and preservation.' He elaborates when asked why he decided to become active in the party:

> At the end of the day it's survival. The bottom line here is survival, you know, your very existence, your survival as an entity, as a race, as a culture, a nation, it's survival, we are fighting for our very survival. We are being ethnically cleansed by force of numbers. I don't believe it's coincidence but that's a matter of debate whether what is actually happening in our country today is by design or by ignorance ... I tend to think that it is a conspiracy but I really hope that it isn't.

As hinted above, Chris traces the threat to his collective group to conspiratorial forces: 'It's essentially communism. Bearing in mind that the present [New Labour] Cabinet, at one time were in the Communist parties and they haven't changed. They are neo-Marxists who seek to establish a New World Order and total state control.' Although only a handful of interviewees hinted at their belief in conspiracy theories, Chris returned to the topic when discussing his family background:

> I can remember a time when I lived in Kent when if a Black person or Asian person walked down the street, everyone would stop, turn and look. Of course, this was before mass immigration got totally out of control to the point where it is now, *and it is totally out of control* [his emphasis] . . . I still say to people, 'look, you do not need to apologise for your existence. Do not allow the enemy to put us on the defensive'. We should be putting *them* on the defensive. It is *they* who are undermining and destroying our culture and our country, trying to re-mould us in their world-view, you know New World Order and all this.

Activists who did reference conspiracy theories almost always focused on the recent Labour Government. Sam, for example, expressed his view that the entire British 'establishment' from trade unions to political parties is 'all one and the same party' and described Labour as 'a completely new Communist Party attaching itself to the old Labour movement'. Pam similarly drew a distinction between the BNP and the 'one world party which all the others seem to be', and Sally expressed her belief that the main parties in British politics seek to represent 'globalist multi-cultural ideals'. Though John claimed he rejects the idea of 'a little cell of Marxists plotting in a basement in Hackney to do us all down', he continued to express his anxiety over a more 'diffuse acceptance of a certain unconsciously neo-Marxist, sub-Gramscian agenda which people aren't even aware of'.

While conspiracy theories were only rarely referenced, virtually every activist cited survivalism. Most framed their active involvement as an opportunity to take action and fight for the survival of the collective white British community. Reflective of most was Neil, who saw his involvement as an attempt to avoid 'ethnic conflict' and 'to do all in my power to try and prevent my fellow British people . . . from being killed and exploited'. When asked what sustains his commitment to the BNP, another activist similarly explained:

> One of the things I often say to people is that, you know, people go on about saving the whale, saving the seal, or making sure the American Indian way of life is maintained, but when you talk about maintaining the traditional way of life of the white British person, people look at you as though that's a racist thing to say but I don't see any difference really.

Most did not view their involvement with the BNP as a conventional form of political participation, or as an attempt to influence policy and enter public office. Rather, most presented their active involvement as a quest to ensure the survival of white Britons. These longer-term motivations were frequently contrasted with those of mainstream party supporters, who were often perceived as unable or unwilling to defend white Britons from a forthcoming and apocalyptic-style conflict. One example was Val when asked why she switched her active support for the UK Independence Party (UKIP) to the BNP: 'This isn't going to be solved politically. I will tell you what's going to happen. You're gonna lose your country, you're gonna lose your life.'

The interviews also reveal the way in which activists often appropriated the party's claim that community-level tensions between groups will soon escalate into a race war. In several cases, activists hinted at their belief in a forthcoming conflict, and framed their active participation in the BNP as the only means through which they can prepare. When asked what drives his commitment, one local organizer responded: 'Well, people always used to say to me that there'll be like a *war*, a civil war in this country. I used to think "yeah maybe there will", but then I think they're a little bit naïve. But now the more and more I think about it, if things don't change maybe there will be. I think there could be, I hope there isn't, but I think there could be.' Another activist similarly explained: 'Nobody *saw* 9/11, nobody *saw* 7/7 the day before. We probably won't see the beginning of the clash of civilizations or recognize it. It could be happening now. If the apocalypse is happening we probably wouldn't know about it until it's too late. Our worry as the BNP is that we might miss the beginning of the war because nobody saw it coming and was ready for it.'

Similar to these views, others expressed their belief that Britain was being deliberately 'Balkanized', and that the mainstream parties are deliberately weakening white Britons by separating them into different parts of the country. Typical of most was one organizer who pointed toward urban disturbances in Australia and Paris as evidence that members of different groups in Britain will soon be 'taking to the streets'. Another expressed a similar view when explaining why she decided to become an activist:

> I know what the end product is. If you can get enough people out on the streets fighting, the Islamics fighting the Jews, fighting the Poles, like in Northern Ireland you'll get worn out and they'll say this can't go on. They say 'this is what we're going to do: this lot can have the West Midlands and the East Midlands; and this lot here can have the South East'. The British people will end up, half of them down the south and the other half up the north. We're finished. The nation is a powerful thing, and they are destroying the nation all over the world. They did it in Bosnia and Yugoslavia with tanks and guns, they're doing it in Iraq and they're doing it here shuffling bits of paper around.

The need to take action: urgency

During one election in 2010, the BNP issued the following warning to supporters: 'Britain's existence is in grave peril, threatened by immigration and multiculturalism. In the absence of urgent action, we, the indigenous British people, will be

reduced to minority status in our own ancestral homeland within two generations.'
It then continued to detail the percentage of the British population which is non-
white, birth rate figures among settled minority groups, the percentage of pupils in
primary schools who are of 'Third World origin', and the number of languages
spoken in schools in London.[36]

If a movement is to persuade its supporters to become active, then it must not
only emphasize the seriousness of problems in society, but also that they require
urgent and radical action. Research on nuclear disarmament movements, for
example, reveals how they compelled supporters to become active by reiterating
statistics about the growing size of nuclear arsenals.[37] Across Europe, extreme
right parties similarly underscore the urgency of the situation by drawing on
statistics, although these focus on different trends in society. The extreme right
often seeks to mobilize active support by emphasizing the rapid growth of minority
ethnic communities and claiming that disproportionately high birth rates among
these groups not only threaten the survival of the in-group but also require urgent
action. One study of supporters of the French National Front (FN), for example,
suggested that 95 per cent agree that 'immigrant women's high fertility endangers
French national identity'.[38]

The BNP similarly cultivates a vocabulary of urgency among its supporters,
claiming urgent action is required to protect white Britons from threatening
out-groups and their high birth rates: 'On current demographic trends we, the
native British people, will be an ethnic minority in our own country within
60 years. By 2020, an extra 5–7 million immigrants will have entered Britain,
whilst immigrant communities already resident here are having more children
than the indigenous British people.'[39] In fact, the vocabulary is evident in virtually
every edition of the party magazine, which regularly features data on the growth
of settled minority ethnic groups: one article warns supporters that in 'less than
80 years white people have gone from being 17% of the world population to 7%.
Extinction is staring us in the face'; another warns them that the number of
foreigners in London will soon exceed the number of white Britons, and within
two decades the latter will become a minority in cities such as Birmingham,
Manchester and Leicester. By 2060, 'the indigenous British will be a minority in
their own country'.[40]

It is against this backdrop that the party underscores the necessity of taking
urgent action. Members are warned they are fast approaching 'the last 20 years in
which present trends can be reversed and all we hold dear preserved', that the
'point of no return' will arrive sometime before 2060, and 'realistically we have
no more than 20 years to avoid fighting and losing a civil war'.[41] This vocabulary
is focused heavily on the expanding presence of settled Muslim communities. As
one article explains, because Muslims 'believe' in having large families it is only
a question of time until they 'achieve their conquest demographically'.[42] Another
titled 'whites must breed or face extinction' warns followers that immigrants will
soon be 'thundering into Europe', that France will become a Muslim country
within 35 years, and the rest of Europe will follow within a century.[43]

As discussed at the outset, movements often attempt to increase the resonance of their claims by citing legitimate sources. The vocabulary of urgency inside the BNP frequently includes data and extracts from external sources. One article cites school census data when claiming white Britons are 'being eliminated' and warning that 'those of us who have been forecasting that we will become a minority in these islands by 2060 need to bring that figure forward by some 30 years'.[44] Another draws on data from the Office for National Statistics (ONS) when claiming minority ethnic groups are 'growing at 15 times the rate of the white population'.[45]

In this way, by stressing urgency, the party attempts to pull supporters into active participation, for example, warning: 'Too much is at stake to just spend our time in the pub or in front of the TV. If we don't get off our backsides and do something now then one day we'll switch on the TV to find that our country no longer belongs to us and that WE are the minority.'[46] The accounts of activists reveal the way in which the vocabulary has been adopted, and used as a rationale for becoming active: Val explained that 'time is running out and I think it's running out quite rapidly'; Peter traced his participation to his view that 'without any change in 20 years' time we'll be looking at another Islamic state'; Michael explained how 'it's perfectly possible for things in my lifetime to have got to a stage where you can't turn them around'; and Clive remarked simply how there is 'not much time left'.

The theme of urgency was prominent throughout the interviews, such as one with a new recruit: 'By 2040, there's going to be twice as many people worshipping in mosques as there is in churches . . . we could be a minority in our country in 50 years' time . . . there's not much time left.' An organizer similarly linked his motive to a belief that white Britons are being 'ethnically cleansed', before asking: 'If 10 per cent of the population are ethnic and things are bad *now*, what will it be like when they're 50 per cent, 60 per cent, 70 per cent?' A fellow activist traced his activism to similar concerns:

> There's a motive particularly for nationalists in that we see that if we don't start to achieve fairly soon we'll be flogging a dead horse . . . if you look at the immigration situation into this country, the multiplication factor in the Asian population means that in not that many years' time we will be a minority and I think once you get to that point then you might as well forget it. So we've got a timeframe effectively.

Some activists directly recited arguments from party literature, such as one recruit: 'There's no force in the country that's coming along to save us all. If we don't save ourselves then no one else is going to save us. I mean, I could give you an example. One hundred years ago, Europeans were one third of the earth's population but now there's a policy called multiculturalism.' Often without prompting, others like Sam recited arguments made by the party: 'Statistics have just been broadcast that say that whites are on course to become a minority by

2050, not 2060 as was previously thought.' Asked what sustains her activism, Val responded in similar fashion: 'If you believe them, it will be 2060. The Somali birth rate in this country is 6.8; the Bangladeshi is something like 6.5; the white British birth rate is 1.54 children. So we aren't even reproducing ourselves two for two.' Like survivalism, these extracts reflect the way in which a vocabulary of urgency is integral to understanding what sustains their active commitment over the longer-term.

Emphasizing collective efficacy: resistance

While these vocabularies might seem unconvincing, to citizens joining the BNP after feeling threatened by immigrants or settled Muslim communities, and experiencing a specific event, it is possible to understand how they might resonate and inspire collective action. The vocabularies are frequently compelling and, based on the accounts of activists, convincing to citizens who first approached the party after feeling that their wider group was under threat. At the same time, however, citizens are unlikely to engage in collective action unless they perceive it has a credible prospect of delivering on their goals. As others have shown, these feelings of individual or collective efficacy – the ability to make a difference – are important motives for political activists.[47] For these reasons, movements often attempt to encourage a belief among supporters that their collective action can make a difference, a task which is especially important for minor parties.[48]

One way in which the BNP attempts to cultivate feelings of efficacy is through a vocabulary of resistance, which seeks to persuade supporters that only active involvement in 'the cause' will enable them to fulfil a historic role in resisting the extinction of their group, and reaching their 'special destiny'.[49] Writing to members following elections to the European Parliament in 2004, for example, this vocabulary was communicated as follows: 'To anyone who has recently wandered into our movement without realising this, I urge long and careful consideration of your position. The BNP is not just a political party: it is the only organisation with the understanding, the courage and the will to lead the native peoples of Britain in our version of the New Crusade that must be organised if Europe is not to sink under the Islamic yoke.'[50] Survivalist movements often portray their followers as fulfilling a pivotal role in national recovery and renewal, and it is no different in the BNP.[51] The party typically presents itself as the only revolutionary party in British politics capable of awakening apathetic white Britons from a 'nightmare of systematic and deliberate destruction'.[52] Only the party and its most active supporters are resisting the 'Islamification' of Britain, and can 'save the nation'.[53] As we shall see, one important aspect in this vocabulary is a strong emphasis on the moral obligation of supporters to participate.

One example of how these vocabularies are cultivated is an article which informs members it is their duty 'to impress upon friends, relatives, work colleagues that it is only the BNP that can do anything effective about the swamping of Britain by the Third World'.[54] Another explains that only active support will enable members to undertake the 'greatest task', which 'is that of saving our race and nation'.[55] This opportunity to resist threatening out-groups and save the wider group is often presented as a stark choice. Either activists assume 'the burden of saving our civilization', or they and their loved ones face racial extinction: 'Your real choice – the only one, apart from having children, that is really going to count for something . . . is to do the best you can to be a player, rather than a spectator, in the long march of sacrifice, persecution and intelligently applied dedication which is the only thing that can save all that we hold dear.'[56]

Political movements of various types often frame their campaigns in terms of resistance. As one sociologist points out, social movements often think and talk in terms of external threats, of ways of life being in danger, of territory and rights needing defence, and of cherished values being assaulted.[57] Unlike other movements, however, in the BNP the vocabulary of resistance is often presented in militaristic terms. During its infancy, the party often presented itself as operating amid 'battle conditions' and as 'an army fighting for its survival'. Recruits were encouraged to adopt a 'soldierly spirit and ethos', and consider themselves 'engaged in a war'.[58] In more recent years, the party has continued this militaristic tradition, for example, telling supporters they are engaged in a 'war without uniforms' and 'a war for our survival as a people'.[59]

These claims often draw heavily on myths, traditions and symbols in national culture. Increasingly, activists are associated with the 'British spirit', the 'spirit of the Blitz' and other historical examples of British resistance against 'foreign invaders'. They are portrayed as the heirs to historical figures such as Nelson, and 'a million and more brave lads who were killed or maimed fighting in every battle to see off every would-be foreign invader'.[60] At other times, they are described as the '*de facto* government of the Free British fighting a war against the forces of captive Britain', and compared to 'knightly crusaders' who resisted the 'Islamic cult' at the battle of Tours in 732.[61] Only by becoming active can members join the crusade and assume a historic role in the 'first stages in the Last Battle'.[62] Another strategy is to contrast heroic activists with apathetic members of the public; while activists are 'lions', the latter are 'sheep waiting to be prodded'.[63] These comparisons are important as they encourage individuals to identify positively with a particular group while strengthening feelings of efficacy.[64]

Most of the activists interviewed saw their involvement with the BNP as a credible opportunity to take action and resist threats to their wider group. This was apparent in the response of Jim, for example, when asked why he has remained an active supporter: 'Well, I suppose the things that are important to me are that I want to see changes in the country and there's absolutely no way that I could affect anything that goes on in this country without being active, in my opinion, in the British National Party.' Like Jim, others similarly highlighted feelings of efficacy when explaining what has kept them involved: 'There is no force in the country that's coming along to save us all. If we don't save ourselves, then no one else is going to save us.'

For most activists, only political activism on behalf of the BNP offered an opportunity to enact change: 'In the BNP, you feel like you're going somewhere, you feel like you are developing and growing . . . it just feels right, it feels that *this is the movement.*' Chris, for example, presented the party as the only vehicle in British politics through which he can take action in the survivalist struggle: 'I care about the fact that we're a country and nation with a thousand years or more of history, and it's going to be destroyed. It *will* be destroyed if we don't do something.' These feelings of efficacy and the vocabulary of resistance were evident in most of the interviews:

> Somewhere down the line there's got to be, I wouldn't say *martyrs* because it's not martyrs, but you've got to have people to stand up at the front and you've got to say 'well I'm going to challenge it and you lot follow us' . . . It's just that some people are willing to sacrifice and stand up and be counted and others, like your next door neighbour, will think it but won't actually say it.

> I'm not interested being a sort of, heroically struggling against the light or a voice crying in the wilderness. If I felt it really was a waste of time and this was running on tramlines toward a sort of Marxist future I wouldn't bother. But I do believe quite honestly that the future is going to be what we make it. I do believe we are at a crossroads.

When discussing their longer-term motives, most activists contrasted their own heroic actions with members of the public who, for example, are 'sheep who take it lying down'. Like most, Sam expressed his bewilderment at how some Britons 'can sit at home and watch Coronation Street while their country is being torn to shreds'. As he continues: 'When I hear people moaning in the pub or at the bus stop or wherever, my attitude is "what are you going to do about it?" "Oh well, what can I do about it?" they say. Well you *can* do something about it. A lot of people don't realise that they can, they don't realise the power that they've got.'

Like Sam, one organizer expressed his exasperation over the lack of response from his fellow citizens: 'You shook your head and thought these people are just mugs, they're being exploited, they don't know what's going on around them . . . If we see ourselves as doing anything, I think it's to say no there is an alternative, it's not all over, the game is not finished.' While distinguishing themselves from the public, activists also contrasted their actions with the perceived weakness of the mainstream parties, describing the latter for example as 'weak' and 'just following the crowd'. Adopting an argument long advocated by the extreme right, one recruit who joined in 2003 explained why he remains active in the party: 'The thing that's conspired against us more than anything else is we've gone soft. A Roman Emperor said I fear for our country because we've been comfortable for too long . . . We've not challenged ourselves, we've been able to sit back and we haven't really been under threat except for the Second World War . . . We've become unable to defend ourselves.'

The militaristic tradition was prominent in most interviews. After describing his active participation as 'standing up with your fellow man in a fight for the survival of this country', one activist continued: 'It's the old British fighting spirit thing which, since the end of the Second World War, seems to have disappeared . . . I don't want to make myself out to be a social hero or whatever but I do feel quite sad that there aren't more people like me who are prepared to actually do something.' Asked about the advantages of BNP membership, others also emphasized militaristic themes:

> I can fling myself into as it were, something that's the modern equivalent of war if you see what I mean and feel really that I am doing something useful. That may sound a bit extreme but I do feel that, you know, even before the [7th July 2005] bombings, for the last 40 years I've been expecting something of this sort. For the first time, one felt one could actually do something about it; one could actually do something for the country. So I see it rather as the nearest thing to volunteering for a coming war.

Moral obligation: to protect future generations

Most activists saw themselves as action-takers, tracing their longer-term motives to a desire to 'do something' against threatening groups. Like most, Michael described feeling as though he 'really wanted to do something', Val stressed the importance of 'just being able to do something' and Neil recalled feeling 'that I wanted to do something'. This perceived need to take action, however, was also often framed in moral terms. Most activists adopted what political scientist Nathan Teske describes as the 'language of no choice'. As Teske reveals in his study of political activists in the United States, for many participants the perceived need to act was 'so deep, so important, or so basic to the sense of self that the term choice does not capture or express it'.[65] The decision to get involved marked an opportunity to act in a way consistent with their inner moral convictions, and to satisfy a sense of moral obligation. For many, the decision to get active was not a choice at all.[66]

The language of no choice was similarly evident among BNP activists. Like most, when asked why she remains active in the party, Michelle explains how the alternatives are not acceptable: 'Because doing nothing is not an option.' As she continues: 'You wait for years and years thinking someone's got to do something about it, someone must see what's happening to us and someone will eventually do something about it. And then you realize that actually nobody's going to do anything about it and you feel like, got to stand up and do something about it.'

Like Michelle, most activists explained how the decision to get active was not a choice. Chris, for example, retraced his steps toward activism as follows: 'I sought out the British National Party knowing that I had to get involved. It was just something that I knew and felt that I had to, that I *must* get involved in something. I had to really; I couldn't *not* do it.' When asked whether he could ever see himself leaving the party, Bob similarly responds: 'I could probably do it tomorrow, but in a week I'd be thinking. I'd see something on the news that's not right. So who's going to do something about it? Oh, it's going to be the BNP so I'll get back involved.' Like these activists, Sally explained how she 'wouldn't be able to get up in the morning and know that I wasn't doing something'. Simon similarly explained: 'I've always regarded myself, and I still regard myself, as nothing more than a nationalist activist. It's just that if roles need to be played, and no other people will step into those roles then, you know, cometh the hour cometh the man.'

Integral to this language of no choice was a sense of moral obligation and duty. As others argue, political movements provide a setting 'in which emotions can be created or reinforced', and where the decision to become active is 'a way of saying something about oneself and one's morals, and of finding joy and pride in them'.[67] When objects of affection are threatened, feelings of moral indignation and outrage lead citizens toward a crossroads: either they resign themselves to feelings of inefficacy or, alternatively, their moral concerns are channelled into political activism. In their quest to influence this decision, movements might seek to cultivate a sense of moral obligation among their supporters to get actively involved.[68]

Through a fourth vocabulary of legacy, the BNP presents active participation as an opportunity to protect future generations. Reflective of this vocabulary is one article which informs supporters that they are the 'only people who can save this country and provide a future for the generations to come'.[69] Another informs activists that their 'trump card' is that, unlike other parties in British politics, only they are dedicated to securing 'the existence of our people and a future for our children'.[70]

This claim that only active involvement will ensure a safe and worthwhile future for their children and grandchildren appears regularly in party literature: in one article, a member of the old guard explains to members how his motive stems from a determination to fight for his grandchildren; another urges supporters to get active so they can emulate the 'struggle and sacrifice' of their ancestors; and in another, active involvement is presented as an opportunity to work for 'unborn generations of the race'.[71]

When discussing their active participation, activists frequently referenced the vocabulary of legacy by framing their involvement as a quest to protect loved ones from threats in society:

> If we don't do something about this, what are we leaving our young people? It's the next generation and the one after that and the one after. I mean my life is all downhill now innit? But I got a grandson so what am I leaving him? He might say to his mother, 'what did you do about this?' But he might say, 'I know what my grandma did about it'.

> I see everything that my ancestors had fought and died for under threat. Members of my family died fighting for the freedom of this country and their blood and toil is in the foundations of the democracy and all other institutions that we hold dear. And I think it would be the greatest betrayal to see that all going down the drain and not do anything about it.

Like these activists, Sam expressed similar views when discussing his motives for staying involved: 'You need an opposition that's worthy to bring us to back to traditions that my father, my grandfather understood. I want to hand them down to my grandsons never mind my sons and it just makes me more adamant to carry on.' The vocabulary was also evident in the account of Clive, an organizer for the BNP and father of two sons: 'We knew there was going to be some kind of legacy left because our grandparents and our great-grandfathers built a great country, made it strong. I suppose my main factor is my children. I brought them into this world and I'm watching them, thinking my god, what lies ahead for them.' Neil also drew attention to the importance of his children when discussing his activism: 'I've got two children, I've got two young daughters and I will do everything to protect them and fight for them, like I would any other person . . . I believe that these people need defending and need protecting . . . I believe I can contribute something.'

The importance of these moral concerns became particularly evident when, toward the end of the interview, activists were asked how involvement with the BNP has changed them personally. For most, the decision to become actively involved was seen as enabling them to fulfil a sense of moral obligation to their collective group. Like most, Bob responded as follows: 'I don't know. I suppose it goes back to the fact that I do feel better about myself for having made that move to put my head above the parapet and get involved and try and do something . . . At least I've stood up and said this is what I believe in and I want to try and change it.' Others similarly explained:

> To me I couldn't sit by . . . without doing something. So you know, when I'm on my deathbed at least I'll be able to say, whatever state the country's in, at least I had a go. Whereas if I'd sat back and done nothing, I'd probably be regretting it when it's my time, I'd think 'well I wish I'd have done so and so'. But at least I can perhaps put my hand on my heart now and say, for whatever involvement I had, I did give it a go and try and encourage people to get involved . . . So it makes you feel as though you're doing something about it.

The perceived sense of moral obligation was perhaps best illustrated in the account of one young recruit. When asked how involvement with the BNP has changed his life, Dean responds: '[It is] just more of a satisfaction, you know, getting something out of life, knowing that I'd contributed something, done something [different] from the majority of people who sit around and do nothing.'

Conclusions

As we saw in the last chapter, activists often framed their initial decision to approach the BNP as an attempt to protect themselves and their wider group from the 'threats' posed by immigration and culturally distinct Muslim communities.

Enrolling in the party offered an opportunity to respond to these threats, both in wider society and the local community. In this chapter, however, we have seen how the motives that initially pushed citizens into the extreme right provide an insufficient explanation for why some become and *remain* actively involved.

Also important is how the party attempts to pull them into active involvement. The motivations driving activists are not static and fixed at one point in time. Rather, they are continually cultivated and nurtured through interaction with the party and fellow members. To encourage their active loyalty, the BNP devotes considerable effort to providing them with a particular rationale for taking action. This includes a specific set of motivational vocabularies which build on the initial push factors, and provide a call to arms for taking action: they underscore the severity of the perceived problems facing white Britons, attach a sense of urgency, promote feelings of efficacy and emphasize the moral obligation to get actively involved. For the activists, only participation in the BNP offered an opportunity to take action against threatening out-groups, save white Britons from the urgent threat of racial extinction and ensure the safety of future generations. In this way, and by building on their initial grievances, the party is providing supporters with a compelling and convincing rationale in the hope of pulling them into becoming committed activists.

Clearly, there remain limitations to this study which future research might overcome. First, not all members become active and more research is needed on exploring why these collective action frames fail to resonate among some followers. Second, some members have abandoned the extreme right, and more research is needed on this process of disengagement.[72] A third additional avenue for future research concerns the possibility that these specific vocabularies which emphasize survivalism and urgency might 'trip' individual activists into violence. For instance, concerns raised by individuals who have been convicted for planning acts of terrorism include similar claims as those espoused above, such as belief in a forthcoming race/civil war, the need for urgent action and to save future generations from perceived threats. Further research is needed to shed light on this link between collective action frames, political participation and the propensity for violence.

CONCLUSIONS

Yet another false dawn?

Writing about the National Front (NF) during its heyday in the 1970s, the academic Christopher Husbands warned against an interpretation of the extreme right that subscribed to Richard Hofstadter's epigram about minor parties in America: 'Third parties are like bees: once they have stung, they die.' Instead, and after examining support for the NF among working-class communities, Husbands found it difficult to escape the conclusion that a successor party which steered clear of its political ineptitude could attract much higher levels of support.[1] Two decades after his prediction, the main offspring of the NF – the British National Party – began polling striking levels of support. While it has not matched the success of similar parties in other European democracies, the BNP has become the most successful extreme right party in British history. Since 2001, its support in general elections increased 12-fold; support in local elections jumped by a factor of 100; and membership grew more than seven-fold. While its rise has been steady rather than spectacular, the party has achieved what none of its predecessors could: a foothold in public office.

This book examined the BNP at a key moment in its almost 30-year history. It adopted an integrated approach to show how changes in the wider arena have created particularly favourable conditions for the extreme right, but also how the BNP has modified its approach in the quest for a wider breakthrough. The party could not have chosen a more promising time to launch an electoral challenge. Never before has the extreme right in Britain encountered such favourable circumstances. While several trends have contributed to this climate, the most important have been the increased importance of immigration in the public mindset and dissatisfaction with the performance of the main parties on this issue.

Particularly since the late 1990s, a striking increase in public anxiety over immigration and rising ethno-cultural diversity has created a more receptive audience for parties which campaign against immigrants and minority ethnic groups. Though immigration first climbed the list of salient public concerns in the late 1960s and 1970s, over the next two decades its importance declined and the issue largely fell off the agenda. It was not until the early years of the twenty-first century when immigration once again emerged as a top priority for Britons.

At this time, most citizens agreed that immigration was one of the most important issues facing the country and reached the same conclusion about how their political representatives should respond: they should reduce the number of immigrants. A significant portion of the population went further by expressing profound concern and scepticism over the impact of immigrants on public services, society and ways of life. Unlike previous decades, the increased salience of immigration also formed part of a wider 'new security agenda' in British politics which, by 2005, was just as important in the public mindset as more traditional issues like public services.[2] As these issues became more important, there also emerged evidence of public anxiety over settled Muslim communities. Amid those trends above, it represented yet another opportunity for the extreme right to rally Britons feeling threatened by the presence of culturally distinct minority groups.

In the political arena, these opportunities have been reinforced by significant levels of dissatisfaction among the electorate over the perceived failure of recent governments and the main parties to deliver a competent response to their concerns over immigration. This is not simply protest politics. Rather, it concerns a perception among some citizens that the main parties are unwilling or unable to deliver an adequate performance on issues about which they care deeply. As large numbers of Britons became anxious over immigration and its effects, majorities also rejected the suggestion that the government had immigration under control, was making progress in this area or was simply being open and honest about the number of immigrants entering the country.

Underlying these more immediate opportunities are deeper trends which have been working in favour of small challenger parties: the continued erosion of bonds between citizens and the political mainstream; a perception among voters that there exists little difference between the two main parties; a reluctance to turn out in elections or join parties; and increasingly volatile voters who are guided more strongly by their attitudes toward issues than partisan loyalties. As elsewhere in Europe, these trends cultivated potential support for parties which launch populist attacks against the 'old gang parties' and appeal to politically dissatisfied citizens, or whom the BNP describes as the 'silent majority'.

When seen as a whole, these changes have produced a particularly favourable climate for parties which aim to attract citizens who feel threatened by immigration and rising diversity, and dissatisfied with the existing political options. In fact, and as we saw in Chapter 5, these two sets of attitudes – anti-immigrant hostility and political dissatisfaction – are the two most important drivers of support for the BNP in elections.

Unlike its predecessors, the BNP launched a more concerted effort to take advantage of these changes. The British extreme right had never invested seriously in electoral politics. Few resources were devoted to developing an electoral strategy, and there was a reluctance to experiment with alternative ways of mobilizing support. Since 1999, however, and under a new leader, the BNP shifted its strategy from one that was focused on building an identity in the public mindset to one that prioritizes the quest for votes. This has entailed increasing its presence in elections, expanding its organization, and extending its reach beyond its core base. Referred to as 'modernization', the strategy holds its roots in community-based campaigns in the inner East End, but gathered pace following the rise of similar and far more successful parties elsewhere in Europe.

The BNP has attempted to rally Britons by downplaying its toxic brand. While large sections of the population are concerned over immigration and are distrustful of the main parties, few Britons have been willing to endorse the extreme right's traditional message of biological racism, anti-Semitism and anti-democratic appeals. In its attempt to detoxify the brand, the BNP has put stronger emphasis on the cultural (rather than racial) threats posed by immigration and minority ethnic groups; adopted a populist (but not overtly anti-democratic) strategy; and sought to circumvent the barriers of the electoral system and its negative image by replacing confrontational tactics with community-based activism. In this way, it hoped to rally Britons who previously might not have supported the extreme right, but who are deeply concerned over immigration and extremely dissatisfied with the response of the main parties on this issue.

The party is not active across the country, but where it has managed to establish a presence its branches are instructed to focus on local elections and embed their campaigns in community issues. Similar to the pavement politics of the Liberal Democrats, the party attempted a breakthrough by concentrating scarce resources on building credibility and bastions of support in specific parts of the country. The search for votes also meant changes to the way in which the party is organized, and an attempt to abandon its beginnings as 'just a little East London party with a couple of odds and sods'.[3] Its infrastructure, membership and electoral support remain heavily concentrated in areas where the extreme right was active some three decades ago, mainly the Midlands and, to a lesser extent, London and its surrounding areas. But its grassroots organization has also experienced significant growth and expanded into the North West and Yorkshire regions. Within these areas, the BNP has polled strongest in deprived districts, where education levels are low and there are large Muslim communities.

However, although wider conditions are favourable, and the BNP has attracted record levels of support, it has continually struggled to realize its potential. Despite operating amid trends which are evident across many European democracies, and which have given birth to similar but far more successful parties, by European standards the BNP remains a failure. Unlike its more successful continental cousins, it has not exercised real power. It has failed to achieve parliamentary representation, or even finish second in a constituency election. It might have captured a few dozen councillors, but it has never controlled a council. The attempt to build a 'modernized' and mainstream BNP, it seems, has failed. For many observers and academics, the story of the British extreme right has not changed: it remains primarily a story about failure.

Clearly, one important factor in the party's limited success has been the British electoral system, which penalizes minor parties and discourages citizens from supporting them in elections. This conventional wisdom, however, often fails to account for evidence that supporters of the extreme right are not influenced strongly by their institutional context. It suggests that either they are unfamiliar with the mechanics of their particular system, or they simply do not care that their votes may be 'wasted'.[4] Even in Britain, BNP candidates have polled strongly in several seats despite little realistic prospect of entering Parliament. Arguments that focus only on the electoral system also fail to explain why the extreme right in Britain has not polled stronger in 'second order' elections, which have more proportional arrangements. The varying fortunes of extreme right parties across a range of different systems in Europe suggests that while the formal rules of engagement are important, they are only one part of the story.

The argument put forward in this book is that the BNP's failure to realize its potential and achieve a breakthrough owes more to its origins. Unlike similar parties on the continent, the BNP is anchored in an overtly extremist and some-times violent tradition of racial nationalism. This tradition is emblematic of what Elisabeth Carter describes as the 'neo-Nazi' tradition within the larger family of European extreme right parties: a tradition which is defined by its biological racism, anti-Semitism, radical xenophobia and hostility toward democracy, parliamentarianism and pluralism.[5] As with other movements in Europe which hold their roots in this tradition, the extreme right in Britain has persistently failed in its quest to escape from the margins of the system.

This was first revealed in the record of the NF which, despite opportunities, proved unable to convince Britons it was a legitimate player in the democratic process. Though a large portion of the electorate was anxious over immigration, most voters were unwilling to endorse the NF's claims of racial supremacism, Jewish-led conspiracies, hints at the need to overthrow democracy and political violence. A large reservoir of potential supporters remained beyond its grasp, and so the NF was instead forced to rely on smaller rumps of support from young, skilled workers in deprived urban areas in the Midlands and London's East End, and who lived in close proximity to immigrant communities.

While the NF soon faded it left an indelible print on its successor. The BNP quickly became a bastion of inexperienced ex-NF activists, who had little desire to abandon or revise the racial nationalist tradition. Disillusioned with their failure to sustain a challenge when confronted with Thatcherism, and faced with a less propitious climate, they withdrew the BNP from elections, relied heavily on the extremist fringe for volunteers, and returned to confrontational tactics. Lacking the resources or inclination to commit to elections, the BNP appeared more street gang than political party. Continuity with the legacy of history reinforced its stigma in society and so, in path-dependent fashion, the party was profoundly shaped by its ancestors. By the time it returned to elections to offer

Britons a 'modernized' brand, surveys revealed the extent to which most citizens had reached the same conclusion about the party: like with the old NF, they do not consider the BNP to be an acceptable political alternative. It short, history matters.

Extreme right supporters in modern Britain

The stigma of the BNP is also reflected in its social bases of support. Despite attempting to set sail in a new direction, like its predecessor the party has fallen heavily dependent on a socially distinct base of 'angry white men'; middle-aged and elderly working-class men who have low levels of education and are deeply pessimistic about their economic prospects.[6] These supporters also congregate in similar social contexts: deprived urban areas, where education levels are low, there are large Muslim communities, and which tend to be in the Midlands, North West and Yorkshire regions.

While it has failed to rally a large coalition of supporters, however, the trends above are enabling the BNP to forge ties with members of particular social groups concerned about specific issues. BNP supporters have clear goals, and are driven by similar motives as supporters of more successful extreme right parties elsewhere in Europe. At first glance, the BNP is rallying Britons who are concerned about a diverse array of issues – they are: insecure about their precarious financial position; distrustful toward a range of institutions in society; hostile toward various minorities; and dissatisfied with the existing political options. Yet the most important predictors of whether somebody will vote BNP are whether they are deeply hostile toward immigration and extremely dissatisfied with the main parties.[7] Even after allowing for their background characteristics, this potent combination of hostility toward immigration and political dissatisfaction has a strong impact on BNP support.

While most Britons do not consider the BNP an acceptable alternative, it is rallying older working-class men who, as a result of their precarious position, feel threatened by immigration and are extremely dissatisfied with the response of the main parties on these issues. Both the quantitative and qualitative evidence strongly suggests that, in some areas of the country, the BNP is becoming a vehicle through which some Britons are 'sending a message' about their concern over a set of issues they care deeply about, but which they feel are not being competently addressed.

The interviews with BNP members provided richer insight into the nature of these concerns. They revealed how supporters are overwhelmingly concerned about immigration, settled Muslim communities and the impact of minority ethnic groups on wider society. Rather than being driven simply by racist hostility, however, most traced their initial decision to support the party to a feeling that immigrants and culturally distinct Muslim communities are threatening British culture, values and ways of life. On joining the party, these supporters were met with a concerted attempt to amplify these initial concerns into a broader and more compelling set of motivational vocabularies: the struggle for survival; the need for urgent and radical action; and to protect their families and wider group from an array of threats, including extinction.

Implications

The findings in this book challenge some popular claims about extreme right parties and the roots of their support. As noted at the outset, there are numerous competing interpretations of the extreme right: some see parties like the BNP as a temporary by-product of rapid and destabilizing economic change; others view them as an outlet for political protestors; and still others see them as single-issue parties rallying racist voters. These arguments gloss the complexity of motives which are driving support for this form of extremism.

Advocates of a protest perspective contend that political dissatisfaction is the major driver of support, suggesting disgruntled citizens will support the extreme right but eventually reunite with their mainstream party of choice. BNP supporters are certainly dissatisfied with the political mainstream – they: express extremely high levels of dissatisfaction with the performance of the government; are more dissatisfied than other citizens with the three main parties; and are deeply distrustful of national and local institutions. Their political dissatisfaction, however, only takes us so far. Supporters of the BNP are also deeply concerned about other issues.

Advocates of an alternative single-issue perspective argue that these supporters are concerned only about immigration and are, essentially, racist voters hostile toward any 'non-white' group. This leads us to expect that the BNP focuses exclusively on immigration, attracts supporters who share no distinct social profile and are driven foremost by their racist hostility toward various minority groups.[8] The BNP certainly devotes much of its attention to immigration and is rallying Britons who are profoundly concerned about this issue and more likely than other citizens to endorse openly racist views. But it has also actively explored ways of downplaying its single-issue image, such as by developing a populist anti-establishment strategy and targeting community-based issues. While racist hostility is an important element of BNP support, its followers are not motivated simply by crude 'anti-black' racism: they are also deeply pessimistic about their financial prospects, extremely dissatisfied with the main parties and profoundly concerned about a settled and culturally distinct minority group (see below).[9]

An alternative perspective suggests the BNP is simply a reincarnation of the NF and, by extension, is rallying identical social bases of support. While there is strong continuity between the two parties, this view ignores important changes which have taken place within the extreme right's bases of support. Unlike their NF-voting ancestors, modern BNP supporters are older, express higher levels of political dissatisfaction and are more likely to be based in northern England. Nor can BNP supporters be dismissed simply as crude racists. While they are fiercely opposed to immigration, they also feel that Muslims are threatening their culture and ways of life. The view that Islam poses a specific threat to Western civilization emerged as a significant predictor of BNP support, while the party tends to recruit most support in areas where there are large Muslim communities. One of the most striking findings is that BNP support is not simply strongest in areas where there are large 'non-white' populations, but where there are large Muslim communities of Bangladeshi or Pakistani heritage. Meanwhile, there is no relationship between BNP support and the presence of non-Muslim Asians (e.g. Buddhists, Hindus and Sikhs), while support is *lower* in areas where there are large black populations.[10]

This is consistent with evidence elsewhere in Europe which points toward the growing importance of anti-Muslim sentiment to understanding what drives support for the extreme right.[11] It suggests that the BNP's embrace of Islamophobia is having an effect, and its appeal is more complex than that of the old NF which tended to poll strongest in areas where there were sizeable 'non-white' communities. Supporters of the modern-day BNP express high levels of hostility toward Muslims and immigrants, but appear less concerned about minority groups which have become more integrated and accepted in British society over recent decades.[12] The interviews provided further evidence that the BNP is rallying Britons who are particularly concerned about the perceived threat posed by Muslims and Islamic values. Seen from the perspective of the average member, only involvement with the BNP offered an opportunity to take action against these threats and 'do something' to protect their collective group and ways of life.

This view of Muslims as a threatening out-group is unlikely to subside in the near future. British Muslims make valuable contributions to social and political life but they also experience disproportionately high levels of deprivation, and therefore have similar economic interests as typical extreme right supporters.[13] Intergroup competition over scarce resources such as jobs and social housing may exacerbate a sense among more deprived communities that Muslims are threatening their economic interests. These local conflicts over resources might also fuel perceptions that Muslims pose a more diffuse threat to liberal democratic values and traditions.

The findings above should be seen within the context of evidence that a significant portion of the British population endorses a conception of national identity that has difficulty incorporating Muslims, and questions where Islamic ideas and values fit within 'British' ways of life.[14] Public anxiety over the commitment of Muslims to British values introduces the prospect of a particularly powerful identity-based symbol around which extreme right or populist anti-immigrant parties might rally much larger support. In contrast to anti-Semitism and crude racial prejudice, the claim that Muslims hold incompatible values surfaces in sections of British media and political debate, which may inadvertently legitimize campaigns by the extreme right. During the campaign in a parliamentary by-election in Oldham in 2011, for example, the BNP cited coverage of 'Pakistani sex gangs' as evidence that 'the controlled media has finally admitted that there are Muslim paedophile gangs operating in Britain which prey on young white females, a fact for which Nick Griffin was twice put on trial for daring to say'.[15]

The electoral potential of anti-Muslim sentiment has been recognized by numerous parties on the European continent, which supplement anti-immigrant campaigns with Islamophobic discourse. The rise of Geert Wilders in the Netherlands or the Sweden Democrats (SD) underscore the way in which campaigns that frame Muslims as a threat to Western liberal democratic values and ways of life can mobilize considerable levels of support. In Britain, this has similarly been recognized by an increased number of parties and groups. The general election in 2010 was contested by almost 1,000 candidates from extreme right or populist Eurosceptic parties. Much like the BNP, the UK Independence Party (UKIP) advocated a halt on immigration (via a five-year freeze), deporting illegal immigrants and ending 'the active promotion of the doctrine of multiculturalism by local and national government and all publicly funded bodies'. It also called for bans on the burka and veiled niqab in certain buildings.[16] UKIP's shift toward anti-Muslim positions was especially apparent under its former leader, Lord Pearson, who invited Wilders to show his anti-Islam film, *Fitna*, in the House of Lords. It is not surprising, therefore, that some find important overlaps between the BNP and UKIP electorates.[17]

Future prospects

Once they have coalesced and their identity and reputation are well established, the political viability of most anti-immigrant groups and parties becomes inextricably linked to the prominence of immigration-related issues. As long as these issues remain salient and mainstream political parties fail to address them to the satisfaction of a critical mass of citizens and voters, anti-immigrant groups are likely to reap the political rewards, returns often . . . dispensed in the form of an increasing number of votes or formal members.[18]

What are the future prospects for the BNP and the extreme right? Seen from one perspective, the extreme right across Europe looks set to continue attracting support from more deprived and less well-educated citizens who are concerned chiefly about immigration and are dissatisfied with the response of the main parties on this issue. Their continuing willingness to endorse anti-immigrant and anti-Muslim campaigns was evident at elections in 2010, which saw strong performances by the Sweden Democrats, Party for Freedom (PVV) in the Netherlands and Jobbik in Hungary.

As elsewhere in Europe, the trends which are fuelling the rise of the BNP – namely anti-immigration sentiment, anxiety over Muslim communities and political dissatisfaction – are unlikely to subside in the near future. On the contrary, by historical standards immigration levels are likely to remain high while settled Muslim communities will continue to expand. For politicians and policy makers, the task of calming public anxiety over these issues is highly complex. The evidence in this book suggests that the perceived inability or unwillingness of governments and the main parties to deliver a convincing response to public concern over immigration is a key driver of support for the extreme right. Unlike in previous decades, however, international treaties mean governments have less control over immigration, whether from within the European Union (EU) or as a result of family reunions. These restrictions combined with competing interests of the private sector became apparent to the Coalition Government in 2010, when the Conservatives were forced to modify a pre-election pledge on immigration. Even when governments have implemented more restrictive policies – for example, legislation by Labour on asylum – they have not necessarily altered public perceptions that the issue is not being effectively managed.[19]

For several other reasons, the main parties are likely to find it difficult to establish an image of competence on immigration-related issues, and satisfy public anxiety over rapidly diversifying communities. Negative coverage of these issues in tabloid newspapers (which supporters of the extreme right tend to read) is likely to embellish perceptions of racial threat. Another factor which may lead citizens to conclude that rising diversity is a result of 'uncontrolled' immigration is natural demographic growth among already-settled and expanding minority ethnic communities. A continuing financial crisis and cuts to local government budgets may also exacerbate perceptions of threatened resources. The cuts announced in 2010, for example, included substantial reductions to grants which supported initiatives to promote community cohesion, tackle racist extremism and prevent violent extremism (PVE).[20]

While the rise of the BNP commenced before the onset of recession, the importance of the financial crisis is reflected in evidence that it benefitted the party at the 2010 general election. As at previous elections, BNP candidates polled strongest in deprived urban constituencies where there were large Muslim communities and low education levels, mainly in the Pennines, West Midlands, East London and nearby seats in Essex. But they also performed strongly in areas which, since 2005, have experienced large increases in unemployment.[21]

In response to these challenges, some have called for 'a greater focus on how to make immigration more acceptable to a sceptical public'.[22] Too often, however, arguments which seek to make the case for the positive contribution of immigration focus only on economic benefits while failing to address public concern over threats to culture, values and ways of life. The evidence in this book suggests that the task of addressing anxiety over the cultural impact of immigrants is equally, if not more, important than addressing concern over their impact on material resources, such as jobs and social housing. This requires more energy to be devoted to exploring ways of highlighting the positive contribution which immigrants and settled minority groups make to wider society, not just the economy.

Seen from an alternative perspective, however, there are good reasons to question whether the BNP will be the main beneficiary of the trends discussed above. Despite its attempts to 'modernize', there is little evidence in this book that the party is successfully widening its appeal among the electorate. While large numbers of Britons are concerned over immigration and dissatisfied with the main parties, they remain unwilling to shift their support behind Griffin's BNP. Unlike more successful parties in Europe, the BNP is failing to extend its reach across society more widely, and into more affluent and better-educated sections of the population.[23] Instead, its appeal is restricted to angry white men: older, less well-educated and pessimistic workers who are more likely than other citizens to endorse the most hostile views toward immigrants and minority groups. Groups which have long been under-represented in the extreme right electorate – women, the middle classes and the better educated – remain so. Nor is the party replenishing its ageing bases of support with fresh young converts who in earlier decades *did* turn out for its predecessor – the NF – in larger numbers. The BNP's attempt to present a family-friendly image which attracts women and young Britons has met little success.

As discussed in Chapter 5, one explanation for why the BNP is struggling to appeal to younger citizens is a generational effect. Unlike their parents and grandparents, more recent Britons are significantly less likely to endorse racially prejudiced and authoritarian views.[24] Research by the political sociologist Robert Ford reveals a steep generational decline in racial prejudice which is especially sharp among Britons who have grown up since mass immigration commenced in the 1950s, or in his words: 'Generations brought up in an ethnically homogenous Britain express high levels of prejudice, while those who have come up since mass migration began express progressively more tolerant attitudes.'[25]

Various factors are contributing to this generational shift in attitudes: improving levels of education; the way in which young Britons have been raised in a society where leaders of political and faith communities support and celebrate diversity; and the increasing geographical and social dispersal of minority ethnic groups. Unlike earlier generations, in some parts of the country young Britons are being socialized amid 'super diversity' and exposed to a plethora of languages, faiths, identities and cultural practices.[26] They are also significantly more likely than their parents and grandparents to experience social contact and build relations with members of different ethnic, cultural and/or religious groups. As decades of research in social psychology has shown, when this contact takes place under certain conditions it can have important effects, such as promoting tolerance, reducing prejudice and countering perceptions of racial threat, all of which are important to understanding what drives support for the extreme right.[27]

If it is the case that a more tolerant generation of Britons are replacing their older and more prejudiced forebears, then political parties which are associated with more socially unacceptable forms of racism will increasingly struggle to rally support. This is not to argue that racial prejudice will disappear. Generational change is a slow process that affects members of different social groups in different ways. Racial prejudice is falling most sharply among women, the better educated and more affluent but remains stronger among more deprived and less well-educated working-class men.[28] Also, while most Britons now distance themselves from crude racism, there remain large pools of xenophobic hostility toward immigrants and minority ethnic groups.

When seen through a wider lens, however, the evidence suggests that 'traditional' right-wing extremist parties like the BNP will increasingly find their appeal restricted to dwindling pools of racially prejudiced angry white men. The fact that the party is not extending its appeal beyond smaller rumps of hostility suggests a bleak future. Indeed, following its failure to engineer a breakthrough at the 2010 general election and support of only 4.5 per cent at a parliamentary by-election in Oldham in January 2011, the party's electoral prospects appear far from promising. Much will depend on whether it can attract a younger and more diverse coalition of supporters. The party's stigma in wider society suggests this is distinctly unlikely.

Yet, while it might not enter Westminster, the BNP does look set to become an enduring fixture on the political landscape. Over the short term, it hopes to solidify its presence in areas of strength by contesting local elections in England, and elections to the Scottish Parliament and National Assembly for Wales. The party aims to sustain its electoral challenge by investing more heavily in canvassing techniques, training activists, databasing results and undertaking personal visits with supporters. It is also continuing to modify its internal structures and constitution, although it remains hampered by factionalism.

Over the longer term, the party has set out plans to develop a social movement model of activism. Griffin warns supporters not to 'fall for the illusion that electoral power on its own is the Holy Grail', and that 'there is more than coming to power and then being able to use it effectively than simply winning elections'. Titled 'Deadline 2014', one article by Griffin sets the scene by predicting global financial catastrophe, grinding poverty, collapse of the manufacturing sector and the end of oil reserves, while also claiming that 'internationalists – everyone from the Bilderbergers to the European Commission, from the would-be One World Government in the United Nations to the brainwashed Common Purpose cultists in your bankrupt local Health Trust – will press on with their rolling power grab'. Griffin argues these trends will soon thrust white Britons into a 'clash of civilizations' that will spread across the continent: 'Glass will be broken. Sirens will wail. Cities will burn. The Tiber, and other urban rivers all over Western Europe, will indeed "flow with much blood".'[29]

To exploit the anticipated period of chaos, Griffin argues the BNP should sink deeper roots in communities, such as through 'civil rights agitation' and challenging local authorities when working-class communities have been marginalized.[30] Other proposals include 'intelligent militancy', such as making greater use of Judicial Review Applications and street-based demonstrations against various issues, for example, 'opposition to the Muslim thugs who are making a habit of abusing army home-coming parades'.[31] He has also reiterated the importance of focusing on a wide array of issues and developing community-based groups, such as a campaign against the war in Afghanistan that was launched in the autumn of 2010 and demonstrations against the 'scandal of the racist sexual grooming of young white girls by Muslim men'.[32] As Griffin elaborates:

It's got to be on community memories . . . using this pub and keeping this pub and not letting it become a madrassa and things like this and sharpening the divisions and pointing out the unfairness. But it is also longer term. If we don't make a really serious breakthrough inevitably it is clear that in ever increasing swathes of the country our people will become a minority and if you look at the demographics of it, when the tipping point comes it'll be incredibly quick because it's not just about birth-rates, it's about death-rates and these things, you see it in Northern Ireland. It's going street by street by street. If we haven't made a really significant breakthrough in 10 or 15 years' time, then if we've already developed the techniques of organizing a minority community to fight for its rights then that's what we increasingly become.[33]

BNP members are used to reading their Chairman's strategies. Writing to supporters shortly after his election as leader, Griffin gave them the following message: 'We are here to build a power-winning machine . . . We have a real chance now to progress in a rapid leap of just a few years from an ineffective pressure group to a potential party of government.' He then proceeded to set out possible victories for those who remained committed to the cause: 'But neither must we become a mere power-winning machine. We do not seek power for its own sake, but so that we can use it to do the things we must do to protect our people and secure a future for white children. That has always been our aim, is our aim, and will always remain our aim.'[34]

APPENDIX 1

Methodology

Gaining access to extreme right parties and their members is notoriously difficult. As one academic has observed, parties like the BNP are 'renowned for refusing to grant outsiders access to their records and personnel'.[1] Only rarely have these types of parties made their membership lists available to the social science community.[2] As a result, researchers have instead often been forced to rely heavily on analysis of party literature, speeches, or elite-level interviews with leaders and official party spokespersons. While these alternative sources of data hold the potential to provide useful insights, they are limited in terms of what they can actually tell us about the parties and their grassroots supporters.

In response, from the outset this study employed a qualitative approach, drawing on extensive interviews with individual members, organizers and leaders. Qualitative interviewing is particularly effective not only in the study of extremist groups, but political participation more generally.[3] Its benefits have been traced to numerous factors. Rather than asking participants to choose from a set of predetermined responses on a survey, open-ended interview questions allow supporters to elaborate more fully, and in their own words about their backgrounds, motivations, beliefs and context. Unlike a survey-based approach, for example, where the aim is to obtain a large and representative sample from which the researcher can generalize to a wider group, qualitative studies focus more heavily on collecting a small but rich sample of data.

In this case, participants were approached through a 'snowballing' strategy. The snowball technique is particularly useful when the focus rests on an organization which tends to refuse access to outsiders, and is comprised of activists who are closely connected and difficult to approach directly.[4] These participants were not drawn from a predetermined sampling frame, but were approached through networks of existing members. The process of building a sample begins when a small number of initial participants (the 'seeds') are invited to participate. It is through these initial seeds that the researcher recruits additional participants, either inviting them personally to participate or forwarding details about the study via other participants. The process continues until the desired sample size is reached.[5]

The contact details of initial seeds were gathered from two sources: first, local, regional and national organizers were approached through the BNP website; second, elected BNP councillors were approached through local councils. This produced a list of 24 potential participants who were invited to participate in the study between January and May 2005. The invitations produced a response rate of 16 per cent. Those who did not respond were contacted one week later, either by e-mail or telephone, which produced an additional four interviews. The interviews commenced in May 2005. While most participants were inquisitive about the aims of the research, a majority provided details of fellow members or agreed to forward information about the study.

These snowball 'chains' in different parts of the country were then continually cultivated over the ensuing two years (for an example of a chain in one region, see Fig. A.1). Meanwhile, additional interviews were organized with the initial wave of participants. This was because a reliance on 'one-shot interviews' has been criticized by some academics for providing insufficient grounds for adequate elaboration and interpretation. Moreover, sensitive topics require a greater level of involvement from the researcher if an adequate level of trust and rapport is to be established.[6] These additional interviews were held either weeks, months or in some cases one year after the first interview. In several cases, activists were interviewed on three or four separate occasions, making an important contribution to the richness and quality of the data.

Clearly, however, there are limitations when relying on snowball sampling. The non-random sample prevents researchers from being able to generalize to a wider population, and there is also a risk of participants influencing who is subsequently recruited to the study. It is possible that this potential bias is further reinforced as the sampling process continues. For instance, members might actively seek to ensure that only one 'type' of member is exposed to the study. These problems arise because the technique is not based on traditional probability sampling, where units are selected from a sampling frame with a known probability of selection.[7]

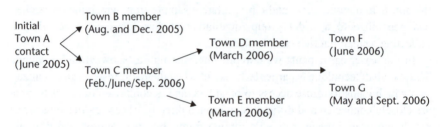

FIGURE A.1 Example of a snowball chain

Note: Date of interview(s) in brackets.

In an attempt to minimize these potential difficulties, several strategies were pursued. First, to minimize the risk of initial seeds influencing the sample, activists were approached throughout England and Wales (Table A.1). Whereas previous studies focused on a single branch or region, the decision to 'cast a wide net' reduced the likelihood of focusing only on one type of member, or a particular faction within the party. Interviewees were located in urban and rural areas; where the BNP has polled strongly in elections but also where it has not; and where there is a history of extreme right party campaigning but also where there is not. Second, rather than focus only on elites, interviews were held with members at every level of the organization, including the BNP Chairman (who was interviewed on four occasions), national and regional organizers, local organizers, elected councillors, ordinary members and former members. Overall, the study draws on data gathered through 49 interviews with 27 activists.

While small, the sample size is comparable to similar studies of extreme right party members in other European states, for example, Belgium, France, Germany,

TABLE A.1 Information about the interviews

	Region	Number and date of interviews
1	South East	(1) May 2005
2	North West	(1) May 2005
3	North West	(2) May 2005 and May 2006
4	South West	(3) June, November 2005 and October 2006
5	South East	(2) August 2005 and December 2005
6	South East	(1) September 2005
7	Yorkshire	(4) September & December 2005, April 2007, March 2008
8	South West	(3) September, December 2005 and April 2007
9	North West	(2) December 2005 and June 2006
10	North West	(1) January 2006
11	South West	(1) February 2006
12	South West	(1) March 2006
13	South West	(4) March, June, August 2006 and April 2008
14	Yorkshire	(2) May 2006
15	East Midlands	(1) May 2006
16	Yorkshire	(2) May 2006 and October 2006
17	North West	(2) May 2006 and October 2006
18	North West	(2) June 2006 and April 2008
19	North West	(1) June 2006 and April 2008
20	South East	(2) June 2006 and September 2006
21	Greater London	(1) December 2006
22	Yorkshire	(2) April 2007 and April 2008
23	Yorkshire	(1) April 2008
24	South East	(1) May 2009
25	South East	(1) May 2009
26	Yorkshire	(1) June 2009
27	BNP Chairman	(4) March, October 2006, December 2009 and June 2010

Note: See also M.J. Goodwin (2010) 'Activism in contemporary extreme right parties: The case of the British National Party', *Journal of Elections, Public Opinion and Parties*, 20(1): 31–54.

Italy and the Netherlands.[8] To improve the comparability of the research, the interview guide followed these latter studies by incorporating similar themes and questions, and employing a 'life-history' approach. The life-history method has proven especially effective in studies of participants in various types of extremist groups.[9] In large part, this is because life-history interviews hold the potential to reveal participants' own interpretation of conditions, events and experiences, and enable researchers to understand how they 'make sense' of the wider world around them. Life-history interviews put strong emphasis on *individual* experiences, views and beliefs, thereby minimizing the likelihood of participants simply 'parroting' party propaganda.[10] These individual accounts were recorded and transcribed, with additional notes being taken following each interview and throughout the fieldwork stage.

In terms of analyzing the data, a template approach was adopted whereby the data and core themes were analyzed through an analysis guide, or 'codebook'.[11] The codebook incorporates categories and themes relevant to the research questions. After each interview was transcribed, the data were coded according to key themes and patterns. The codes which emerged through this thematic analysis came to represent the link between the raw data and theoretical concepts.[12] The interviews were supplemented with qualitative analysis of internally oriented party literature which, unlike externally oriented literature, provided rich insight into the development, culture and evolution of political parties.[13] In the case of the BNP, analysis of the BNP website or monthly newspaper was avoided on the basis that these put stronger emphasis on populist themes and issues, which are designed more for potential supporters and voters. Instead, qualitative analysis of textual data was restricted to the monthly subscription magazine (*Identity*), which is tailored for an internal audience of members and activists.[14]

While some are critical of the subjective and idiosyncratic nature of qualitative textual analysis, suggesting for example it does not produce the 'hard' results associated with quantitative content analysis, the qualitative approach is especially useful in the case of research that is more exploratory in nature, and which is aimed at 'understanding rather than explanation, and at discovering rather than constructing'.[15] A straightforward form of content analysis was employed, with magazine extracts highlighted and reduced to broad analytic categories and codes. As others note, when analyzing qualitative data, codes are items selected by the researcher which 'can be expanded, changed, or scrapped altogether as our ideas develop through repeated interactions with the data'.[16] The role of coding was three-fold: to identify relevant information and phenomena; to collect examples; and to analyze these items so as to identify commonalities, differences, patterns and structures.[17] In retrospect, as interviews commenced an iterative process ensued, with the researcher oscillating between interview data and primary literature as codes and concepts emerged.

As one academic noted in the mid-1990s, traditionally studies of extreme right parties were highly politicized, with anti-fascists and journalists producing a plethora of opinionated, speculative and emotional studies.[18] However, the experiences of academics who have undertaken detailed qualitative research (and their findings) have often undermined the conventional wisdoms concerning these more committed supporters of the extreme right. Kaplan and Weinberg, for example, refer to the activists they interviewed as being more 'complicated, considerably more personable and far more nuanced than is suggested by the caricatures'.[19] Reflecting on her experience of interviewing members of the Ku Klux Klan (KKK) in the United States, Kathleen Blee recalled in similar terms: 'Far from being the stock characters of popular portrayals of Klan members – uniformly reactionary, red-neck, mean, ignorant, operating by an irrational and incomprehensible logic – many of the people I interviewed were interesting, intelligent, and well-informed.'[20]

In similar fashion, few of the BNP members who were interviewed in this study conformed to the popular stereotypes of them as being irrational and uninformed crude racists. While most were certainly hostile toward immigration and rising ethno-cultural diversity, their hostility was framed in more subtle terms. Also, most appeared relatively at ease throughout the interviews and, contrary to initial expectations, it was not especially difficult to gain access to them (which perhaps owed much to the author being a white male). Consequently, the qualitative accounts which members provided during the interviews enable us to explore the views and voices of citizens who are typically under-represented in public debate and discourse. While further research is needed to make broader generalizations about what drives citizens toward extremist parties, the often neglected voices which emerge in this book provide a useful point from which to start.

APPENDIX 2

TABLE A.2 Socio-economic variables: principal components analysis varimax-rotated component loadings

Attitudinal items	C1 Anti-immigration	C2 Euro-scepticism	C3 Political protest	C4 Homophobia
Benefits of immigration	–		–	–
Immigration economy	–		–	–
Immigration halted	–		–	–
Immigrants leave country	–		–	–
Immigrants cause crime	–		–	–
Immigrants jump queues	–		–	–
EU withdraw		0.62	–	–
EU important policy		0.61	–	–
EU decision making		0.58	–	–
EU prosperity		0.65	–	–
Local MP		–	0.65	–
Political corruption		–	0.67	–
Parties all the same		–	0.67	–
Civil partnership		–	–	0.78
Gays/lesbians unfair advantage		–	–	0.81
Variance	29.7%	8.8%	8.1%	6.7%
Accumulated value – % Total variance	29.7%	38.6%	46.6%	53.3%

Note: Components with eigenvalues >1 are retained. Rotated component loadings (varimax rotation) greater than 0.5 shown. All variables are Strongly Agree + Agree/Strongly Disagree + Disagree = 1; all other responses = 0.

Question wording:

'Benefits of immigration' = Do you agree or disagree with the following statement? 'Britain has benefitted from the arrival in recent decades of people from many different countries and cultures'; 'Immigration economy' = Do you agree or disagree with the following statement? 'Immigration in recent years has helped Britain's economy grow faster than it would have done'; 'Immigration halted' = Do you agree or disagree with the following statement? 'All further immigration to the UK should be halted'; 'Immigrants leave country' = Do you agree or disagree with the following statement? 'The Government should encourage immigrants and their families to leave Britain (including family members who were born in the UK)'; 'Immigrants cause crime' = Do you agree or disagree with the following statement? 'Most crimes in Britain are committed by immigrants'; 'Immigrants jump queues' = Do you agree or disagree with the following statement? 'Local councils normally allow immigrant families to jump the queue in allowing council homes';

'EU withdraw' = Do you agree or disagree with the following statement? 'The UK should withdraw completely from the European Union'; 'EU important policy' = rating European Union (EU) as one of the top four important issues facing the country; 'EU decision making' = Here are some statements that different people have made. In each case, do you think the statement is completely true, partially true but is exaggerated, or is completely untrue? 'A great majority of the important decisions that affect our daily life are taken by the European Union, not by Britain's parliaments, assemblies or councils' (Completely true/Partially true but exaggerated/Completely untrue/Don't know); 'EU prosperity' = Do you agree or disagree with the following statement? 'The existence of the EU promotes prosperity throughout Europe';

'Local MP' = How much do you trust each of the following to tell the truth? Your local MP (Trust a great deal/Trust a fair amount/Do not trust much/Do not trust at all/Don't know); 'Political corruption' = Do you agree or disagree with the following statement? 'Most British politicians are personally corrupt'; 'Parties all the same' = Do you agree or disagree with the following statement? 'There is no real difference these days between Britain's three main parties – Labour, Conservative and Liberal Democrat';

'Civil partnership' = Do you agree or disagree with the following statement? 'It is a good thing that gay and lesbian couples are able to enter into "civil partnership" and have rights similar to married couples'; 'Gays/lesbians unfair advantage' = Which, if any, of these groups do you often think benefit from unfair advantages in Britain these days? Gay and lesbian men and women.

NOTES

Introduction

1 BNP (2010) *Democracy, Freedom, Culture and Identity: British National Party General Election Manifesto 2010*, Welshpool: British National Party, p. 90.
2 Interview 3 with Nick Griffin, December 2009.
3 *Voice of Freedom*, 77: 9.
4 'Welcome to Barking – new far right capital of Britain', *The Guardian*, Saturday, 6 May 2006.
5 C. Milmo, 'The battle for Barking', the *Independent*, Saturday, 10 April 2010.
6 According to the poll, 53 per cent of respondents were 'very worried' or 'fairly worried' about the increasing popularity of the BNP. YouGov/the *Sun*, fieldwork, 21–22 March 2010.
7 Electoral turnout in Barking increased from 50.1 per cent (2005) to 61.4 per cent (2010).
8 Interview 4 with Nick Griffin, June 2010.
9 M. Taylor and H. Muir (2010) 'General election 2010: The defeat of the BNP', the *Guardian*, Friday, 14 May 2010; on collapse of the BNP vote, see F. Hamilton, 'BNP hopes of a breakthrough dashed as party defeated in target seats', *Times Online*, 7 May 2010. On coverage more generally, see also C. Milmo, 'Griffin's future in doubt as BNP campaign implodes', the *Independent*, Saturday, 8 May 2010.
10 A.M. Messina (2007) *The Logics and Politics of Post-WWII Migration to Western Europe*, Cambridge: Cambridge University Press, p. 231.
11 See, for example, T. Bale (2003) 'Cinderella and her ugly sisters: The mainstream and extreme right in Europe's bipolarising party systems', *West European Politics*, 26(3): 67–90; A. Zaslove (2004) 'Closing the door? The ideology and impact of radical right populism on immigration policy in Austria and Italy', *Journal of Political Ideologies*, 9(1): 99–118; T. Bale, C. Green-Pedersen, A. Krouwel, K.R. Luther and N. Sitter (2009) 'If you can't beat them, join them? Explaining Social Democratic responses to the challenge from the populist radical right in Western Europe', *Political Studies*, 58(3): 410–426.
12 W. van der Brug, M. Fennema and J. Tillie (2005) 'Why some anti-immigrant parties fail and others succeed: A two-step model of aggregate electoral support', *Comparative Political Studies*, 38(5): 538.
13 P. Norris (2005) *Radical Right: Voters and parties in the electoral market*, Cambridge: Cambridge University Press, p. 4.

14 On cross-national variations in extreme right support, see E.L. Carter (2005) *The Extreme Right in Western Europe: Success or failure?* Manchester: Manchester University Press; H. Kitschelt (with A. McGann) (1995) *The Radical Right in Western Europe: A comparative analysis*, Ann Arbor, MI: University of Michigan Press; Norris, Note 13 *supra*; W. van der Brug *et al.*, 'Why some anti-immigrant parties fail and others succeed: A two-step model of aggregate electoral support', The Hague: University of Amsterdam.

15 Two candidates from the Stamford Fascists were elected in 1924, one BUF councillor was elected in 1938 and a breakaway party from the National Front (NF) – the National Party (NP) – elected two councillors in Blackburn in 1976.

16 D. Butler and M. Westlake (2000) *British Politics and European Elections 1999*, London: Macmillan, p. 227.

17 Anti-fascist groups such as Searchlight detail these links extensively, see www. searchlightmagazine.com.

18 'UK news in brief: London car bomb charge', the *Guardian*, 4 November 1985; 'Gaol for own goal bomber', the *Guardian*, 28 November 1986; S. Tye, ' "I've turned over a new leaf" claims the racist', *Swindon Advertiser*, 18 January 2007; A. Osborne, 'Man admits firebombing mosque', *Swindon Advertiser*, 23 October 2006; 'Racist gave bomb tips to BNP thug', *Eastbourne Herald*, 6 July 2006; 'BNP member jailed for string of racist attacks', *Eastbourne Herald*, 16 March 2005.

19 'Who are the English Defence League'. Available online: www.englishdefenceleague. org/Who-are-the-edl-english-defence-league.html (accessed 10 January 2010).

20 'Five jailed for trying to stir up race hate violence', the *Guardian*, Saturday, 5 November 2005. For readers interested in extra-parliamentary forms of right-wing extremism, see, for example, T. Bjørgo (ed.) (1995) *Terror from the Extreme Right*, London: Frank Cass Ltd; T. Bjørgo and J. Horgan (eds) *Leaving Terrorism Behind: Individual and collective disengagement*, London and New York: Routledge; K.M. Blee (1996) 'Becoming a racist: Women in contemporary Ku Klux Klan and Neo-Nazi groups', *Gender and Society*, 10(6): 680–702; D.P. Green and A. Rich (1998) 'White supremacist activity and crossburnings in North Carolina', *Journal of Quantitative Criminology*, 14(3): 263–282; M.W. Watts (2001) 'Aggressive youth cultures and hate crime', *American Behavioral Scientist*, 45(4): 600–615.

21 Copeland, for example, admitted to police that his 'main intent was to spread fear, resentment and hatred throughout this country, it was to cause a racial war'. 'Profile: Copeland the killer', *BBC News*, 30 June 2000. Available online: http:// news.bbc.co.uk/1/hi/uk/781755.stm (accessed 10 March 2010); also Campbell, 'Ex-BNP council candidate is jailed for stockpiling explosive chemicals', the *Guardian*, Wednesday, 1 August 2007; 'Neo-Nazi convicted of terror plan', *BBC News*, 15 July 2009. Available online: http://news.bbc.co.uk/1/hi/8152159.stm (accessed 10 March 2010); 'BNP member jailed over terror cache', the *Independent*, 15 January 2010.

22 Academics have invested considerable effort in attempting to reach a consensus on this concept and its core features. See C. Mudde (2007) *Populist Radical Right Parties in Europe*, Cambridge: Cambridge University Press; J. Rydgren (2004) *The Populist Challenge: Political protest and ethno-nationalist mobilization in France*, New York and Oxford: Berghahn; J. Rydgren (2007) 'The sociology of the radical right', *Annual Review of Sociology*, 33: 241–262; also U. Backes (2010) *Political Extremes: A conceptual history from antiquity to the present*, London and New York: Routledge; C. Mudde (2000) *The Ideology of the Extreme Right*, Manchester: Manchester University Press; T. Saalfeld (1993) 'The politics of national-populism: Ideology and politics of the German Repulikaner Party', *German Politics*, 2(2): 177–199.

23 Carter, Note 14 *supra*.

24 On populism, see P. Taggart (2000) *Populism*, Buckingham: Open University Press; D. Canovan (1999) 'Trust the people! Populism and the two faces of democracy', *Political Studies*, 42: 2–16.

25 L. Weinberg and A. Pedahzur (2004) 'Introduction', in L. Weinberg and A. Pedahzur (eds) *Religious Fundamentalism and Political Extremism*, London: Frank Cass, pp. 6–7; see also S.M. Lipset and E. Raab (1971) *The Politics of Unreason: Right-wing extremism in America, 1790–1970*, London: Heinemann, p. 5; for further discussion, see also R. Eatwell and M.J. Goodwin (2010) 'Introduction', in R. Eatwell and M.J. Goodwin, *The New Extremism in 21st Century Britain*, London and New York: Routledge, pp. 1–20.
26 BNP (2010) *Democracy, Freedom, Culture and Identity: British National Party General Election Manifesto 2010*, Welshpool: British National Party, pp. 22–23.
27 Nick Griffin (2010) 'What is going to be done'. Available online: www.bnp.org.uk/ news/what-going-be-done (accessed 20 September 2010).
28 P. Ignazi (1992) 'The silent counter-revolution: Hypotheses on the emergence of extreme right-wing parties in Europe', *European Journal of Political Research*, 22(1): 10.
29 See, for example, R. Griffin (1991) *The Nature of Fascism*, London: Routledge.
30 Carter, Note 14 *supra*, p. 17. On the features of fascism see notably Griffin, Note 29 *supra*.
31 On the impact of ideology on extreme right performance, see Carter, Note 14 *supra*; A. Cole (2005) 'Old right or new right? The ideological positioning of parties of the far right', *European Journal of Political Research*, 44(1): 203–230; M. Golder (2003) 'Explaining variation in the success of extreme right parties in Western Europe', *Comparative Political Studies*, 36(4): 432–466; Ignazi, Note 28 *supra*, pp. 3–34; H. Kitschelt (with A. McGann) (1995) *The Radical Right in Western Europe: A comparative analysis*, Ann Arbor, MI: University of Michigan Press.
32 Based on their attitudes toward democracy, parliamentarism and pluralism, Carter identifies three groups in the wider European extreme right family, namely: (1) a first group of parties that reject outright the fundamental values, procedures and institutions of the democratic constitutional state, and which seek to replace the existing democratic system altogether; (2) a second group which display anti-system properties but which demand significant reform to strengthen the executive and curtail the rights and freedoms of organized interests and individuals; and (3) a third group which also favours reform of the democratic system but in order to have less state intervention rather than more, and which calls for greater measures to safeguard the rights and freedoms of individuals. Carter, Note 14 *supra*, p. 41.
33 For further discussion, see J. Rydgren (2005) 'Is extreme right-wing populism contagious? Explaining the emergence of a new party family', *European Journal of Political Research*, 44(3): 416.
34 On the historic failure of the extreme right, see R. Eatwell (1998) 'Britain, the BNP and the Problem Of Legitimacy', in H.G. Betz And S. Immerfall (eds) *The New Politics Of The Right: Neo-populist parties and movements in established democracies*, New York: St Martin's Press, pp. 143–155; and (2000) 'The extreme right and British exceptionalism: The primacy of politics', in P. Hainsworth (ed) *The Politics of the Extreme Right: From the margins to the mainstream*, London: Pinter, pp. 172–192; M.J. Goodwin (2007) 'The extreme right in Britain: Still an "ugly duckling" but for how long?' *Political Quarterly*, 78(2): 241–250; H. Kitschelt (with A. McGann) *The Radical Right in Western Europe: A comparative analysis*, Ann Arbor, MI: University of Michigan Press.
35 YouGov/*Daily Telegraph* poll, fieldwork, 20–22 July 2005.
36 G.A. Almond and S. Verba (1963) *The Civic Culture: Political attitudes and democracy in five nations*, Princeton, NJ: Princeton University Press, p. 455; see also p. 179.
37 It should be noted that evidence on the impact of electoral institutions on extreme right support is mixed, for example, K. Arzheimer and E.L. Carter (2006) 'Political opportunity structures and right-wing extremist party success', *European Journal of Political Research*, 45(3): 419–443; W. van der Brug *et al.*, Note 14 *supra*, pp. 537–573; Carter, Note 14 *supra*; Mudde (2007), Note 22 *supra*, p. 234; E.L. Carter (2004) 'Does PR

promote political extremism? Evidence from the West European parties of the extreme right', *Representation*, 40(2): 82–100; Norris, Note 13 *supra*.

38 R. Griffin (1996) 'British fascism: The ugly duckling', in M. Cronin (ed) *The Failure of British Fascism: The far right and the fight for political recognition*, Basingstoke and New York: Macmillan and St Martin's Press, p. 163; also M.J. Goodwin (2007) 'The extreme right in Britain: Still an ugly duckling but for how long?' *Political Quarterly*, 78(2): 241–250.

39 The BNP polled 16.4 per cent in Oldham West and Royton, 11.3 per cent in Burnley and 11.2 per cent in Oldham East and Saddleworth.

40 BNP (2001) 'The BNP and the general election', *Identity*, 7: 7.

41 'Gains by far right but relief for ministers', the *Guardian*, Saturday, 4 May 2002. The 'monkey' elected Mayor was a populist mascot of a local football team.

42 ICM/*BBC News* race poll 2002, fieldwork, 7–11 May.

43 BNP Statement of Accounts 2003, p. 1. Available online: www.electoralcommission. org.uk (accessed June 2010).

44 BNP, *Rebuilding British Democracy*, p. 4.

45 N. Griffin (2004) 'Chairman's article', *Identity*, 48: 4; N. Griffin (2005) 'New target that's going to make it special', *Identity*, 52: 4.

46 The four constituencies were Dagenham, Dudley North, Keighley and West Bromwich West.

47 'BNP to contest racial hotspot', the *Guardian*, 11 January 2005.

48 At the 1979 general election the National Front polled 191,719 votes and averaged 1.3 per cent of the vote in seats contested.

49 BNP Statement of Accounts 2006, p. 1. Available online: *www.electoralcommission.org.uk* (accessed June 2010).

50 In local elections the next year the party's number of local election candidates more than doubled to over 700, its number of votes reached almost 300,000 and its tally of councillors increased to 50.

51 Interview with Nick Griffin, June 2010.

52 BNP Statement of Accounts 2008, p. 1. Available online: www.electoralcommission. org.uk (accessed June 2010). Elections for Mayor of London were held at the same time as elections to the GLA. The BNP candidate received over 69,000 1st preference votes (2.9 per cent) and more than 128,000 second preference votes (6.4 per cent). Compared with the previous result in 2004 this represented a −0.2 per cent decline on 1st preference votes and a 2 per cent increase in 2nd preference votes.

53 N. Cohen. 'Forget these Londoners and the BNP reaps the harvest', *Evening Standard*, 7 May 2008.

54 The BNP became the second largest group on Burnley Council with eight councillors following the local elections in May 2003. The BNP's period as second largest group lasted less than two months. In June 2003, the Liberal Democrats gained one seat following a local by-election, thereby equalling the number of BNP councillors. In October 2003, the Lib Dems gained an additional seat from the BNP. In May 2007, the number of BNP councillors in Burnley declined to four.

55 BNP Statement of Accounts 2004. Available online: www.electoralcommission.org.uk (accessed June 2010).

56 A. Lecomber (2004) 'June 10th: What happened?', *Identity*, 47: 6.

57 BNP (2009) *British Jobs for British Workers* leaflet, Worcester: British National Party.

58 Meanwhile in local elections the party also won its first two county council seats in Lancashire and Leicestershire.

59 The parties I am referring to are the Austrian Freedom Party, the Vlaams Belang in Belgium, Ataka in Bulgaria, the Danish People's Party, the True Finns in Finland, the National Front in France, LAOS in Greece, Jobbik in Hungary, the Lega Nord in Italy, the Greater Romania Party in Romania, the Slovak National Party in Slovakia and the British National Party.

60 B. Macintyre, 'If history is any guide, the BNP will follow Mosley's Fascists down the plughole', *The Times*, 23 October 2009.

61 On 22–23 October 2009, the poll asked a representative sample of 1,314 adults the following: 'Are there any circumstances in which you might seriously consider voting BNP in a future local, general or European election?' Respondents were given an option of 'Yes, definitely consider voting BNP' (4%), 'Yes, probably' (3%), 'Yes, possibly' (15%), 'No, under no circumstances' (66%) and 'Not sure' (12%). In the same poll 72 per cent of respondents said they had 'fairly negative' or 'very negative' feelings toward the BNP while only 9 per cent said they had 'very positive' or 'fairly positive' feelings toward the party. YouGov/*Daily Telegraph* poll. Available online: http://today.yougov.co.uk (accessed 20 August 2010).

62 Interview 3 with Nick Griffin, December 2009.

63 The National Front (NF) also fielded 17 candidates who received a total of 10,784 votes (averaging 634 votes per candidate). The NF's strongest performance was 4.9 per cent in Rochdale. The Bradford-based Democratic Nationalists (DN) stood two candidates in Bradford West (1.1 per cent) and Bradford South (0.8 per cent)

64 N. Lowles (2010) 'Record breakers', *Searchlight*, May, 419: 17; N. Lowles (2010) 'Routed', *Searchlight*, June, 420: 6; N. Lowles (2010) 'The politics of Hope and Hate', *Searchlight*, April, 418: 7.

65 The *Mirror*, 5 May 2010.

66 YouGov/*Sunday Times*, fieldwork, 16–17 April 2010.

67 In general elections in 2010, for example, Sweden Democrats (SD) polled 339,000 votes and Flemish Interest (VB) polled 506,000 votes.

68 Some of these data were gathered by commercial polling agencies such as Ipsos-MORI and YouGov. The author would like to express a debt of gratitude to Bobby Duffy at Ipsos-MORI and Joe Twyman at YouGov for making the data available. For more technical analysis of BNP voters, see R. Ford and M.J. Goodwin (2012) *Voting for Extremists* (forthcoming with Routledge).

69 See, for example, R. Eatwell (2003) 'Ten theories of the extreme right', in P.H. Merkl and L. Weinberg (eds) *Right-Wing Extremism in the Twenty-First Century*, London: Frank Cass, pp. 47–73; H. Kitschelt (with A. McGann) (1995) *The Radical Right in Western Europe: A comparative analysis*, Ann Arbor, MI: University of Michigan Press; C. Mudde (2007), Note 22 *supra*; Norris, Note 13 *supra*; Rydgren (2004), Note 22 *supra*.

70 S. Berman (1997) 'The life of the party', *Comparative Politics* 30(1): 101–122. For a wider discussion of these approaches, see C. Mudde (2007), Note 22 *supra*, pp. 232–276.

71 See, for example, H.G. Betz (1994) *Radical Right-Wing Populism in Western Europe*, New York: St Martin's Press.

72 The 'ethnic threat model' stems from earlier research on 'group threat' and 'realistic group conflict' theories, for example, H. Blumer (1958) 'Race prejudice as a sense of group position', *Pacific Sociological Review*, 1: 3–7; and L. Bobo (1983) 'Whites' opposition to busing: Symbolic racism or realistic group conflict?' *Journal of Personality and Social Psychology*, 45: 1196–1210.

73 This is also sometimes referred to as the 'valence model', see notably H.D. Clarke, D. Sanders, M.C. Stewart and P.F. Whiteley (2009) *Performance Politics and the British Voter*, Cambridge: Cambridge University Press, p. 5. See also H.D. Clarke, D. Sanders, M.C. Stewart and P. Whiteley (2004) *Political Choice in Britain*, Oxford: Oxford University Press.

74 In adopting this integrated approach the book is informed by pre-existing studies, notably W. van der Brug, M. Fennema and J. Tillie (2005) 'Why some anti-immigrant parties fail and others succeed: A two-step model of aggregate electoral support', *Comparative Political Studies*, 38: 537–573; H. Kitschelt (with A. McGann) (1995) *The Radical Right in Western Europe: A comparative analysis*, Ann Arbor, MI: University of Michigan Press; Mudde, Note 22 *supra*; Norris, Note 13 *supra*; Rydgren (2004), Note 22 *supra*, p. 5.

75 Y. Alibhai-Brown, 'BNP supporters do not merit sympathetic understanding, just outright condemnation', the *Independent*, 24 April 2006; R. Liddle, 'Labour's heartland won't be fooled on immigration again', *The Sunday Times*, 15 November 2009; T. Gold, 'General election 2010: One dark day with the BNP in Dagenham', the *Daily Telegraph*, 12 April 2010; T. Parsons, 'No matter how let down you feel, the BNP will not make life better – for anyone', the *Daily Mirror*, 5 May 2010.

1 The legacy of history

1 Originally quoted in P. John, H. Margetts, D. Rowland and S. Weir (2006) *The BNP: The roots of its appeal*, Essex: Democratic Audit, p. 12.
2 E. Ivarsflaten, 'Reputational shields: Why most anti-immigrant parties failed in Western Europe, 1980–2005.' Paper presented at the 2006 Annual Meeting of the American Political Science Association, Philadelphia 2006. For example, Ivarsflaten points to the way in which the Scandinavian Progress Parties emerged out of anti-tax movements, the Swiss People's Party (SVP) was initially established to represent agrarian interests and the Northern League (LN) in Italy and Flemish Bloc (VB) in Belgium hold their roots more directly in regionalist campaigns. On evidence that studies emerging from neo-Nazi traditions have performed less strongly, see D. Art (2008) 'The organizational origins of the contemporary radical right: The case of Belgium', *Comparative Politics*, 40(4): 421–440; E.L. Carter (2005) *The Extreme Right in Western Europe: Success or failure?*, Manchester: Manchester University Press; M. Golder (2003) 'Explaining variation in the electoral success of extreme right parties in Western Europe', *Comparative Political Studies*, 36(4): 432–466; P. Ignazi (1992) 'The silent counter-revolution: Hypotheses on the emergence of extreme right-wing parties in Europe', *European Journal of Political Research*, 22(1): 3–34; H. Kitschelt (in collaboration with A. McGann) (1995) *The Radical Right in Western Europe: A comparative analysis*, Ann Arbor, MI: University of Michigan Press.
3 N. Griffin (2006) 'The convergence of catastrophes', *Identity*, 68: 7 (July).
4 For a detailed history of these early groups, see T. Lineham (2000) *British Fascism 1918–39: Parties, ideology and culture*, Manchester: Manchester University Press, pp. 38–83, 124–149; R.C. Thurlow (1998) *Fascism in Britain: From Oswald Mosley's Blackshirts to the National Front*, revised paperback edition, London and New York: I.B. Tauris, pp. 30–61.
5 For example, William Joyce, Arnold Leese and Neil Francis-Hawkins were all members of the BF. G. Webber (1984) 'Patterns of membership and support for the British Union of Fascists', *Journal of Contemporary History*, 19: 575–606.
6 On this point and BUF ideology, see S.M. Cullen (1987) 'The development of the ideas and policy of the British Union of Fascists, 1932–40', *Journal of Contemporary History*, 22: 114–136; R. Eatwell (1995) *Fascism: A history*, London: Chatto & Windus, pp. 227–242.
7 R. Griffin (ed) (1995) *Fascism*, Oxford and New York: Oxford University Press, p. 172.
8 Eatwell, Note 6 *supra*, pp. 182–183.
9 *Blackshirt*, 5 October 1934, cited in N. Nugent and R. King (1979) 'Ethnic minorities, scapegoating and the extreme right', in R. Miles and A. Phizacklea (eds) *Racism and Political Action in Britain*, London: Routledge & Kegan Paul, p. 35.
10 The Public Order Act of 1936 prohibited the wearing of political uniforms, the establishment of paramilitary organizations and the use or display of physical force to promote political objectives, and enabled authorities to regulate or potentially ban political processions.
11 In the 1931 general election, 24 NP candidates received 36,000 votes, or 0.2 per cent of the total vote.
12 Lineham, Note 4 *supra*, pp. 99–103.

13 R.C. Thurlow (1987) *Fascism in Britain: A history, 1918–1985*, Oxford and New York: Basil Blackwell, p. 107.
14 Nugent and King, Note 9 *supra*, pp. 32–33.
15 In local elections in 1937, BUF candidates polled over 20 per cent in North East Bethnal Green, 19 per cent in Stepney and 14 per cent in Shoreditch. In municipal elections held six months later the BUF contested eight seats across five London boroughs and finished second in six (polling its strongest result of 22 per cent in Bethnal Green East). The movement polled less strongly outside of London with BUF candidates finishing bottom of the poll in Leeds, Manchester, Sheffield and Southampton. R.C. Thurlow, Note 13 *supra*, p. 116. Lineham also notes how in the Metropolitan Borough Council elections in November 1937, the 56 BUF candidates in the Metropolitan police district all failed to get elected. Lineham, Note 4 *supra*, p. 112.
16 Thurlow, Note 13 *supra*, pp. 123–124.
17 There were also sizeable BUF units in Birmingham, Leeds, South Wales, Bristol, Reading, Edinburgh and Aberdeen. N. Fielding (1981) *The National Front*, London and Boston: Routledge & Kegan Paul, p. 41; Thurlow, Note 13 *supra*, p. 124.
18 Thurlow, Note 13 *supra*, p. 124.
19 Eatwell, Note 6 *supra*, p. 233. Lineham's study of BUF membership in east London and south west Essex was based on a sample of 311 Mosleyites, 36 per cent of whom were unskilled and semi-skilled workers, and 15 per cent skilled workers. T. Lineham (1996) *East London for Mosley: The British Union of Fascists in East London and South-West Essex, 1933–40*, London: Frank Cass, p. 216. On BUF membership see J. Brewer (1984) *Mosley's Men: The BUF in the West Midlands*, Aldershot; Webber, Note 5 *supra*; Lineham, Note 4 *supra*, pp. 150–175; S. Rawnsley (1980) 'The membership of the British Union of Fascists', in K. Lunn and R.C. Thurlow (eds) *British Fascism: Essays on the radical right in inter-war Britain*. London: Croom Helm, pp. 150–166.
20 Although because of data limitations these estimates should be treated with caution. Eatwell, Note 6 *supra*.
21 For a more analytical discussion see J. Rydgren (2005) 'Is extreme right-wing populism contagious? Explaining the emergence of a new party family', *European Journal of Political Research*, 44: 413–437.
22 Mosley returned from exile to contest the 1959 general election, standing in the constituency of Kensington North where he polled 8 per cent of the vote. On the UM call for a 'white Brixton', see Thurlow, Note 4 *supra*, p. 216.
23 Carter, Note 2 *supra*.
24 Lineham, Note 4 *supra*, p. 71.
25 A.S. Leese (1951) *Out of Step: Events in the two lives of an anti-Jewish camel-doctor*, Guildford: Arnold Leese, p. 50. For more detailed studies of Leese, see D. Baker (1996) 'The extreme right in the 1920s: Fascism in a cold climate or "conservatism with knobs on"?', in M. Cronin (ed) *The Failure of British Fascism: The far right and the fight for political recognition*, London and New York: Macmillan, pp. 12–28; J. Morell (1980) 'Arnold Leese and the Imperial Fascist League: The impact of racial fascism', in K. Lunn and R.C. Thurlow (eds) *British Fascism: Essays on the Radical Right in Inter-War Britain*, New York: St Martin's Press; Thurlow, Note 13 *supra*, pp. 70–77.
26 Thurlow, Note 13 *supra*, p. 71.
27 Lineham, Note 4 *supra*, p. 159.
28 Lineham, Note 4 *supra*, pp. 72, 74.
29 Lineham, Note 4 *supra*, p. 76.
30 Morell, Note 25 *supra*, p. 5.
31 In the BUF, Chesterton was an organizer in the Midlands, member of the policy directorate, director of publicity and propaganda, editor of the movement's journals and biographer of Mosley. N. Hillman (2001) "Tell me chum, in case I got it wrong. What was it we were fighting during the War?" The re-emergence of British Fascism, 1945–58', *Contemporary British History*, 15(4): 1–34.

32 Eatwell suggests that most of the 2,000–3,000 members of the LEL 'were Colonel Blimpish rather than fascist: in fact, many members saw it as a Conservative ginger group rather than a radical rival, an attempt to keep the Conservatives true to the imperial way'. Eatwell, Note 6 *supra*, p. 265.

33 Tyndall described his debt to Chesterton as follows: '[W]ithout hesitation, what understanding of political affairs I have I owe much more to A.K. [Chesterton] than to any other person.' *Spearhead*, 71, originally quoted in D. Baker (1996) *Ideology of obsession: A.K. Chesterton and British fascism*, London and New York: Tauris Academic Studies, p. 198.

34 M. Walker (1977) *The National Front*, Glasgow: Fontana/Collins, p. 40.

35 The *Guardian*, 8 January 1974, as quoted in Hillman, Note 31 *supra*, p. 16.

36 National Socialist Movement, Internal Bulletin (July) 1964, originally cited in N. Copsey (2004) *Contemporary British Fascism: The British National Party and the Quest for Legitimacy*, London: Palgrave Macmillan, p. 13.

37 Michael Billig (1978) *Fascists: A social psychological view of the National Front*, London and New York: Harcourt Brace Jovanovich, pp. 6, 127.

38 The 'National Front' was not a completely new name as a National Front Movement had been founded in 1951 by Andrew Fountaine, although this existed for only a few months. S. Taylor (1982) *The National Front in English politics*, London and New York: Macmillan, p. 18.

39 Hillman, Note 31 *supra*, p. 2.

40 The NF executive committee included John Tyndall and Martin Webster who were both active in the Greater Britain Movement (GBM), Andrew Fountaine who had been involved with the first British National Party (BNP), Peter Williams who was a former BUF Blackshirt and Andrew Brons who had been in the National Socialist Movement and GBM. Taylor, Note 38 *supra*, pp. 53–63.

41 Carter, Note 2 *supra*, pp. 51–52. On the ideology of the NF, see Billig, Note 37 *supra*; Taylor, Note 38 *supra*; Thurlow, Note 13 *supra*.

42 This was in the period 1977–79, see Taylor, Note 38 *supra*, p. 97.

43 Walker, Note 34 *supra* p. 186.

44 Nugent and King, Note 9 *supra*, p. 42.

45 Taylor, Note 38 *supra*, p. 65.

46 On biological racism in the NF, see Taylor, Note 38 *supra*, pp. 65–68.

47 On Holocaust revisionism and the NF, see R. Eatwell (1996) 'The esoteric ideology of the National Front in the 1980s', in M. Cronin (ed) *The Failure of British fascism*. Basingstoke: Macmillan, pp. 99–117. On urging followers to become 'Jew wise' see *Spearhead*, 3, as cited in Billig, Note 37 *supra*, p. 128.

48 J. Tyndall (1988) *The eleventh hour*, London: Albion Press, p. 11.

49 S. Small and J. Solomos (2006) 'Race, immigration and politics in Britain: Changing policy agendas and conceptual paradigms, 1940s–2000s', *International Journal of Comparative Sociology*, 47(3–4): 237

50 Z. Layton-Henry (1984) *The Politics of Race in Britain*, London: George Allen and Unwin, p. 24.

51 Layton-Henry, Note 50 *supra*, p. 23; D. Butler and D. Stokes (1974) *Political Change in Britain: The evolution of electoral choice*, 2nd edn, London and Basingstoke: Macmillan, p. 219; A.M. Messina (2007) *The Logic and Politics of Post-WWII Migration to Western Europe*, Cambridge: Cambridge University Press, pp. 109–110.

52 Butler and Stokes, Note 51 *supra*, pp. 303, 415, 462.

53 These figures are taken from the British Election Study (BES): in 1964, 27% of voters said the Conservatives, 22% said Labour and 52% said there was not much difference; in 1966, 28% of voters said the Conservatives, 15% said Labour and 57% said there was not much difference. According to this data, in the 1970s the Conservatives increasingly took the lead, but still around one third of voters in 1970 (34%) and over half in 1979 (59%) said there was not much difference between the two main parties.

54 D.E. Schoen (1977) *Enoch Powell and the Powellites*, London and Basingstoke: Macmillan, p. 37.
55 Walker, Note 34 *supra*, pp. 115, 136–137.
56 Layton-Henry, Note 50 *supra*, p. 92.
57 According to the British Election Study (BES), the per cent of respondents who thought the Conservatives were most likely to stop immigration increased sharply from 28 per cent in 1966, to 58 per cent in 1970 and 61 per cent in 1979. For further evidence and discussion of this point, see R. Ford (2007) *British attitudes towards ethnic minorities 1964–2005: Reactions to diversity and their political effects*, University of Oxford: unpublished DPhil thesis.
58 Butler, Note 51 *supra*, p. 303.
59 I am referring here to those respondents in the BES who felt either 'very strongly' or 'strongly' that immigration should be reduced.
60 B. Särlvik and I. Crewe (1983) *Decade of Dealignment: The Conservative victory of 1979 and electoral trends in the 1970s*, Cambridge: Cambridge University Press, pp. 170, 172, 306, 242.
61 R. Eatwell (1996) 'The esoteric ideology of the National Front in the 1980s', in M. Cronin (ed.) *The Failure of British Fascism*, Basingstoke: Macmillan, p. 102.
62 Walker, Note 34 *supra*, p. 150.
63 D. Butler and D. Kavanagh (1975) *The British General Election of February 1974*, London and Basingstoke: Macmillan, p. 164.
64 Although they polled slightly higher in constituencies with no Liberal candidate. In seven constituencies where there was no Liberal opponent, the NF polled an average of 6.2 per cent, compared to an average of 2.7 per cent in 27 constituencies where there was a Liberal candidate. Butler and Kavanagh, Note 63 *supra*, p. 336.
65 On average NF candidates spent £236 on their campaign, compared to £254 in the general election in February. Butler and Kavanagh, Note 63 *supra*, p. 243.
66 Walker, Note 34 *supra*, p. 174.
67 In Leicester 48 NF candidates averaged 18 per cent, in Bradford 21 candidates averaged 12 per cent, in Blackburn two candidates won 33 per cent and in Sandwell 11 candidates averaged 17 per cent. The NF had been active in Leicester and Wolverhampton since 1969–70.
68 The party did have a branch in Belfast and in Cardiff. In Scotland one local organizer complained how it was impossible to outmanoeuvre the Scottish National Party (SNP), cited in Fielding, Note 17 *supra*, p. 41.
69 Taylor identifies areas based on the NF polling over 10 per cent of the vote in the three general elections held in the 1970s, or in local elections in 1976–77. S. Taylor (1979) 'The National Front: Anatomy of a political movement', in *Racism and political action in Britain*, edited by R. Miles and A. Phizacklea. Boston: Routledge & Kegan, p. 138.
70 There were approximately 11 branches and 8 smaller groups in London and 5 branches and 22 groups in the South East. Walker estimates that there were also 5 branches and 3 groups in the Midlands, 7 branches and 11 groups in the North, 1 branch and 7 groups in the South West and 1 group each in Scotland and Northern Ireland. Walker, Note 34 *supra*, pp. 149–150.
71 C.T. Husbands (2006) *Racial Exclusionism and the City: The urban support of the National Front*, London: Routledge, p. 14 and pp. 7–11. In the London borough council elections in 1978, the NF fielded a full slate of candidates in Haringey and Waltham Forest, and came close to replicating the feat in Enfield, Islington and Tower Hamlets. However, as Husbands notes, the NF had not always focused on districts in East London. In the period 1967–74, the Front stood in sporadic fashion in areas of West London, such as Brent, Ealing, Hillingdon and Hounslow. It was only after the London borough elections in 1974, which saw NF candidates poll strongly in East End areas such as Haringey, Islington and Newham, that NF strategists turned toward the East End.

72 Taylor, Note 69 *supra*, p. 135.
73 For the main studies of NF voting, see M. Harrop, J. England and C.T. Husbands (1980) 'The bases of National Front support', *Political Studies* 18(2): 271–283; Husbands, Note 71 *supra*; Taylor, *The National Front and English Politics*; P. Whiteley (1979) 'The National Front vote in the 1977 G.L.C. elections: An aggregate data analysis', *British Journal of Political Science*, 9: 370–380; see also R. Ford and M.J. Goodwin (2010) 'Angry white men: Individual and contextual predictors of support for the British National Party', *Political Studies*, 58(1): 1–25.
74 Taylor, Note 38 *supra*; Butler and Kavanagh, Note 63 *supra*, p. 337; D. Butler and D. Kavanagh (1980) *The General Election of 1979*, London and Basingstoke: Macmillan, p. 419.
75 H. Kitschelt (in collaboration with A. McGann) (1995) *The Radical Right in Western Europe: A comparative analysis*, Ann Arbor, MI: University of Michigan Press, p. 255.
76 Harrop *et al.*, Note 73 *supra*. In another individual-level study of NF sympathizers in areas of disproportionate NF strength, Husbands similarly found strong sympathy for the Front among skilled *and* unskilled male workers, and findings indicated that the party appeared to have a more even age distribution (though when taken as a whole these socio-demographic factors had weak explanatory power). Husbands, Note 71 *supra*.
77 Harrop *et al.*, Note 73 *supra*.
78 W. van der Brug and M. Fennema (2003) 'Protest or mainstream? How the European anti-immigrant parties developed into two separate groups by 1999', *European Journal of Political Research*, 42(1): 55, 69; also W. van der Brug, M. Fennema and J. Tillie (2005) 'Why some anti-immigrant parties fail and others succeed', *Comparative Political Studies*, 38(5): 537–73.
79 There were, however, geographical variations in the depth of hostility toward blacks: concern was more pronounced in London locations, Slough and Leicester, while less pronounced in Bradford and Wolverhampton. Husbands, Note 71 *supra*, pp. 98–109.
80 Husbands, Note 71 *supra*, pp. 26–28. Husbands evokes the term 'political tradition' to refer to the fact 'that NF voting often either continued an episodic history of race-related mobilization (one that might go back to before the turn of the century) or else took advantage of a specific and distinctive local political culture', pp. 34, 54.
81 Harrop *et al.*, Note 73 *supra*, pp. 277–278.
82 Layton-Henry, Note 50 *supra*, p. 104.
83 There is evidence in the 1979 general election of a large shift of support toward the Conservatives in areas previously associated with high levels of support for the National Front, notably in London's North East and other areas that were predominantly white but which were in close proximity to more ethnically diverse areas. See J. Curtice and M. Steed (1980) 'An analysis of voting', in Butler and Kavanagh, Note 63 *supra*. In their 1979 analysis (p. 399), Curtice and Steed note particularly large swings to the Conservatives in areas of previously high National Front support in North-East London and in other areas that were overwhelmingly white, but bordered areas with large ethnic minority populations. The volatility of the NF vote was also highlighted by one academic who observed how support for the NF often surged quickly to a peak before quickly slumping back down again, suggesting that the party was failing to attract enduring loyalty from its voters. Stan Taylor noted how in four cases where it is possible to compare the NF vote across three sets of local elections, the general pattern was for this support to rise from an average of 3.6 per cent to a peak of over 16 per cent, and then slump back down to 8 per cent. While boundary changes should be taken into account, this general pattern was also followed in Leicester where the comparison across elections is less swayed by such difficulties. Taylor, Note 38 *supra*, p. 136.
84 Sixty-four per cent thought the NF had a 'Nazi side' and 56 per cent thought the party wanted a 'dictatorship not democracy', see Harrop *et al.*, Note 73 *supra*, p. 279.

85 Walker, Note 34 *supra*, p. 25.
86 Walker, Note 34 *supra*, p. 149.
87 NF candidates spent on average £227. Butler and Kavanagh, Note 63 *supra*, p. 315.

2 In the ghetto: 1982–1999

1 *Spearhead*, 169: 20, Nov. 1982.
2 BNP (2009) *Constitution of the British National Party*, 11th edn, Welshpool: British Heritage/BNP, p. 1.
3 John Tyndall (1998) *The eleventh hour*, 2nd edn, Welling, Kent: Albion Press, p. 483.
4 On national officers, see *BNP Members' Bulletin*, Feb. 1984. Charles Parker was NF candidate in Ravensbourne constituency in February 1974, Walsall South in October 1974 and Walsall North in 1979; also *Spearhead*, 134: 19, Dec. 1979; see also *New Frontier* (n.d. Mar. 1982?).
5 *Spearhead*, 140: 19, June 1980; also 'David Bruce: Obituary', *British Nationalist*, Jan. 1999, p. 4; 'John Peacock: Obituary', *British Nationalist*, May 1999, p. 4.
6 J. Tyndall (1998) 'The movement in Britain: Time to bury some myths', *Spearhead*, Oct. 1992, p. 4.
7 *Spearhead*, Jan. 1992.
8 *Spearhead*, Mar. 1998, p. 7; *British Nationalist*, May 1998, p. 2.
9 The *League Review* was the journal of the group League of St George. 'Was Hitler a capitalist tool?' *Spearhead*, 193, Nov. 1984; *Spearhead*, 190: 18, Aug. 1984; also R. Hill with A. Bell (1988) *The other face of terror: Inside Europe's neo-Nazi network*, London: Grafton, p. 184.
10 Tyndall, Note 3 *supra*, p. 244.
11 *British Nationalist*, June 1984, p. 2.
12 *British Nationalist*, Nov. 1997, p. 6; *British Nationalist*, Oct. 1997, p. 4.
13 *British Nationalist*, Apr. 1997, p. 2; *British Nationalist*, Jan. 1999, p. 9.
14 *Spearhead*, 161: 6–7, Mar. 1982.
15 'Repatriation: another view', *Spearhead*, July 1995, p. 7.
16 *British Nationalist*, May 1983, pp. 1, 3.
17 M. Billig (1978) *Fascists: A social psychological view of the National Front*, London: Harcourt Brace Jovanovich, p. 166.
18 On the first quote see *Spearhead*, Jan. 1991, p. 7; on the second see *Spearhead*, 174: 5, Apr. 1983.
19 *British Nationalist*, Aug. 1983, p. 3; *British Nationalist*, June 1984, p. 2; *British Nationalist*, June 1985, p. 2; *British Nationalist*, May 1993, p. 2; on the book see *British Nationalist*, Jan. 1998, p. 5.
20 *Spearhead*, 278: 16, Apr. 1992. On the Bilderberg group in other parties see C. Mudde (2000) *The ideology of the extreme right*, Manchester: Manchester University Press, pp. 73, 161.
21 *British Nationalist*, Jan. 1992, p. 6.
22 Interview with John Tyndall, 23 November 2002, cited in K. Thomson, 'All change on the British "extreme right"? Nick Griffin and the "modernization" of the British National Party (BNP)', PhD Diss (University of Bath), p. 43.
23 *British Nationalist*, June 1984, p. 3; *British Nationalist*, Oct. 1984, p. 2; *British Nationalist*, Mar. 1986, p. 2; *British Nationalist*, Apr. 1998, p. 3.
24 *British Nationalist*, Dec. 1983, p. 1.
25 *British Nationalist*, Oct. 1984, p. 2.
26 *British Nationalist*, Aug. 1988, p. 1; *British Nationalist*, July 1989, p. 1; *British Nationalist*, Aug./Sep. 1989, p. 1; *British Nationalist*, Nov. 1989, p. 4; *British Nationalist*, July 1998, p. 5; *British Nationalist*, Mar. 1990, p. 8; *British Nationalist*, June 1997, p. 1.
27 *British Nationalist*, Aug. 1983, p. 3; *British Nationalist*, Apr. 1984, p. 1; *British Nationalist*, May 1984, p. 1; *British Nationalist*, Mar. 1985, p. 3; *British Nationalist*,

May 1985, p. 1; *British Nationalist*, June 1986, p. 1; *British Nationalist*, May 1993, p. 2; *British Nationalist*, May 1993, p. 2; *British Nationalist*, Aug. 1995, p. 3. On the prominence of this theme in NF News, see S. Taylor (1982) *The National Front in English Politics*, London: Palgrave Macmillan, pp. 97–98.

28 *Spearhead*, Dec. 1998, p. 15.

29 *British Nationalist*, Jan. 1999, p. 1.

30 *BNP Members' Bulletin*, Jan. 1985; *Spearhead*, Dec. 1998, p. 15; *British Nationalist*, Nov. 1997, p. 1; *British Nationalist*, Dec. 1997, p. 4.

31 *British Nationalist*, Mar. 1999, p. 1.

32 *Spearhead*, 168: 11, Oct. 1982.

33 *Spearhead*, 169: 19, Nov. 1982.

34 *British Nationalist*, July 1983, p. 1.

35 E. Carter (2008) *The Extreme Right in Western Europe: Success or failure*, London: Routledge, p. 52.

36 R. Harmel (2002) 'Party organizational change: Competing explanations?', in K.R. Luther and F. Müller-Rommel (eds) *Political Parties in the New Europe: Political and analytical challenges*, Oxford: Oxford University, pp. 119–142; also R. Harmel and L. Svåsand (1993) 'Party leadership and party institutionalization: Three phases of development', *West European Politics*, 16(1): 67–88.

37 *British Nationalist*, July 1983, p. 4; on 'ghost campaigns', see Tyndall, Note 3 *supra*, p. 504.

38 *BNP Membership Bulletin*, Dec. 1982.

39 The strongest performances were in Walsall South (1.3 per cent), Broxbourne (1 per cent), Leicester West (1 per cent) and Woolwich (1 per cent).

40 *BNP Members' Bulletin*, Feb. 1984.

41 *BNP Members' Bulletin*, Jan. 1985.

42 *Spearhead*, Feb. 1991, p. 13. For example, BNP candidates appeared in two council by-elections in Bradford and Sunderland in 1985.

43 Two unofficial candidates did represent the BNP in the outer-London constituency of Ravensbourne (polling 0.4 per cent) and the constituency of Tonbridge and Malling located in Kent (polling 0.6 per cent).

44 *British Nationalist*, Jan. 1990, p. 7. Academics generally share this interpretation. Kitschelt suggests that the Conservatives' radical positioning toward immigration effectively 'removed a critical catalyst that might otherwise have permitted the crystal-lization of a right-wing protest party'. H. Kitschelt (in collaboration with A. McGann) (1995) *The radical right in western Europe: A comparative analysis*, Ann Arbor, MI: University of Michigan Press, p. 249.

45 Figures taken from Ipsos-MORI Issues Index. Available online: www.ipsos-mori.com (accessed 10 March 2010).

46 *Spearhead*, 164: 9, June 1982.

47 See Tyndall, Note 3 *supra*, pp. 488 and 583.

48 'Action in Harwich wins big publicity', *British Nationalist*, Sep. 1987.

49 *BNP Members' Bulletin*, Feb. 1983.

50 *Spearhead*, June 1982, p. 9.

51 *British Nationalist*, Jan. 1993, p. 1.

52 *British Nationalist*, May 1983, p. 4; *BNP Members' Bulletin*, Feb. 1984. The party claimed that 100–150 activists attended the London march.

53 *British Nationalist*, Dec. 1989, p. 7; see also Q. Cowdry, 'Immediate action urged over war crime allegations', *The Times*, 24 October 1989.

54 *BNP Members' Bulletin*, Feb. 1984; *BNP Members' Bulletin*, Jan. 1985; *British Nationalist*, Feb. 1986, p. 4.

55 'Law threat to council after fight', the *Guardian*, 15 April 1985.

56 *BNP Members' Bulletin*, Jan. 1985.

57 I. Smith, 'Law urged to ban rival race protests', *The Times*, 26 June 1989.

58 E. Morrison (n.d.) *Memoirs of a street soldier: A life in white nationalism* (part 14), available online: www.white.org.uk/memoirs14.html (accessed 10 May 2005).

59 See Thomson, Note 22 *supra*, p. 48.
60 See Tyndall, Note 3 *supra*, p. 490.
61 *BNP Members' Bulletin*, Oct. 1985.
62 Interview 1 with 'Jimmy', May 2009.
63 It is difficult to assess the extent of this cooperation and the number of activists involved, although in principle both movements agreed to jointly organize activities, exchange publications and form an electoral pact.
64 *West London Members and Supporters Bulletin*, Aug. 1991.
65 *Spearhead*, Feb. 1990, p. 18.
66 'The general election: no big breakthrough but steady progress', *Spearhead*, 278, Apr. 1992.
67 See Morrison, Note 58 *supra* (part 13).
68 *Spearhead*, Mar. 1996, p. 13.
69 *Spearhead*, 281: 9, 1992. See also M.J. Goodwin (2010) 'In search of the winning formula: Nick Griffin and the "modernization" of the British National Party', in R. Eatwell and M.J. Goodwin (eds) *The new extremism in twenty-first century Britain*, London and New York: Routledge, pp. 169–190.
70 For more detailed discussion of these campaigns, see N. Copsey (1996) 'Contemporary British fascism in the local arena: The BNP and the "Rights for Whites" ', in M. Cronin (ed) *The failure of British fascism: The far right and the fight for political recognition*, Basingstoke: Macmillan, pp. 118–141; R. Eatwell (1998) 'The dynamics of right-wing electoral breakthrough', *Patterns of Prejudice*, 32(3): 3–31.
71 *Spearhead*, Mar. 1996, p. 12.
72 *British Nationalist*, June 1997, p. 5; *British Nationalist*, Sep. 1997, p. 4; *British Nationalist*, Oct. 1997, p. 1; *British Nationalist*, Dec. 1997, p. 3; *British Nationalist*, Feb. 1998, p. 5; *British Nationalist*, Mar. 1998, p. 5; *British Nationalist*, June 1998, p. 4; *British Nationalist*, Aug. 1998, p. 4; *British Nationalist*, Oct. 1998, p. 1.
73 *Spearhead*, July 1994, p. 10.
74 *Spearhead*, Mar. 1994, p. 18.
75 *Spearhead*, May 1995, p. 13.
76 *Spearhead*, June 1995, pp. 9–11.
77 *Spearhead*, Mar. 1996, p. 11.
78 H. Kitschelt (in collaboration with A. McGann) (1995) *The radical right in Western Europe: A comparative analysis*, Ann Arbor, MI: University of Michigan Press; also J. Rydgren (2005) 'Is extreme right-wing populism contagious? Explaining the emergence of a new party family', *European Journal of Political Research*, 44: 413–437.
79 See, for example, C. Mudde (2007) *Populist Radical Right Parties in Europe*, Cambridge: Cambridge University Press; also Rydgren, Note 78 *supra*.
80 Carter, Note 35 *supra*, p. 37; see also M. Barker (1981) *The new racism: Conservatives and the ideology of the tribe*, London: Junction books; C. Mudde (1995) 'Right-wing extremism analyzed: A comparative analysis of the ideologies of three alleged right-wing extremist parties (NPD, NDP, CP'86)', *European Journal of Political Research*, 27(2): 203–224.
81 P. Hainsworth (2000) 'Introduction: the extreme right', in P. Hainsworth (ed) *The politics of the extreme right: From the margins to the mainstream*, London and New York: Pinter, p. 1.
82 Rydgren, Note 78 *supra*.
83 Carter, Note 35 *supra*; M. Golder (2003) 'Explaining variation in the success of extreme right parties in Western Europe', *Comparative Political Studies*, 36(4): 432–466; Kitschelt, Note 78 *supra*.
84 *Spearhead*, Aug. 1996, p. 23. On the NPD see *Spearhead*, Dec. 1993, p. 19.
85 *Spearhead*, Mar. 1996, p. 12.
86 *Spearhead*, Mar. 1996, p. 11.
87 *Spearhead*, Mar. 1996, pp. 11–12.
88 *British Nationalist*, Nov. 1997, p. 5.

89 *British Nationalist*, Mar. 1997, p. 8.
90 *Patriot*, 1 'editorial'.
91 *Patriot*, 2: 22–26, Winter 1997; *Spearhead*, May 1995, p. 12; *Patriot*, 6, Autumn 1999; *British Nationalist*, Oct. 1999, p. 2; *Spearhead*, Feb. 1997, pp. 10–11.
92 On the mega-phone culture see *Patriot*, 1: 6; on the stupid statement see *Patriot*, 1: 17.
93 *Spearhead*, Mar. 1996, p. 12.
94 *Spearhead*, Mar. 1996, p. 12.
95 For example *Spearhead*, Jan. 1998, p. 16; *Patriot*, 3: 2, Summer 1998.
96 *British Nationalist*, Aug. 1997, p. 6; *British Nationalist*, Oct. 1997, p. 7; *British Nationalist*, Aug. 1998, p. 7; *British Nationalist*, Apr. 1999, p. 9; *British Nationalist*, Oct. 1998, p. 9.
97 *British Nationalist*, June 1998, p. 7.
98 *British Nationalist*, Jan. 1998, p. 1; *British Nationalist*, Feb. 1998, p. 6.
99 *British Nationalist*, Oct. 1998, p. 3.
100 *British Nationalist*, Apr. 1998, p. 5.
101 *British Nationalist*, Aug. 1999, p. 9.
102 *British Nationalist*, Sep. 1998, p. 9; *British Nationalist*, Apr. 1999, p. 10.
103 *British Nationalist*, Dec. 1997, p. 5.
104 *Spearhead*, June 1998, p. 17.
105 *British Nationalist*, June/July 1999, p. 9.
106 *British Nationalist*, Feb. 1998, p. 3.
107 *Spearhead*, June 1998, p. 17.
108 *Spearhead*, May 1998, p. 5.
109 *British Nationalist*, Dec. 1997, p. 7.
110 *Spearhead*, Mar. 1996, p. 13.
111 *British Nationalist*, Sep. 1998, p. 6. On these links see M.J. Goodwin (2010) 'In search of the winning formula: Nick Griffin and "modernization" of the British National Party', in R. Eatwell and M.J. Goodwin (eds) *The new extremism in 21st century Britain*, London and New York: Routledge.
112 *Spearhead*, Dec. 1998, p. 11.
113 *Spearhead*, Oct. 1998, p. 11. On Tyndall's opposition to the abandonment of marches, see interview with Tyndall, cited in Thomson, Note 22 *supra*, p. 63.
114 *Spearhead*, Apr. 1996, p. 8.
115 *British Nationalist*, Aug. 1997, p. 8.
116 *British Nationalist*, May/June 1990, p. 8.

3 From street gang to political party: 1999–2009

1 J. Wood (1982) 'The British National Party: A step towards unity', *Spearhead*, 167: 17 (Sep.).
2 N. Griffin (2002) 'Moving forward for good', *Identity*, 21: 4–7.
3 'BNP elects new leader', *British Nationalist*, Oct. 1999, p. 1.
4 For instance, Labour liberalised work permits, encouraged an increase in foreign students and facilitated family reunion migration. For further discussion of these factors, see A.M. Messina (2007) *The logics and politics of post-WWII migration to Western Europe*, Cambridge: Cambridge University Press; also R. Ford (2007) *British attitudes toward ethnic minorities, 1964–2005: Reactions to diversity and their political effects*, University of Oxford: unpublished DPhil thesis.
5 The highest figure of 596,000 was recorded in 2006.
6 This figure subsequently declined to 31,000 by 2008. Office for National Statistics (ONS) (2008) *Migration statistics 2008: Annual Report*, Surrey: Office of National Statistics.
7 Home Office (2007) *Accession monitoring report A8 countries May 2004–June 2007*, London: Home Office.

8 Office for National Statistics (2010) *Migration Statistics Quarterly Report*, August, London: Home Office/Department for Work and Pensions.

9 ONS (2008), Note 6 *supra*.

10 S. Vertovec (2006) *The emergence of super-diversity in Britain*, Working paper no. 25, University of Oxford.

11 Messina, Note 4 *supra*, p. 115.

12 'Tories "whipping up anti-asylum vote" ', *BBC News*, 8 April 2000; 'Hague fuels asylum row', *BBC News*, 30 April 2000.

13 'Tory leader attacks asylum system', *BBC News*, Sunday, 10 April 2005. Available online: http://news.bbc.co.uk (accessed 20 October 2009). Conservative Party (2005) *Conservative election manifesto 2005*, London: Conservative Party.

14 'Blunkett stands by "swamping" remark', *BBC News*, 25 April 2002; 'Hodge attacked for "BNP language" ', *BBC News*, 25 May; 'What does "British jobs" pledge mean?' *BBC News*, Friday, 16 November 2007. Available online: http://news.bbc.co.uk (accessed 20 October 2009).

15 B. Duffy and A. Pierce (2007) *Socio-political influencers: Who they are and why do they matter?* London: Ipsos-MORI.

16 The Ipsos-MORI issues index recorded a peak of 46 per cent in December 2007. Respondents are asked: 'What would you say is the most important issue facing Britain today?' and 'What do you see as other important issues facing Britain today? (Unprompted – combined answers). Available online: www.ipsos-mori.com (accessed 20 June 2010).

17 Data on immigration as the *most* important issue collected from the British Election Study (BES).

18 For example, in the period 1989–2008 the percentage of voters who agreed (i.e. either 'strongly agree' or 'tend to agree') with the statement 'there are too many immigrants in Britain' never dropped below 54 per cent. See Ipsos-MORI 'Attitudes toward immigration'. Available online: www.ipsos-mori.com (accessed 20 December 2009).

19 H.D. Clarke, D. Sanders, M.C. Stewart and P.F. Whiteley (2009) *Performance politics and the British voter*, Cambridge: Cambridge University Press, p. 5. See also H.D. Clarke, D. Sanders, M.C. Stewart and P. Whiteley (2004) *Political choice in Britain*, Oxford: Oxford University Press. On the valence model of electoral choice, see also D.E. Stokes (1963) 'Spatial models of party competition', *American Political Science Review*, 57: 368–377.

20 This refers to British Social Attitudes (BSA) data. For further discussion, see L. McLaren and M. Johnson (2007) 'Resources, group conflict and symbols: Explaining anti-immigration hostility in Britain', *Political Studies*, 55: 709–732.

21 British Social Attitudes (BSA) 2003 survey. For further discussion, see R. Ford (2010) 'Who might vote for the BNP? Survey evidence on the electoral potential of the extreme right in Britain', in R. Eatwell and M.J. Goodwin (eds) *The new extremism in twenty-first century Britain*, Abingdon and New York: Routledge, pp. 145–168.

22 YouGov/*Tonight with Trevor McDonald* survey, 30 Aug.–1 Sep. 2006.

23 Ipsos-MORI/BBC *Rivers of Blood* Survey, 11–13 April 2008.

24 Fourteen per cent of voters considered immigration the most important issue, behind the economy (47 per cent). Meanwhile, less than 2 per cent of voters considered the NHS, education and pensions as the most important issues compared with more than one third in 2001; see R. Ford and W. Somerville (2010) 'Immigration and the 2010 General Election: More than meets the eye', in T. Finch and D. Goodhart (eds) *Immigration under Labour*, London: Institute for Public Policy Research, pp. 10–14.

25 In October 2010, immigration remained the third most important issue for voters overall and second most important for public sector workers. 'Ipsos-MORI Issues Index: Trends since 1997: The most important issues facing Britain today', available online: www.ipsos-mori.com. YouGov/the *Sun* survey, 21–22 March 2010. According

to the Ipsos-MORI Issues Index in October 2010, 27 per cent of respondents considered race relations/immigration/immigrants one of the most important issues facing Britain.

26 J. Cruddas (2010) 'A clear and present peril', in T. Finch and D. Goodhart (eds) *Immigration under Labour*, London: Institute for Public Policy Research, p. 40.

27 As Clarke and colleagues note, by the time of the 2005 general election 39 per cent of voters mentioned one of these 'new' issues as their top priority, up almost eight-fold since 2001. H.D. Clarke *et al.* (2009) *Performance politics and the British voter*, Cambridge: Cambridge University Press, pp. 55–77.

28 'Attitudes towards British Muslims: A survey commissioned by the Islamic Society of Britain and conducted by YouGov', November 2002. YouGov questioned a representative sample of 1,890 electors throughout Britain on 31 October–1 November 2001.

29 YouGov/*Daily Telegraph* poll, 20–22 July 2005.

30 ICM/*Daily Telegraph* poll, January 2008.

31 YouGov/Channel 4, May–June 2009. See also D. Cutts, R. Ford and M.J. Goodwin (2011) 'Anti-immigrant, politically disaffected or still racist after all? Examining the attitudinal drivers of extreme right support in Britain in the 2009 European elections', *European Journal of Political Research* (forthcoming).

32 On this point see, for example, M. Sobolewska (2010) 'Religious extremism in Britain and British Muslims: Threatened citizenship and the role of religion', in R. Eatwell and M.J. Goodwin (eds) *The new extremism in twenty-first century Britain*, London and New York: Routledge, pp. 23–46.

33 McLaren and Johnson, Note 20 *supra*, p. 720.

34 D. Voas and R. Ling (2010) 'Religion in Britain and the United States', in A. Park, J. Curtice, K. Thomson, M. Phillips, E. Clery and S. Butt (eds) *British Social Attitudes: The 26th Report*, London: Sage, pp. 65–86.

35 See, for example, J. Rydgren (2004) *The populist challenge: Political protest and ethno-nationalist mobilization in France*, New York and Oxford: Berghahn, p. 193.

36 On 'dissatisfied democrats', see H.D. Klingemann (1999) 'Mapping political support in the 1990s: A global analysis', in P. Norris (ed) *Critical Citizens: Global support for democratic governance*, Oxford: Oxford University Press.

37 G. Stoker (2010) 'The rise of political disenchantment', in C. Hay (ed) *New directions in political science: Responding to the challenges of an interdependent world*, Basingstoke: Palgrave Macmillan, pp. 47, 50. For a fuller discussion of the 'Stoker thesis', see G. Stoker (2006) *Why politics matters: Making democracy work*, Basingstoke: Palgrave Macmillan.

38 In fact, even including individuals who 'fairly strongly' identify with the three main parties alongside those who 'very strongly' identify, there has been a striking decline from 84 per cent in 1964 to 49 per cent in 2005. Data gathered from the British Election Study; see also I. Crewe and K. Thomson (1999) 'Party loyalties: Dealignment or realignment?', in G. Evans and P. Norris (eds) *Critical elections: British parties and voters in long-term perspective*, London: Sage, p. 70.

39 Stoker (2010), Note 37 *supra*, pp. 57–58. On party convergence and extreme right support, see J. Rydgren (2006) *From tax populism to ethnic nationalism: Radical right-wing populism in Scandinavia*, New York: Berghahn, p. 19; see also H. Kitschelt (in collaboration with A. McGann (1995) *The radical right in Western Europe: A comparative analysis*, Ann Arbor, MI: University of Michigan Press.

40 For further discussion of these trends see, for example, A. Heath and B. Taylor (1999) 'New sources of abstention?' in G. Evans and P. Norris (eds) *Critical Elections: British parties and voters in long-term perspective*, Sage; J. Curtice (2005) 'Turnout: Electors stay home – again', *Parliamentary Affairs* 58(4): 776–785.

41 Clarke *et al.*, Note 27 *supra*, p. 306.

42 Clarke *et al.* (2004) *Political Choice in Britain*, Oxford: Oxford University Press, pp. 123–125.

43 Respondents were asked: 'Please tell me whether you are confident in the current government, or not, when it comes to promoting the integration of foreign populations into your country's society?' The percentages expressing confidence in their government in descending rank order were Spain (45%), France (37%), Germany (34%), the United States (34%), Italy (32%), Great Britain (25%), with an average of 34%. Ipsos-MORI interviewed a representative sample of 1,000 adults aged 18 years or more in each country. Ipsos-MORI (2006) *A new British model?* London: Ipsos-MORI.

44 Ford and Somerville, Note 24 *supra*.

45 Further evidence is produced by Ford who averages polls between 2001–05 which asked voters what party was best on immigration. These polls were carried out by a range of different companies, namely ICM, Ipsos-MORI, Populus and YouGov. In 2001 the average percentage selecting Conservative was 30 per cent compared with 47 per cent who said neither/don't know; in 2003 these figures were 30 per cent versus 34 per cent; in 2004 it was 31 per cent versus 34 per cent; and in 2005 this was 35 per cent versus 25 per cent. Ford (2007), Note 4 *supra*. See also Ford (2010), Note 21 *supra*, p. 158.

46 Rydgren, Note 39 *supra*, p. 21.

47 On the political history of Nick Griffin and influence of the new radical right, see M.J. Goodwin (2010) 'In search of the winning formula: Nick Griffin and the "modernization" of the British National Party', in R. Eatwell and M.J. Goodwin (eds) *The new extremism in 21st century Britain*, London and New York: Routledge, pp. 191–210; also M.J. Goodwin (2007) 'The extreme right in Britain: Still an "ugly duckling" but for how long?', *Political Quarterly*, 78(2), pp. 241–250.

48 Interview 4 with Nick Griffin, 24 April 2009.

49 N. Griffin (1996) 'The unholy alliance', *Spearhead*, Nov., pp. 12–13; N. Griffin (1996) 'Still 'no electoral road'?', *Spearhead*, Dec., p. 13; N. Griffin (1997) 'Time to go to the ball', *Spearhead*, Jan. Also see N. Griffin (2002) 'Editorial: what we have to learn from France', *Identity*, 22 (July).

50 The book was J. Marcus (1995) *The National Front and French politics: The resistible rise of Jean Marie Le Pen*, Houndmills: Macmillan.

51 For further discussion see, for example, Rydgren, Note 35 *supra*, p. 158; also M. Wieviorka (1998) *Le racisme, une introduction*, Paris: La Découverte.

52 *British Nationalist*, July 1998, p. 4.

53 N. Griffin (2005) 'Manifesto launch – just the beginning', *Spearhead*, 55 (June), p. 6.

54 Interview 1 with Nick Griffin, 13 March 2006.

55 BNP (2005) *Rebuilding British Democracy: British National Party General Election Manifesto 2005*, Powys: British National Party, pp. 17–20.

56 See Griffin, Note 53 *supra*.

57 BNP (2001) 'Time to declare: where we stand!' *Identity*, 9: 6–7 (May).

58 See BNP (2000) *Identity*, 1: 2 (Jan./Feb.).

59 P. Golding (2001) 'British: through and through!' *Identity*, 8: 3.

60 On earlier hostility toward Muslims see, for example BNP (1989) 'Moslems try to lay down the law', *British Nationalist*, Feb., p. 3; (1989) ' "We should break Britain's laws", says Asian', *British Nationalist*, May, p. 3.

61 Interview 4 with Nick Griffin, 24 April 2009.

62 BNP (2001) 'BNP launches campaign against Islam!', *Identity*, 14 (Oct.).

63 BNP European Election Broadcast 2004.

64 BNP Statement of Accounts – Regional Accounting Unit (2005), p. 1.

65 BNP, Note 55 *supra*, p. 51.

66 BNP European Election Broadcast 2009.

67 BNP (2010) *Democracy, freedom, culture and identity: British National Party general election manifesto*, Welshpool: British National Party, p. 5.

68 BNP, 'BNP general election manifesto 2010'. Previously, the party campaigned on the themes of freedom, security, identity and democracy.

69 N. Griffin (2003) 'At the crossroads', *Identity*, 34: 4–7 (July); Griffin, Note 53 *supra*, p. 7; BNP, Note 55 *supra*, p. 19.
70 D. Hamilton (2005) 'In defence of the British tradition' *Identity*, 51: 16–18 (Jan.).
71 N. Griffin (2002) 'Grasping the future today', *Identity*, 25: 4–5 (Oct.).
72 BNP European Election Broadcast 2009.
73 BNP, Note 55 *supra*.
74 BNP (2009) *British National Party: 2009 County council elections manifesto*, London: British National Party.
75 Interview 2 with Nick Griffin, October 2006.
76 N. Griffin (2001) 'The British National Party (BNP) and the National Front (NF)', *Identity*, 12: 11 (Aug.); Interview 1 with Nick Griffin, 13 March 2006.
77 Interview 3 with Nick Griffin, 24 April 2009.
78 Interview 2 with Nick Griffin, October 2006.
79 Interview 2 with Nick Griffin, October 2006.
80 N. Griffin (2000) 'The way ahead', *Identity*, 1 (Jan./Feb.); N. Griffin (2000) 'Wagons roll!' *Identity*, 2: 4.
81 Interview 4 with Nick Griffin, 24 April 2009.
82 J. Russell (2002) 'The road to victory in Blackburn', *Identity*, 27: 14–15.
83 N. Griffin (2002) 'How democracy triumphed in Halifax', *Identity*, 29: 4–5. 'BNP takes council seat from Labour', the *Guardian*, Friday, 24 January 2003; 'Collective responsibility', Guardian Unlimited, Friday, 24 January 2003, available online: www.guardian.co.uk (accessed January 2008).
84 Interview 3 with Nick Griffin, 17 June 2008.
85 *Burnley Express*, 22 June 2004; *Voice of Freedom*, Feb. 2004, p. 5; *Voice of Freedom*, May/June 2004, p. 2; *Voice of Freedom*, Oct. 2004, p. 8.
86 E. Butler (2006) 'We are the management', *Identity*, 68: 10.
87 *Voice of Freedom*, 77: 9; *Voice of Freedom*, 98: 13; *Voice of Freedom*, 104: 11.
88 Interview 1 with Nick Griffin, 13 March 2006.
89 Interview 4 with Nick Griffin, 24 April 2009.
90 N. Griffin (2004) 'Chairman's article', *Identity*, 48: 4; N. Griffin (2005) 'New target that's going to make it special', *Identity*, 52: 4; On BNP strategy in 2005, see also A. Lecomber (2004) 'Mapping out a winning strategy', *Identity*, 48; BNP (2005) 'General election 2005: the final review', *Identity*, 56: 24–25; E. Butler (2005) 'The 100 seat campaign', *Identity*, 53: 16–17; A. Lecomber (2005) 'General election 2005', *Identity*, 55: 8.
91 A. Lecomber (2005) 'General election 2005', *Identity*, 55: 9.
92 N. Griffin (2006) 'Keeping the ball rolling: Target 100', *Identity*, 67: 6.
93 One aggregate-level study finds that where the BNP had contested a ward in 2002 we should expect its vote share in 2004 be at least 24 per cent larger than in a comparable ward which did not have a BNP candidate in 2002. G. Borisyuk, C. Rallings and M. Thrasher (2007) 'Voter support for minor parties: Assessing the social and political context of voting at the 2004 European elections in Greater London', *Party Politics*, 13(6): 670; Joseph Rowntree Charitable Trust (2004) *539 voters' views: A voting behaviour study in three northern towns*, York: JRCT.
94 J. Rydgren (2005) 'Is extreme right-wing populism contagious?' *European Journal of Political Research*, 44(3): p. 416.

4 Organizing for elections

1 For further discussion see, for example, A. Abedi and T.C. Lundberg (2009) 'Doomed to failure? UKIP and the organisational challenges facing right-wing populist anti-political establishment parties', *Parliamentary Affairs*, 62(1): 72–87; also R. Harmel and K. Janda (1994) 'An integrated theory of party goals and party change', *Journal of Theoretical Politics*, 6(3): 259–287.

2 E.L. Carter (2005) *The extreme right in Western Europe: Success or failure?* Manchester: Manchester University Press, p. 202.

3 C. Mudde (2007) *Populist radical right parties in Europe*, Cambridge: Cambridge University Press, p. 267.

4 M. Duverger (1964) *Political parties: Their organization and activity in the modern state*, London: Methuen.

5 On NF organization, see S. Taylor (1982) *The National Front in English Politics*, London and Basingstoke: Macmillan, pp. 82–96.

6 Abedi and Lundberg, Note 1 *supra*; also R. Heinisch (2003) 'Success in opposition – failure in government: Explaining the performance of right-wing populist parties in public office', *West European Politics*, 26(3): 91–130.

7 *Spearhead*, Mar. 1993, p. 6; also J. Tyndall (1998) *The eleventh hour*, Welling: Albion, p. 203 and pp. 557–558.

8 On one-man band, see *Identity*, June 2001, p. 12; on activist see *Spearhead*, Apr. 1990, p. 8.

9 Although it did reorganize its East London Branch into four separate units – Tower Hamlets, Newham, Hackney, Waltham Forest and Redbridge. See *British Nationalist*, Aug. 1995, p. 7; also *Spearhead*, Nov. 1993.

10 N. Copsey (1996) 'Contemporary British fascism in the local arena: The BNP and "rights for whites" ', in M. Cronin (ed) *The failure of British fascism: The far right and the fight for political recognition*, Basingstoke: Macmillan, p. 124.

11 Interview 3 with Nick Griffin, 24 April 2009.

12 *Identity*, Dec. 2005, p. 4.

13 Griffin, 'How the BNP works'. Griffin would reiterate this view, for example, in 'The convergence of catastrophes', *Identity*, July 2006, p. 7.

14 BNP, *Statement of accounts 2007*, p. 4.

15 BNP (2009) *Constitution of the British National Party*, 11th edn, Welshpool: British Heritage/BNP.

16 BNP (2001) *British National Party constitution*, Powys: British National Party, pp. 4–5; 'Party structure and organisation', available online: www.bnp.org.uk/donate (accessed 21 February 2008).

17 Regional Accounting Unit 2005.

18 On branches, groups and contacts, see BNP (2010) *Activists' and Organisers' Handbook*, Powys: British National Party. For example, one review resulted in the closure of five units due to inactivity, the promotion of eight contacts to group status, and 13 groups to branch status. Shortly afterward, more than 30 units were closed or amalgamated into larger units. See *Identity*, 51, Jan. 2005, p. 27; BNP *Statements of Accounts 2006*.

19 *Identity*, Feb. 2006, pp. 10–11.

20 C. Mudde (2007) *Populist radical right parties in Europe*, Cambridge: Cambridge University Press, p. 269.

21 *Spearhead*, 164: 18, June 1982; *Spearhead*, 163: 18, May 1982; also *Spearhead*, 164: 18, June 1982.

22 *BNP Members' Bulletin*, Feb. 1983; also *Spearhead*, 164: 18, June 1982.

23 *BNP Members' Bulletin*, Dec. 1982. Nor was the BNP alone in targeting London – more than half of the NF's candidates also appeared in the capital.

24 *British Nationalist*, Dec. 1989, p. 7; *Spearhead*, 176: 17, June 1983; also *BNP Members' Bulletin*, Jan. 1985.

25 *BNP Members' Bulletin*, Jan. 1984.

26 *British Nationalist*, Dec. 1989, p. 7.

27 *Spearhead*, July 1994, p. 10; *Spearhead*, May 1996, p. 23.

28 The data is drawn from party literature and self-reported data submitted to the Electoral Commission. Each edition of the private journal of the BNP founder and the BNP newspaper would direct potential new recruits to a branch or group in their local area. The

data which is reported by the party should be treated with caution, yet it seems unlikely that the party would direct possible new recruits toward non-existent units. Where possible, this is cross-checked with more recent data submitted by the BNP to the Electoral Commission in its Statement of Accounts. Regional Accounting Unit 2005.

29 *Identity*, Nov. 2001, p. 13; *Identity*, Dec. 2001, p. 13; *Identity*, Mar. 2002, p. 19; *Identity*, Apr. 2002, p. 23; *Identity*, Mar. 2003, p. 18; *Identity*, Apr. 2001, p. 12; *Identity*, May 2001, p. 12; *Voice of Freedom*, Aug. 2000, p. 12; *Identity*, June 2001, p. 12; *Voice of Freedom*, Sep. 2002, p. 5.

30 *British Nationalist*, July 1997, p. 7; *British Nationalist*, Aug. 1997, p. 7; *British Nationalist*, Jan. 1998, p. 7.

31 *Voice of Freedom*, 72: 14, May 2006.

32 Ten candidates stood in Newham and six stood in Tower Hamlets, *British Nationalist*, May 1998, p. 7.

33 Interview 1 with Nick Griffin, March 2006.

34 *Identity*, June 2001, p. 11.

35 *Voice of Freedom*, Oct. 2000, p. 11.

36 Organizers in Gloucestershire were similarly criticized for their lacklustre performance. *BNP Organisers' and Activists' Bulletin*, May, 1985.

37 *Spearhead*, Oct. 1992, p. 19.

38 *British Nationalist*, Dec. 1998, p. 9.

39 For example, in Burnley, Wilks-Heeg notes how in nine sets of local elections between 1992–2003 the Conservatives failed to field a full slate of candidates, and that the popularity of a local independent politician (Harry Brook) who launched hostile attacks against the local council created a more receptive audience for the active local BNP branch. S. Wilks-Heeg (2009) 'The canary in a coalmine? Explaining the emergence of the British National Party in English local politics', *Parliamentary Affairs*, 62(3): 390; M.J. Goodwin (2008) 'Backlash in the 'hood: Determinants of support for the British National Party at the local level', *Journal of Contemporary European Studies*, 16(3): 349–363.

40 *Identity*, Dec. 2001, p. 15; *Identity*, June 2002, p. 18 *Identity*, Mar. 2001, p. 12; *Identity*, Apr. 2001, p. 12; *Identity*, May 2001, p. 12.

41 *Identity*, May 2002, p. 21.

42 *Voice of Freedom*, May 2002, p. 2.

43 Interview 1 with Nick Griffin, 13 March 2006; on new units see *Identity*, Apr. 2003, p. 15.

44 Interview 1 with Nick Griffin, 13 March 2006; see also *Identity*, Oct. 2006, p. 5.

45 *Identity*, Dec. 2005, p. 7.

46 N. Griffin (2006) 'British nationalism: Political party or broad-based popular movement?', *Identity*, 71, Oct., pp. 4–5; see also L. Barnes (2006) 'A Europe of folk nations', *Identity*, 69: 10–11, Aug.

47 *Identity*, June 2001, p. 12; *Identity*, Apr. 2002, p. 23.

48 *Identity*, 36: 10, Sep. 2003.

49 *Identity*, Sep. 2001, p. 6. See also *Blood and Honour*, 19, 2000. Interview with Nemesis available online: www.bloodandhonourcentral.co.uk/interviews/nemesis.html (accessed 10 January 2010).

50 'Relaunch of the Young BNP: The BNP Crusaders'. Available online: www.bnp.org.uk/news/relaunch-young-bnp-bnp-crusaders (accessed 5 August 2010).

51 BNP *2002 Statement of Accounts*.

52 Interview 3 with Nick Griffin, 24 April 2009.

53 'BNP membership report for advisory council September 14 2008'. Available online: http://bnp.org.uk/acmeetings (accessed 7 October 2009).

54 BNP Regional Accounting Unit, *Statement of Accounts 2006*.

55 *Voice of Freedom*, Oct. 2000, p. 11; *Identity*, 8: 13, Apr. 2001; *Identity*, 14: 12, Oct. 2001; *Identity*, Sep. 2003, p. 10; *Identity*, Mar. 2004, p. 13; *Voice of Freedom*, June 2005, p. 9; *Identity*, Sep. 2005, p. 14; *Identity*, 80: 14, July 2007.

56 Interview 3 with Nick Griffin, 24 April 2009.
57 Interview 3 with Nick Griffin, 24 April 2009.
58 Interview 2 with Nick Griffin, October 2006.
59 *Identity*, 70: 5, Sep. 2006.
60 Interview with Jackie Griffin, June 2005.
61 *Identity*, 84: 6, Nov. 2007.
62 *Identity*, 61: 5, Dec. 2005.
63 *Identity*, 61: 7, Dec. 2005; *Identity*, 68: 7, July 2006; *Identity*, 75: 5, Feb. 2007.
64 *Identity*, 70: 6, Sep. 2006.
65 *British Nationalist*, Jan. 1992, p. 8; *Spearhead*, Aug. 1993, p. 19.
66 *British Nationalist*, Apr. 1997, p. 8.
67 *British Nationalist*, Dec. 1997, p. 8.
68 Interview 3 with Nick Griffin, 24 April 2009.
69 The party has also received several large individual donations (although these are small compared to donations received by the main parties). In 2001 the BNP received a bequest of £8,000 and three years later received bequests totalling over £60,000. Over the period 2003–09, one supporter donated more than £32,000 to the party and, according to declared donations, in 2009 received approximately £35,000. Data collected from the Electoral Commission.
70 BNP Statement of Accounts 2004; Statement of Accounts 2005, p. 17.
71 Interview 4 with Nick Griffin, December 2009.
72 N. Griffin (2006) 'Facing the end of liberalism', *Identity*, 70: 5–6, Sep.
73 Interview 1 with Nick Griffin, 13 March 2006.
74 *Spearhead*, Jan. 1998, p. 6.
75 This data has been collected from the BNP's annual Statement of Accounts that are submitted to the Electoral Commission.
76 In its 2007 Statements of Accounts, the BNP notes that the Director of Group Development, Director of Excalibur Promotions, Director of Internet Operations, the North East regional organizer, the South East regional organizer and Director of the Administration Department were all removed from the Advisory Council.
77 'Leadership challenge 2008', 6 May 2008. Available online: http://enoughisenough-nick.blogspot.com (accessed 1 March 2010).
78 N. Griffin (2010) 'What is going to be done'. Available online: www.bnp.org.uk/news/what-going-be-done (accessed 16 September 2010).
79 BNP, 'Rapid Expansion Campaign' video, presented at the launch of BNP 2009 European Election campaign.
80 These claims appeared on a website established by renegade activists. Available online: http://yourbnp.com/ (accessed 14 May 2010). On the statement by Griffin, see 'Leadership challengers 2010'. Available online: www.bnp.org.uk/leadership (accessed 11 January 2011).
81 According to the party, the total number of members with two or more years, continuous membership (and hence were eligible to vote) was 4,200. The three challengers – Derek Adams, Richard Barnbrook and Eddy Butler – failed to secure the support of 20 per cent of this group (i.e. 840 signatures on their nominations). Derek Adams received 4 signatures, Richard Barnbrook 23, Eddy Butler 214 and Nick Griffin 995. 'Chairman Nick Griffin receives huge vote of confidence to continue as leader.' Available online: www.bnp.org.uk (accessed 16 September 2010). Some rebels alleged that Derek Adams was a Griffin loyalist who stood to split the anti-Griffin vote.
82 The committee consists of the national treasurer and several regional organizers. 'Finances, new regional treasurer, Richard Barnbrook, structural reorganisation and a new autumn anti-War campaign: A report from the BNP's Advisory Council meeting'. Available online: www.bnp.org.uk (accessed 19 September 2010).
83 'Party debts have dropped from £560k to £220k in three months'. Available online: www.bnp.org.uk (accessed 16 December 2010).

84 Four proposals were voted on at the conference: (1) to leave the party constitution in its current state, (2) for the Chairman to be advised and assisted by a nationally elected executive of eight members, while remaining the governing body, (3) to establish a governing body to be a national executive comprising a chairman plus eight separately elected members of an executive committee, and (4) to establish a governing body of an executive committee which comprised the Chairman, two representatives from each of the party's regions, plus three members who are appointed by the Chairman (the National Nominating Officer, National Treasurer and National Organiser). According to Brons, option (1) received three votes, options (2) and (3) together received 17 votes, and option (4) received 42 votes and would subsequently go before an EGM in 2011. Also 'British National Party adopts constitutional reform outline', 12 December 2010. Available online: www.bnp.org.uk (accessed 10 January 2011).

85 Brons expressed these views through a special online blog established to help manage the consultation process; see 'Outcome of annual conference', Monday, 13 December 2010. Available online: http://bnpconstitutionalconsultation.blogspot.com (accessed 11 January 2011).

5 Voting for the BNP

1 C. Moreton, 'Richard Barnbrook: The art-school liberal who now won't allow blacks into his party', the *Independent*, 1 June 2008.

2 'BNP secures two European seats', *BBC Online News*, 9 June 2009. Available online: http://news.bbc.co.uk/1/hi/8088381.stm (accessed 10 August 2009).

3 See, for example, H.G. Betz (1994) *Radical right-wing populism in Western Europe*. London: MacMillan; also J.G. Anderson and T. Bjørklund (1990) 'Structural changes and new cleavages: The progress parties in Denmark and Norway', *Acta Sociologica*, 33(3): 195–217. On problems within this approach, see C. Mudde (2007) *Populist radical right parties in Europe*, Cambridge: Cambridge University Press, pp. 202–205.

4 There is no question that Labour has struggled to sustain the loyalty of the old left, who provided around half of its vote in 1974 but less than one third in 1997. A. Heath, R. Jowell and J. Curtice (2001) *The Rise of New Labour: Party policies and voter choices*, Oxford: Oxford University Press, p. 123.

5 See, for example, Mudde, Note 3 *supra*; P. Norris (2005) *Radical right: Voters and parties in the electoral market*, Cambridge: Cambridge University Press.

6 In Belgium, for example, Coffé *et al.* find that the share of people from the Maghreb countries or Turkey has a highly significant positive impact on the extremist vote share but that the share of minority groups from countries other than the Maghreb or Turkey has a negative insignificant effect. H. Coffé, B. Heyndels and J. Vermeir (2007) 'Fertile grounds for extreme right-wing parties: Explaining the Vlaams Blok's electoral success', *Electoral Studies*, 26, pp. 142–155.

7 See, for example, S. Saggar (2009) *Pariah politics: Understanding Western radical Islamism and what should be done*, Oxford: Oxford University Press, pp. 39–48.

8 For a useful summary of the protest model and other approaches, see R. Eatwell (2003) 'Ten theories of the extreme right', in P. H. Merkl and L. Weinberg (eds) *Right-wing extremism in the twenty-first century*. London: Frank Cass, pp. 47–73.

9 This is also referred to as the 'valence' model of electoral choice; see H.D. Clarke, D. Sanders, M.C. Steward and P.F. Whiteley (2009) *Performance politics and the British voter*, Cambridge: Cambridge University Press.

10 G. Borisyuk, C. Rallings and M. Thrasher (2007) 'Voter support for minor parties: Assessing the social and political context of voting at the 2004 European elections in Greater London', *Party Politics* 13(6): 670; P. John, H. Margetts, D. Rowland and S. Weir (2006) *The BNP: The roots of its appeal*, University of Essex: Democratic Audit.

11 The two sources of individual-level data are the following. The first are aggregated data from the twice-monthly omnibus survey carried out by Ipsos-MORI between mid-2002

and mid-2006. Analysis is restricted to white British respondents in England, producing a sample of 965 self-identified BNP supporters in a combined sample of almost 150,000 white English respondents aged 15 or over. The second are data gathered in the YouGov online nationally representative panel, one week prior to the European elections in June 2009. The panel contained only adults eligible to vote and the data is weighted to the profile of eligible voters in the UK, including people without internet access. YouGov draws a sub-sample of the panel that is representative of the electorate by age, gender, social class and type of newspaper. Only this sub-sample has access to the questionnaire and respondents can only answer this questionnaire once. The survey contains 32,268 respondents, and questions about voting intention produced 985 self-identified supporters of the BNP (i.e. respondents were asked: 'If you do vote, which party do you intend to vote for in the election to the European Parliament?'). The author would like to express his gratitude to Ipsos-MORI and YouGov for their cooperation. For more technical analysis of the data and further discussion, see R. Ford and M.J. Goodwin, *Voting for Extremists* (forthcoming with Routledge); R. Ford and M.J. Goodwin (2010) 'Angry white men: Individual and contextual predictors of support for the British National Party', *Political Studies*, 58(1): 1–25; D. Cutts, R. Ford and M.J. Goodwin (2011) 'Anti-immigrant, politically disaffected or still racist after all? Examining the attitudinal drivers of extreme right support in Britain in the 2009 European elections', *European Journal of Political Research* (in print).

12 Aside from the studies in Note 12, see R. Ford and M.J. Goodwin (2011) *Voting for Extremists* (forthcoming with Routledge); G. Borisyuk, C. Rallings, M. Thrasher and H. van der Kolk (2007) 'Voter support for minor parties – Assessing the social and political context of voting at the 2004 European Elections in Greater London', *Party Politics*, 13: 669–693; B. Bowyer (2008) 'Local context and extreme right support in England: The British National Party in the 2002 and 2003 local elections', *Electoral Studies*, 27: 611–620; M.J. Goodwin, R. Ford, B. Duffy and R. Rea (2010) 'Who votes extreme right in twenty-first century Britain? The social bases of support for the National Front and British National Party', in R. Eatwell and M.J. Goodwin (eds) *The new extremism in 21st Century Britain*, New York and Abingdon: Routledge; P. John and H. Margetts (2009) 'The latent support for the extreme right in British politics', *West European Politics*, 32(3): 496–513; John *et al.*, Note 10 *supra*; JRRT (2005) *The Far Right in London: A challenge to local democracy?* York: Joseph Rowntree Reform Trust; J. Rhodes (2006) 'Far right breakthrough: The support for the BNP in Burnley', PhD Diss. Manchester: University of Manchester Press; S. Wilks-Heeg (2009) 'The canary in the coalmine: Explaining the emergence of the British National Party in English local elections', *Parliamentary Affairs* 62(2): 377–398.

13 P. Norris (1999) 'Gender: a gender-generation gap?', in G. Evans and P. Norris (eds) *Critical Elections:British parties and voters in long-term perspective*, London: Sage. On the gender gap and extreme right support, see Mudde, Note 3 *supra*, pp. 111–118.

14 R. Ford (2008) 'Is racial prejudice declining in Britain?', *British Journal of Sociology*, pp. 609–636.

15 'A glimpse into the dark recesses of Middle England', the *Independent*, 27 April 2004.

16 Forty-four per cent were aged 35–54 years old and 32 per cent were 55 years or older but only 25 per cent were 18–34 years old. Aggregate-level studies find that the BNP performs strongest in areas with older populations, for example, Borisyuk *et al.*, Note 12 *supra*, p. 678; JRRT, Note 12 *supra*, p. 19.

17 For a useful discussion of these effects, see D. Denver (2007) *Elections and Voters in Britain*, Basingstoke: Palgrave Macmillan, p. 54; also R. Ford and M.J. Goodwin (2010) 'Angry white men: Individual and contextual predictors of support for the British National Party', *Political Studies*, 58(1): 9–10.

18 On family socialization effects and extreme right party support, see B. Klandermans and N. Mayer (eds) (2005) *Extreme Right Activists in Europe: Through the magnifying glass*, London and New York: Routledge.

19 For a review of contact theory, see M.J. Goodwin (2009) 'Can we promote cohesion through contact? Intergroup contact and the development of "cohesive" local communities', in C. Durose, S. Greasley and L. Richardson (eds) *Local Governance, Changing Citizens?* Bristol: Policy Press, pp. 91–110. On education and prejudice, see P.M. Sniderman, P. Peri, R.J.P. Fiueiredo and T. Piazza (2000) *The Outsider: Prejudice and politics in Italy*, Princeton, NJ: Princeton University Press; D.L. Weakliem (2002) 'The effects of education on political opinions: An international study', *International Journal of Public Opinion Research*, 14: 141–157.

20 Ford, Note 14 *supra*; J.R. Tilley (2005) 'Research Note: Libertarian-authoritarian value change in Britain, 1974–2001', *Political Studies* 53: 442–453.

21 See Bowyer, Note 12 *supra*; Ford and Goodwin, Note 17 *supra*; John *et al.*, Note 10 *supra*, p. 15; Borisyuk *et al.*, Note 12 *supra*, p. 678.

22 Unfortunately, the 2009 survey did not ask respondents about education.

23 Overall, 61 per cent of BNP voters came from the lower social classes (i.e. C2, D, E), compared with 48 per cent of UKIP voters, 47 per cent of Labour voters and 45 per cent of the overall sample.

24 Borisyuk *et al.*, Note 12 *supra*, p. 685; J. Curtice, S. Fisher and M. Steed (2005) 'An appendix: An analysis of the results', in D. Butler and M. Westlake, *British Politics And European Elections 2004*, Basingstoke: Palgrave Macmillan; John *et al.*, Note 10 *supra*, pp. 14–15.

25 These data are presented in Table 5.8; 69% of BNP voters agreed that the economy will get worse, compared with 56% of UKIP voters, 52% of Conservative voters, 42% of Liberal Democrat voters and 27% of Labour voters.

26 BNP supporters were also only second behind supporters of the UK Independence Party (UKIP) in terms of the percentage expecting the financial situation of their family to worsen over the following year (53% compared to 55% of UKIP voters). Voters were asked: 'How satisfied are you with your own, and your immediate family's, lives at the moment in each of the following areas?' When given the statement: 'Having enough money to live comfortably', 74% of BNP voters expressed dissatisfaction (i.e. 'fairly' or 'very' dissatisfied) compared to 52% of the total sample who were dissatisfied. When given the statement: 'Having access to high-quality local public services in your area such as schools and hospitals', 44% of BNP voters expressed dissatisfaction compared with 33% overall. When given the statement: 'Feeling safe going out in your area', 49% of BNP voters expressed dissatisfaction compared with 29% overall. When given the statement: 'Feeling confident that my family will have the opportunities to prosper in the years ahead', 75% of BNP voters expressed dissatisfaction compared with 53% overall. When asked: 'How do you think the financial situation of your household will change over the next 12 months?' 75% of BNP voters said it would get worse (i.e. 'get a little worse' or 'get a lot worse') compared with 41% of the overall sample. When asked: 'Do you fear that you or a close member of your family will lose their job as a result of the current financial crisis?' 49% of BNP voters said: 'Yes, I do fear this' compared with 40% of the sample overall.

27 Respondents were asked, 'Some people talk about "left", "right" and "centre" to describe parties and politicians. With this in mind, where would you place each of the following . . .?' In terms of ranking themselves, 40% of BNP voters ranked themselves 'right wing' (12% said they were slightly right-of-centre, 17% said they were fairly right wing and 11% said they were very right wing), 21% said they were centre, and 14% said they were 'left-wing' (3% said they were very left-wing, 4% said they were fairly left-wing and 6% said they were slightly-left-of-centre), and 26% said they didn't know.

28 In terms of Labour, 54% of BNP voters agreed that Labour 'used to care about the concerns of people like me, but doesn't nowadays', compared with 45% of the sample overall; 31% agreed that Labour 'used NOT to care about the concerns of people like me, and still does not do so nowadays' (compared with 23% of the sample overall).

BNP voters were much less likely to agree with the statements that Labour 'used to care about the concerns of people like me, and still does nowadays (5% versus 17% overall), that Labour 'used NOT to care about the concerns of people like me, but DOES nowadays' (1% compared to 2% overall). In terms of the Conservatives, 45% of BNP voters agreed that the Tories 'used NOT to care about the concerns of people like me, and still does not do so nowadays' (compared with 36% overall), 17% agreed that the Conservatives 'used to care about the concerns of people like me, but doesn't nowadays' (compared with 8% overall), but were less likely to agree that the Conservatives 'used NOT to care about the concerns of people like me, but DOES nowadays' (12% compared to 16% overall) and to agree that the Conservatives 'used to care about the concerns of people like me, and still does nowadays' (10% compared to 20% overall).

29 Respondents were asked: 'Which if any of the following groups do you often think suffer unfair discrimination in Britain these days? [Please tick all that apply].' In descending rank order, 77% of BNP voters selected 'white people' (compared to 40% of the sample overall), 17% of BNP voters selected 'people educated at state comprehensive schools' (compared with 16% overall) and 15% of BNP voters selected women (compared with 29% of the sample overall). Respondents were also asked: 'And which if any of these groups do you think benefit from unfair advantages in Britain these days?' In descending rank order, 70% of BNP voters selected Muslims (compared with 39% of the total sample), 62% of BNP voters selected 'non-white people' (compared with 36% of the total sample) and 36% of BNP voters selected 'gay and lesbian men and women' (compared with 23% of the sample overall).

30 Voters were asked: 'Are you a member of any of the organisations or associations listed below? [Please tick all those to which you belong].' 59% of BNP voters said they were 'not a member of any of these kinds of organisation or association', compared with 52% of the total sample, so they were only slightly more likely to say they were not a member. Voters were then asked: 'And which of the following have you done in the past five years? [Please tick all that apply].' BNP voters were more likely than the sample overall to have boycotted a product or service (35% compared to 30%), written to a newspaper (21% compared to 17%) and phoned a talkback radio programme (8% compared to 5%).

31 J. Rhodes (2006) 'Far right breakthrough: The support for the BNP in Burnley', PhD Diss. Manchester: University of Manchester, p. 136.

32 It is worth highlighting, however, that the percentage of BNP voters who identified 'political party websites' as one of their main sources of information was four-fold higher than the percentage for the sample overall. This provides some tentative evidence that the BNP website is a more important tool for their voters than the websites of other parties are for their supporters. Voters were asked: 'And which of these are your main sources of political news and information these days? [Please tick all that apply].' In descending rank order, BNP voters selected television (82% compared to 83% overall), newspapers (62% compared to 62%), news websites (51% compared to 48%), radio (48% compared to 51%) and 12% selected political party websites (compared to 3% overall).

33 Voters were asked: 'Which daily newspaper do you read most often?', to which 34% of BNP voters selected the *Sun/Star* (compared to 22% of the total sample) and 19% selected the *Express/Mail* (compared to 16% of the total sample). On research elsewhere in Europe see, for example, K. Arzheimer (2009) 'Contextual factors and the extreme right vote in Western Europe 1980–2002', *American Journal of Political Science*, 53(2): 259–275; E. Ivarsflaten (2005) 'Threatened by diversity: Why restrictive immigration and asylum policies appeal to Western Europeans', *Journal of Elections, Public Opinion and Parties*, 15(1): 21–45.

34 For a more technical discussion of these results, see Ford and Goodwin, Note 17 *supra*; also R. Ford and M.J. Goodwin, *Voting for Extremists* (forthcoming with Routledge).

The model includes a period trend term to control for the significant rising trend in BNP support since 2002, and a dummy for 2005, the only election year in the sample.

35 For a more technical discussion of the importance of racist hostility to the BNP vote, see D. Cutts, R. Ford and M.J. Goodwin (2011) 'Anti-immigrant, politically disaffected or still racist after all? Examining the attitudinal drivers of extreme right support in Britain in the 2009 European elections', *European Journal of Political Research* (in print).

36 Bowyer, Note 12 *supra*.

37 Curtice, Fisher and Steed, Note 24 *supra*, pp. 196–197.

38 For a more technical discussion of these results, see Ford and Goodwin, Note 17 *supra*.

39 Clarke *et al.*, Note 9 *supra*, p. 307.

40 The exceptions are levels of distrust among UKIP voters in senior civil servants.

41 Respondents were asked: 'Do you agree or disagree with the following statement: Most British politicians are personally corrupt.' Agree combines those who said 'agree strongly' or 'tend to agree'. Seventy-eight per cent of BNP voters agreed, compared with 67 per cent of UKIP voters, 51 per cent of Conservative voters, 49 per cent of Green voters, 47 per cent of Liberal Democrat voters, 35 per cent of Labour voters and 54 per cent of the sample overall.

42 Respondents were asked: 'Do you agree or disagree with the following statement: There is no real difference these days between Britain's three main parties – Labour, Conservative and Liberal Democrat.' Agree combines those who said 'agree strongly' or 'tend to agree'. Sixty-nine per cent of BNP voters agreed, compared with 61 per cent of Green voters, 60 per cent of UKIP voters, 45 per cent of Lib Dem voters, 30 per cent of Labour voters, 25 per cent of Conservative voters and 46 per cent of the sample overall.

43 Due to potential collinearity between various attitudinal items, the data were analysed using a principle components analysis. The factor classification axes were rotated and three components were extracted using orthogonal rotation, ensuring that the factors stayed uncorrelated. Four factors were required to reproduce 53 per cent of the variance (all with eigenvalues greater than one based on the Kaiser Criterion). The four factors produce a rather clear pattern describing individual attitudinal characteristics. Factor 1 captures anti-immigration sentiment; Factor 2 Euro-scepticism; Factor 3 political dissatisfaction and Factor 4 homophobic attitudes. Factor scores were saved and introduced as independent variables in the logistic regression models (see Appendix 2).

44 Model 2 controls for standard socio-economic influences on BNP support, including gender, age, social class, region, public sector employment and also other measures including anti-immigrant papers, political socialization, associational membership, political activism and financial expectations.

45 J. Curtice, S. Fisher and R. Ford (2010) 'Appendix 2: An Analysis of the Results', in D. Kavanagh and P. Cowley, *The British General Election of 2010*, New York: Palgrave Macmillan, pp. 385–426; also D. Denver (2010) 'The results: How Britain voted', *Parliamentary Affairs*, 63(4): 588–607.

46 P. Norris (2005) *Radical Right: Voters and parties in the electoral market*, Cambridge: Cambridge University Press, p. 256; A. Russell and E. Fieldhouse (2005) *Neither Left nor Right? The Liberal Democrats and the electorate*, Manchester and New York: Manchester University Press, p. 141; see also M. Duverger (1954) *Political Parties: Their organization and activity in the modern state*, New York: Wiley.

47 YouGov/*Mail on Sunday* poll, fieldwork, 2–3 April 2004.

48 YouGov/Sky News, fieldwork, 21–24 April 2004; also M.J. Goodwin (2010) 'In search of the winning formula: Nick Griffin and the "Modernization" of the British National Party', in R. Eatwell and M. Goodwin (eds) *The New Extremism in Twenty-First Century Britain*, London: Routledge, pp. 169–190.

49 Respondents were asked: 'Do you generally feel positive or negative towards the following political parties?' With regard to the BNP, 11 per cent said they felt 'very' or 'fairly' positive, 72 per cent said they felt 'very' or 'fairly' negative toward the party,

13 per cent said they felt 'neither positive nor negative', and 4 per cent said they didn't know. YouGov/Channel 4 News Survey, 29 May–4 June 2009.

50 The poll, conducted by YouGov for the *Daily Telegraph* in October 2009, asked respondents: 'Are there any circumstances in which you might seriously consider voting BNP in a future local, general or European election?' Four per cent of respondents would 'definitely consider voting BNP', 3 per cent would 'probably' consider voting BNP, 15 per cent would 'possibly' consider voting BNP while 66 per cent would 'under no circumstances' consider voting BNP, and 12 per cent were not sure. Available online: www.yougov.co.uk (accessed 10 November 2009). On the NF, a NOP survey conducted in February 1978 asked voters whether they agreed or disagreed with the statement: 'I might seriously consider voting for the National Front.' Six per cent agreed (i.e. 'strongly agree' or 'tend to agree', 3 per cent neither agreed nor disagreed, 85 per cent said they 'tend to disagree' or 'strongly disagree' and 7 per cent said they don't know, see M. Harrop, J. England and C.T. Husbands (1980) 'The bases of National Front support', *Political Studies*, 28(2): 2719.

6 Membership

1 BNP (2010) *Activists' and Organisers' Handbook*, Powys: British National Party.
2 P. Whiteley (2009) 'Where have all the members gone? The dynamics of party membership in Britain', *Parliamentary Affairs* 62(2): 242–257; also P. Whiteley and P. Seyd (1994) 'Local party campaigning and voting behaviour in Britain', *Journal of Politics*, 56: 242–251; see also S. Scarrow (1996) *Parties and their Members: Organizing for victory in Britain and Germany*, Oxford: Oxford University Press, pp. 27–51.
3 In 1983, almost 4 per cent of the electorate was a member of one of the three main parties but by 2005 this figure had fallen to 1.3 per cent. On party membership in Britain, see J. Marshall (2009) *Membership of UK Political Parties*, House of Commons Library Standard, Note SN/SG/5125; Power Inquiry (2006) *The Report of Power: an Independent inquiry into Britain's democracy*. London: The Power Inquiry; and Electoral Commission. For academic studies of membership of the main parties, see P. Whiteley, Note 2 *supra*; P. Seyd and P. Whiteley (1992) *Labour's Grassroots*, London: Clarendon Press; P. Seyd and P. Whiteley (2002) *New Labour's Grassroots*, London: Palgrave-Macmillan; P. Whiteley, P. Seyd and J. Richardson (1994) *True Blues: The politics of Conservative Party membership*, Oxford: Oxford University Press; P. Whiteley and P. Seyd (2002) *High Intensity Participation: The dynamics of party activism in Britain*, Ann Arbor, MI: University of Michigan Press; P. Whiteley, P. Seyd and A. Billinghurst (2006) *Third Force Politics: Liberal Democrats at the grassroots*, Oxford: Oxford University Press. On the downward trend in party memberships across Europe, see P. Mair and I. van Biezen (2001) 'Party membership in twenty European democracies, 1980–2000', *Party Politics* 7(1): 5–21; S. Scarrow and B. Gezgor (2010) 'Declining memberships, changing members? European political party members in a new era', *Party Politics* (forthcoming in print).
4 BNP (2004) 'Activism and publicity, *Identity*, 41: 7.
5 As quoted on BNP life membership scheme. Available online: http://secure.bnp.org.uk/life (accessed 5 October 2009).
6 According to its constitution, the BNP seeks to represent 'the indigenous Anglo-Saxon, Celtic and Norse folk communities of Britain', and those it regards 'as closely related and ethnically assimilated or assimilable aboriginal members of the European race also resident in Britain'. These indigenous British ethnic groups include the Anglo-Saxon, Celtic Scottish, Scots-Northern Irish, Celtic Welsh, Celtic Irish, Celtic Cornish, Anglo-Saxon-Celtic, Celtic-Norse, Anglo-Saxon-Norse and Anglo-Saxon European folk communities. BNP (2009) *BNP Constitution 11th Edition*, Welshpool: British National Party. Available online: http://bnp.org.uk/resources/constitution-1th-edition (accessed 8 October 2009).

7 For instance, Griffin argued: '. . . if we are going to be forced to take them [non-white members] in the end, why not bite the psychological, moral, and ideological bullet now . . . and then go on to benefit from the fact that our media spokesmen would have an extra weapon with which to rebut charges of "racism"?' N. Griffin (2004) 'The great debate – the end of the road', *Identity*, 46: 4–7 (Aug.).

8 'BNP "whites-only" membership rules outlawed', the *Guardian*, Saturday, 13 March 2010.

9 'BNP membership rules still discriminatory, court rules', BBC, 12 March 2010. Available online: http://news.bbc.co.uk/1/hi/uk_politics/8564742.stm (accessed 12 March 2010).

10 Interview with Nick Griffin, BBC 5live phone-in, 19 April 2010.

11 On the problems of collecting membership data, see L. Billordo (2003) 'Party membership in France: Measures and data-collection', *French Politics*, 1: 137–151; also Mair and van Biezen, Note 3 *supra*.

12 Unlike Britain, however, extreme right parties in other European states have attracted relatively large memberships, for example, B. Klandermans and N. Mayer (eds) (2006) *Extreme Right Activists in Europe: Through the magnifying glass*, London and New York: Routledge.

13 M. Walker (1977) *The National Front*, Glasgow: William Collins, p. 9.

14 J. Wood (1982) 'The British National party: A step towards unity', *Spearhead*, 167: 17 (Sep.).

15 'London rally a triumph', *Spearhead*, 169: 19 (Nov. 1982).

16 BNP (1983) *Members' Bulletin* (Feb.); 'New local units set up', *Spearhead*, 164: 18 (June 1982).

17 In areas such as Bath, Bristol and Croydon, individuals with a long history of involvement with the extreme right signed up, see BNP (1992) 'BNP recruitment now breaking records', *British Nationalist*, p. 7; J. Tyndall (1996) No Title, *Spearhead*, 323: 9 (Jan.); T. Wells (1991) 'The next election: what we must aim at', *Spearhead*, p. 20 (Feb.); see also BNP (1983) 'Robin May joins!', *British Nationalist*, p. 4 (Jan.); BNP (1991) 'Nationalist group merges with BNP', *British Nationalist*, p. 7 (Feb.). ND members also began helping BNP campaigns in Merseyside. A. Lecomber (1998) Editorial, *Patriot*, 3: 2 (Summer); BNP (1999) *British Nationalist*, p. 10 (Apr.).

18 J. Tyndall (1995) 'Doing the enemy's work', *Spearhead*, p. 6 (Sep.). On proscribing membership of Combat 18, see *Spearhead*, p. 19 (Jan. 1994).

19 'Conference sets aims for 1994', *Spearhead*, p. 18 (Mar. 1994).

20 J. Tyndall (1998) 'Unity – now!' *Spearhead*, p. 7 (Mar.); N. Griffin (1998) 'No need to worry', *Spearhead*, p. 9 (Mar.).

21 J. Tyndall (1998) 'Give us the ammunition and we'll do the job!', *Spearhead*, p. 6 (Jan.).

22 Figures obtained from BNP statement of accounts submitted to the Electoral Commission and from internal party literature. Available online: www.electoralcommission.org.uk (accessed 8 October 2009).

23 BNP statement of accounts 2007, p. 7. Available online: www.electoralcommission. org.uk (accessed 8 October 2009); BNP membership report for advisory council meeting September 2008. Available online: http://bnp.org.uk/acmeetings (accessed 9 October 2009).

24 I. Cobain, E. Addley and H. Siddique, 'BNP membership list posted online by former "hardliner" ', the *Guardian*, 19 November 2008.

25 I. Cobain, E. Addley and H. Siddique, Note 24 *supra*.

26 'BNP crashes through 14,000 membership mark – Party larger than UKIP', 28 May 2010. Available online: www.bnp.org.uk (accessed 15 December 2010).

27 Interview 4 with Nick Griffin, December 2009.

28 Note 26 *supra*.

29 J. Marshall, Note 3 *supra*, p. 18.

30 Data drawn from data submitted by individual parties to the Electoral Commission. At the time of writing, all of these parties were registered with the Electoral Commission.

In addition there are a number of organizations which appear to be active on the extra-parliamentary fringe but are not formally registered as political parties, such as Combat 18 (C18), the International Third Position (ITP), the League of St George and the Racial Volunteer Force (RVF).

31 It is important to note that across Europe more generally, parties' members often differ from their voters; members are more likely to be older men who have more resources to invest in politics, for example, they tend to be middle class, better educated and have higher incomes. Similarly, in Britain party members are more likely than their fellow citizens to be men, retired, better educated and have a higher occupational status. See, for example, S. Scarrow and B. Gezgor (2010) 'Declining memberships, changing members? European political party members in a new era', *Party Politics* (forthcoming in print). On party members in British politics see P. Whiteley, Note 2 *supra*.

32 R. Booth, S. Rogers and P. Lewis, 'Analysis of a party – what the BNP list says about its members', the *Guardian*, 20 October 2009; for coverage of the list leaked in November 2008, see 'BNP membership list by postal district', *The Times*, 29 November 2008.

33 For more technical analysis, see M.J. Goodwin, D. Cutts and R. Ford, 'Neighbourhood deprivation, political legacies and extreme right party membership', paper presented at the *60th Political Studies Association (PSA) Annual Conference*, Edinburgh, 29 March–1 April 2010.

34 Note 33 *supra*.

35 I am referring here to the general election in 2001, the general election in 2005, elections to the European Parliament in 2009 and the general election in 2010. While the party's grassroots is dominated by men, it is worth noting that each of the women interviewed occupied relatively senior positions within the party. Of the six women interviewed, one was a national organizer, three organized BNP activities at the regional or local level and two were elected BNP councillors. Some of these data were collected from the minutes of meetings of the BNP advisory council. Available online: http://bnp.org.uk/resources/ac-meetings (accessed 7 October 2009).

36 This means that 'he' is 15 years younger than the average Conservative member, 12 years younger than the average Liberal Democrat and four years younger than the average Labour member. See Seyd and Whiteley, Note 2 *supra*; Whiteley, Seyd and Billinghurst (2006), Note 2 *supra*; Whiteley, Seyd and Richardson (1994), Note 2 *supra*.

37 Unfortunately, an attempt to obtain data on the socio-economic profile of activists proved unsuccessful. A brief questionnaire distributed to each activist following the interview was returned by only 11 participants (a response rate of 45 per cent). It is worth noting that over half of survey respondents (55 per cent) owned their own property, and a further 35 per cent lived in rented accommodation. In terms of education, 64 per cent did not pursue education beyond secondary school.

38 A. Linden and B. Klandermans (2007) 'Revolutionaries, wanderers, converts and compliants', *Journal of Contemporary Ethnography* 36(2): 184–201; Klandermans and Mayer, Note 12 *supra*.

39 Klandermans and Mayer, Note 12 *supra*, pp. 270–271.

40 On Italy, see P. Milesi, A. Chirumbolo and P. Catellani (2006) 'Italy: The offspring of fascism', in Klandermans and Mayer, Note 12 *supra*, p. 73.

41 In addition to the interview data, qualitative analysis of internal membership bulletins and literature has been undertaken to further substantiate the typology.

42 J. Bean (1999) *Many Shades of Black: Inside Britain's far right*, London: New Millennium, p. 57.

43 Bean, Note 42 *supra*, p. 83.

44 BNP (2006) 'John Bean: A true nationalist', obtainable via BNPTV. Available online: www.bnptv.org.uk (accessed May 2007); Bean, Note 42 *supra*, p. 119.

45 Bean, Note 42 *supra*, p. 150.

46 *Identity*, p. 15 (Dec. 2007).
47 A. Lecomber (2003) '2002 – best year for British nationalism', *Identity*, 28: 20–21 (Jan.).
48 Interview 2 with Nick Griffin, October 2006.
49 Interview 2 with Nick Griffin, October 2006.
50 BNP minutes of the advisory council meeting, September 2008. Available online: http://bnp.org.uk/acmeetings/September%20AC%20Minutes.doc (accessed 9 October 2009).
51 N. Teske (1997) *Political Activists in America: the identity construction model of political participation*, Cambridge: Cambridge University Press, p. 55.

7 Initial motivations: why join?

1 J. Tyndall (1995) 'Doing the enemy's work', *Spearhead*, p. 8.
2 See, for example, J. van Spanje and W. van der Brug (2007) 'The party as pariah: The exclusion of anti-immigration parties and its effect on their ideological positions', *West European Politics*, 30(5): 1022–1040.
3 W. Brustein (1996) *The Logic of Evil: The social origins of the Nazi Party, 1925–1933*, Yale: Yale University Press, CT, pp. 27–28.
4 B. Klandermans and N. Mayer (eds) (2006) *Extreme Right Activists in Europe: Through the magnifying glass*, Abingdon and New York: Routledge; B. Klandermans and A. Linden (2007) 'Stigmatisation and repression of extreme right activism in the Netherlands', *Mobilization*, 11(2): 213–228.
5 These cases have been documented in media, for example: 'Petition calls for sacking of lecturer named on leaked BNP members' list', *The Times Higher Education Supplement*, 2 April 2009, p. 11; 'Sacked; the radio host exposed in BNP leak', the *Evening Standard*, 19 November 2008, p. 7; 'Ban teachers who are BNP supporters; union calls for action after far-right party's 12, 000 members are listed online', the *Independent*, 20 November 2008, p. 8; 'Racist firefighters to be sacked', *The Times*, 18 March 2005; 'Racist party headmaster quits multi-cultural school', the *Observer*, 22 September 1991, p. 9; ' "Rights for whites" man says sacking was unfair', the *Independent*, 24 August 1994, p. 4; 'Protest after sacking of store worker', the *Northern Echo*, 1 July 2002, p. 5; 'Union fights tribunal over BNP expulsion', the *Guardian*, 31 May 2003, p. 17; 'BNP teacher suspended', *The Times Educational Supplement*, 30 April 2004, p. 3; 'We want BNP fireman sacked', *This is Hampshire*, 10 June 2004; 'Two Midland teachers quit BNP', *Sunday Mercury*, 13 June 2004, p. 15; 'BNP ballerina defies rising clamour to sack her', the *Guardian*, 1 January 2007, p. 9.
6 'BNP members "targeted by threats" ', BBC News online, 19 November 2008. Available online: www.bbc.co.uk (accessed 19 November 2008).
7 For a useful survey of early theories and their critics, see D. McAdam (1982) *Political Process and the Development of Black Insurgency, 1930–1970*, Chicago and London: University of Chicago Press, pp. 5–19.
8 R. Hofstadter (1963) 'Pseudo-Conservatism revisited: A postscript', in D. Bell (ed) *The Radical Right*, New York: Doubleday, p. 100.
9 I.S. Rohter (1969) 'Social and psychological determinants of radical rightism', in R.A. Schoenberger (ed) *The American Right Wing: Readings in political behavior*, New York: Holt, Rinehart and Winston, p. 198. Toch similarly interpreted the rightist belief in conspiracy theories as 'the final effort to maintain an unrealistic self-concept, on behalf of which one's own weaknesses, failures, and inadequacies have to be explained away'. H. Toch (1965) *The Social Psychology of Social Movements*, Indianapolis, IN: The Bobbs-Merrill Company, p. 57. Perhaps the best-known study, *The Authoritarian Personality* (1950), suggested that 'the antidemocratic individual, because he has had to accept numerous externally imposed restrictions upon the satisfaction of his needs, harbors strong underlying impulses . . . one outlet for this

aggression is through displacement onto outgroups leading to moral indignation and authoritarian aggression'. T.W. Adorno, E. Frenkel-Brunswick, D.J. Levinson and R.N. Sanford (1950) *The Authoritarian Personality*, New York: Harper and Row, p. 239. For more recent work on authoritarianism, see R.A. Altemeyer (1981) *Right-Wing Authoritarianism*, Winnipeg, MB: University of Manitoba Press.

10 R.D. Putnam (2000) *Bowling Alone: The collapse and revival of American community*, New York: Simon & Schuster, p. 289, cited in E.S. Wellhofer (2003) 'Democracy and fascism: Class, civil society and rational choice in Italy', *American Political Science Review* 97(1): 91–106. For further discussion of this approach, see R. Eatwell (2003) 'Ten theories of the extreme right', in P.H. Merkl and L. Weinberg (eds) *Right-Wing Extremism in the Twenty-First Century*, London and New York: Routledge, pp. 47–73.

11 W. Kornhauser (1959) *The Politics of Mass Society*, Glencoe, IL: Free Press, p. 32.

12 H. Arendt (1951) *The Origins of Totalitarianism*, New York: Harcourt Brace Jovanovich, pp. 323–324.

13 P. Selznick (1970) 'Institutional vulnerability in mass society', in J.R. Gusfield (ed) *Protest, Reform and Revolt*, New York: John Wiley, p. 264.

14 N. Teske (1997) *Political Activists in America: The identity construction model of political participation*, Cambridge: Cambridge University Press, p. 10; see also A.C. Elms (1969) 'Psychological factors in right-wing extremism', in R.A. Schoenberger (ed), *The American Right Wing*, New York: Holt, Rinehart and Winston, p. 144.

15 Klandermans and Mayer, Note 4 *supra*, p. 267.

16 H.K. Anheier (2003) 'Movement development and organizational networks: The role of "single members" in the German Nazi Party, 1925–30', in M. Diani and D. McAdam (eds) *Social Movements and Networks: Relational approaches to collective action*, Oxford: Oxford University Press, pp. 49–76; S. Berman (1997) 'Civil society and the collapse of the Weimar Republic', *World Politics*, 49(3): 401–429; also H. de Witte (2006) 'Extreme right-wing activism in the Flemish part of Belgium: Manifestation of racism or nationalism?' in Klandermans and Mayer, Note 4 *supra*, p. 149; K. Blee (1991) *Women of the Klan: Racism and gender in the 1920s*, Berkeley, CA: University of California Press, p. 3.

17 This approach draws on 'realistic group conflict' theory and 'social identity' theory. Realistic group conflict theory posits that competition between groups over resources and values induces intergroup conflict and exclusionary attitudes. Social identity theory applies a socio-psychological perspective to explain the development of negative attitudes toward out-groups. It assumes individuals have a need to perceive their own in-group as superior to other out-groups, and will attach negative characteristics to out-groups. For an extended discussion, see J. Tolsma, M. Lubbers and M. Coenders (2008) 'Ethnic competition and opposition to ethnic intermarriage in the Netherlands: A multi-level approach', *European Sociological Review*, 24(2): 215–230; M. Semyonov, R. Raijman and A. Gorodzeisky (2006) 'The rise of anti-foreigner sentiment in European societies, 1988–2000', *American Sociological Review*, 71(3): 426–449.

18 See K. Arzheimer (2009) 'Contextual factors and the extreme right vote in Western Europe, 1980–2002', *American Journal of Political Science* 53(2): 259–275; V.M. Esses., L.M. Jackson and T.L. Armstrong (1998) 'Intergroup competition and attitudes toward immigrants and immigration: An instrumental model of group conflict', *Journal of Social Issues*, 54: 699–724.

19 L. McLaren and M. Johnson (2007) 'Resources, group conflict and symbols: Explaining anti-immigration hostility in Britain', *Political Studies*, 55: 714.

20 See, for example, J. Rhodes (2006) 'Far right breakthrough: The support for the BNP in Burnley', PhD Diss., Manchester: University of Manchester; also H.M. Blalock (1967) *Toward a Theory of Minority Group Relations*, New York: Wiley.

21 P.M. Snidermans, L. Hagendoorn and M. Prior (2004) 'Predisposing factors and situational triggers: Exclusionary reactions to immigrant minorities', *American Political Science Review*, 98(1): 35–49.

22 McLaren and Johnson, Note 19 *supra*, p. 727.
23 L. Bennie (2004) *Understanding Political Participation: Green Party membership in Scotland*, Aldershot: Ashgate, p. 117.
24 H. de Witte (2006) 'Extreme right-wing activism in the Flemish part of Belgium: Manifestations of racism or nationalism?' in Klandermans and Mayer, Note 4 *supra*, pp. 127–150.
25 All names of interviewees and locations have been changed to protect anonymity.
26 R. Hart (2008) 'Practicing Birchism: The assumption and limits of idiocultural coherence in framing theory', *Social Movement Studies*, 7(2): 121–147.
27 B. Klandermans and N. Mayer, Note 4 *supra*.
28 D.P. Green, D.Z. Strolovitch and J.S. Wong (1998) 'Defended neighbourhoods, integration, and racially motivated crime', *American Journal of Sociology*, 104(2); also J. Rieder (1985) *Canarsie: The Jews and Italians of Brooklyn against Liberalism*, Cambridge, MA: Harvard University Press; G.D. Suttles (1972) *The Social Construction of Communities*, Chicago, IL: University of Chicago Press. The central tenets of the 'defended neighbourhoods approach' are also evident in C. Husbands (1983) *Racial Exclusionism and the City: The urban support of the National Front*, London: Taylor and Francis.
29 Other studies also highlight the importance of 'situational triggers'. According to Sniderman and colleagues, concerns over immigration and ethnic threat can manifest in two ways: either an individual develops an ongoing concern about a particular issue (such as immigration) which leads to a generalized readiness to be concerned about the impact of immigration and increased ethnic diversity; or some aspect of their immediate circumstances triggers concerns about immigrants and minority ethnic groups. These triggers galvanize those already concerned about a particular problem and who are already predisposed to support a particular response. Alternatively, triggers mobilize citizens regardless of whether they were predisposed to be concerned about the problem. Snidermans, Hagendoorn and Prior, Note 21 *supra*.
30 E. Ivarsflaten (2005) 'Threatened by diversity: Why restrictive asylum and immigration policies appeal to Western Europeans', *Journal of Elections, Public Opinion and Parties*, 15(1): 21–45. On this approach, see also G. Lavav (2004) *Immigration and Politics in the New Europe: Reinventing borders*, Cambridge: Cambridge University Press; S.L. Schneider (2008) 'Anti-immigrant attitudes in Europe: Outgroup size and perceived ethnic threat', *European Sociological Review*, 24(1): 53–67.

8 Sustaining commitment: why stay?

1 L. Nunn (2002) 'Selling the BNP', *Identity*, 22: 12–13 (July).
2 P. Whiteley (2009) 'Where have all the members gone? The dynamics of party membership in Britain', *Parliamentary Affairs*, 62(2): 242–257; see also P.B. Clarke and J.Q. Wilson (1961) 'Incentive systems: A theory of organizations', *Administrative Science Quarterly*, 6: 134–137.
3 M. Olson (1965) *The Logic of Collective Action*, New York: Schocken. For an extended discussion and how this applies to the British case see, for example, P. Seyd and P. Whiteley (1992) *Labour's Grass Roots: The politics of party membership*, Oxford: Clarendon Press, pp. 56–59.
4 Seyd and Whiteley, Note 3 *supra*, p. 61.
5 On this point, see also Bennie, *Understanding Political Participation: Green Party membership in Scotland*, Aldershot: Ashgate Publishing Ltd, p. 55.
6 Goffman describes 'frames' as 'schemata of interpretation' which enable individuals 'to locate, perceive, identify, and label' occurrences within their life and the world at large. E. Goffman (1974) *Frame Analysis: An essay on the organization of the experience*, New York: Harper Colophon, p. 21, originally cited in R.D. Benford and D.A. Snow (2000) 'Framing processes and social movements: An overview and

assessment', *Annual Review of Sociology*, 26: p. 614. On frame theory, see also D.A. Snow, E.B. Rochford, S.K. Worden and R.D. Benford (1986) 'Frame alignment processes, micromobilization and movement participation', *American Sociological Review*, 51(4): 464–481; R.D. Benford and D.A. Snow (2000) 'Framing processes and social movements: An overview and assessment', *Annual Review of Sociology*, 26: 611–39; W.A. Gamson (1988) 'Political discourse and collective action', in B. Klandermans, H. Kriesi and S. Tarrow (eds) *From Structure to Action: Comparing social movement research across cultures*, Greenwich, CT : JAI Press, pp. 219–44.

  7 R.D. Benford and D.A. Snow (2000) 'Framing processes and social movements: An overview and assessment', *Annual Review of Sociology*, 26: p. 614; see also R.D. Benford (1993) ' "You could be the hundredth monkey": Collective action frames and vocabularies of motive within the nuclear disarmament movement', *Sociological Quarterly*, 34(2): p. 199; D.A. Snow and R.D. Benford (1988) 'Ideology, frame resonance, and participant mobilization', *International Social Movement Research*, 1: 197–217.

  8 Benford, Note 7 *supra*, p. 201.

  9 On vocabularies of motive, see in particular Benford, Note 7 *supra*, pp. 199–200; also C. Wright Mills (1940) 'Situated actions and vocabularies of motive', *American Sociological Review*, 5(6): 904–913; M.B. Scott and S. Lyman (1968) 'Accounts', *American Sociological Review*, 33: 1268–1275.

10 Benford and Snow refer to these three criteria as ideational centrality (i.e. do these frames draw on beliefs, traditions, values and myths that are culturally relevant?), experiential commensurability (i.e. do the frames resonate with the personal everyday life experiences of potential recruits?), and empirical credibility (i.e. does the party support its frames with an evidence base?); Benford and Snow, Note 7 *supra*, pp. 611–639.

11 J. Tyndall (1998) *The Eleventh Hour*, Aberdeen: Albion Press, p. 485.

12 Tyndall, Note 11 *supra*, p. 505.

13 N. Griffin (1996) 'Apocalypse soon?' *Spearhead* (Mar.), p. 17.

14 Griffin, Note 17 *supra*.

15 N. Griffin (2005) 'On "nationalist" unity', *Identity*, 55: 6.

16 N. Griffin (2004) 'Closing a dangerous gap', *Identity*, 50: 4–7.

17 Griffin, Note 16 *supra*.

18 Interview 2 with Nick Griffin, October 2006.

19 These frames have been identified on the basis of how often they appear in party literature and interview data. For further discussion, see Benford, Note 7 *supra*.

20 BNP (2010) *Democracy, Freedom, Culture and Identity: British National Party general election manifesto 2010*, Welshpool: British National Party, p. 4.

21 BNP (2005) *Rebuilding British Democracy*, Powys: British National Party, p. 13.

22 Benford, Note 7 *supra*, p. 201.

23 Benford, Note 7 *supra*, p. 202.

24 See for example N. Griffin (2005) 'The death of multi-cultural fantasy', *Identity*, 58: 6 (Sep.); J. Bean (2003) 'Census – who are the missing millions?', *Identity*, 31: 3 (Apr.); Paul Golding (2001) 'British: through and through!', *Identity*, 8: 3; P. Golding (2001) 'Freedom, security, identity and democracy!', *Identity*, 7: 3; N. Griffin (2001) 'A long hot summer!', *Identity*, 11: 4–5; S. Johnson (2003) 'Implications of racial differences', *Identity*, 33: 11; C. Liddel (2006) 'Multiculturalism: The engine of genocide', *Identity*, 68: 14; J. Maddox (2003) 'The left sees sense on migration', *Identity*, 33: 14; (2003) 'Racial extinction for the Ruddy Duck', *Identity*, 33: 20; BNP (2006) 'We will be an ethnic minority', *Identity*, 70: 22.

25 L. Barnes (2006) 'A Europe of folk nations', *Identity*, 69: 10.

26 N. Griffin (2010) 'Deadline 2014: The convergence of catastrophes and what the BNP needs to do'. Available online: www.bnp.org.uk (accessed 7 July 2010), p. 4; D. Hamilton (2005) 'Making the wasteland bloom again', *Identity*, 56: 12.

27 N. Griffin (2005) 'All is changed, utterly changed', *Identity*, 57: 4.

28 C. Liddel (2006) 'Multiculturalism: The engine of genocide', *Identity*, 68: 12; L. Watts (2006) 'Wake up and smell the cocoa', *Identity*, 72: 8; see also D. Baxter (2006) 'Marxist left and global capitalist right push integration', *Identity*, 63: 24.

29 Griffin, Note 27 *supra*, p. 6.

30 D. Hamilton (2006) 'Asylum invaders and the anti-British fifth column', *Identity*, 67: 12.

31 J. Bean (2006) 'John Bean's nationalist notebook', *Identity*, 70: 20–21.

32 N. Griffin (2006) 'The white dragon: The flag of England', *Identity*, 68: 27; J. Maddox (2006) 'Christianity in Britain: Self-harm or suicide? Part 4', *Identity*, 69: 27; N. Griffin (2005) 'New target that's going to make it special', *Identity*, 52: 5; BNP (2005) 'Just the Beginning', *Identity*, 55: 6; P. Golding (2001) 'March of the Titans: A history of the white race reviewed by Paul Golding', *Identity*, 13: 15; BNP (2006) 'History speaks: March of the Titans reviewed', *Identity*, 71: 10–12.

33 As advertised in *Spearhead*, 124: 18, cited in S. Taylor (1982) *The National Front in English Politics*, London and Basingstoke: Macmillan, p. 104.

34 N. Griffin (1996) 'The spectre of communal violence', *Spearhead* (June), p. 4; N. Griffin (1996) 'Provocations and diversions', *Spearhead* (Sep.), p. 14; N. Griffin (1996) 'The unholy alliance', *Spearhead* (Nov.), pp. 12–13.

35 J. Tyndall (1995) 'This "extremist' thing", *Spearhead* (Apr.), p. 6–8; J. Tyndall (1995) 'Truths and myths about British decline', *Spearhead*, 316: 9; J. Tyndall (1996) 'The anatomy of moderation', *Spearhead* (Apr.), p. 8.

36 BNP (2010) *Democracy, Freedom, Culture and Identity: British National Party general election manifesto 2010*, Welshpool: British National Party, pp. 16–19.

37 Benford, Note 7 *supra*. Also C. Berlet (2004) 'Hate, oppression, repression and the apocalyptic style: Facing complex questions and challenges', *Journal of Hate Studies*, 3(1): 145–166.

38 J. Rydgren (2004) *The Populist Challenge: Political protest and ethno-nationalist mobilization in France*, New York and Oxford: Berghahn, p. 177; on the survey, see P. Ignazi and C. Ysmal (1992) 'New and old extreme right parties: The French Front National and the Italian Movimento Sociale', *European Journal of Political Research*, 22: 101–121.

39 BNP (2005) *Rebuilding British Democracy: British National Party General Election Manifesto 2005*, Powys: British National Party.

40 Barnes, Note 25 *supra*, pp. 10–11; J. Maddox (2003) 'A suicidal death wish', *Identity*, 28: 3.

41 Griffin, 'Stand, men of the West', pp. 4–6; Griffin, 'Nationalist groups of the British Isles', pp. 4–5.

42 Bean, Note 31 *supra*, p. 20.

43 E. Harstein (2005) 'Whites must breed or face extinction', *Identity*, 58: 11 (Sep.).

44 Bean, Note 31 *supra*, p. 20.

45 BNP (2006) 'July's news', *Identity*, 68: 2; Bean, Note 31 *supra*.

46 BNP (2002) 'People Like You . . . .', *Identity*, 27: 10–11.

47 See studies cited in Note 8 *supra*.

48 See, for example, W.A. Gamson (1992) *Talking Politics*, Cambridge: Cambridge University Press; B. Klandermans (1984) 'Mobilization and participation: Social-psychological expansions of resource mobilization theory', *American Sociological Review*, 49(5): 583–600.

49 BNP (2002) 'Projecting the party forward', *Identity*, 24: 3 (Sep.).

50 N. Griffin (2004) 'Attacks on the BNP', *Identity*, 46: 8–10 (Aug.).

51 R.G. Mitchell (2002) *Dancing at Armageddon: Survivalism and chaos in modern times*, Chicago, IL: University of Chicago Press, p. 10.

52 N. Griffin (2002) 'Grasping the future today', *Identity*, 25: 4–5.

53 Heydon, 'Turkey in Europe', p. 12; also J. Bean (2006) 'Muslim impudence', *Identity*, 70: 3 (Sep.); J. Maddox (2006) 'Christianity in Britain: Self-harm or suicide? Part 4', *Identity*, 69: 26; Bean, Note 31 *supra*.

54 Bean, Note 31 *supra*.
55 P. Golding (2001) 'British: through and through!', *Identity*, 8: 3 (Apr.); see Griffin, Note 52 *supra*.
56 Griffin, 'Career opportunities?', p. 7
57 R. Flacks (1988) *Marking History: The American left and the American mind*, New York: Columbia University Press, p. 73.
58 Tyndall, Note 11 *supra*, pp. 204–205, 484; 'Prepare to stand by these men!', *Spearhead* (Oct. 1990), p. 18.
59 D. Baxter (2006) 'Marxist left and global capitalist right push integration', *Identity*, 63: 26.
60 BNP, 'Your help is needed and needed NOW!'
61 L. Nunn (2002) 'Selling the BNP', *Identity*, 22: 12–13 (July); BNP (2004) 'Islamic awareness week is launched' available online: www.bnp.org.uk/news (accessed 28 February 2006); also BNP (2004) 'A double challenge to the Muslim council of Britain', available online: www.bnp.org.uk/news_detail.php?newsId=52 (accessed 28 February 2006).
62 See Griffin, 'Career Opportunities?', p. 4; N. Griffin (2002) 'Can you afford to wait any longer?', *Identity*, 22: 4–5 (July).
63 See Nunn, Note 61 *supra*.
64 H. Tajfel and J.C. Turner (1985) 'The social identity theory of intergroup behaviour', in S. Worchel and W.G. Austin (eds) *Psychology of Intergroup Relations*, 2nd edn, Chicago, IL: Nelson-Hall, pp. 7–24.
65 N. Teske (1997) *Political Activists in America: The identity construction model of political participation*, Cambridge: Cambridge University Press, pp. 127–130.
66 Teske, Note 65 *supra*, p. 129.
67 J.M. Jasper (1998) 'The emotions of protest: Affective and reactive emotions in and around social movements', *Sociological Forum*, 13(3): 414.
68 Benford, Note 7 *supra*. p. 206.
69 N. Griffin (2005) 'The death of the multi-cultural fantasy', *Identity*, 58: 7 (Sep.).
70 BNP (2005) 'They're trying to close you down', *Identity*, 51: 9 (Jan.).
71 J. Bean (2005) 'John Bean's Nationalist notebook', *Identity*, 58 (Sep.), p. 22; F. Bowley (2006) 'For their future I can make a difference', *Identity*, 63 (Feb.), p. 10; J. Bean (2006) 'John Bean's nationalist notebook', *Identity*, 70: 20–21 (Sep.); BNP (2005) 'Speakers corner: A dangerous addiction', *Identity*, 53: 23 (Mar.); see Baxter, Note 59 *supra*; see L. Barnes (2006) 'A Europe of folk nations', *Identity*, 69: 10–11 (Aug.) See J. Tyndall (1992) 'Outlook favourable!', *Spearhead* (Oct.), p. 4.
72 On disengagement from the extreme right in other case studies see, for example, T. Bjorgo (2009) 'Processes of disengagement from violent groups of the extreme right', in T. Bjorgo and J. Horgan (eds) (2009) *Leaving Terrorism Behind: Individual and collective disengagement*, Abingdon and New York: Routledge, pp. 30–48.

Conclusions: yet another false dawn?

1 C.T. Husbands (1983) *Racial Exclusionism and the City*, London: George Allen & Unwin, p. 147.
2 H.D. Clarke, D. Sanders, M.C. Stewart and P.F. Whiteley (2009) *Performance Politics and the British Voter*, Cambridge: Cambridge University Press.
3 Interview 4 with Nick Griffin, 24 April 2009.
4 Evidence on the impact of electoral systems on extreme right support is mixed, for example, K. Arzheimer and E.L. Carter (2006) 'Political opportunity structures and right-wing extremist party success', *European Journal of Political Research*, 45(3): 419–443; W. van der Brug, M. Fennema and J. Tillie (2005) 'Why some anti-immigrant parties fail and others succeed: A two-step model of aggregate electoral support', *Comparative Political Studies*, 38(5): 537–573; E.L. Carter, *The Extreme Right in*

Western Europe; C. Mudde (2007) *Populist Radical Right Parties in Europe*, Cambridge: Cambridge University Press, p. 234; E.L. Carter (2004) 'Does PR promote political extremism? Evidence from the West European parties of the extreme right', *Representation*, 40(2): 82–100; P. Norris (2005) *Radical Right: Voters and parties in the electoral market*, Cambridge: Cambridge University Press, p. 4.

5 E.L. Carter (2005) *The Extreme Right in Western Europe: Success or failure?* Manchester: Manchester University Press, pp. 51–52.

6 For further technical discussion of BNP voters, see R. Ford and M.J. Goodwin (2011) *Voting for Extremists* (forthcoming with Routledge); R. Ford and M.J. Goodwin (2010) 'Angry white men: Individual and contextual predictors of support for the British National Party', *Political Studies*, 58(1): 1–25.

7 On the importance of these motives in other European cases see, for example, W. van der Brug, M. Fennema and J. Tillie (2000) 'Anti-immigrant parties in Europe: Ideological or protest vote?', *European Journal of Political Research*, 37: 77–102; J. Rydgren (2008) 'Immigration sceptics, xenophobes or racists? Radical right-wing voting in six West European countries', *European Journal of Political Research*, 47(6): 737–765.

8 C. Mudde (1999) 'The single-issue thesis: Extreme right parties and the immigration issue', *West European Politics*, 22(3): 192–197.

9 For a more technical discussion of racist hostility and the BNP vote, see D. Cutts, R. Ford and M.J. Goodwin (2011) 'Anti-immigrant, politically disaffected or still racist after all? Examining the attitudinal drivers of extreme right support in Britain in the 2009 European Elections', *European Journal of Political Research* (in press/forthcoming).

10 R. Ford (2008) 'Is racial prejudice declining in Britain?', *British Journal of Sociology*, 59(4): 609–636.

11 On evidence, see Chapter 5 but also B. Bowyer (2008) 'Local context and extreme right support in England: The British National Party in the 2002 and 2003 local elections', *Electoral Studies*, 27: 611–620; H. Coffé, B. Heyndels and J. Vermeir (2007) 'Fertile grounds for extreme right-wing parties: Explaining the Vlaams Blok's electoral success', *Electoral Studies*, 26: 142–155; R. Ford and M.J. Goodwin (2010) 'Angry white men: Individual and contextual predictors of support for the British National Party', *Political Studies*, 58(1): 1–25.

12 On this point, see Ford, Note 10 *supra*.

13 S. Saggar (2009) *Pariah politics: Understanding Western radical Islamism and what should be done*, Oxford: Oxford University Press; see also R. Eatwell and M.J. Goodwin (eds) (2010) *The New Extremism in Twenty-First Century Britain*, London and New York: Routledge.

14 See L. McLaren and M. Johnson (2007) 'Resources, group conflict and symbols: Explaining anti-immigration hostility in Britain', *Political Studies* 55(4): 709–732.

15 BNP, 'Media admits that Nick Griffin has been right all along over Muslim paedophile gangs'. Available online: www.bnp.org.uk/news/media-admits-nick-griffin-has-been-right-all-along-over-muslim-paedophile-gangs (accessed 6 January 2011).

16 UKIP (2010) *UKIP Manifesto: Empowering the People*, Devon: UK Independence Party.

17 On the comparison between BNP and UKIP support, see R. Ford and M.J. Goodwin (2011) *Voting for Extremists* (forthcoming with Routledge); also R. Ford, D.C. Cutts and M.J. Goodwin (2011) 'Strategic Eurosceptics and polite xenophobes: Support for the UK Independence Party (UKIP) in the 2009 European Parliament Elections', *European Journal of Political Research* (forthcoming).

18 A.M. Messina (2007) *The Logics and Politics of Post-WWII Migration to Western Europe*, Cambridge: Cambridge University Press, pp. 74–75.

19 For further discussion of this point see, for example, R. Ford and M.J. Goodwin (2010) 'Angry white men: Individual and contextual predictors of support for the British

National Party', *Political Studies*, 58(1): 1–25; also R. Ford and M.J. Goodwin (2011) *Voting for Extremists* (forthcoming with Routledge).

20 The estimated reductions released in June 2010 include –£19.1 million for 'Connecting Communities', –£5 million for other cohesion funding and –£7 million for preventing violent extremism (PVE) work. See CLG (2010) *Local Government Contribution to Efficiencies in 2010–11*, London: Communities and Local Government.

21 J. Curtice, S. Fisher and R. Ford (2010) 'An analysis of the results', in D. Kavanagh and P. Cowley, *The British General Election of 2010*, Basingstoke and New York: Palgrave Macmillan, pp. 385–426.

22 Tim Finch and David Goodhart (2010) 'Introduction', in T. Finch and D. Goodhart (eds) *Immigration Under Labour*, London: Institute for Public Policy Research, p. 9.

23 See, for example, A.J. McGann and H. Kitschelt (2005) 'The radical right in the Alps: Evolution of support for the Swiss SVP and Austrian FPÖ', *Party Politics*, 11(2): 147–171.

24 See, for example, J.R. Tilley (2005) Research, note: Libertarian–authoritarian value change in Britain, 1974–2001', *Political Studies*, 53(2): 442–453.

25 R. Ford (2008) 'Is racial prejudice declining in Britain?' *British Journal of Sociology*, 59(4): 620. On similar trends in other European states, see T. Pettigrew and R. Meertens (1995) 'Subtle and blatant prejudice in Western Europe', *European Journal of Social Psychology*, 25: 57–75; M. Gijsberts, L. Hagendoorn and P. Scheepers (2004) *Nationalism and the Exclusion of Migrants: Cross-national comparisons*, Aldershot: Ashgate.

26 On super-diversity, see S. Vertovec (2007) 'Super diversity and its implications', *Ethnic and Racial Studies*, 30(6): 1024–1054. On the dispersion of minority ethnic communities, see L. Simpson (2007) 'Ghettos of the mind: The empirical behaviour of Indices of Segregation and Diversity', *Journal of the Royal Statistical Society series A*, 170(2): 405–424; also N. Finney and L. Simpson (2009) *Sleepwalking to Segregation? Challenging myths about race and migration*, Bristol: Policy Press; A Simon (2010) 'Do ethnic groups migrate toward areas of high concentration of their own group within England and Wales?' in J. Stillwell and M. van Ham (eds) *Ethnicity and Integration: Understanding population trends and processes*, Vol. 3, Dordercht: Springer.

27 See, for example, T.F. Pettigrew and L.R. Tropp (2006) 'A meta-analytic test of intergroup contact theory', *Journal of Personality and Social Psychology*, 90(5): 751–783; also M.J. Goodwin (2009) 'Can we promote cohesion through contact? Intergroup contact and the development of "cohesive" local communities', in C. Durose, S. Greasley and L. Richardson (eds) *Local Governance, Changing Citizens?* Bristol: Policy Press, pp. 91–110.

28 Ford, Note 25 *supra*, p. 632.

29 N. Griffin (2010) 'Deadline 2014: The convergence of catastrophes and what the BNP needs to do'. Available online: www.bnp.org.uk (accessed 7 July 2010).

30 N. Griffin (2010) 'General election 2010 analysis by BNP leader Nick Griffin'. Available online: www.bnp.org.uk (accessed 20 September 2010).

31 N. Griffin (2010) 'What is going to be done'. Available online: www.bnp.org.uk/news/what-going-be-done (accessed 20 September 2010).

32 Griffin, Note 30 *supra*.

33 Interview with Nick Griffin, June 2010.

34 N. Griffin (2003) 'Knowing who we are and where we have to go', *Identity*, 30: 4–7 (Mar.).

Appendix 1: Methodology

1 E.L. Carter (2005) *Extreme Right Parties in Western Europe: Success or failure?* Manchester: Manchester University Press, pp. 65–66.

2 See, for example, P. Ignazi and C. Ysmal (1992) 'New and old extreme right parties: The French Front National and the Italian Movimento Sociale', *European Journal of*

Political Research, 22(1): 101–121; G. Ivaldi (1996) 'Conservation, revolution and protest: A case study in the political cultures of the French National Front's members and sympathizers', *Electoral Studies*, 15(3): 339–362.

3 See, for example, J.A. Aho (1990) *The Politics of Righteousness: Idaho Christian Patriotism*, Washington: University of Washington Press; T. Bjørgo (1993) *Racist Violence in Europe*, New York: St Martin's Press; K. Blee (1996) 'Becoming a racist: Women in contemporary Ku Klux Klan and neo-Nazi groups', *Gender and Society*, 10(6): 680–702; E. DeClair (1999) *Politics on the Fringe: The people, policies and organization of the French National Front*, Durham: Duke University Press; B. Klandermans and N. Mayer (eds) *Extreme Right Activists in Europe: Through the magnifying glass*, London and New York: Routledge; N. Fielding (1981) *The National Front*, London: Routledge & Kegan Paul Ltd. On the strengths of qualitative research more generally, see F. Devine (1995) 'Qualitative methods', in D. Marsh and G. Stoker (eds) (2002) *Theory and Methods in Social Science*, 2nd edn, Basingstoke: Macmillan. On the strengths of qualitative research in the study of party activism see, for example, N. Teske (1997) *Political Activists in America: The identity construction model of political participation*, Cambridge: Cambridge University Press.

4 For example, Aho, Note 3 *supra*; Blee, Note 3 *supra*; R. Futrell and P. Simi (2004) 'Free spaces, collective identity and the persistence of U.S. white power activism', *Social Problems*, 51(1): 16–42.

5 For more technical discussion of the method see, for example, M.J. Salganik and D.D. Heckathorn (2004) 'Sampling and estimation in hidden populations using respondent-driven sampling', *Sociology Methodology*, 34(1): 193–240; also J.S. Coleman (1958) 'Relational analysis: The study of social organization with survey methods', *Human Organization*, 17: 28–36.

6 E.G. Mishler (1986) *Research Interviewing: Context and narrative*, Cambridge, MA: Harvard University Press, p. 24; R.M. Lee (1993) *Doing Research on Sensitive Topics*, London: Sage.

7 Salganik and Heckathorn, Note 5 *supra*, p. 197; see also S. Berg (1988) 'Snowball sampling', in S. Kotz and N.L. Johnson (eds) *Encyclopedia of Statistical Sciences*, vol. 8, New York: Wiley, pp. 528–532.

8 Recent studies of extreme right party activists are based on qualitative interviews with 24–28 activists, see Klandermans and Mayer, Note 3 *supra*, pp. 51–64.

9 K. Fangen (1999) 'On the margins of life: Life stories of radical nationalists', *Acta Sociologica*, 42(4): 357–374.

10 K. Blee and V. Taylor (2002) 'Semi-structured interviewing in social movement research' in B. Klandermans and S. Staggenborg (eds) *Social Movement Research*, Minneapolis: University of Minneapolis Press, p. 104.

11 See B.F. Crabtree and W.L. Miller (1992) 'A template approach to text analysis: Developing and using codebooks', in Crabtree and Miller (eds) *Doing Qualitative Research*, Newbury Park, CA: Sage, pp. 93–109.

12 For further discussion, see M.B. Miles and A.M. Huberman (1994) *Qualitative Data Analysis: An Expanded Sourcebook*, 2nd edn, Thousand Oaks, CA: Sage; also N. King (1994) 'The qualitative research interview', in C. Cassell and G. Symon (eds) *Qualitative Methods in Organizational Research*, London, California and New Delhi: Sage, pp. 14–36.

13 On this distinction between internal- and external-orientated literature, see the discussion by C. Mudde (2000) *The Ideology of the Extreme Right*, Manchester: University of Manchester Press, p. 21.

14 The complete back-catalogue of *Identity* was made available to me by a local BNP organizer to whom I am grateful.

15 For further discussion of this point and related studies, see Mudde, Note 13 *supra*, p. 22.

16 A. Coffey and P. Atkinson (1996) *Making Sense of Qualitative Data: Complementary Research Strategies*, Thousand Oaks, CA: Sage, p. 32.

17 J. Seidel and U. Kelle (1995) 'Different functions of coding in the analysis of textual data', in U. Kelle (ed) *Computer-Aided Qualitative Data Analysis: Theory, methods and practice*, London: Sage.
18 C. Mudde (1996) 'The war of words: Defining the extreme right party family', *West European Politics*, 19(2): 225–248.
19 J. Kaplan and L. Weinberg (1998) *The Emergence of a Euro-American Radical Right*, New Brunswick, NJ: Rutgers University Press, p. 2.
20 K.M. Blee (1993) 'Evidence, empathy, and ethics: Lessons from oral histories of the Klan', *The Journal of American History*, 80(2): 604–605.

INDEX